SUSTAINABLE HOMEBREWING

SUSTAINABLE HOMEBREWING

AN All-Organic APPROACH to CRAFTING Great Beer

Amelia Slayton Loftus

Storey Publishing

The mission of Storey Publishing is to serve our customers by
publishing practical information that encourages
personal independence in harmony with the environment.

Edited by Margaret Sutherland and Lisa H. Hiley
Cover design by Kimberly Glyder
Text design and production by Tina Henderson
Art direction by Carolyn Eckert

Cover photographs by © LICreate/iStockphoto.com (carboy); © Photoevent/
iStockphoto.com (glass of beer); © Richard Loader/Getty Images (hops)
Decorative illustrations and lettering (cover and interior) by Kimberly Glyder
How-to illustrations by Michael Gellatly

Indexed by Christine R. Lindemer, Boston Road Communications

Storey Publishing
210 MASS MoCA Way
North Adams, MA 01247
www.storey.com

Printed in the United States by Versa Press
10 9 8 7 6 5 4 3 2 1

Library of Congress Cataloging-in-Publication Data on file

Dedication

This book is dedicated to everyone who ever inspired and/or encouraged me to brew, and indulged me in my single-minded need to make every homebrew as eco-friendly as possible!

And to my late father, Peter Slayton, who taught me the joys of tinkering and invested in me a steadfast belief in renewable energy, especially solar power.

Also to women beer makers everywhere who are rediscovering our ancient role as brewers, medicine women, and creators of wonderful tasty things. And to the organic farmers who are growing wonderful, high-quality organic hops and brewing grains. Your products are proof that you do not need to rely on chemicals to make great beer! And the organic breweries who are putting great, high-quality organic craft beers out there for everyone who cannot brew their own to enjoy.

Last but not least, to my husband, Patrick, who had to live with my crazy writing schedule for the two years that I worked on this book!

Acknowledgments

This book would never have come about without the people who inspired me to pursue sustainable brewing for the past 19 years:

Charlie Papazian for his book *The Joy of Homebrewing*. It gave me the passion to brew that has sustained me for all these years! Also the authors of many other great brewing guides, especially John Palmer (*How to Brew*), Ray Daniels (*Designing Great Beers*), Sandor Katz (*The Art of Fermentation*), and Stephen Harrod Buhner (*Sacred and Herbal Healing Beers*).

Friends I have brewed with and shared homebrews with through the years, especially Ben P., Dan S., John G., and everyone at Sparge. The founding members of Seven Bridges Cooperative, who believed in the sustainable brewing dream enough to launch an organic homebrew business and invest in it for over 15 years. And finally, the friends, acquaintances, and heroes in the environmental movement who have instilled in me a great reverence for the earth that sustains us.

CONTENTS

PART 1 THE ALLURE and the ART of HOMEBREWING

PART 2   SUSTAINABLE BREWING in the KITCHEN and GARDEN

PART 3   BREWING ORGANIC BEER

INTRODUCTION

To me, being a good brewer means not only making excellent, even award-winning, beer, but also being conscious of the impact your activity has on the environment and incorporating sustainable practices into your brew routine. Sustainable brewing means choosing ingredients and supplies that have a lower impact on the environment, using equipment that is made from durable, nontoxic materials, and employing brewing practices that use as little energy and water as possible. It involves reusing and recycling spent brewing grain, cooling water, and beer bottles or kegs. Just as importantly, sustainable brewing means making great beer, which is the most efficient and sustainable use of ingredients possible — because it will never be wasted! Not to mention that always having fresh organic beer on hand greatly enhances your quality of life.

Today, organic beer is no longer a novel idea. But 20 years ago, just a small handful of organic beers were available to North American beer drinkers, and many of those were imports. Some of the first to hit the scene were from Caledonia Brewing in Scotland (Golden Promise, Organic Lager, Organic Premium Ale), Samuel Smith's in Great Britain (Organic Lager, Organic Best Ale), and Pinkus Müller in Germany (Original, Pinkus Spezial, Hefeweizen). These imports encouraged a handful of American brewers to take the plunge and in the late '90s, beers began to appear from Wolaver's (Brown Ale, Pale Ale, and IPA), Butte Creek (Organic Ale, Organic Porter, and IPA), Eel River Brewing (Organic Amber Ale) — all located in California — as well as Fish Brewing in Washington (Amber Ale, River Run, and IPA) and Lakefront Brewery in Wisconsin (ESB).

Since then, the number of organic beers on the market has exploded. Nowadays, almost every grocery or liquor store with a decent selection of beer and wine has several organic offerings. Small organic breweries continue to pop up all over North America. Portland's Organic Beer Festival, established in 2003, attracts thousands of attendees every year.

All this commercial organic brewing activity has greatly benefited aspiring organic homebrewers: the demand has dramatically improved the selection and quality of organic ingredients, and the price gap between organic and nonorganic ingredients has dropped significantly. Choosing organic ingredients over conventionally grown ones is arguably one of the most important steps a brewer can take towards being truly sustainable.

There are so many great reasons to brew organic, but these are my top three:

1. It supports organic agriculture and small-scale farming. Most people agree that the top reason to choose organic anything, beer included, is to support organic agriculture because it is better for the environment. Organic farms in North America tend to be smaller and more community based than conventional operations. They give back to their communities in the form of fresh, healthy food, local jobs, and better stewardship of the local ecology.

2. Beer is food. If you eat organic food whenever possible, you should also drink organic beer whenever possible. Moderate consumption of beer, one or two beers a day, has been discovered to offer health benefits, including lowering the risk of cardiovascular disease. Drink organic beer, and you will have even less to worry about!

3. It's cheaper in the long run. Some organic ingredients cost more (in some cases a lot more), but brewing your own organic beer is still cheaper than buying it. You can reduce costs by buying in bulk and building your own recipes, brewing from scratch with whole grains instead of extract, and seeking out local sources for heavy base ingredients such as barley malt and malt extract. Then you can order by mail only the ingredients you cannot buy (or grow) locally. If you are willing to be creative about substituting ingredients, you can use more locally grown counterparts and still create beers that are true to the style intended.

PART

1

THE ALLURE

and the

ART

of

HOMEBREWING

1

LOOKING at Essential Equipment and SUPPLIES

Being a sustainability-minded homebrewer means keeping your brewery as efficient, environmentally sound, and worker friendly as possible. When it comes to buying equipment and supplies, there are many factors to consider. What are the costs to the environment, human health, and human rights for the materials you are about to purchase?

It is kind of hard to feel like a truly sustainable brewer if you know that the factory that makes your plastic bucket fermenter dumps toxins into local water supplies, contributing to serious health problems for nearby residents. Your amazing homebrewed beer will taste even better if you can sip with confidence, knowing a 10-year-old kid did not have to work a 10-hour day in a factory so the manufacturer could keep the cost of your brewing gizmo low while turning a tidy profit.

When you start out as a homebrewer, the equipment is the largest investment you will make, unless you are very resourceful at repurposing cheap or free items. Some of the items are familiar kitchen tools, while others are more unusual. Racking cane? Wort chiller? Airlock? What the heck? Fear not — by the time you finish this chapter you will be ready to equip your home brewery in style and with a clear conscience.

Developing Your Personal Ecosystem

What in the world is a personal ecosystem? I use this phrase to describe the sum total of all the interactions with the environment that one individual has. Driving a car has a negative impact. Growing organic veggies has a positive impact. Just like a checkbook register, you can add up all the positive and negative impacts. Ideally you can live a life that has a net positive impact on the environment. Achieving the goals of near-perfect homebrew nirvana and keeping your personal ecosystem balance sheet out of the gutter is a challenge.

A personal ecosystem is all about your relationship with the environment and how your actions relate to the whole. Instead of getting too complicated about it, it is always good to focus on the positive impacts you can have and try to minimize the negative impacts without getting the carbon meters and calculators out. My philosophy is, "Live a good life, and life will be good!"

The Cost of Manufacturing

Humans manufacture an unbelievable array of goods that have advanced civilization and improved the lives of many, but there is a cost beyond dollars for many of the wonderful products we have become accustomed to. Unfortunately that cost is often borne by people making those goods, not the ones using them. Fortunately, progress is being made toward addressing these problems, much of it driven by consumer awareness. As we demand more environmental and human rights responsibility in the manufacture of the goods we buy, industry innovates to meet that demand. This is especially true in the controversial world of plastics.

The U.S. Department of Commerce has a Sustainable Manufacturing Initiative (SMI), which provides tools and support to small, medium, and large manufacturing companies looking to improve their environmental report card. The fact that this agency exists is proof that government and industries are starting to take industrial pollution, municipal and industrial waste, the manufacturing carbon footprint, and energy efficiency seriously. It often turns out that improving performance for environmental reasons also improves a company's competitiveness and its profit margin by reducing its energy and waste disposal costs. Every year more companies incorporate the SMI sustainability goals into their overall planning.

It's important to consider whether your equipment is made from materials that contain toxic ingredients, generates hazardous waste in the manufacturing process, or has a short life span. The location of the factory where the item was made also has an environmental effect. The shipping distance between the production plant and your home represents a carbon emissions cost that might influence your decision. When purchasing equipment that uses fuel, electricity, or water, consider the efficiency of the item. The savings gained by choosing cheaper, less efficient gear might not be as much as you would save by buying a more expensive item that uses less water, fuel, or electricity.

Basic Brewing Equipment

Here is a handy checklist to help you organize your brew equipment shopping.

- Brew pot (3 to 6 gallons)
- Thermometer [32 to 220°F (0–104°C)]
- Strip thermometer (optional)
- Stirring spoon
- Funnel
- Strainer and/or colander
- Hop- and grain-straining bags
- Wort chiller (optional)
- Fermenting container (5 gallons)
- Second fermenting container (optional)
- Airlock(s)
- Stopper(s)
- Hydrometer and test jar
- Racking cane
- Siphon tubing: 5 or 6 feet
- Siphon tube clamp
- Large cleaning brush (carboy brush)
- Bottle brush
- Bottling wand
- Bottles and caps
- Bottle capper
- Brewery cleanser
- Sanitizing solution

Fair Wage Produced and Fairly Traded

One step beyond sustainability is the human rights equation. Did the workers that made your brew pot earn a fair wage, and were they able to do their job in a safe and respectful work environment? These are hard questions without simple answers, yet the first step toward improving workers' rights is to ask such hard questions. The facts are not always easy to come by when looking at a product that has had a long chain of custody before reaching your backyard home brewery.

Many durable goods for the homebrew market are made in such far-flung places as China or Italy and are shipped to a distributor, who then ships it to a retailer. So when you ask at your local homebrew shop if the brew pot you are about to buy is made under Fair Trade standards, you will most likely find they have no idea. Brand names are often a good way to keep track of the manufacturing trail, but many homebrew items are not sold under a particular brand.

There is so little information available about working conditions in factories that for now the best way to approach the problem is to look at the general regions of production. For instance, quite a lot of homebrew gear is made in Italy, where fairly decent labor laws guarantee workers a minimum wage, paid overtime, and decent workplace safety.

In recent years, however, many items previously manufactured in North America or Europe are being made more cheaply in China. China's mandated 11-hour workday is routinely ignored, and many factory workers toil 12 hours a day, 7 days a week, for weeks on end. Injuries are frequent because safety standards are low and training is not a priority, and ill-paid workers are often docked pay for minor infractions.

Supporting smaller-scale craftsmanship can offer a significant improvement in the quality of life for people that make homebrewing equipment. There are dozens of examples of handcrafted brewing equipment. Unfortunately, many of these smaller businesses have fallen by the wayside in recent years thanks to the increased centralization within the industry. Many homespun brewing implements, such as the Bazooka screen, were once crafted by their inventors but are now being mass-produced in Chinese factories. There are still some small companies that focus on craftsmanship and local production rather than trying to outcompete everybody on price. A good example is Blichmann Engineering in Lafayette, Indiana.

Homebrewing Equipment in Detail

Your largest expenditure will be in your equipment, and it makes sense to spend money for quality items that will last. Let's start with a discussion of the equipment itself. If you know what you need but want more information on eco-friendly choices, see Choosing Eco-Friendly Materials, page 15.

BREW POT

You need a large pot that will fit your batch size. Most batches are 5 gallons. A 6- or 7-gallon pot is ideal for extract and partial mash recipes, but for brewing all-grain recipes, you may need a larger pot. Stainless steel is best. Ceramic-on-steel is acceptable as long as there are no scrapes or gouges in the coating.

You can use aluminum, but be aware that there is some controversy regarding the health risks of using aluminum cookware with acidic foods such as beer wort. Depending on the pH of your brew water, aluminum can also contribute undesirable flavors to your beer unless an oxidized layer has built up over time on the inside of the pot. This will keep metallic flavors out of the brew and can help prevent flavor transfer between batches as long as this layer is not stripped off with the use of oxygen-based cleansers.

Since the brew pot is usually the most expensive piece of brewing equipment (a quality 6- to 10-gallon stainless steel one can cost between $100 and $250), some folks make do with a smaller pot. A 3- or 4-gallon pot (12- to 16-quart) can be used for extract brewing with acceptable results. You can boil a concentrated brew, then add sterilized water to top it up to five gallons in the fermenter before adding the yeast. There are some drawbacks to this method, and it doesn't work for all-grain brewing.

Whatever size pot you have, a long-handled brew spoon will make your life easier. The best choice is a stainless steel one that can be sanitized by boiling and will not melt or potentially leach harmful plastic residues into your beer.

Brew pot and long-handled spoon

THERMOMETER

Beer making requires some precision in temperature reading, so invest in a good-quality thermometer; you will not regret it. It should be immersible and have a temperature scale of at least 30 to 220°F (–1 to 104°C). Metal-probe thermometers give you fast results and are easy to read, but they need to be calibrated or adjusted regularly to remain accurate. Glass thermometers are consistently reliable, but do not use one filled with mercury. Most glass thermometers sold for brewing and cooking are alcohol filled. They do not need to be calibrated, but test yours in boiling water before brew day so that if it is off by a few degrees you can compensate accordingly.

Digital-probe thermometers are very easy to use, but choose wisely — many of the cheap thermometers on the market are not highly reliable, are tricky to program, and are just about impossible to repair. A majority of the homebrew thermometers are made in Asia nowadays, including American brands. A few companies such as Tel-Tru Manufacturing in Rochester, New York, still manufacture thermometers in the United States.

Most homebrew suppliers also sell inexpensive, reusable strip thermometers that stick to the outside of the fermenter so you can monitor the temperature during fermentation. Most of these thermometers have a temperature range of 35 to 80°F (2–27°C). These are very useful for maintaining consistent fermenter temperatures and to troubleshoot problems with fermentation. They are worth the two or three dollars apiece if you brew regularly.

STRAINING EQUIPMENT

A good funnel is essential for fermenting homebrew in containers with narrow openings. The most common funnel sold by homebrew shops is a large (8– to 10-inches in diameter) hard plastic funnel made of nylon, a form of plastic that is very durable and impact resistant. These funnels usually cost under $15. Most of them come with a snap-in screen that is very helpful for filtering out hops and other solid ingredients when transferring the cooled brew from the brew pot to the fermenter. Another funnel I really like is sold by major retailers for the home canning industry. It is a small stainless steel funnel with a stainless steel screen insert. These funnels cost between $10 and $15, and are about 6 inches in diameter, meaning you have to aim carefully

Straining equipment

when pouring the wort (unfermented beer) into the fermenter!

The type of straining gear you need will depend on the quantity of material you have to strain. Straining the large amounts of grain for all-grain recipes requires mashing and lautering equipment, which is described in more detail in chapter 4.

Straining bags are a great option if you are dealing with a smaller amount of grains. The bag should be large enough to loosely hold the grains while allowing for expansion as they swell. If the grains are packed too tightly, water will not flow freely through the bag and you will not extract all the goodness from the malt. It is better to have too large a bag than too small. A bag that is at least 9 by 12 inches can hold up to 4 pounds of crushed grain. If possible, choose a bag made from organic cotton.

Hop-boiling bags are also useful, but you should have at least three because many recipes call for adding hops at three separate times. If you only have one bag, you have to fish the bag out of the boiling wort, open it, and add more hops. This is hard to do without getting burned, and the temporary removal of the hops could influence the flavor and bitterness extraction.

Colanders are useful for straining small amounts of grains. The size depends on the type of brewing you do and the batch size you will be brewing.

Brew Tip

IF THE STRAINER IS ALL STAINLESS, you can sterilize it by putting it in the brew kettle during the last 20 minutes of boiling. The heat will sterilize it, and you will not have to use chemicals or expend more energy with a different heat source. If you use an immersion wort chiller, throw that, the thermometer, and your (nonplastic) stirring spoon into the pot as well. When the brew is finished, you will not need to scramble around sanitizing these items at the last minute!

A large kitchen colander, at least 4 quarts, can be used for any of the beginning recipes in chapter 7. If you already own a colander with larger holes, you can line it with a piece of cheesecloth to filter out the smaller particles. Stainless steel equipment is preferable if it will be used in both your kitchen and your brewery. Plastic strainers can trap flavors and oils from cooking that you may not want transferred to your homebrew.

Strainers are useful for filtering out hops. Many brewers simply throw the loose hops into the brew kettle and strain them out at the end. For this method you will need a large funnel (if your primary fermenter has a narrow mouth) and a fine-mesh strainer that fits inside the funnel and strains out the hops as the beer is being poured into the fermenter. A regular 6- to 8-inch kitchen strainer works well. Some homebrew funnels have a handy snap-in screen. These are convenient, but often the mesh is so small that the screen clogs easily. Both the funnel and the strainer should be stainless steel or plastic so they can be sanitized.

WORT CHILLER

A wort chiller is optional, but using one will make the process go much faster and can help you produce better beer, because rapid chilling reduces off-flavors and the risk of infection. A wort chiller functions as a heat exchanger and will cool 5 gallons of boiling-hot wort in about 20 minutes. The most common type is an immersion chiller made from about 25 feet of copper tubing coiled into a cylinder that fits most large brew pots. The ends stick out and have attachment points for water hoses. As cold water runs through the coils, the brew is cooled quickly. Wort chillers use a lot of water to cool hot wort, but you can recycle it for cleaning or irrigation so it isn't wasted.

Immersion wort chiller

FERMENTER

This large container, usually holding 5 gallons, should have a single opening that can be sealed with an airlock or vent tube. Carboys — large glass bottles

Fermenter with draining stand and carboy with airlock and stopper

with narrow necks — are a popular choice and the option I recommend if you cannot afford stainless steel. You should have at least one fermenter. Two is better, so you are able to have more than one brew fermenting at a time or have the option to transfer the beer to a second stage (secondary fermenter), which can help produce a cleaner finished beer and prevent off-flavors.

Glass, stainless steel, and food-grade plastic are commonly used materials. A fermenter should be free from scratches, major dents, rust patches, or non-beer-friendly residues. Residue is bad when it comes to brewing, especially the toxic kind or the kind that can introduce bacteria to your fermenting beer. A spoiled batch will cost you more than the money you saved on a cheap or improperly repurposed fermenter!

AIRLOCK AND STOPPER

Airlocks are one-way valves that allow fermenting gases to escape while preventing unwanted bacteria from getting into your beer. For a tight seal, most fermenters need a rubber stopper with a hole that perfectly fits the airlock.

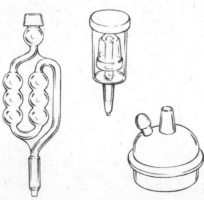

Airlocks and stoppers

HYDROMETER

A hydrometer is a simple glass instrument used to measure the density of liquid as compared to water. It is a fragile glass tube with a weighted bottom and a narrow neck with scale markings on it. The most common scales for brewing are *specific gravity, balling,* and *potential alcohol.* Triple-scale hydrometers that include all three scales are readily available.

Unfermented beer has a high sugar content. Sugar solution has a higher density than water, and so does wort. Alcohol, on the other hand, has a lower density than water. As the beer ferments, sugars are converted into alcohol by the yeast, and the density drops. To take a hydrometer reading, place a sample in a test jar, which is a narrow tube of plastic or glass with a stand to hold it up. Read the scale at eye level. Once you know the original gravity and final gravity, it is a simple matter to calculate the alcohol percentage of the finished beer.

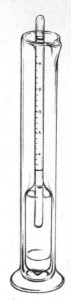

Hydrometer

SIPHONING AND TRANSFER GEAR

Simply pouring the beer from one vessel to another mixes in an excessive amount of oxygen, which can ruin the beer, so most brewers use a siphoning device called a racking cane. This is a long tube that reaches all the way to the bottom of the fermenter and has a curved top to prevent the tube from collapsing, which could cause the siphon to fail. It also has a removable tip

Racking cane

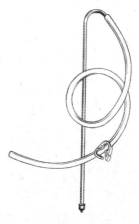

Bottling wand

shaped like a little inverted cup that prevents the gunk at the bottom of the fermenter from being sucked into the racking cane. The flatter bottom of the tip also helps the cane rest on top of the sediment layer instead of sinking down into it, another feature that contributes to a clean, sediment-free flow of beer from one vessel to the next.

To go with the racking cane, you will need some food-grade siphon tubing sized to fit it. A tubing clamp that threads over the siphon tube is a very useful addition; it can help you control the flow rate and stop the flow if needed. If your fermenter has a narrow opening, you still need a funnel to assist you in filling the fermenter with fresh-brewed wort or to help with cleanup.

BOTTLING EQUIPMENT

Most homebrewers package their homebrew in glass bottles that are specifically designed to hold the high pressure of a carbonated beverage. There are other options for packaging beer, but none is quite as reusable, cheap, and readily available as the humble glass beer bottle. Beer bottles require a lot of energy and materials to manufacture and transport. Reusing them is far better than recycling because the amount of energy it takes to wash and sanitize old bottles is much less than that needed to melt down and make new ones. Unfortunately, much of the energy required is human and comes in the form of scrubbing. For most of us homebrewers, scrubbing bottles is our least favorite task.

Bottles come in all shapes and sizes, but one thing must be true for any bottle that will hold beer: it must be strong enough to contain the pressure of a carbonated beverage. Any bottle that once held beer or sparkling wine is sufficient. Champagne bottles are wonderful. Flip-top bottles are great because the caps are also reusable, although the rubber washers will have to be replaced when they wear out.

A bottling wand is an inexpensive plastic tube that has a valve on the end. The valve opens to allow the beer to flow when the wand is pressed down, and the flow stops when the valve is lifted up. It allows the bottles to fill from the bottom up, which can help prevent oxidation of the beer.

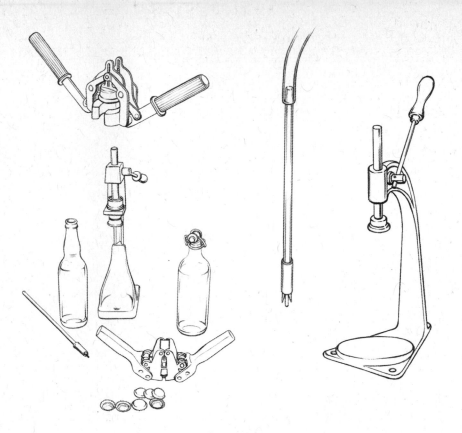

Bottling equipment

Bottle cappers come in several different styles. The least expensive version is a wing or hand capper. To use it, you place a cap on the bottle, position the capper over the top, and pull down the handles to crimp the edges. Bench cappers are slightly more expensive but a bit more durable, and most provide a more consistent, higher-quality crimp than hand cappers. They can be freestanding or can be clamped onto a counter; they adjust to the height of the bottles being used. Bottle capper technology has changed little in the past hundred years. Thus it is possible to find an antique capper that is still fully functional, and these are often more durable than ones made today.

CLEANING TOOLS

A large brush, often called a carboy brush, is indispensable when it comes to cleaning narrow-mouthed fermenting vessels. The long handle and bent

Efficient Use of Raw Materials

Thrifty homebrewers often repurpose bottles and soda kegs to package beer in. Here are some other ways to use materials more efficiently:

Brewing ingredients. I would never tell anyone to skimp on ingredients, but being smart about your purchases can save resources. Start by buying high-quality fresh ingredients, and only buy as much as you can realistically use over the shelf life of the ingredient. Then brew smart, paying attention to detail to lessen the chances that a batch will go wrong, provoking an irresistible urge to toss it down the drain.

Cleaners. Make only as much solution as you really need, and use it for multiple tasks until it is inactive or too dirty to be useful. You can often make do with slightly lower concentrations than the manufacturer recommends. They are in the business of selling you as much cleaner as you will buy, after all!

Bottle caps. Technically, it is possible to recrimp them, but the plastic liners are designed for onetime use. Metal crimp-on bottle caps can be recycled, however, and some resourceful artisans use them to make jewelry or fashionable belts or other decorative items. Flip-top bottles can be reused indefinitely, though they cost more initially. The rubber washers can also be reused, but they do wear out; when they show tiny cracks or start to become brittle from repeated use, replace them. I find I only need to replace mine about once a year, or after 6 to 12 uses.

Miscellaneous supplies. Most peel-and-stick labels are attached to shiny paper that cannot be recycled. Make your own labels from recycled or recyclable paper and attach with a glue stick or an eco-friendly craft glue. Labeling only the beers you give away and marking your private stash with a Sharpie will save you a bit of time and money while conserving resources.

Colored electrical tape makes handy reusable keg labels that can be peeled off easily and stuck back on multiple times. I have one for just about every kind of beer I have ever brewed, and I store them on the side of my refrigerator when they're not in use. Sometimes when I am wondering what to brew next I'll peruse my collage of keg stickers, which almost always helps me decide!

If you regularly use acid test kits or pH papers, save money and packaging by buying replacement papers and solutions in bulk. You can also develop some less scientific methods of testing, such as increasing your reliance on taste and smell.

brush are designed to reach the sloped inside shoulder of a carboy and remove minute particles that you can't see but that will harbor a healthy population of unwanted bacteria. A carboy brush is essential for making sure the bottles you use are really clean. A bottle brush is much like a carboy brush, except it is smaller and the brush is straight, not bent.

Tubing, bottle, and carboy brushes

Choosing Eco-Friendly Materials

Stainless steel, glass, plastic, wood, aluminum, and copper are materials commonly used to make homebrewing equipment. Sometimes you have a choice of several materials for a given application. For instance, fermenters are available in plastic, glass, or stainless steel.

It makes good sense to choose durable quality items that have a long service life and thus do not have to make an early one-way trip to the landfill. It may be more expensive initially to buy high-quality equipment, but it generally saves money over time. I still own the very first 4-gallon stainless steel stockpot I purchased in 1994. It cost twice as much as the ceramic-on-steel canning pot my then brewing partner bought, but it outlasted that canning pot by about 15 years. Spread out over a 20-year service life, even a two-hundred-dollar brew kettle does not add very much to your beer cost!

The winner of the durability challenge is definitely stainless steel, followed by copper, then glass. Unless you break it glass will last a lifetime. Plastic is sturdy but will develop scratches and become brittle within a few years, curtailing its life, though plastic is often the only choice for some smaller items. There are many types of plastic, some of which are controversial, and a few, such as PVC, that are known to be unsafe for food contact. I recommend doing your research (see Resources) before choosing to brew in plastic containers.

The best choice for your home brewery will often depend on a combination of other factors as well, including how often you plan to brew, what your brewing system volume will be, and physical limitations such as limited storage space or a limit to how much weight you can lift. A 5-gallon glass carboy full of beer weighs in at over 50 pounds, which is definitely one important fact to consider!

Finding Equipment and Supplies

The first places to shop for homebrewing equipment are flea markets, thrift stores, yard sales, and online marketplaces such as Craigslist. Many folks who used to brew at some point no longer do it. You might think them nuts to give up such an awesome hobby, but why not take advantage of the cost savings and the benefit to the environment by buying used? You might find a complete homebrewing setup on Craigslist for a fraction of the cost of buying everything new.

Boiling pots, wort chillers, glass carboys, bottle cappers, and home draft equipment (for kegging) are all great items to pick up used. Some gently used plastic items are okay, but I would be wary of purchasing a used plastic fermenter. Who knows if the last batch fermented in it was infected?

Your next stop should be your local homebrew shop, if you have one within reasonable driving distance. Even if you find some used equipment, chances are you will need to fill some gaps and you also need fresh supplies like cleaner, sanitizers, and bottle caps. The staff at the brew shop can answer your questions, and they just might stock organic or locally produced items. You can connect with other brewers in your area through the shop and get involved with a local homebrew club, if there is one.

Other sources for homebrewing equipment include restaurant supply stores, general houseware stores, and even science or lab supply stores. The local hardware store is a good place to pick up materials and parts if you plan on making some of your own items, but definitely check the label on plastic parts, as many plastic goods sold in hardware stores are not made of food-grade material.

After you exhaust your local sources, there are plenty of reputable homebrew mail-order suppliers. Choose one that is as geographically close to you as possible; this reduces the shipping cost as well as the carbon footprint of the goods that are shipped to you. See Resources for a partial list of suppliers.

How to Be Clean and Green

A critical step in the homebrewing process is cleaning and sanitizing your equipment. Cleaning physically removes contaminants that might encourage bacterial growth and sanitizing kills most microbes. Sterilization kills all living organisms. Understanding what makes a brewing sanitization regime effective can also help you to be more environmentally friendly. First, realize that it is nearly impossible to work in a sterile environment, especially when brewing beer at home. This is okay. Most commercial breweries don't operate under completely sterile conditions either. Brewers must sanitize to keep unwanted organisms at manageable levels; the alcohol level, hops content, and natural antimicrobial behavior of living yeast do the rest.

As eco-savvy folks know, many traditional cleaning solutions have the potential to damage our health and the environment through chemicals that are designed to kill microorganisms. While it's necessary to kill off the bugs that can sour a batch of beer or encourage fungus or mold, the gunk that results from the cleaning process has to end up somewhere when you are done with it. Sending it down the drain usually just makes it someone else's problem.

Cleaners and sanitizing agents may include ingredients that can cause eye, skin, or respiratory irritation, and some ingredients can contribute to longer-term health issues. The concentrated forms of some commercial cleaning products are classified as hazardous, creating potential handling, storage, and disposal issues. Some chemicals found in cleaning products or generated in their manufacture persist in the environment, meaning they do not easily break down and can accumulate in the environment or our bodies over time. Fortunately, many eco-friendly cleansers are available, including some that are made specifically for the beer-brewing crowd.

Maintaining a clean, green home brewery involves a two-step process:

1. Remove grime and deposits from equipment, using a low-sudsing cleaner and hot water. Pay special attention to items that will remain in contact with the beer for a long time, such as the fermenter, and any items that will come in contact with the beer after it has been boiled. Thoroughly rinse all equipment with clean water to remove any residue.

2. Sanitize all equipment that will touch the beer after the boiling stage, and rinse immediately before use. Some sanitizers, such as Star San, are available in no-rinse formulas, in which case the equipment can be allowed to drip-dry, leaving a protective film. If using a low-toxicity sanitizer such

as hydrogen peroxide, rinsing is not necessary. It is also safe to skip rinsing after iodine sanitizer has been used, but some find the smell strong enough to warrant a final rinse. If you do rinse, use sterile water (boiled for 15 to 20 minutes), waiting until just before you use the equipment, as surfaces do not remain sanitary for long after the sanitizer has been rinsed away.

Follow the Directions!

Knowing how critical sanitation is, beginning homebrewers often make a common error: they use too much cleaning product! It is important to stick to the guidelines on the label and dilute any cleaning product to the recommended levels. Some products actually lose effectiveness if mixed incorrectly, and others become toxic if the solution is stronger than recommended.

ECOLOGICALLY SOUND CLEANSERS AND SANITIZERS

Here is a rundown of cleansers and sanitizers that can be used safely in brewing without generating overly toxic residue or waste.

Sodium percarbonate, a combination of sodium carbonate (soda ash) and hydrogen peroxide, is stable until mixed with warm water, at which point it splits back into its constituent ingredients, resulting in a strong cleaning solution. The peroxide provides bleaching action, while the sodium carbonate acts as a descaling agent to lift deposits from equipment. These no- or low-foaming cleaners rinse off easily. They have a low level of toxicity, so that if you take normal precautions, follow the directions, and refrain from drinking the stuff, you will suffer no ill effects. They can be a mild skin irritant. If you have sensitive skin or will be washing a lot of bottles, use gloves as a reasonable precaution.

Soda ash has been regarded as a reasonably benign cleanser since the late 1800s. It was commonly manufactured from salt brine and limestone, with the main by-products being calcium chloride and ammonia, which are sold for other uses or recycled to manufacture more soda ash. A significant amount of solid waste is produced in the manufacture of soda ash, primarily large amounts of unrefined limestone with a high sodium and chloride content, which caused water pollution near some factories. Sodium carbonate can also be refined from natural deposits of the mineral ore trona. Refining is a much less resource-intensive process that produces very little hazardous waste. In the United States most sodium carbonate is now produced by the latter, more environmentally friendly method.

I have used several brands of sodium percarbonate–based cleaners, and all are quite effective. Five Star's PBW is my personal favorite, because it leaves no residue after long soaking periods and is very effective at removing labels. It is formulated specifically for the brewing industry and is widely available at homebrewing supply stores. Straight-A cleaner is a close second, and the only negative mark in my experience is from a film left on bottles left to soak in a Straight-A solution overnight. Many brewers swear by OxiClean, which is cheaper than the homebrew cleaners. It is widely available where household goods and laundry detergent are sold.

White distilled vinegar is acetic acid produced by the fermentation of alcohol by acetic acid bacteria and then distilled, which renders it sterile. It is cheap and effective at cutting grease, lifting deposits, and reducing stains and odors. It dissolves *beer stone* and other mineral buildup and is great for cleaning stainless steel and removing oxidation from copper. However, acetic acid bacteria can ruin a batch of beer by unintentionally turning it into vinegar, so if you use raw, undistilled vinegar, you must sterilize it by boiling for at least 20 minutes and allow it to cool before using. You don't want vinegar-causing bacteria anywhere near your home brewery!

White distilled vinegar can also be used as a sanitizer, but it is only effective at temperatures over 130°F (54°C). It must be used full strength (at least 5 percent acetic acid, the minimum required acid level for commercially produced vinegars) and must remain in contact with the surface for at least 1 minute. This works for small items such as stoppers, but for large items such as carboys, a solution such as iodophor is more practical.

Vinegar has been found to be 99.9 percent effective against food-borne pathogens such as *E. coli* and salmonella, but its effectiveness as a homebrew sanitizer has not been fully documented. To be on the safe side, I use boiled vinegar to clean countertops and the sink area before brewing and stick to other sanitizers for my fermenter and other brewing equipment. If you have access to an industrial chemical supplier, you may be able to obtain 99 percent pure acetic acid, which can be diluted to make the large quantities necessary for sanitizing all your brewing equipment.

Hydrogen peroxide is an effective sanitizer when used in concentrations of 3 percent or more, and it is approved for use as a sanitizer by the U.S. Environmental Protection Agency (EPA). Hydrogen peroxide breaks down into oxygen and water, leaving no harmful residue. When applied at sufficient strength, it acts as a disinfectant by oxidizing the cell membranes of microorganisms, effectively burning them to death. The 3 percent solution found in retail drugstores is just strong enough to be used without dilution. Soak small items for at least 60 seconds. To sanitize a container, fill it to the brim, or slosh the solution around for a couple of minutes. For a 5-gallon carboy, use at least a pint and slosh it around so all surfaces inside are contacted many times.

Industrial strength hydrogen peroxide (35 percent) is available through industrial suppliers and sometimes through pool supply companies or janitorial supply companies that cater to hospitals. To use it, mix 1 part peroxide with 10 parts water. If you decide to sanitize regularly with hydrogen peroxide, it may be worth the effort to find 35 percent peroxide, as it will be more economical in the long haul and will significantly reduce the amount of packaging required.

Handle with Care

Technical-grade peroxide must be handled with care, as must other full-strength cleaning chemicals (such as bleach or acetic acid). At full strength it can burn skin, and the vapor can be a potent irritant to the eyes and respiratory system. Ask for the Material Safety Data Sheet (MSDS) when you purchase any industrial-strength chemicals, so you have all the facts you need to safely handle them.

Iodophor sanitizer is a preparation of iodine bound with a surfactant carrier so the iodine readily dissolves when mixed with water. Iodophor can be used as a no-rinse sanitizer because the iodine breaks down so rapidly that by the time it dries there is little to no residue. It is a very effective sanitizer at low concentrations. The recommended dilution is 12.5 parts per million (ppm) of iodophor in cold water, which is sufficient to sanitize items with 60 seconds of contact time. To err on the safe side, I recommend a contact time of 5 to 10 minutes to make up for less than perfect cleaning. Iodophor is easy to use because when mixed to the proper dilution it has a light brown or amber color not unlike a light beer. When the solution loses its color, or if it has been longer than 24 hours since it was prepared, it is no longer effective as a sanitizer, and a fresh batch should be made. Because iodophor solution breaks down so quickly, it can be allowed to stand until clear and then be used for irrigation or cleaning.

How Safe Is Iodine?

A naturally occurring mineral, iodine by itself is nontoxic in small quantities. An iodine solution of 12.5 ppm is safe enough to drink, although it has an alarmingly unpleasant flavor. The added surfactant used in iodophor is basically a strong form of soap that is not suitable for human consumption; you wouldn't want to drink soap either.

In 2006 the U.S. EPA reviewed iodine and iodine complexes, including iodophor, and determined that they are noncarcinogenic and nontoxic for skin exposure. Internal intake in acute levels above the Recommended Daily Allowance generally has a temporary effect, and healthy individuals readily excrete the excess through action of the thyroid gland.

Star San is an acid-based, self-foaming sanitizer formulated for the homebrewing market by Five Star Chemicals. It is a blend of phosphoric acid and dodecylbenzenesulphonic acid. When used with a spray bottle, the foaming action increases contact time on surfaces. Acid-based sanitizers are very effective at killing microorganisms by rupturing cell walls within 30 seconds. It leaves no odor and doesn't stain, which is why many homebrewers prefer it over iodophor. Because of its acid-based nature, surfaces remain sanitary for a longer period of time than with other no-rinse sanitizers.

Like other sanitizing agents, Star San and other acid-based sanitizers are powerfully strong and require dilution in water before use. At full strength the acid can eat away soft metals, rubber, plastic, and your skin and clothes. It should be treated as a hazardous material until diluted, and any spills should be cleaned up immediately with plain water. Once diluted to the recommended strength, acid-based sanitizers are reasonably safe to work with and will not damage clothing or furniture, but if your skin is sensitive, wearing gloves is recommended. Diluted, it is safe for most septic systems and municipal sewer systems.

Chlorine Bleach — Not for Eco-Brewers!

From the beginning of my homebrew adventure, back in 1994, I have been advised to use bleach as a sanitizer. I tried it a few times but ditched it in favor of iodophor, alcohol, and peroxide. Although bleach is certainly effective, cheap, and readily available, from an eco-brewing perspective it is really not a good option. Here are my top three reasons not to use it:

1. Bleach is toxic and highly corrosive. It can damage skin and eyes, and if left in contact with stainless steel can corrode and pit this otherwise virtually impervious metal. Chlorine gas is listed as a hazardous pollutant by the EPA.

2. Bleach smells and tastes bad. The odor of chlorine is detectible at 3 ppm; it can be absorbed by plastic items, which transfer that awful taste to your beer. If you are in a bind and bleach is all you have available, rinse everything extremely well with boiled water.

3. Chlorine manufacturing pollutes. The chlorine manufacturing industry has created some of the deadliest toxins known. Persistent toxic chemicals such as dioxin bioaccumulate in plants and animals and eventually wind up in human bodies.

Although dodecylbenzenesulphonic acid is a scary sounding name, it is widely used in laundry detergent and billions of pounds of it are produced each year. It biodegrades rapidly. Phosphoric acid is also considered to be readily biodegradable, with low bioaccumulation potential.

Ethyl or isopropyl alcohol can aid in keeping the home brewery sanitary, but by itself it is not the most effective sanitizer. Because of its general toxicity, methyl alcohol is not recommended, and isopropyl alcohol, because of its nasty taste, should not be allowed near your homebrew. Interestingly, pure alcohol is slightly less effective than diluted, so use it at 70 to 80 percent. Ethyl alcohol, in the form of 140 proof vodka kept in a spray bottle, is my spot sanitizer of choice.

Soaking items in 70 percent alcohol for 5 to 10 minutes is normally sufficient to kill most microorganisms, but it will not kill all bacterial spores or viruses. As with all sanitizers, alcohol's success as a sanitizer is contingent on the initial cleanliness of the surface. It is handy for quickly spritzing the mouth of a carboy or yeast starter vessel or for providing a sterile lubrication when attaching keg disconnects. It is an effective hand sanitizer as well.

I use it as a supplemental sanitizer, rather than replacing anything else in my regimen, because it is much more expensive than the other options and not quite as effective. And a word of caution: 140 proof or 70 percent alcohol is very flammable!

SANITIZING WITH HEAT

Using heat, either dry or wet, is a time-honored method of sterilization that has been around since the 1800s, when cloth was boiled to provide sterile bandages. Used properly, heat completely eliminates all microorganisms, making it the only true sterilization technique that is readily accessible to homebrewers, as most other methods just sanitize, not sterilize. The level of sterilization achievable with heat is not necessary for homebrewing equipment, but we do use this method when boiling the wort every time we brew.

Heat is useful for sterilizing porous items, such as the cloth bags used for steeping hops or spices in the fermenter, because it is very effective and does not leave any chemical residue whatsoever. Plus, there are no chemical solutions to dispose of. On the other hand, heat sterilization does require energy

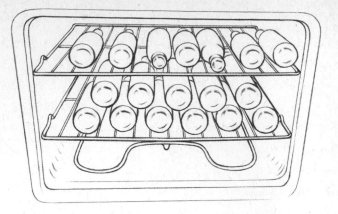

Sterilizing bottles in an oven

— a lot of it — in the form of fuel, whether it is a fossil fuel, wood, or electricity that is most likely generated by oil, coal, or natural gas.

Dry heat sterilization can be done in a home oven. This is a popular method for sterilizing bottles. Most ovens can hold enough bottles for one 5-gallon batch of beer. Most bottles are made of a type of glass that can become brittle with rapid heating or cooling. To minimize structural damage, stack the bottles in the oven before turning the heat on. Leave the bottles in the oven after the heat is turned off, and let them cool completely before removing them. They will stay sterile indefinitely as long as the openings are sealed. Small bits of tinfoil placed on the openings before heating work well for this purpose.

TIMING DRY HEAT STERILIZATION

The amount of time required to heat-sterilize bottles depends on oven temperature and whether you're using a convection oven. It uses less energy to run the hotter cycle for a shorter time period. Use the following chart as a guide:

Temperature	Heating time, regular oven*	Heating time, convection oven*
340°F (171°C)	60 minutes	45 minutes
320°F (160°C)	120 minutes	90 minutes
285°F (141°C)	180 minutes	140 minutes

*Start timing from the point when the sterilizing temperature is reached, not from when the oven is first turned on.

Wet heat sterilization is a faster method. A boiling water bath effectively kills most bacteria and viruses, but boiling does not render items completely sterile. Bacterial and fungal spores can survive boiling for shorter periods, but these are of no great concern for homebrewing, as anything harmful that could survive in fermented beer will be killed in a boil of 20 minutes or longer.

Wet heat works most effectively as pressurized steam. A pressure cooker or an autoclave is required for steam sterilization. To fully sterilize items with steam, hold them at a temperature of 250°F (121°C) for at least 15 minutes. At 275°F (135°C) 3 to 5 minutes is sufficient for most items. Most homebrewers do not have access to full-size autoclaves, but a home pressure cooker can be useful for sterilizing small items such as rubber stoppers or flasks used for yeast culturing, when sanitary equipment is especially important.

Reuse Cleaning Solution and Sanitizers

After brew day is done, think twice before dumping that batch of cleaner!

1. Use it to soak kegs or scorched brew pots or bottles that need delabeling. Soaking for several days in a percarbonate cleaner such as PBW or OxiClean will remove all but the most stubborn labels and leave your bottles spotlessly clean. Just make sure the cleaner is not the type that will leave any mineral deposits on your bottles. When in doubt, soak a single bottle overnight to be sure.

2. Used cleaner is also very effective in the kitchen for removing coffee stains from glass and stainless steel and removing stubborn deposits from pots and pans with an overnight soak.

3. Let your iodophor sanitizing solution sit outside in buckets for a few days and it will naturally deactivate, after which you can use it to irrigate. Dilute acid-based sanitizers by mixing with wort chiller water or grey water (at least double the water volume) so it is safe to water the garden with. You can also do this with cleaning solutions. Just to be safe, I suggest watering a single plant of each type with a small amount, wait a few days to be sure the plant does not have an adverse reaction, then continue to use it if the plants seem okay.

4. Think of ways to combine cleaning and sanitizing chores. Doing this will reduce the number of batches of cleaner and sanitizer needed for each batch of brew, saving water and supplies. For instance, if you time things right, on brew day you can also bottle or rack off a previous batch, or attend to some bottle- or keg-washing chores, using the same batch of solution for each task. This has the added benefit of saving time, because there is normally a lot of waiting while the mash sits or during the boil.

2

FINDING Organic BREWING INGREDIENTS

Great home-crafted beers are the result of high-quality ingredients, good recipes, and good brewing practices. If you want your beer to excel, not just in flavor but in kindness to the environment, you will also want to choose locally grown and/or organic ingredients as much as possible. Organic ingredients are sometimes more expensive and can be a bit harder to find, and the selection of organic brewing ingredients is not as wide as the selection of conventionally grown ingredients.

Despite these inconveniences, with a little diligence and creativity, it is possible to brew virtually every beer style imaginable using just organic ingredients, and do it well. Many organic beers, a few of mine included, have won blue ribbons in competitions going head to head with beers made with nonorganic ingredients. The main ingredients for any beer are malt, yeast, and hops. Here is an overview of each, along with a discussion of adjunct ingredients.

Barley Malt

Next to water, malt makes up the largest percentage of any beer and thus contributes much of the flavor, so it's critical that you start with the best malt possible. Malting is the process of sprouting grain, typically barley, then drying it at low temperatures. The process converts most of the grain starches to fermentable sugars, primarily maltose, and makes the barley more digestible by yeast. Other grains can be malted — wheat and rye are also malted for the brewing industry — but barley is the base for virtually every commercial beer style.

Barley malt is available in whole kernel, as a liquid extract, or as a powdered extract. Beer made from whole kernel malt has to be mashed — a process of steeping the grains in water, which activates enzymes that convert starches in the grains to fermentable sugar. This more advanced brewing process is fully explained in chapter 4. It is much easier to brew beer with extract because the starches have already been converted to sugars, then condensed into a syrup or powder. Many brewers find it convenient to brew with extract even after they have brewed for years.

MALT EXTRACTS

The quality of malt extracts varies widely. As of this writing, there is just one brand of organic malt extract on the market, a pale unhopped extract made by Briess Malt and Ingredients Company. This extract is very good when fresh but will darken with age, as do all brands. Older extracts can have a stronger flavor, often called an "extract tang," and may produce a darker-colored beer. Seek suppliers who maintain fresh inventory, order by mail, or buy dry extract when in doubt, as it is much more shelf stable.

Powdered malt extract should flow freely. If it has clumped into a brick, it has been exposed to too much moisture, which degrades the quality. Liquid malt extract is harder to evaluate, especially if it is packaged in a bucket or can. Check for a "packed on" or "sell by" date on the package. Give obviously dusty, dented, or swollen packages a pass.

WHOLE-KERNEL MALTS

Whole-kernel barley malts fall into two main categories. The first is *base malts*, lightly kilned malts such as pale ale, pilsner, wheat malt, and Munich malt.

These malts contain starches that need to be mashed to extract fermentable sugars from the grains. A few pounds of this type of malt can be mashed together with some specialty grains and combined with extract to produce full-strength beer (see chapter 3). This partial-mash method is fairly easy for new brewers and does not require much special equipment. Alternatively, beer can be brewed entirely with base malts and no added extract using the all-grain process covered in chapter 4. Specialty malts can be added to the all-grain malt bill as needed to create certain beer styles.

The other main category of malts is usually called *specialty malts* and includes crystal, caramel, and chocolate malts. These malts have had the grain starches converted to sugars right inside the grain kernel. They are heated to starch conversion temperatures while still wet from the germination phase of the malting process and before being dried in the kiln. Then the grains, which now contain fermentable sugars, are kilned at higher temperatures to create caramelization. The longer the caramelized grains are roasted, the darker and more complex are the flavors that develop. (See pages 192–200 for information on kilning your own specialty malts.)

Brewing Across the Centuries

For millennia humans have been making fermented beverages from grains they could gather or grow locally. Some historians even theorize that agriculture actually began because people were producing larger quantities of grain for drinking purposes. Each culture evolved a way of converting the starchy grain to fermentable sugar, in many cases by chewing the grain and spitting it out, letting the enzymes present in saliva break down the starch. Some traditional fermented recipes that are still being brewed today include *chicha*, the South American beer made primarily from corn; *sake*, made from rice in Japan; and Bantu or Kaffir beer made from millet or sorghum in Africa.

Some caramel or crystal malts are roasted to amber shades to produce light, sweet caramel color and flavor, while others are roasted to dark reddish brown colors with more intense burnt caramel, plum, and raisin flavors. These malts are often given a color rating in the Lovibond color scale ranging from 10°L to 140°L. Lovibond is an international standard of measure commonly used in the beer industry. Specialty malts can be roasted even longer to produce the dark chocolate or almost black color and chocolaty, roasted flavors desired for dark beers such as stouts. Specialty malts are often blended to achieve a complex mix of flavors, and exact quantities are used to develop the precise color of finished beer that the recipe designer is looking for. See chapter 6 for a simple guide to malting your own grain and chapter 9 for recipe creation tips.

Local Flavor

Malt produced in different areas of the world can contribute different and unique properties to a beer. The term *terroir*, often heard in wine circles, describes the effect of climate, soil, and local water on the taste of the crops from a given area. This term can be rightly applied to a grain if it is grown in a single area and is not commingled with grain from other areas when it is processed into malt.

Now that small malt houses are reviving the craft of malting grains from distinctive regions, unlike large houses that blend the grains from many different regions for the sake of uniformity, the possibilities for distinctive regionally produced beers have grown significantly in recent years. Some homebrewers have taken this effect even further by growing and malting their own brewing grain (see chapter 6).

Just as the gourmet craft beer trend is fostering the start-up of small hop growers, a few grain producers are leaping into the challenging field of small-scale grain malting. For example, the Riverbend Malt House in North Carolina grows and malts varieties of grain that are still virtually unheard of in the brewing world: Thoroughbred Barley, Appalachian Wheat, and Carolina Rye.

FINDING ORGANIC MALT

Because commercial malting of barley has become very centralized, there are only a few producers of organic barley malt in North America. Unless you live near one, the chances are you will not be able to buy barley malt that has been grown and processed locally. The reality is that most barley growers have no hand in the malting process. They grow the barley to the specifications required by the malt house and ship the raw grain to the malt house, where it is malted, dried, and sometimes processed into extract.

The finished malt is then shipped to distribution points around the country. From the distributors the malt travels once again to breweries or homebrew shops. All of this travel adds up to a significant carbon footprint. However, the energy expended per glass of beer produced is much less than it would be to ship the finished beer, so by the simple act of making your own beer, you are doing something to help the environment. Cheers to that!

PURCHASING QUALITY MALT

The most important factor when purchasing malt is to make sure it is fresh. Obviously, you do not want to use musty, stale, or damp malt, or grains that are crawling with bugs, but it does take some experience to tell fresh, high-quality ingredients from stale ones. Start by smelling every grain and hop that you use. At first you might not be able to detect the highest quality, but it is not too hard to smell when a grain is off.

Good-quality malt has a pleasant smell. Base malt grains smell malty, grassy, or biscuity when fresh, but more like stale crackers or cereal when they are not in great shape. Flaked grains such as oats and rye that have a high oil content develop a rancid odor as they age. Crystal and dark malts can transform from a malted candy, raisiny, or fresh-roasted coffee smell to one that is bitter and sour smelling. Taste a small amount of the grains, too (unless there are bugs crawling in it).

If your community supports a homebrew store, the shop probably turns its inventory over frequently enough to maintain fresh stocks of popular grains. This is not always the case with organic ingredients because the demand for organic is lower than for conventionally grown, primarily because of higher prices. When buying organic malt, ask to see a sample or buy a small quantity the first time to make sure the quality meets your expectations.

If your local homebrew shop doesn't stock many organic ingredients or has a limited selection, it makes sense to divide your purchases between what you can obtain locally and what you can order by mail. You can save shipping costs by ordering 50-pound bags of base malt through your local shop, then ordering specialty grains and hops by mail. If you are an extract brewer, you may be able to special-order a 50-pound sack of dry malt extract or a 60-pound bucket of liquid malt extract. Since these make up the base of each batch of homebrew, you can expect to brew between five and ten 5-gallon batches of beer from each bulk bag or bucket.

STORING MALT

Malt is quite shelf stable as long as it is stored properly. Whole-grain malt should be stored whole, and if possible crushed just before use. If you do not have a grain mill and buy your grain milled by the homebrew supplier, store it in airtight containers until use.

Whole grains and dry malt extract can be stored in a refrigerator as long as precautions are taken to prevent moist air from entering the packaging. Double-bag the product and remove excess air to avoid condensation. Dampness will offset the benefit of the cooler temperatures, because damp malt loses quality very rapidly. It is fine to store malt at temperatures of 50 to 70°F (10 to 21°C) instead of refrigerating, as long as the temperature does not regularly exceed 70°F.

Store grains in a clean dry area that is protected from rodent and insect pests. Grains can be stored in their original 50-pound sacks until opened and then transferred to buckets or bins with securely sealed lids. If your storage area is dry and ventilated, the bag tops can be rolled down and taped securely shut.

Liquid and dry malt extract store well for up to 2 years under the right conditions, but both varieties will slowly darken with age. Dry malt extract tends to cake up over time and can turn into a solid brick if exposed to moisture. Make sure it is in an absolutely airtight package and keep in a cool place or even a refrigerator. Liquid malt extract can develop some undesirable flavors as it ages, ranging from a mild effect, such as licorice or molasses, to more unpleasant wet-cardboard or sherrylike flavors. If you need to store it for longer than a few months, refrigerate liquid malt extract to extend the shelf life and maintain the best quality.

Using Old Extract

Any off-flavors imparted by old liquid extract are much more noticeable in lighter-bodied beers. As an eco-conscious brewer, you want to avoid throwing anything away, so recycling older ingredients into a dark, hoppy, or spicy beer is one solution. You can end up with a drinkable beer this way, but it is always best to buy ingredients that you will be able to use within a few months.

Hops

Hops are the flowers from the hop plant (*Humulus lupulus*), a climbing vine that grows quite prolifically in many parts of the world but does best between 35 and 55 degrees latitude, where most of the world's commercial hop production is concentrated. Most hops produced for the brewing industry are processed into pellets, which preserves the quality and blends all of the hops in a given harvest to produce uniformity of alpha acids and aroma compounds. For large-scale commercial brewing, this consistency is invaluable.

Hops are available to the homebrewer in two main forms: whole and pelleted. **Whole hops** are simply the dried flowers. Often they are vacuum

Whole hops

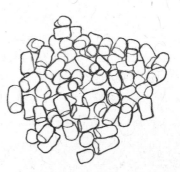

Hop pellets

sealed or compressed into plugs to preserve freshness. Whole hops are sometimes inaccurately called *leaf hops*. Since the flower is the part used for beer making, the correct term is *hop flowers* or *hop cones*, which refers to the pine-cone shape of the hop flower.

Hop pellets are simply hops that have been partially dried, then finely ground at low temperatures and compressed into small pellets, similar in appearance to rabbit food. Hop pellets are widely available, and often there is a larger selection of varieties. Although many eco-minded brewers instinctively prefer whole-flower hops, the pelleted form can often be of higher quality because the tight compression of the pellet better preserves the delicate hop oils.

Hops are very aromatic when fresh, and though the aroma depends on the variety of hop, they should never smell dusty or cheesy. Most hops are bright green when fresh, although some pellets may have a dark exterior. To release the full aroma of hop pellets, crumble a few between your fingers to release the aromas trapped inside the dense pellets.

FINDING ORGANIC HOPS

Because most hop buyers demand pelletized hops and hop-pelleting machinery is expensive and difficult to operate, there are only a few hop processors in North America, primarily located in the Pacific Northwest, where most modern hop cultivation takes place. However, hop shortages in 2008 and 2009 had an interesting effect: in response to the rising demand for organic hops, which most of the large established growers seemed to have little interest in filling, many small start-ups decided to cultivate organic hops to meet this new niche market (see Resources). Although organic hops are often more expensive, harder to find, and available in fewer varieties than conventionally grown hops, as demand rises, new varieties of organic hops find their way to market every year.

Short of growing your own hops, supporting growers who are practicing sustainable, organic agriculture is an excellent way to green up your brewing! Using creativity and the hop variety chart in chapter 9, you should be able to brew a wide variety of organic beers with hops that are grown reasonably close to home.

STORING HOPS

Once your hops are dried, they need to be properly packaged for storage. The longer you plan to store your hops, the better the packaging should be. The best storage conditions remove light, heat, and oxygen — all factors that speed deterioration. Over time, most hops lose alpha acid value and the aroma oils break down. As the hops oxidize, their fresh, clean aroma is lost, while stale, rancid, or even cheesy ones develop. Some varieties degrade faster than others — in general, higher-alpha hops have more natural antioxidants and retain alpha acid levels and freshness longer, while the low-alpha-aroma hops are more delicate and require the most careful storage.

There are several ways to avoid exposure to damaging elements including vacuum sealing, freezing, compressing, and using specially designed packaging. One easy and inexpensive method is to compress as many hops as you possibly can into mason jars or other airtight glass containers and freeze them. This method has a few drawbacks, however: it requires significant freezer space; there is the danger of broken glass; less oxygen is removed than with vacuum sealing; and if you remove some of the hops and store a partially emptied jar, more air is introduced. However, glass is more airtight than most plastic and is infinitely reusable.

I prefer to use the zippered foil pouches that are widely available online. For a small investment you can purchase enough of these bags to meet your hop storage needs for many years. These heavy-duty bags can be washed and reused many times, and they can be used without a vacuum sealer: simply stuff full of hops, seal the zipper almost all the way, then press flat to push out excess air before sealing completely. To prevent the bags from tearing during their life in your freezer, keep them in a heavy paper bag or other protective wrapper. If you have a vacuum sealer, it might be possible to use it with these bags, depending on the model of sealer you have.

Yeast

Without yeast, beer would not be beer. Yeast is a type of fungus that consumes simple sugars such as glucose and maltose and excretes alcohol, carbon dioxide, and other gases. Brewer's yeast is quite different from bread yeast, and you will want to use a good-quality version if you care about the

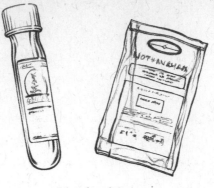

Liquid and dry yeast

flavor of your homebrew. Unless you want to make a singularly bad-tasting batch of beer, you should never use bread yeast to brew beer.

There are two main types of brewer's yeast, ale and lager. Ale yeast thrives at room temperature, and most ale yeast performs best between 60 and 70°F (16 and 21°C). Lager yeast thrives best at much cooler temperatures, usually ranging between 40 and 50°F (4 and 10°C). Brewer's yeast is commonly available in both dry and liquid form.

Dry yeast is a powder or granular form of dehydrated yeast that looks like baking yeast. Dry yeast survives shipping over long distances better than liquid and if refrigerated has a shelf life of several years, but the variety available to brewers is limited compared to the selection of liquid yeast.

Yeast in liquid form is in its natural living state. Liquid yeast is usually available to homebrewers as a pure culture packaged in a foil pouch or plastic vial. Brewers in North America, parts of Europe, and a few other lucky places have access to dozens of liquid yeast strains through homebrew retailers. Liquid yeast has a limited shelf life of 3 to 6 months but can often be revived after 6 to 18 months by making a starter culture. Liquid yeast absolutely must be stored under refrigeration, which adds a slight energy-cost premium. Because of its high perishability and more complex packaging, liquid yeast is typically three times more expensive than dry yeast.

If you live near a smaller-scale craft brewery, you might be able to obtain liquid yeast directly from it. Most such breweries have a surplus of yeast, and most brewers are receptive to sharing with homebrewers. Brewers have busy schedules, so contact the company to arrange a time, and have your container ready when you pick up the yeast. If you show up unannounced without a sanitized container, you should not be surprised if you are turned away. Mason jars, pub growlers, or Erlenmeyer flasks all make good transport containers for liquid yeast. Store the yeast in the refrigerator in a well-sealed container until use. If the yeast is more than a few weeks old, you should revive it with a starter (see page 53).

The cost of liquid yeast can be ameliorated somewhat by culturing it and making starters. Yeast can also be propagated and stored for future use, or harvested from beer bottles from commercial breweries that bottle-condition their beer or pasteurize it. Yeast culturing and harvesting goes beyond the scope of this book, but if you love science-geeky brew stuff, there are some excellent online tutorials.

Spices, Herbs, and Other Flavors

When it comes to enhancing a beer's flavor by adding herbs, spices, and other flavors, the possibilities are almost endless. Culinary spices, fresh or dried herbs, freshly grated citrus peel, chocolate, vanilla, and coffee add great flavor to select beer styles. Organic spices and flavors are widely available, although some of the more unusual flavors may be harder to find. Things like mugwort and heather that have long been used in traditional beer recipes are hard to pick up, even at the local health food store (see Resources).

Most beer recipes calling for herbs, spices, or other flavors use a small amount, and just as when brewing with hops, it is important to be careful about weights. Many flavors can easily overpower a beer — sometimes the difference between a great beer with wonderful aroma and flavor nuances and one that makes you cringe could be as little as a few grams too much of a given spice.

As with other ingredients, you want these additives to be organically grown and minimally processed whenever possible. Luckily there is a great selection of high-quality organic herbs and spices available to homebrewers — check farmers' markets and health food stores or grow your own! The quality and depth of flavor of the organic version is typically far superior to the conventionally grown counterpart.

THE ORGANIC NATURE OF YEAST

As of this writing organic beer yeast is not commercially available, though there is real interest in making organic yeast strains available to craft and homebrewers, and I fervently hope it will happen soon. Meanwhile, we are not going to worry too much about it, because once you understand how yeast works, you'll realize that if you feed the yeast organic food the yeast itself becomes organic. In fact, commercial organic beers are produced with the same yeast as nonorganic beers, within strict guidelines, of course.

If you follow best practices, you will be in the habit of making a yeast starter for each batch using organic malt. When the starter is pitched (added) into an organic beer, the vast majority of yeast cells will pretty much be organic by the time they finish fermenting. When the beer is finished, most of the yeast cells go dormant and sink to the bottom of the fermenter, leaving very little residue. So by the time you pop the cap of that beer made with "nonorganic" yeast, you are looking at a faint trace of nonorganic material, if any, in the finished beer.

One environmental concern, however, is that the manufacture of dry yeast does create some hazardous by-products that can have a detrimental effect on the environment if the waste is not treated properly. Production of dry yeast releases a significant amount of acetaldehyde, which is considered a hazardous air pollutant under the Clean Air Act. Volatile organic compound (VOC) emissions are also a concern, and most yeast manufacturing plants do not have wastewater treatment sufficient to handle the volume of waste produced. This is more of a concern in the production of dry yeast for the baking industry than it is for the brewing industry, because the scale of baking production is much higher and some of the aging production facilities in the United States currently lack state-of-the-art pollution controls.

STORING YEAST

Yeast degenerates most rapidly at room temperature, and overly high temperatures can kill yeast. Thus, it is best to store yeast in a refrigerator except when it is actively growing (as in a starter or in your fermenter). Dehydrated or freeze-dried yeast may be stored in the freezer with very little detriment. Liquid yeast should not be stored in a freezer unless it is suspended in a glycerin solution. This is an advanced procedure, usually not necessary unless you want to preserve a specific strain of yeast for a long time.

The Importance of Water

Water is an often overlooked ingredient, yet it accounts for at least 90 percent of the weight and volume of beer and often exceeds 95 percent of the total. A simple guideline when it comes to brewing is this: if you think your tap water is good enough to drink, it is probably sufficient for brewing most basic beers. Mineral content of the water is a consideration, but the extract used in beginner recipes usually has enough minerals to provide the foundation for a good beer. For a deeper discussion of water chemistry, see Looking at Water Chemistry, page 96.

If you use tap water for your beer, you should filter it to remove the added chlorine. A basic charcoal filter is sufficient to remove chlorine and any heavy metals or other toxic compounds while leaving most of the beneficial minerals in the water. Unless you are concerned about possible toxins or contaminants in the water, it is not necessary to filter water for cleaning or chilling. If you are very lucky, you have a well or a local spring provides your brewing water! I advise against using distilled water as it doesn't have the mineral profile necessary to make good beer (see Use Local Brewing Water, page 40). See chapter 4 for more information about the mineral content of water used for brewing.

Fermentable Adjuncts

In modern brewer's lingo *adjuncts* are unmalted grains used in beer recipes to add flavor or other characteristics not found in base malt or specialty grains. Buckwheat, corn, millet, oats, quinoa, rice, rye, sorghum, unmalted barley, and wheat are all adjunct grains that can be used to make beer. Some large commercial brewers add adjuncts such as corn or rice to cut costs and to make the beer lighter in color or flavor.

Most homebrewers use adjuncts to add texture, such as the silky mouthfeel that oats can add, or unique flavors, such as the crisp, dry, slightly sour flavor from rye. Flaked grains are the easiest form of adjunct grains to use, as they can be added directly to the mash. Whole grains such as rice or corn

Use Local Brewing Water

The most sustainable approach is to use your own tap water and filter it. A basic activated carbon water filter should be all you need. It works with simple water pressure, retains beneficial minerals, and does not waste water. Sometimes you can find a local spring to collect water from.

Some homebrewers brew most of their beers with distilled or reverse osmosis–filtered water, then add minerals to adjust the water mineral profile to exact specifications. Although this is a very scientific approach, it is costly — both to the environment and to the wallet. Making distilled water uses a lot of energy, and the last time I checked, it was selling for three dollars a gallon at the local supermarket. Mining, processing, packaging, and shipping mineral additives also requires energy and resources. From an eco-brewing standpoint it does not make much sense to remove minerals from water, then put more minerals back in.

If your style of brewing calls for a low mineral profile, you can build a solar still, plans for which can be found in many good survival guides or online. *When Technology Fails* by Matthew Stein includes plans for a basic one you can make with a sheet of plastic, a few rocks, a container, and a hole in the ground.

Another option is to buy water in bulk from the filtered water–dispensing machines found at many grocery stores (try Whole Foods) that allow you to use your own containers. Many of these machines do have an option to dispense reverse osmosis (RO)–filtered water, which is probably a cheaper and more sustainable option than buying distilled water in plastic jugs. The most important thing is to avoid buying bottled water.

If your house is equipped with a reverse osmosis system, you're not really ahead of the game. Most household RO water filters discharge between 4 and 18 gallons of wastewater for every gallon of purified water produced, and some systems use electric power as well. If water conservation is a part of your eco-brewing regime, using RO–filtered water is a bit counterproductive.

should be cooked and ground up before adding, as they are too tough to be broken down into fermentable sugars without this extra step.

Almost any grain can be added to the mash and the starches in the grains will be broken down into fermentable sugars as long as there are enough enzymes present in the base malts to break them down. If you are using a good-quality base malt such as a pale ale malt or a pilsner malt, it is possible to use up to two-thirds adjunct to one-third base malt. This is a useful capability when brewing partial mash recipes with a large portion of adjunct grains.

Organic adjunct grains are readily available, and here is where the bulk bin department of a well-stocked health food store is an organic brewer's best friend. The prices are usually reasonable, and you can buy exactly the amount you need. It is always a good idea to check for freshness, especially when buying in bulk. Although the reduced packaging is great for the environment, bulk bins allow more rapid oxidation, so the natural oils in the grains could cause them to turn rancid if the stock is not turned over regularly. If your local stores do not stock organic grains, see Resources.

Fermentable Sugars

A myriad of other sugar sources can be put to good use as brewing ingredients. Corn sugar, beet sugar, cane sugar, and honey are the ones used most often. Maple syrup, agave syrup, palm sugar, and molasses can also contribute fermentable sugar, as well as a unique flavor profile. Many of these sugars are available in organic form in health food stores or by mail order. These sugars are usually used in conjunction with barley malt to add flavor or other characteristics. They can be used on their own to make fermented beverages — these are gluten-free but do not usually closely resemble beer!

Corn sugar creates a fine bubble, is neutral in flavor, and is highly fermentable, leaving little sediment in the bottle. Corn sugar is often called dextrose, although dextrose can be made from ingredients other than corn. Dextrose is almost 100 percent glucose, which is nearly 100 percent fermentable by yeast. Organic dextrose made from corn or from tapioca is available from Internet retailers that sell organic brewing supplies.

Beet sugar is commonly used to make candi sugar syrup, an ingredient in many popular Belgian styles. Organic beet sugar is not readily available, although several sources of conventional (nonorganic) beet sugar exist for the household market. Candi sugar can be easily made from organic cane sugar, which is widely available (see page 333 for directions).

Honey is widely used in brewing, both as a fermentable sugar and as the base for mead, an ancient wine made entirely from honey. Honey is 95 percent fermentable. It should be pasteurized before adding to beer, as it contains wild yeast, bacteria, and enzymes that could interfere with the fermentation of lower-alcohol beers.

In recent years bee populations have been dropping dramatically, which is an alarming development because pollination by bees is essential to the future of sustainable agriculture and the stability of our ecosystem. The recent decline in bee populations has been linked to heavy agricultural pesticide use. You can help reverse this problem by buying honey that is locally produced and organically farmed if possible.

Although the idea of organic honey may seem somewhat problematic since foraging bees can fly anywhere, it may be labeled as such if the hives are located on certified land and are not within two miles of a sanitary landfill, incinerator, power plant, golf course, town or city; or of any crops sprayed with prohibited substances or genetically modified crops; or other sources of contamination. This is better for the bees, and the honey is better for your brew!

ADDING SUGAR WITH FRUIT

Fruit has been used in beer recipes for a very long time. Lambics are the oldest and perhaps the most well-known styles that use fruit to produce exceptional beers. Brewing with fruit can be a little tricky — it is best not to boil it, as this can cause the natural pectins to develop and gelatinize, which lead to cloudiness. Pasteurization is a good idea to kill unwanted bacteria.

Buying fresh fruit for your homebrew is where you can truly shop local and add to your organic brewing ingredients list. Farmers' markets, farm stands, and even the produce sections of some large grocery stores are great places to obtain fruit for brewing. When it comes to buying organic fruit, most of us have a variety of options close to home, and choosing organic fruit is a wise move, since many commercial fruit crops are heavily sprayed.

GMO Sugars

I would be remiss in my discussion of organic sugar if I did not bring up the issue of genetically modified organisms, commonly referred to as GMOs. The industry that promotes genetic engineering of food crops uses the argument that GMOs produce higher yields and will thus solve the world's food shortage problems. This is a laudable theory, but it has yet to be fully backed up in practice, with little real evidence that GMO crops are indeed producing higher yields or lower food production costs in any meaningful way.

The problems associated with GMO crops include a heightened reliance on pesticides and herbicides, which increases contamination of cropland and water supplies. Over 75 percent of GMO crops in production today are engineered to have increased tolerance to being sprayed with herbicide. GMOs can also create unexpected toxins or allergens in genetically modified food crops. The full extent of the potential health effects of consuming GMOs has not been fully studied, but these crops are steadily being released into the general food supply anyway.

Companies that sell food products containing GMOs in the United States are not required to disclose the presence of GMOs on the label, even though the same foods must contain GMO information on the label when exported to about 50 other countries. Some states have put forth ballot initiatives to require labeling of GMOs, but thus far such initiatives have been defeated by the companies that stand to gain the most profit by keeping consumers uninformed.

At the moment the only way to be completely sure the food products you consume are free from GMOs is to buy organic or to buy conventional single-ingredient foods that are known to be GMO-free. A number of consumer guides are available to help those of us concerned about avoiding GMOs (see Resources). However, much of the corn and sugar beet crop in the United States has been converted to GMO crops. Because of poor labeling laws and the industry-wide practice of shipping crops to a central facility for processing, GMO crops are mixed with non-GMO crops, so most sugars cannot be guaranteed to be GMO-free by the manufacturer.

The potential for chemical residues reaching harmful levels on sprayed fruit is amplified when you start using the large quantities of fruit that some beer recipes call for. A handful of berries seems harmless enough, but any chemical residues are multiplied with 5 pounds of them. See chapter 6 for a more thorough discussion of adding fruit to beer.

Sources for Brewing Ingredients

It is always a great idea to check in with your local homebrew retailer if you have one. A homebrew retailer is a great asset to any community that has a strong interest in homebrewing. These shops serve as a hub of homebrewing activities and often sponsor events or contests. Many shops offer low-cost or free classes taught by avid homebrewers. You may be able to find locally grown hops and other ingredients at your retailer; if not, the staff will know about growers in the area and may have a bulletin board where local sellers can advertise. They may also stock a few organic ingredients and might be willing to special-order others for you.

Ordering through the local shop supports your own homebrewing community, and it may save you money on shipping costs. Even if you cannot buy organic ingredients at your local shop, it will stock all the basic homebrewing essentials, from yeast to glass carboys, so I encourage you to shop locally for such needed supplies.

Another good source for ingredients such as flaked grains, honey, agave syrup, and rice syrup is your local health food store or the natural foods section of some large supermarkets. A farmers' market is a great resource for fresh fruit, herbs, honey, or brewing-friendly produce such as pumpkins, especially if you are seeking large quantities. Often you can get a bulk price on such things as honey or fruit when you buy directly from the farmer. It certainly never hurts to ask!

Brew Tip

FOR THE BEST HONEY FLAVOR and fermenting performance, add honey to the secondary fermenter after pasteurizing: Heat the honey to 180°F (82°C) and hold at that temperature for at least 20 minutes; then cool to room temperature, and add to the fermenter.

3

The BASICS of Brewing GOOD BEER

If you have never brewed beer before or are still a beginner, this chapter outlines the fundamentals of brewing. By the end of it, you will be ready to brew any of the recipes in chapter 7. If you are already homebrewing at the intermediate to advanced level, feel free to skip this chapter!

Brewing beer is a bit like growing a garden. To grow a garden you till the soil, add compost and organic fertilizer, and plant seeds. While the garden grows, you must make sure the plants have a good growing environment with plenty of water and sunlight. Eventually you harvest the vegetables or have a beautiful flowering plant. The basic principles of brewing beer are just as straightforward: You prepare the malt sugar, season with hops, and inoculate with brewer's yeast. While the beer ferments, you must provide the ideal growing conditions of temperature, nutrients, and a dark environment. The

yeast eats the sugars and excretes alcohol and gas, mostly carbon dioxide. In as little as a few weeks, your beer harvest is ready!

As in gardening, although the fundamental concepts are easy to understand, the details of brewing are just as important and a bit more complex. There will be a learning curve, so it makes good sense to start with the basics and follow proven procedures very carefully. Brewing from scratch (all-grain brewing) is a challenge most people are not well equipped to handle right away. An understanding of why each detail is important will come with experience. If you are like most folks who start homebrewing, you will find yourself getting excited about advancing your skills and trying new beer styles as you learn the craft.

Getting Started

You will need to do some preparation to make sure the first batch of beer you make is successful. The following checklist will help you make sure you are ready on brewing day:

Ingredients. To make good beer, you must use good ingredients, primarily malt, hops, and yeast. See chapter 2 for a complete discussion.

The absolute easiest way to begin brewing is to use only a malt extract, but I find that most beginning brewers are willing to put in the extra effort and add some whole grains to their batch. The improvement in quality is worth it, and most organic recipes call for the addition of grain.

Equipment. If you buy a starter package, it should contain all the gear you will need. If you are cobbling together the required equipment on your own, read chapter 1 to help you choose the best equipment. To help in your planning, the usual batch size for American homebrewers is 5 gallons (all the recipes in this book are for 5 gallons). It is possible to scale down to 2.5 or even 1 gallon, or to scale up to 10, 15, or even 50 gallons. Small batches usually consume more energy and water per gallon produced. Larger batches require more equipment than most beginning brewers have available but are typically more cost-effective both in price and resource impact (water and fuel) per gallon.

Recipe. To make sure your first batch tastes great, the first thing to do is choose a proven recipe. Brewing great beer requires precision in measuring the ingredients, especially the hops. You want to have a good balance of hop aromas and bitterness to the sweetness and body in the beer that come from malt and other sugars. You could choose one of the recipes from this book (which have been test-brewed for accuracy), a recipe you have found on the Internet or from a friend, or a prepackaged ingredient kit. The Pale Rider Ale on page 235 is a good recipe for starting out (or you can follow the one provided in your kit, if you go that way).

Time. Allow plenty of time to brew your first batch. Most beginner batches take 2 to 4 hours, plus time for the beer to ferment and to age in the bottle. If you like to multitask, you will find ways to streamline your brewing process as you gain experience. For the first batch, however, it is a really good idea to focus on one step at a time!

Space. You will need space in the kitchen or outdoor cooking equipment to cook up the brew, clean and sanitize equipment, and fill the fermenting container with fresh-brewed beer. You will also need a cool, dark space to keep the beer while it ferments. The fermentation takes 2 weeks to several months, depending on the type of beer. Certain beer styles, such as lambic and Belgian ale or mead, can take as long as a full year to brew. You probably don't want to wait that long for your first brew to be ready! A basic pale ale, porter, brown ale, or stout is usually ready to drink in about 4 weeks.

Are Kits Okay?

There is nothing wrong with choosing a kit to make beer, although I do caution you against using a prehopped, no-boil kit, as in my experience they produce dubious results. Most homebrew kits are of excellent quality and contain exactly the right amount of ingredients needed for the batch, so you will not have left-overs to worry about. Kits sold by reputable homebrew shops are your best bet, as they usually feature fresh ingredients and are put together by experienced home-brewers who love good beer.

Step 1. Assemble the Ingredients

Virtually every beer recipe uses just four key ingredients: barley malt, hops, yeast, and water. Brewing is a lot like baking in that it is important to measure each ingredient accurately. This is especially important with hops. Hops have powerful bittering properties, and a mistaken measurement of a fraction of an ounce can significantly affect the resulting beer. Before you brew, double-check that you have every ingredient on hand in sufficient quantity and that everything is fresh and in good condition.

Step 2. Clean Your Equipment

Cleaning is the least glamorous aspect of brewing, but it is critical. You will never regret doing a good job of it, but you might regret doing a poor job! Rinse everything well, as soap and oil residues can adversely affect a batch of beer. So can the residual flavors from that smoked cherry porter you brewed the last time. Any equipment that touches the beer during or after the boil must also be sanitized. The best procedure is to scrub all items in warm cleaning solution, rinse thoroughly, then do a final rinse with an effective sanitizer.

The most commonly used sanitizers are iodophor, which is iodine based, and acid-based sanitizers such as Star San (see chapter 1 for a complete discussion of sanitizers). With any sanitizer, follow the instructions for proper

Use Fresh Ingredients

If you purchased ingredients 6 months ago, it might be a good idea to replace any whole grains and hops, especially if they were stored at room temperature. Yeast should always be as fresh as possible; if in doubt either replace it or make sure you have some backup yeast. It is not a bad idea to keep a package or two of dry beer yeast in your fridge as cheap insurance. Dry (dehydrated) yeast stores well for up to a year if refrigerated, and if the beer you are making with 50 dollars' worth of ingredients does not start fermenting, you will have some more readily available to salvage the batch.

dilution carefully. If you are concerned about residues, you can rinse again with boiled, sterile water. I emphasize good old-fashioned scrubbing or a good long soak over relying too heavily on chemical remedies. Your equipment should look, feel, and smell clean.

After each brew, clean equipment before storing it, especially if you do not brew often. A missed bit of extract can grow into a nasty patch of mold that will ruin anything made of a semiporous material, including rubber and plastic. If your tubing develops mold, it is too risky to use it again unless it is silicone or high-heat tubing that can be boiled. When in doubt, replace inexpensive items such as plastic tubing or airlocks, and reclean and sanitize metal or glass items.

Step 3. Prepare the Yeast

How you handle the brewing yeast makes a considerable difference in the quality of the beer that you produce. Once you understand that yeast is a living organism that needs to be nurtured and treated gently, you should have little trouble coaxing your yeast to a great performance each time you brew.

Bad Bacteria = Bad Beer!

Most bacteria and wild yeast that commonly infect beer are undesirable, but the good news is that the presence of alcohol in the beer prevents an infection that could make you really ill. In fact, before modern sanitizing technology became available, beer was often safer to drink than the municipal water supply. Wild yeast can impart an unpleasant barnyard flavor to your beer, but bacterial infections, which are far more problematic, will turn your brew into vinegar or something even worse (see Making the Best of a Bad Batch [Vinegar!], page 154). Bacteria that most commonly infect beer include lactic acid bacteria, acetic acid bacteria, Obesumbacterium proteus, Pectinatus, and Megasphaera.

Fortunately, many bacteria find the typical environment in wort and beer to be less than ideal. Most fermented beer has a low pH, high alcohol content, antimicrobial compounds from hops, and little oxygen. Thus, using healthy yeast and practicing good sanitation techniques are normally all it takes to prevent an infected batch.

Yeast is sold in either dry or liquid form; the form you use determines how you handle it. The stronger the beer, the more important it is to start with an adequate amount of yeast.

USING DRY YEAST

When using dry yeast (which is dehydrated or freeze-dried), many brewers simply open the packet and sprinkle it on top of the wort. Although this can work, I recommend rehydrating dry yeast with water before pitching it. When introduced to liquid, dehydrated yeast draws some of the liquid inside its cell walls. If that liquid happens to be wort, it can slow down the yeast, especially if it is a high-gravity or heavily hopped brew such as an IPA. Water rehydrates the yeast but doesn't interfere with its action, allowing it to do a better job of fermenting. To rehydrate yeast follow these steps (doing this all in the same pot greatly reduces the risk of contamination).

1. Boil a few ounces of water for 15 to 20 minutes in a small stainless steel saucepan with a lid. You need about 4 fluid ounces to rehydrate 5 to 20 grams of yeast.
2. Cool the water to 80°F (27°C).
3. Sprinkle the yeast onto the water and let it completely dissolve — this usually takes about 10 minutes.
4. Gently stir, then add the rehydrated yeast solution to the fermenter and give the fermenter a good shake to distribute completely and aerate.

Dry yeast tends to start fermenting rapidly soon after pitching, because there is a large population of yeast cells, but the fermentation can slow down more quickly, and incomplete fermentations are slightly more frequent with dry yeast. Some dry yeast packets suggest a warmer pitching temperature than I recommend. The pitching temperature should always be the same as the fermenting temperature for ales, and in any case should never be higher than 80°F (27 °C).

USING LIQUID YEAST

Most liquid yeast packages have basic instructions for use printed right on the label. Most homebrew yeast manufacturers have excellent websites that should be able to answer any questions you have about their product. Here is an outline of what to expect.

Liquid yeast is sold in a couple of different forms. Under the brand name Wyeast, it comes in a foil bag with an inner pouch of nutrients that is commonly referred to as a "smack pack." This inner pouch is popped 6 to 24 hours before it is time to pitch the yeast. The amount of time depends on the age of the pack since the manufacturing date. A good rule of thumb to follow is to allow 6 hours plus 2 hours for every month past the manufacturing date for the yeast to grow.

As the yeast feeds on the nutrients, it creates gas, causing the pouch to swell. The optimum time to pitch is when the pouch is fully swollen. You can pitch the yeast before then, but it is a good idea to let it swell at least a little to show that the yeast is viable. If the pouch swells more quickly than expected and you will not be ready to brew for a day or more, you can store the pouch in a refrigerator for a few days before use. Any longer, and you should probably make a yeast starter.

Other brands of liquid yeast, such as White Labs, are sold in plastic tubes that are ready to pitch, meaning you open the cap and dump it into the wort. The yeast will perform better if you remove it from the refrigerator and allow it to slowly come to room temperature before pitching it.

When direct-pitching yeast from a pack or vial, the total quantity of yeast in one dose is generally less than what is considered optimal. The lag time can range from a few hours to as much as 48 hours. Stronger beers, lagers, and beers with a large amount of hops or spices may exhibit a longer lag time between the time the yeast is pitched and the first signs of active fermentation. A lag time of up to 24 hours is usually not cause for alarm, but a faster start to fermentation is more desirable.

As long as your cleaning and sanitizing routine was good, the yeast should be present in sufficient numbers to ferment the beer to completion without allowing an infection to take hold. If the lag time is longer than 24 hours, the yeast population was too low to start with, and the initial reproductive stage of the yeast was longer than advisable. A longer lag time means a higher risk that the beer will be infected. See page 58 for a guide to optimal yeast pitching rates for homebrewing.

PROOFING YEAST BEFORE USING

If you are uncertain whether the yeast is viable, proofing it before you brew can give you great peace of mind and save you the money of a ruined batch. Yeast failure can result from yeast that is too old, yeast that has been frozen (especially liquid yeast), or yeast that has been exposed to temperatures over 100°F (38°C).

To proof the yeast add about a tablespoon of malt extract that has been boiled in half a cup of water to sterilize, then cooled to room temperature. (If using dry yeast, rehydrate it first.) You can use cane sugar in a pinch, but malt is preferable because it contains nutrients necessary to healthy beer yeast metabolism; cane sugar does not. Within an hour the yeast should show signs of life by foaming up. If it shows no change, the yeast is probably no good. If you plan to pitch this proofed yeast in your batch, make sure to keep everything sanitary.

Sometimes it is advisable to proof a small sample of yeast days in advance of your planned brew day, so that you have time to buy fresh yeast if the yeast turns out to be bad. In this case remove a small portion of the yeast from the packet or vial and reseal carefully so your yeast is still pure for brewing.

Two Key Points

When it comes to yeast, the two most important details are (1) to keep everything as sanitary as possible and (2) to keep the temperature of the wort and the yeast under 80°F (27°C).

Many texts and online tutorials and forums mistakenly borrow advice from the baking world and recommend proofing and rehydrating yeast at 100°F (38°C) or higher. This is not the best practice for handling brewing yeast, which thrives at a lower temperature range of 55 to 78°F (13–26°C). Keeping the temperature within the comfort zone of the yeast ensures a healthy, active fermentation.

MAKING A YEAST STARTER

First on the list of good brewing practices when making a yeast starter is being extra scrupulous about cleanliness. A package of yeast, even a nice, fresh one, is somewhat dormant and will have some work to do before reaching optimal performance levels. Making a yeast starter is not necessarily the single most important thing you can do to make better beer, but a large dose of healthy yeast makes for a vigorous fermentation without the problems associated with under-pitching yeast.

Why Making a Yeast Starter Is a Good Idea

Whether you use dry or liquid yeast, it's important to make sure you have a viable, healthy yeast culture. Starting with a high cell count of active and healthy yeast always makes better beer. Starting out with too little yeast or old yeast with a low cell count is referred to as *under-pitching* and can result in a sluggish fermentation, increased risk of infection, and off-flavors. Making a yeast starter increases the yeast cell count (the population of yeast bodies).

Yeast starters are usually recommended when working with liquid yeast but are often unnecessary when using dry yeast, because 10-gram or larger dry yeast packets typically have a high enough live yeast cell count to provide a healthy pitch rate, unless the yeast is old or has been stored improperly. The process of making a starter is basically the same for liquid or dry yeast, except that it is a good idea to rehydrate the dry yeast before adding it to the starter solution.

In a nutshell, making a starter is like making a tiny batch of beer, except you do not add hops and it is not necessary to boil for a full hour. Keeping everything sanitary is extremely important. A contaminated yeast starter will ruin the entire batch of beer, and your extra effort will be wasted. Making a starter is also another way to proof the yeast.

Under-pitching can result in stuck fermentations, beers with higher than expected final gravity, a higher risk of infection, loss of consistency from batch to batch, and off-flavors because of higher fusel alcohols, esters, and sulfur compounds. It is also possible, though rare, to pitch too much yeast, which can result in too-rapid fermentation, thin-tasting beer, and yeasty flavors due to yeast autolysis.

Most brewers make the starter the day before brewing, unless they suspect the yeast is not very active because of age or possible heat damage. In this case, starting 2 or 3 days ahead of time will give the yeast plenty of time to regenerate, and it will give you enough time to seek a replacement in case the yeast fails to start.

A yeast starter sufficient to inoculate 5 gallons of beer should be 2 to 4 cups in volume. It should also have a relatively low specific gravity, as this makes it easier for the yeast to reproduce. Achieving healthy yeast reproduction is the desired goal here, not alcohol production. The best specific gravity range for a healthy yeast starter is 1.030 to 1.040. To make a 2-cup starter that has a specific gravity of about 1.033, use ½ cup of dry malt extract (3 ounces by weight). To make a larger starter, simply multiply the water and extract volumes equally. Refer to the chart below.

AMOUNT OF MALT USED IN YEAST STARTER

Starter volume	Dry extract (ounces/grams)	Liquid extract (ounces/grams)	Specific Gravity (SG)
2 cups/500 ml	3 oz/85g	3.6 oz/100g	1.033
1 quart/1,000 ml	6 oz/170g	7.2 oz/200g	1.033
3 pints/1,500 ml	9 oz/255g	10.8 oz/300g	1.033
2 quarts/2,000 ml	12 oz/340g	14.4 oz/400g	1.033

Here are the basic steps to making a yeast starter.

Sterilize the starter solution. For the healthiest yeast possible, or if you are concerned that the yeast is not very fresh, you can add yeast nutrient powder to the starter solution before boiling. Use about ¼ teaspoon per cup of starter. Boil the solution for 20 minutes in a small stainless steel saucepan or an Erlenmeyer flask. After the mixture boils, cool it rapidly in an ice bath to 70°F (21°C); cooling it too slowly can increase the risk of contamination.

Add the yeast. When the starter solution is cool, transfer it to a sanitized glass jar or bottle that is large enough to hold the starter solution and the yeast with additional space to allow for foaming while the yeast is at peak activity. A 1-quart or 1-liter container is a good size for a 2-cup starter. Add the yeast, mix well to provide oxygen, and cover with sterile foil (spray with sanitizer or hold over a flame) or a sanitized airlock and stopper. If you use foil, double it and cover the top of the container and at least 1 inch down the sides to block airborne bacteria.

If you boil the solution in an Erlenmeyer flask, you do not need to sterilize a separate container. Simply place the flask in a cold-water bath until sufficiently cooled, add the yeast when cooled, and cover. This method has the added advantage of a lower risk of contamination that could result from transferring the yeast or inadequate cleaning and sanitizing.

Using an Erlenmeyer flask

Monitor activity. It usually takes 1 to 6 hours to see signs of activity. If the yeast is very weak or very old, it can take as long as 24 hours. Gently shaking the starter every few hours or using a stir plate can accelerate the growth rate of the yeast. If you don't see any activity after 24 hours, throw it out and get some fresh yeast. After the yeast activity is visible, it takes 10 to 20 hours for the yeast cell population to grow to its maximum density. The best time to use the yeast starter is when it is at peak activity. Accomplishing this requires both luck and good timing.

If your starter is ready before you are ready to brew, you can still use it for 1 or 2 days. If you need to hold the starter for more than 2 days, keep it in the refrigerator. Once it has settled and cleared, a starter will perform best if you decant most of the clear and not-so-tasty liquid off the yeast slurry (the beige muck at the bottom of the jar). That is the stuff you really want to ferment your beer. After 5 days it is best to make a new starter with the yeast slurry from the old starter.

Step 4. Steep the Grains

Most guides to beginning homebrewing don't cover brewing with grains, but when it comes to brewing with organic and homegrown ingredients, using whole grains is essential for beer styles that require color and flavor from specialty malts. This is because there is, as of this writing, just one brand (Briess) of brewing-quality organic barley malt extract available in the United States. I hope this will change as the demand for organic brewing ingredients increases.

Steeping grain does add extra steps to the brewing process, but it is quite easy to do. There are a few ground rules, however. First, the grains must be crushed or cracked before brewing. Most brewing supply shops can do this for a very small charge, usually 10 to 20 cents per pound. If you have a grain mill with a loose enough setting, you can do it yourself. With very small amounts of grain, it is possible to crack the grains with a rolling pin, a wooden or rubber mallet, or a mortar and pestle. It is important to crack each grain, but the crush should be loose enough so the grains are not ground into a powder.

Barley malt is processed in two different ways, so there are two ways to extract fermentable sugars from the grains. Most barley malt is unconverted, which means it is mostly starch and requires a special soaking process called mashing to convert the starches to sugars. This process is fully described in chapter 4. It is fairly complicated and requires extra equipment if large quantities are involved. Some barley malt, often categorized as specialty malt, is converted to sugar during processing. The great thing about most specialty malts is that the sugars are already present in the grain, so to extract the sugars all you need to do is steep it in hot water, then strain it, just as you do with tea or coffee. Caramel, crystal, Carafa, chocolate, and Cara-Pils are all types of malt that can be steeped.

Whole grains

Crushed grains

Note that steeping and mashing are two different things. Steeping extracts sugars already present in the grain, while mashing converts starches in the grain into sugars and is done within a more narrow temperature range, mostly between 150 and 155°F (66 and 68°C). Extract brewing with specialty grains only requires steeping. Both partial-mash and all-grain brewing require mashing. Partial-mash brewing is the intermediate, best-of-both-worlds approach to brewing. Typically one-quarter to one-half of the fermentable sugars is derived from a small mash of a few gallons (which requires less equipment than a full all-grain mash), then supplemented with extract. Most of the recipes in this book require a partial or full mash, but some of the easier beginner recipes just require a short steeping stage.

STEPS FOR STEEPING

The optimum temperature range for steeping grains is 150 to 170°F (66–77°C). At lower temperatures some of the sugars may not dissolve, leaving color, flavor, and fermentable sugars behind. At temperatures exceeding this range, the heat starts to extract undesirable compounds such as tannins from the grain husks, which can leave an astringent aftertaste. As long as you stay within the "sweet spot" temperature range, this is all you need to do when steeping grains.

Most of the beginner recipes in chapter 7 call for just a few pounds of grain, so you'll need a straining bag that measures at least 9 by 12 inches. The simplest method of brewing with specialty grains and extract is the one-pot brewing method described here.

Fill the brew kettle with the full amount of water your batch requires. This is usually 5 gallons for the final product, plus an additional amount to allow for evaporation during the boil and water absorbed by the grains. The amount of water lost depends on the dimensions of the brew kettle and the force of the boil. If your pot can hold 6 gallons, this is a good measure to start with. If you cannot boil the whole 5 gallons, you will need to boil the wort in less water and add water after the boil to make up the difference. When steeping grains in a smaller pot, about 6 quarts of water is the minimum required for most recipes.

Pack the grains loosely in the grain bag. I like to mix them thoroughly for a balanced extraction. That way, if there are any sugars trapped in the center of the bag, at least the flavor ratios will be correct. Tie the bag closed so the grains will not spill out. I like to tie a bow with a long loop so I can hang the loop over the edge of the brew pot and tie it to the handle to keep the bag off

How Much Yeast to Pitch?

The ideal amount of yeast to pitch varies depending on the beer type and also on which expert you ask! It is not necessary to be overly precise, but the following guidelines assume that you are making your yeast starter with a healthy yeast culture. If your starting yeast is sluggish or old, or the starting volume of yeast is low, it is a good idea to increase the amount of starter you pitch.

In the case of really old or sluggish yeast, ferment the starter for a few days, decant the clear liquid off the top, and make a fresh starter with this yeast. A few extra days of growing and feeding can really help resuscitate a culture that has been inactive for a long time. This method is useful if you have an old culture you want to revive or if you are attempting to harvest a yeast strain from a bottle-conditioned beer.

In my experience these rough guidelines work quite well:

Normal-gravity ales (up to 1.60 starting gravity): 100 to 200 billion cells, or 2 pints of active starter

High-gravity ales (over 1.60 starting gravity): 150 to 300 billion cells, or 2 quarts of active starter

Lagers (up to 1.60 starting gravity): 120 to 250 billion cells, or 1.5 quarts of active starter

High-gravity lagers (over 1.60 starting gravity): 200 to 350 billion cells, or 3 quarts of active starter

For certain styles, such as wheat beers and certain Belgian styles, a lower pitch rate than that for most ales is desirable. A lower pitch rate will allow more esters to develop, which will help produce fruity flavors like banana that are desirable in these beers.

the bottom. If the bag is resting on the bottom of the pot while the burner is on, the fibers might burn (if cotton) or melt (if nylon), making a mess and possibly imparting some unpleasant flavors to the beer.

Heat the water slowly, monitoring the temperature carefully until it reaches 160°F (71°C). Turn the heat off, and allow the grain to steep for an

If precision is what you want, most experts agree on a pitching rate of 1 million cells of viable yeast for every milliliter of wort, for every degree Plato. One degree Plato is roughly equivalent to 1.004 SG. So this is the calculation for a 5-gallon wort with an SG of 1.048 (about 12° Plato):

12 plato × 1,000,000 = 12 million cells per mL of wort
1 gallon of wort is about 3,785 mL × 5 = 18,925 mL
18,925 mL × 12,000,000 = about 227 billion yeast cells

If this kind of precision makes your head spin, just work with the rough guide given above and you will do fine. It has not failed me yet. You can even dispense with the calculations altogether and pitch a 1- to 1.5-liter starter of healthy yeast every time you brew, and I doubt you will experience any under-pitching-related problems with your beer. Or you can use an online pitching-rate calculator or a phone app.

If for some reason you do not have time to make a yeast starter, you can always pitch two packages or vials of yeast instead of one. This is more expensive and not so environmentally friendly (because of the excess packaging), so I don't recommend it.

additional 10 or 15 minutes. The total steeping time should be 20 to 30 minutes from when you started heating the water. If you are brewing with a small amount of grain, under 2 pounds, the shorter time is enough, but for more than 2 pounds of grain, the full 30 minutes is recommended.

Steeping the grain

Drain the bag of grains over the brew pot (use a colander that fits over the pot or hang the bag from something over the pot), or place it in a colander over a bowl or pan to catch the sweet liquid. The longer you let it drain, the more liquid you will collect. Although it is tempting to squeeze the bag to wring out every last drop, this is not generally worth the effort, and you may end up extracting too many tannins and other undesirable flavors. I simply let the bag drain for a good 15 to 30 minutes. You can start boiling the bulk of the liquid right away, and add the small amount that drains out later as much as halfway through the boil.

Some recipes are simply impossible to brew without doing some sort of starch conversion with a mash. Some of the beginning recipes in this book call for a mini mash or partial mash because they have some unconverted grains or adjuncts (unmalted grains such as corn, rice, rye, or oats) that are essential to the recipe; oatmeal stout, for instance. The process is similar to the above steeping instructions, except the temperature at which you turn off the heat should be between 150 and 155°F (66 and 68°C) instead of 160°F (71°C), and a specific amount of water should be used. The correct amount of water is usually included in the recipe and should be 1½ to 2 quarts of water per pound of grain. It is fine to use a little more water if needed to cover the grains. A longer steep time is also required to make sure a complete starch conversion takes place — 45 minutes to an hour is good for most recipes.

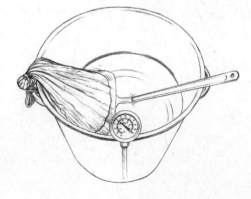

Draining the grain

Step 5. Add Extract and Other Sugars

Many homebrew recipes call for malt extract, also known as malt syrup. Whatever you call it, it is messy stuff! Here are a few techniques that will help you get everything into the pot without making a giant sticky mess.

Since extract dissolves more quickly in hot water, it makes sense to start with really hot water. After removing the grains, continue heating the water until it is just under the boiling point, or 190 to 200°F (88–93°C). Then turn the heat off, add the extract, and stir well until it is completely dissolved. This allows the extract to dissolve without scorching on the bottom of the pot. Burned-on extract is extremely difficult to remove and will leave a burnt aftertaste in your homebrew.

WORKING WITH DRY MALT EXTRACT

Dry malt extract (DME) is a little easier to work with, but because it is hygroscopic (meaning it readily attracts moisture from the surrounding air), it will ball up when exposed to the steam coming off the hot brew kettle. It will also form clumps in the water that take a while to dissolve. For this reason it is a good idea to keep your DME sealed airtight until just before you use it. Otherwise it might form a big brick that will take a painfully long time to dissolve unless you are able to break it up, which might require a sledgehammer! Follow the same procedure as for liquid malt extract, and make sure the extract is completely dissolved before turning the burner back on.

ADDING SUGARS

Other sugars should be treated the same way as the extract: dissolve in the hot water with the extract, then turn the heat back on, unless you are

---

Brew Tip

IF THE EXTRACT IS IN A TUB, ladle some of the hot water into the container, let it sit for a few minutes, then slosh it around to dissolve the extract. If the extract is in a flexible pouch or plastic bag, you can fold the bag onto itself lengthwise several times so it forms a narrow strip, then squeeze out the extract just as you do with a toothpaste tube.

adding a small amount or are ready to stir it constantly until all the sugars are completely dissolved. Once all the sugars are dissolved and the grains are extracted, you have *wort*, the hot sweet liquid that is the base of all beer recipes.

Step 6. Boil the Wort

Some extract-based homebrew recipes call for a boil time of 20 to 30 minutes, but the standard boil time for most recipes is 60 minutes. Whatever the timing, achieving a good rolling boil is the key to success. With experience you will gain a sixth sense about the temperature needed to get the desired result. Too much heat, and zing! — boilover, which is not fun. On the other hand, not enough heat will lead to inadequate hop utilization, insufficient protein coagulation, and the presence of too many undesirable volatiles in your finished beer.

A proper boil has an agitated, churning surface, usually with some foam, and a decent amount of steam rolling from the pot.

There are a couple of points during the boiling process when the chance of a boilover is greatly increased. When the wort first starts to boil, there are still quite a few dissolved proteins that have not yet precipitated out; these proteins create a thick foam when the boiling point is reached. Skimming off the foam as it first forms and diffusing it with a spray bottle are two good ways to prevent it from boiling over. Another critical moment is when the hops are added, because of the additional air and oils that are introduced into

Brew Tip

TO HELP AVOID BOILOVERS keep a spray bottle of water near the stove, with the nozzle set to a fine mist. If the foam starts to rise out of the kettle, a few bursts of spray will make the surge subside and give you a chance to adjust the heat.

If a boilover does occur, it is best to stop everything and clean it up rather than allowing the boil to continue while the sugars cook onto the stovetop. A blackened sugar crust is extremely difficult to remove.

Solar Heat Your Brew Water

If working with tools is not your strong suit, with a little ingenuity you can still take advantage of the heating power of the sun to reduce your fuel or electricity requirements. On a hot sunny day, you can fill your brewing vessel the morning you plan to brew, wrap it in a dark-colored blanket or beach towel (a sheet of black plastic or a large black trash bag will do), and put it in direct sunlight. Pick a spot out of the wind, as moving air can reduce the heating effect quite a bit. In some cases rigging a windbreak may increase the heating potential of this system.

In a few hours your water temperature will have increased, and you will need less heat energy to bring the water up to brewing temperature. I have raised water temperature to as high as 120°F (49°C) using this method on a really hot day. This is not a very efficient water-heating method, but it has two great things going for it: it takes very little effort, and it is free.

the boiling liquid. Again, the spray bottle and judicious temperature control are very helpful when adding ingredients to a kettle at full boil.

During the boil, depending on the recipe, you may have several different hop additions, each requiring a different boiling time. You may have spice additions as well. Most recipes call for a total boiling time for each individual hop or other ingredient. Unless otherwise noted, once an ingredient is added, it remains in the wort for the rest of the boil.

It is important to follow each recipe as closely as possible, especially when it comes to hop additions. Hops add bitterness to beer, and the potential bitterness imparted by a particular hop should be listed on the package as AAU, which stands for alpha acid units. Sometimes it is simply listed as AA, for alpha acid. The AAU value is the amount of alpha acid units in 1 ounce of hops. If you want to make a certain recipe but do not have the hop variety that the recipe calls for, or if your hops have a significantly different

AA, you will need to adjust the hops in your batch of beer. See Adjusting Hop Additions, page 67, for more on how to make those adjustments.

A typical 60-minute boil: If you have a recipe that calls for one type of hop to be boiled for 60 minutes, followed by one to be boiled for 20 minutes,

Why Boiling the Wort Is So Important

Boiling kills unwanted bacteria and other microorganisms. In the almost sterile environment created by boiling, the yeast will have optimum conditions to be fruitful and multiply without competition from other microbial critters. When the yeast does well, the beer is clean tasting and has the flavor characteristics appropriate to its style.

Boiling extracts the desired bitterness from the hops. The oils in hops are not truly water soluble, thus they will not contribute enough bitterness and flavor if just steeped in warm water. The boiling action helps break down the oils so they can be partially dissolved. This is especially important in hoppy beers, such as IPA, which may call for a boil time of 90 minutes or more.

Boiling produces a clearer beer. Proteins present in malt can cause haziness in the finished beer unless they are removed. If the proteins are fine enough, they will not settle out of the beer, even with a long aging time. A good, rolling 45- to 60-minute boil causes these proteins to clump together and sink to the bottom. The process is enhanced with the addition of Irish moss, a seaweed with characteristics similar to those of gelatin, that is added for the last 15 to 20 minutes of the total boil.

Boiling drives off unwanted volatile compounds that can cause off-flavors. The most common detractor is dimethyl sulfide (DMS), which is notorious for its "cooked corn" flavor. It is formed from compounds usually present in the wort that evaporate during a good rolling boil.

and finishing with one that is steeped at the end of the boil, your hop schedule should look like this:

- When the wort starts boiling, add the 60-minute hops.
- After 40 minutes, add the 20-minute hops.
- After another 20 minutes add the final hops, and immediately turn the heat off.

It is common practice to give the wort one final good stir so that all the hop pieces and settled pieces swirl around and collect in a pile at the bottom of the pot, making removal a little easier. This is especially useful when the wort will be removed via a spigot at the bottom of the pot. In any case, it is best to strain out the hops and any other solid ingredients that were added during the boil before the beer is fermented. Before straining, however, the wort should be cooled.

Step 7. Chill the Wort

Cooling the wort quickly to fermentation temperature is an important step toward making high-quality beer. You can stick the pot in a snow bank if you happen to have one handy, but most folks use a cold-water bath, ice, or a wort chiller. Ideally, the beer should be cooled down to yeast-pitching temperature within 30 minutes. This is easier said than done when you are talking about cooling 5 gallons of boiling hot liquid to 70°F (21°C).

There are three main reasons that cooling the wort quickly makes better beer:

- It dramatically reduces the risk of infection by unwanted bacteria or wild yeast.
- It facilitates the precipitation of proteins, hop and grain bits, and other solids that can interfere with a clean-tasting, clear beer. This precipitation is called "cold break" in brewing lingo. Without rapid cooling the cold break is greatly reduced or does not occur at all — and the resulting beer could be cloudy.
- It prevents oxidation and reduces the volume of the dreaded DMS, which continues to be produced while the wort is still hot.

The method you use to cool the wort depends on the equipment you have access to, the amount of wort you have to cool, and whether water can be added after the boil. In addition to using a wort chiller (see page 69), there are two other basic methods.

ADDING COLD WATER TO A PARTIAL BOIL

When you have a small brew pot and must do a partial boil of only 2½ to 3 gallons, you have to add nearly the same amount of cold water to make up the full 5-gallon batch, which helps to chill the wort quickly. Use the same high-quality water you used in your recipe, filtered if needed and boiled to sterilize it.

If you have a large enough extra pot (one with a tight lid), you can boil the extra water at a full boil for at least 20 minutes, cover it, and let it cool overnight undisturbed. On the morning of brew day, if you have room in the refrigerator, you can chill the water more, which will further speed up the wort-chilling process.

Before adding the chilled water to your partial-boil batch in the fermenter, it helps to cool the wort first with a cold-water bath. You will achieve a more rapid cooling when there is a higher temperature difference between the hot wort and the bath, and it is not likely that your cold-water addition will be sufficient to cool the wort to yeast-pitching temperature by itself. By simply setting the brew pot carefully in a sink filled half full of cold water, you will see the temperature drop from over 200°F (93°C) to around 150°F (66°C) in about 10 minutes. Adding the prechilled water should bring it down the rest of the way, especially if it is as cool as 40 or 50°F (4 or 10°C).

What about ice, you may be thinking? You *can* add ice directly to your homebrew instead of water, but caution is strongly advised. Freezing does not kill all bacteria, so ice is a potential source of infection. To be on the safe side, you should boil the water first and freeze it in sanitized containers or trays. Keep in mind that large blocks of ice will not cool as rapidly as smaller blocks, so the extra effort to turn the water into ice may not be worth it; also, it uses extra electricity. But if this method works well for you, go for it.

Adjusting Hop Additions

As long as you use the same (or very similar) ingredients and use the AAUs of hops that each recipe calls for, your homebrews will come out as intended. Every recipe in this book lists the AAU value for each hop. Because alpha acid levels for hops vary from crop to crop and the alpha acid percentage contributed by the hops affects the bitterness of the beer, it is more accurate to use the total AAUs than a simple hop weight.

To determine the total AAUs for a recipe, multiply the weight of the hops by the AA percentage. For instance, if a recipe calls for 8 AAUs of Cascade hops and your hops have 4, you need 2 ounces to equal 8 AAUs. Stick to the form of hop called for to achieve the most accurate results. If the recipe calls for pellet hops, use pellet hops if possible, because boiling extracts bitterness from whole hops at a slightly different rate. If you must substitute whole hops for pellets, or vice versa, you must adjust the quantity of hops.

The most accurate method for doing this is to calculate the IBUs, which is somewhat advanced. When brewing for your own enjoyment, slight differences in the final bitterness may not be important enough to make the extra effort. Here is a rough conversion I find useful for making quick recipe adjustments based on the type of hops available. To adjust for hops boiled for 15 to 90 minutes: Use 10 percent more AAUs of whole hops than pellet hops or use 10 percent less AAUs of pellet hops than whole hops. For example, to substitute whole Perle hops (6 AAUs) for the Perle hop pellets (8 AAUs) called for in the Pale Rider Ale recipe (page 235): First, calculate the total AAUs (8 total AAUs = 1.33 oz at 6% AA), then adjust for whole hops ($1.33 \times 110\% = 1.47$ oz).

Rounding up to 1.5 oz. is fine if your scale does not read two decimal places. In 5 gallons of beer there is some wiggle room for minor adjustments, as long as you don't start throwing handfuls of hops into the kettle with abandon! Aroma and flavor hops that are boiled for less than 15 minutes do not need to be adjusted because the short boiling time extracts too little bitterness relative to the total bitterness of the recipe.

To calculate IBUs, see the hops charts beginning on page 318. You can also use one of the many recipe calculation programs that are available online.

USING A COLD-WATER BATH

While not the most efficient way to cool hot liquids, this is sometimes the best method available. It can take up to an hour to cool 5 gallons of beer using a cold-water bath.

The basic procedure is to fill the sink halfway with cold water, gently rest the brew pot in the sink, and carefully stir the contents. As soon as the water bath is warm to touch, drain the sink, refill it, and repeat. The heat transfer will be rapid (about 5 minutes) at first when there is a large temperature difference, but as the wort cools it will happen more slowly, and the final cooling stage can take up to 30 minutes. Stirring speeds up the process but also increases the risk of introducing airborne bacteria. Give the wort a quick stir, and quickly replace the lid. Adding ice to the bath will speed the process, but to economize I suggest first doing two changes of cold tap water to bring the initial temperature down.

The most important thing to remember when employing a cold-water bath is to avoid splashing any cooling water into your brew pot. Keep the pot covered when not stirring, remove it before refilling the sink or tub, and avoid splashing. Once the beer is cool, wipe the sides and bottom of the pot before pouring it into the fermenter. If your brew pot has a spigot, add sanitizing solution to the last-stage cold-water bath to make sure the inside parts of the spigot are sanitized. It doesn't hurt to discard a few ounces before filling the fermenter from a spigot, just to make sure any contaminated liquid around the valve does not find its way into your beer.

Brew Tip

IF YOU ONLY HAVE ONE POT for boiling, transfer the boiled water you will be adding to your partial-boil batch to another container to cool. Half-gallon canning jars work really well and have a multitude of uses besides holding brewing water. If you have a canner, you can boil the jars with water already in them, then remove them from the canner to cool. Otherwise, clean and sanitize whatever containers you are using and rinse them with boiling water just before filling.

Improve Your Wort-Chilling System

Buy or make the most efficient chiller you can afford, and it will pay for itself over time in water savings. Counterflow chillers are more efficient than immersion chillers, and plate chillers are more efficient than counterflow chillers.

Recirculate the water used for wort chilling. To do this you need two wort chillers or an ice-cooled recirculating wort chiller.

Use ice or snow to speed the process. Making ice in a freezer that is already in use or making it outside when conditions permit won't add much to your energy usage, and it can speed up cooling time and reduce water consumption. If you live in snow country, you can just stick your brew pot in a snow bank to cool it down. Speed the cooling process by stirring every so often with a sanitized spoon and relocating the pot to a new spot several times.

USING A WORT CHILLER

Wort chillers work as simple heat exchangers by running cold tap water through metal tubing that is immersed in the brew pot. A wort chiller with a longer coil length and regular stirring will speed up the cooling time considerably. There are two different kinds of wort chillers available.

Immersion chillers are the most common and the less expensive type. They are simply a coil of copper or stainless steel tubing with a water inlet and outlet at each end. They should be constructed so that the water inlet and outlet are not submerged in the beer when being used. Good ones have bent ends so the water connection hangs outside rather than inside the pot. This way, if there is a leak in the water connection, the water that could potentially contaminate your beer drips outside the pot. Copper immersion chillers are fairly easy to make.

Using an immersion chiller is a simple and straightforward process. To sterilize the chiller, clean it and place it in your pot of boiling wort at least 20 minutes before the end of the boil. Hook up the water connectors to a garden hose or sink with an adapter. Test for leaks, so if there is any spray into the brew pot, you can fix it before the boil is done — when it could contaminate the homebrew. Place a stirring spoon and thermometer in the pot at the same time as the chiller, so that everything is sterilized.

At the end of the boil, turn the heat off. Once the boiling has stopped, turn the water on. If you can regulate the water pressure, a slower flow rate will use less water, but the beer will also cool more slowly. There is an optimum heat transfer flow level. Too fast, and the water will not capture all of the heat; too slow, and the process will take too long. The best technique is to start out with a fast flow rate, because when the wort is still very hot, the heat transfer will be rapid. As the wort cools down, reduce the flow rate, because the lower temperature differential will slow the heat transfer rate, and the extra water will just be wasted.

You can greatly reduce the amount of water needed to chill a batch of homebrew with an immersion chiller by using a recirculating wort chiller.

A counterflow wort chiller is a self-contained heat exchanger through which the beer and the water flow in opposite directions to provide the most efficient cooling method available to homebrewers. To use one you will need to either pump the wort through the chiller using a heat-tolerant, waterproof pump that can be sterilized, or let it flow through a spigot by way of gravity. To use gravity you will also need to make sure your brew pot is placed well above both the chiller and the fermenter so the wort will always flow downhill. If the flow is too slow, which can happen if the distance between the spigot and the bottom of the fermenter is too short, the chances of clogging

Brew Tip

A STERILIZED SPOON AND THERMOMETER are indispensable during the cooling process. The easiest way to sterilize them is to put them in the brew pot during the last 15 to 20 minutes of boiling time.

Water Conservation

The water from a cold-water bath is perfectly usable for dish or clothes washing, or for watering thirsty hop plants. If you have a double sink, it is a simple trick to leave the heated water from the first water bath to clean all the brewing equipment at the end of your brew session. I advise against doing this while the pot of wort is sitting in the other half of your sink, though — the risk of splashing is just too great!

You can use a big tub of water rather than a sink if you want to reuse the cooling water, as it is easier to dump the tub than to scoop the water out of a sink by hand or siphon it out.

are greatly increased. Because counterflow chillers are more expensive than immersion chillers and are more complicated to sanitize and operate, beginning homebrewers rarely use them.

Step 8. Pitch the Yeast and Aerate

Once you have cooked up a batch of beer and chilled it to the proper temperature, the next step is to pitch the yeast. Before you do, double-check that the wort is cooled to between 65 and 75°F (18 and 24°C). The lower range is suitable for lager beers, and the higher range is acceptable for most ales.

After it is sufficiently cooled, pour the beer into the sanitized fermenter. If you did not use hop-boiling bags, pour the wort through a strainer to filter out the hops and any other large particles that should not go into the fermenter. If your primary fermenter has a narrow opening, you will need a funnel (also sanitized!) to make sure every precious drop ends up in the fermenter.

Incidentally, some folks don't bother straining out pellet hops, as they normally just sink to the bottom, but you should definitely strain out whole hops, which could clog your spigot or siphoning gear. I prefer to strain out all hops and other spices at this stage; otherwise they can continue steeping in the fermenting beer, contributing more flavor than intended and possibly more bitterness than desired.

Before pitching the yeast, make sure the package of yeast or the starter is about room temperature. If you pitch yeast right out of the refrigerator into hot wort, the temperature difference could shock the yeast, just when you are depending on it to do a phenomenal job fermenting your best homebrewed beer ever.

Now for the fun part: go ahead and pour the yeast into the fermenter. Once you have added the yeast, it is very important to aerate the wort. Shake or stir the wort thoroughly to make sure the yeast has the oxygen it needs for the all-important reproductive stage. It is perfectly fine to aerate the wort before adding the yeast if you prefer.

There are several different techniques for aerating wort, and it's hard to overdo it unless you're using pure oxygen. The method you use depends on what kind of primary fermenter you have and what tools you have available. Several methods of wort aeration are described in chapter 4 (see page 103), but the two most commonly used are agitating the fermenter by rocking it back and forth, or using a sanitized spoon or whisk to whip air into the wort. Aerate the wort only at yeast-pitching time, before fermentation begins. Never aerate wort during or after fermentation!

If there is less than 12 inches of space between the top of the wort and the stopper, it is wise to employ a blowoff tube during the first few days of fermentation rather than an airlock. A blowoff tube is simply a sanitized length of tubing that runs from the top of the fermenter and into a container of

Brew Tip

THOROUGHLY CLEAN AND SANITIZE any object that might touch the yeast, the wort after the boil, or the inside of the fermenter. For instance, before cutting a packet of yeast open with scissors, sanitize the blades. Common sense at every step can save you the heartbreak of a ruined batch in a few weeks.

sanitizer or sterile liquid that sits on the floor next to the fermenter to collect the excess foam that is created in the first few days. It is important to put this container *below* the liquid level of the fermenter; putting it higher makes it possible that the liquid could siphon backward into your beer.

Although the blowoff system is essentially a giant airlock, the risk of contamination from a blowoff system is higher than that from an airlock because the liquid that the blowoff collects into is open to the air and dust can fall into it. There is also more surface area in a blowoff system, and more surface area equals more chances for bacteria to survive the cleaning and sanitizing process.

Step 9. Monitor Primary Fermentation

After you've pitched the yeast, you just have to sit back and wait. Very high heat or very low temperatures will cause problems with fermentation, so the ideal space to store the beer while it is fermenting is dark and has a steady temperature of 60 to 70°F (16–21°C). The space needs some ventilation, as carbon dioxide is emitted during fermentation. An uninsulated area such as a garage or outdoor storage shed is less than ideal, because such spaces typically undergo dramatic temperature changes from day to night. If you are not sure about a given space, put a thermometer in it and check the temperature several times in a 24-hour period. Do this for several days. If there is consistently less than a 30°F (17°C) difference between the coolest and hottest times of day, your chosen location should work well.

When the yeast is first added, nothing appears to happen. This is because the first stage of yeast activity is reproduction, a process that is not visible to the naked eye. This stage usually lasts from a few hours up to several days. For the sake of good beer, it's better if it happens within 24 hours. Once the yeast has created a miniature army large enough to start fermenting your newly brewed beer, it will switch into high gear and start eating the sugars in the wort. This is when you will notice activity.

In a glass fermenter you will see clumps swimming around in the beer during the most active stage, and there is normally a thick layer of foam on top. The fermentation activity also creates a large quantity of gas, primarily carbon dioxide, which is expelled at a furious rate. Certain yeast strains,

Fermenter with airlock

especially lager yeast, also produce sulfur compounds, which can create some awful odors. Excessive sulfur production during fermentation can be a sign that the yeast is not performing at optimal levels, which can happen when there is a deficiency of nitrogen or other nutrients in the wort, or if the yeast is too stressed because of other environmental factors. Good aeration and the use of a yeast nutrient can help prevent this.

After several days the activity slows considerably, and the foam layer starts to dissipate. Once the foam level has dropped and the rate of bubbling has slowed significantly (a few burps per minute), the primary stage of fermentation is essentially done, and you can replace the blowoff tube (if you used one) with an airlock. The transition from primary to secondary fermentation is gradual, generally happening from 3 to 7 days from the first signs of activity. It is not necessary to pinpoint the exact moment of transition.

Step 10. Monitor Secondary Fermentation

Once the beer reaches the second stage of fermentation, it might be time to transfer it to a secondary fermenter, a step known as *racking* the beer. In some cases this is not really necessary, but in others racking can make the crucial difference between great beer and not-so-good beer. For example, it is not necessary to rack a lighter ale with an expected fermentation time of 2 weeks or less that is in a glass or stainless steel fermenter with a very tight-fitting lid. Because of the increased risk of contamination and oxidation presented by the act of transferring the beer from one vessel to another, it could actually be detrimental. In some cases, however, racking the beer is highly recommended. For example:

- If the beer is in a plastic bucket with a snap-on lid
- If it requires 3 weeks or more of fermentation time
- If there are added ingredients steeping in the fermenter
- If there is a large amount of debris at the bottom

If your fermenter has a spigot at the bottom, simply attach a bit of tubing to the spigot and allow the beer to run into the secondary fermenter. If not, you'll need an airtight siphon to transfer the beer. A rigid racking cane with curved top and a sediment tip is extremely helpful here. The curve prevents the tubing from collapsing on itself, which could stop the flow of beer, and the sediment tip helps to prevent the siphon from clogging. Whichever method you use, it is important that the tubing reach all the way to the bottom of the secondary fermenter so aeration is minimized.

Siphoning can be a little tricky at first. Though sucking on the tube to start the liquid flowing might seem like the obvious method, it is a huge no-no, as lactic bacteria and other nasties from your mouth would contaminate the beer. The trick is this:

1. Put the sanitized racking cane in the primary fermenter. Fill the flexible tubing completely with either sterile water or sanitizing solution. Hold the ends level so the water does not spill out.
2. Connect one end of the filled tubing to the racking cane, and drop the other end into a small cup. The weight of the liquid in the tubing will draw the beer and start the siphon. Discard the first bit of liquid that comes through the siphon.
3. As soon as the beer starts flowing out and all air bubbles have been purged from the line, clamp the tube near the end (or pinch it by bending it back on itself), then drop it into the secondary fermenter and unclamp the tube so the beer starts flowing again.

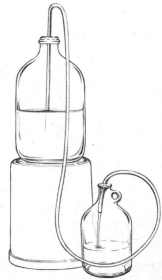

Racking-off setup

Once the beer is racked to a secondary container, there's nothing to do but wait for the beer to finish fermenting. Right after racking you may notice a resurgence in the rate of bubbling and the reappearance of foam on the top. This is because the process remixes the yeast back into suspension, where it can consume residual sugars. This is one benefit of siphoning; it can speed up the fermentation slightly and may increase attenuation slightly. *Attenuation* is the percentage of the fermentable sugars that are converted during the fermentation process. If this referment occurs, it usually subsides quickly, and the rate of bubbling will decline steadily. The beer will also start to clear from the top down as the yeast and solids start to drop out of suspension and slowly settle to the bottom.

Step 11. Bottle Your Beer

Whether you clean your bottles ahead of time or not (see Bottle Prep, page 82), you must sanitize them on bottling day. Most sanitizers, especially the nontoxic kind, are only effective for a short duration. A 5-minute soak in your chosen sanitizer is usually sufficient — follow the instructions for the product. After sanitizing, stack the bottles upside down on a bottle rack or a clean dish rack. Unless you have a helping hand on bottling day, it will make your life easier to do all the bottle prep and have the sanitized bottles within reach before you start filling them.

To prepare for bottling you also need to sanitize your bottling wand, racking cane and tubing, and bottling bucket if you plan to use one. A bottling bucket is simply a bucket with a spigot on it so you do not have to rely on a siphon to get the beer into bottles.

ADDING PRIMING SUGAR

Unless you want flat beer, you must add priming sugar just before bottling so the beer becomes carbonated in the bottle. Dextrose, or pure corn sugar, is the most common priming sugar for homebrewing. Priming sugar must be sterile when added to the beer. The easiest way to sterilize it is to boil the sugar in 1 to 2 cups of water. Mix the sugar and water, bring to a boil, and simmer for 15 to 20 minutes. The solution must be cooled to under 80°F (27°C) before adding it to the beer.

If you are bottling directly from the fermenter, pour the priming sugar into the fermenter a few minutes before you start filling bottles. Stir gently with the sanitized racking cane held an inch or two above the bottom of the vessel so you don't disturb too much sediment. If you are racking the beer to a bottling bucket before bottling, pour the cooled priming solution into the bucket, then rack the beer. The agitation of the siphon flow will mix the priming sugar gently into the beer.

The most obvious reason to add priming sugar for a final referment in the bottle is to add a controlled amount of carbon dioxide to the finished product so the beer becomes fizzy. But bottle-conditioned beers sometimes exhibit slightly different flavor profiles from the same beer that has been carbonated artificially. The yeast produces flavor compounds and gases besides carbon dioxide that can add a complexity to the finished beer that cannot be achieved through forced carbonation. Almost all Belgian beers are bottle conditioned, and many of these beers are famous for their unique and complex flavors.

Bottle-conditioned beers, especially stronger ones, also have an amazingly long shelf life if the bottling is properly done. It is not unusual to pry open a bottle of year-old homebrew that tastes better than the 2-week-old version. Of course the opposite can also happen. If too much oxygen was present at bottling, or there is a slight contamination, or the caps did not seal properly, the beer could be oxidized, sour, or just downright awful.

Adding Fresh Yeast at Bottling

If your beer has been in the fermenter for a long time, or has a very high alcohol content, it is likely there is not enough residual yeast to create ample carbonation. Strong Belgian-style ales, barley wines, and long-aged lagers are examples of beers that need a boost of fresh yeast just before bottling.

Choose a yeast strain that can handle the alcohol level of the beer; if bottling a lager, use a lager yeast so the bottles can condition at lower temperatures. It is best to make a small yeast starter a day before bottling, but you should at least rehydrate dry yeast before adding it. To make a starter, follow the procedure on page 53, but make just 2 or 3 cups and use a small amount of malt extract (about ¼ cup) so the extra sugar does not contribute too much carbonation. Add the yeast with the priming sugar just before bottling. Stir well and fill the bottles right away.

When Is My Beer Ready to Bottle?

The time line for the second stage of fermentation can vary quite a bit, depending on the beer style being brewed. A simple ale will finish fermenting in as little as 7 days from the yeast pitch, while a Belgian Tripel or a lager can take months to complete. Since there is not a catchall blueprint for fermentation length, part of becoming a good brewer is developing the detective skills to know when your beer is ready to bottle.

It is especially important not to bottle too early. If beer is bottled before the fermentation process is fully complete, it will become over-carbonated because fermentation will continue inside the sealed bottles. The worst-case scenario here is — you guessed it — bottle bombs! You do not want a bottle to blow up in your face, although it is more likely it will blow up in the closet, basement, or wherever you stored it, making a giant mess. If the bottles do not blow up, you may have a gusher on your hands when you open one. Also, beer bottled prematurely will often have a thick layer of sediment on the bottom instead of a slight layer that compacts well.

The most reliable method for testing if fermentation is complete is to use a hydrometer to take a gravity reading. If the specific gravity is within the range for final gravity of the beer recipe you are following, it is safe to go ahead and bottle. However, if you are unsure that all fermentation is done because you have observed some bubbling or the beer still looks cloudy, it does not hurt to wait a day or two longer and take another reading. If the measurement has not changed — and as long as your reading is accurate — you can be sure the fermentation is fully complete.

Some sources advise homebrewers to watch the bubbles coming from the airlock and go ahead with bottling when there are fewer than a couple of bubbles per minute. This advice is flawed because many factors affect the rate of bubbling, rendering this method inaccurate. For instance, warming temperatures or movement can cause some of the carbon dioxide that is dissolved in the beer to bubble out, creating a temporary increase in the burp rate. A poor seal can prevent airlock bubbles, since the gas will escape through other openings. Gas under pressure will always vent through the path of least resistance. The water in the airlock presents a slight barrier to the gas, thus a slight amount of pressure must build up before it can pass through the water chamber of the airlock.

Part of what makes a good brewer is having the patience to develop good instincts that will help you know when each batch is ready for bottling or racking to a keg. This is one of the reasons I advise using glass fermenters. Apart from their other benefits, they give you a clear view of what is going on in the fermenter throughout the fermentation process. Here's a rundown of what to expect.

- **Look for color changes.** When you first add the yeast, not much changes until the yeast reproduces. When the yeast has multiplied enough, the beer actually becomes lighter and will appear cloudy or milky. The difference is usually the most pronounced with a very dark beer such as a stout.

- **Watch for clarity.** As the fermentation slows down, the yeast becomes dormant and starts to settle to the bottom. The foam layer subsides and in most cases disappears completely, and the beer starts to clear from the top down. As it clears, the color becomes darker and more vibrant, so if you check it daily, you will notice that band of color widen each day.

- **Keep track of the time.** The clearing process can take from a few days to 2 weeks. Many variables come into play, including ambient temperature, the viscosity of the beer (full-bodied beers take longer), and the specific strain of yeast being used. Once the beer has cleared at least two-thirds of the height of the liquid level, it is pretty much finished, and you can proceed with bottling. Take a final hydrometer reading just to be sure.

FILLING THE BOTTLES

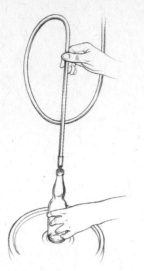

Using a bottling wand

After stirring in the priming sugar, let the beer settle for a few minutes. Then start your siphon, attach the bottling wand, and start filling the bottles. If using a bottling bucket, you just need to attach a short piece of tubing to the spigot and attach the bottling wand to the other end.

Fill each bottle to about an inch from the top. If you're using flip-top caps or corks, leave extra room. Slight variations are acceptable, but too much headspace can leave too much oxygen in the bottle, which can have a detrimental effect on flavor. It is better to slightly overfill than to underfill.

Some old-fashioned homebrewing guides tell you to use a funnel to pour the beer into the bottles, but don't do this unless you are fine with mediocre beer! This method mixes oxygen into the beer, which will cause the flavor to degrade significantly.

Once the bottles are filled, place the caps on the bottles quickly. If you are using oxygen-absorbing caps that have been wet-sanitized, crimp the caps down right away to maximize the oxygen-scavenging benefit of these caps. It makes the job far easier to have one person filling bottles while another caps them. If you are using plain caps or flip-top-style bottles, here is a trick

Brew Tip

PRACTICE SIPHONING WITH WATER so that no homebrew will be sacrificed to the learning curve. There are a few siphoning gizmos on the market that you may find worth the money if you find yourself struggling. The best is a plunger-style device marketed under the brand name Auto-Siphon. I have many brewing friends who swear by it, even though mine collects dust in my brewing closet because I am used to the old-school way, and I am loath to clean and sanitize any more equipment than I absolutely have to.

to reduce the amount of oxygen left in the bottles: Place a cap on each bottle as you fill it but don't crimp it down. Let the bottles stand for 10 minutes or so to allow the first carbon dioxide gas that forms to fill the headspace and help to purge oxygen. After all the bottles are filled, go back and seal them. Placing the caps on the bottles prevents any nasties from falling into the beer.

Step 12. Age Your Beer

The final stage on your journey to bubbly, delicious homebrewed goodness is conditioning and aging your brew, which typically takes a couple of weeks. It normally takes at least 1 week at room temperature for carbonation to develop, but it can take as long as 4 weeks if the temperatures are cool, the beer is very strong (which slows the yeast down), or the beer has sat in the fermenter for too long, allowing most of the yeast to go dormant. For natural carbonation you need some active yeast! If the beer did sit for a long time in the secondary fermenter or was cold-lagered for many weeks, the remedy is to add some fresh yeast.

After the minimum 2 weeks have passed, crack a bottle and taste the fruit of your labors. It may seem obvious, but you probably do not want to drink the yeast sediment on the bottom of the bottle. Although it has plenty of nutrition, it does not taste all that good and will likely give you indigestion. So decant your brew slowly into a drinking glass to enjoy it.

Some beers require aging for longer than a few weeks to reach their full flavor potential. If the beer does not taste as good as you were hoping it would, give it a few more weeks — or even a few more months, depending on the style, then sample it again.

Bottle Prep

I'll let you in on a little secret: I don't wait until bottling day to clean my bottles. I let time do most of the work for me. On brew day I make a batch of cleaning solution to wash my fermenter and other tools. Instead of throwing gallons of slightly used cleaner away, I pour it into some 5-gallon plastic buckets and soak the bottles for a few days or until I get around to rinsing them out. It usually takes three to four buckets to clean enough bottles for 5 gallons of beer. Most labels fall right off, and a quick swish with a bottle brush does the rest. I rinse each bottle, let it dry upside down, then store it on its side or upside down in a box or bag to keep dust out.

Most brewers also sanitize bottle caps. A good method is to soak them in sanitizing solution, then rinse them with freshly boiled water that is still hot but not boiling. Most good-quality caps have a soft liner that might be damaged by boiling water.

Some homebrewers do not sanitize bottle caps and find that they have good results, so after due consideration, this may be a fine option if you know where those caps have been. Most commercial breweries do not sanitize bottle caps because they buy full 70-gross boxes of caps (that's 10,080 bottle caps) that are sealed at the manufacturing plant. Using unsanitized caps for homebrew bottling is taking a bit of a risk, because most caps sold in homebrew shops are in small packages that are packed by the shops themselves or by a homebrew shop distributer. You can inquire about the packaging process to see if the proprietors maintain sanitary conditions that you are comfortable with. If you do skip the step of sanitizing bottle caps, you have saved yourself a bit of effort, so it just makes good sense to be careful handling the caps while bottling to keep them as clean as possible.

Some caps have oxygen-absorbing liners, and sanitizing them this way activates them and uses some of their oxygen-scavenging ability. If you spent the extra money on the caps, you want them to work, so you basically have two options besides not sanitizing them. Option one is to sanitize the caps with iodophor or Star San and do this just before using so as little as possible of the oxygen-absorbing power in the cap lining is lost.

Option two is to use dry heat. Set your oven to 180°F (82°C) — any hotter and the plastic lining of the caps might melt. Place the caps face down on a baking tray in the oven for 20 minutes. Remove the tray, and allow to cool, leaving the caps in place to keep them clean.

4

KICKING IT UP: Brewing from SCRATCH

Most eco-brewers are motivated to use freshly malted grains because doing so has the lowest cost to the environment. Manufacturing extract from fresh grains is an intermediary step that takes resources, including significant amounts of power and water. Commercial extract production is a centralized operation that requires expensive equipment and trained specialists, thus it usually requires more shipping of raw materials than does producing whole malt. Skipping this intermediary step reduces the total amount of fossil fuel and water needed to produce a pint of beer.

Although you can make almost any beer using the partial-mash brewing method described in the previous chapter, brewing with all grain makes it possible to brew a much wider range of beer styles than with extract and specialty grains alone. Here are some other reasons that all-grain brewing is a good thing to do.

- The cost of ingredients is usually lower.
- You have more finely tuned control over the entire brewing process.
- You can use homegrown and locally grown grain (if you malt it yourself).
- You can use spent grain for food, animal food, or soil improvement.

As with any process there are pros and cons to weigh. Here are some of the drawbacks to all-grain brewing.

- It's more time-consuming.
- It's messier, with more equipment to clean.
- More equipment entails higher start-up costs.
- There's the potential for more to go wrong.
- It requires more water and fuel at the brewing stage.
- You have more spent grain to dispose of (a disadvantage if you do not want to reuse it and cannot compost it).

The Process of Making All-Grain Beer

Although it involves a lot of fascinating scientific details and complicated-sounding methods, making beer from scratch is quite easy. And for most of us it is fun! Seriously, all you do is mix the grains with hot water and hold at a temperature of about 150°F (66°C) for 30 to 60 minutes, then rinse out the mixture with some fresh hot water and collect all the liquid that results. In essence you are making your own extract before proceeding with your usual brewing routine.

Making good beer from all grain really can be this straightforward, though, of course, once you figure out the basics, there is a lot more to learn before you master all the possibilities. These are the basic steps for obtaining beer from whole grains:

1. Weigh and crush grains and other ingredients. Measure out water and adjust minerals if needed.
2. Heat water and mix with grains to start mash. The usual ratio is 2 quarts of water for each pound of grain.
3. Mash for 30 to 60 minutes, according to the recipe. For most brews the best temperature range is 150 to 155°F (66–68°C).

4. Rinse the grains with hot water to flush out the sugars. This process is known as *lautering* or *sparging*. The liquid is collected to make beer; the grains are discarded.

5. Boil for 60 to 90 minutes, following the hopping and flavor schedule.

6. Cool the wort to 65 to 75°F (18–24°C).

7. Transfer to a fermenter, and pitch the yeast.

8. Allow the beer to ferment.

9. Bottle your brew or transfer to a keg.

10. Enjoy the fruits of your labor!

Special Equipment for All-Grain Brewing

To brew from scratch you do need a few pieces of specialty equipment, but they are not complicated and for the most part not particularly expensive.

MASH TUN

The mash *tun* (from an Old German word) is just a container that you do the mash in; it can double as your brew pot. A very basic mash tun is a pot, bucket, or tub large enough to hold at least the amount of mash mixture required by your recipe. For a 5-gallon batch, the capacity should be at least 5 gallons to accommodate the volume of mash required for a strong beer. Ideally, you want the tun to hold at least as many gallons as your all-grain system will brew. If it is a few gallons larger, that is better. You never know when you will want to brew an imperial IPA or a barley wine, which could require a capacity of up to double the batch size. If you plan on setting up a 10-gallon brewing system, you can do just fine with a 10-gallon mash tun if you scale down to a 5-gallon batch size for really big beers.

Because most recipes require holding the mash at a constant temperature in the 150 to 155°F (66–68°C) range for up to an hour, a mash tun should be either insulated to hold heat or flameproof so it can be heated if needed. With an insulated but not flameproof vessel, temperature adjustments can be made by adding hot or cold water. Many homebrewers use large plastic water or picnic coolers for a mash tun, but a stainless steel, ceramic, or wooden vessel is preferred in most eco-friendly home breweries.

Many mash tuns are actually dual purpose because they have a built-in filtering system that allows them to function as a lauter tun as well.

LAUTER TUN

All or most of the fermentable sugars in all-grain beer come from the grains, so it is important to strain out the grains properly. The lauter tun must be at least as large as the mash tun and have a strainer or filter built into it. The most efficient setups have a straining apparatus directly above a spigot at the bottom of the lauter tun. It is preferable to have the straining apparatus at the bottom of the container because more sugars will be extracted as the liquid flows through the grain. If the rinsing water can flow out the sides, such as with a colander or straining bag, some of it will miss the dissolved sugars rather than flushing them all out the bottom.

A lauter tun can be as simple as a 5-gallon bucket made of food-grade plastic with a number of ⅛-inch holes drilled in it, nested inside another bucket that has a spigot installed in it. This is a reasonable option for all-grain brewing on a budget, and you can get plastic buckets for free from a grocery store or deli. Just avoid any plastic that held pickles or any other strong-smelling ingredients, because these flavors are easily transferred to your beer.

When using a separate lauter tun, most homebrewers simply use their brew pot as a mash tun. Once the mash is ready for sparging, the grains are transferred to the lauter tun, and the brew pot then can be rinsed out and used to collect the wort for boiling. If you have concerns about toxins leeching from plastic buckets used for lautering, this method is preferable to doing the whole mash in plastic because it limits the amount of time the hot liquid is in contact with plastic.

Combined Mash/Lauter Tun

Often the lautering filter is built into the mash tun; thus the mash tun also serves as the lauter tun. During the mash it is called a mash tun. While the wort is being strained out of the grains, it is called a lauter tun. Most of us just call it a mash/lauter tun, and we're good. What you call it is not all that important, although having fancy names for every piece of brewing gear you own is sure to impress your friends and family. The filter can be a false bottom, a coil of slotted copper tubing, a braided stainless steel tube with the plastic liner removed, or any other ingenious filtering device you can invent that will strain the sweet wort out from the grains.

The ideal choice for a combo mash/lauter tun is a stainless steel pot with a false bottom. Very nice examples of these are manufactured specifically for homebrewers by several different companies, including Polar Ware and Blichmann Engineering. Although more expensive up front, stainless steel is the easiest material to keep sanitary and will last for a lifetime of brewing quality beers. (See DIY Mash/Lauter Tun, page 91.)

HOT LIQUOR OR SPARGE WATER TANK

A hot liquor or sparge water tank holds the water that is used for lautering or sparging the grains. (In this sense "liquor" has the old meaning of "liquid," not necessarily alcohol.) The tank often has a spigot and is placed above the lauter tun so the hot water can be fed by gravity into the top of the mash tun. A sparge arm or other sparging accessory is commonly used to set up a really efficient lautering cycle. The method of sparging or lautering that you use will dictate what type of sparge water tank you need. If you are hand ladling the sparge water or batch sparging, you do not need a special hot liquor tank at all; any pot large enough to heat up the required amount of sparge water will do.

The objective of sparging is to have the water flow gently over the top of the grain bed so the grains are disturbed as little as possible. You can ladle the hot water over the grain bed by hand, which can be a Zen-like experience if you are the patient type. If you brew often or do large batches, however, it can become rather tedious. Buying or making a simple sparging device can be a worthwhile time-saving investment.

A sparge arm, a sprinkler type of device (think of a showerhead), or ring of copper tubing with holes punched in the bottom that the hot sparge water is run through can help automate the task of lautering and improve the final yield from a mash. Rotating sparge arms are miniature versions of sparging arms often employed in large breweries and are rather fun to use but are usually the more expensive option.

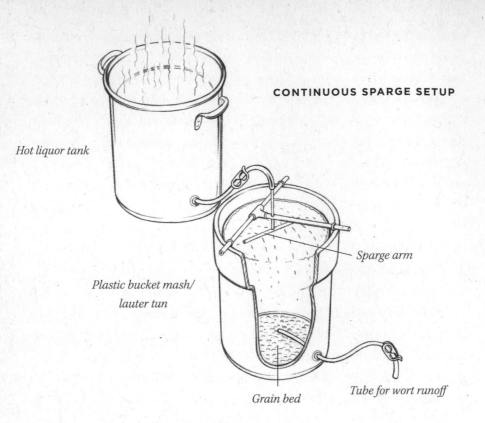

CONTINUOUS SPARGE SETUP

Hot liquor tank

Sparge arm

*Plastic bucket mash/
lauter tun*

Grain bed

Tube for wort runoff

PH-TESTING EQUIPMENT

Because water pH is influenced by many different factors and can change dramatically when combined with malt in the mash, the best time to measure the pH when brewing a new style of beer is at the very start of the mash. You should have supplies on hand to make adjustments if needed. To test pH you can use pH test strips or a pH meter, both of which are available at most homebrew supply stores or via Internet suppliers.

Precision pH strips such as the ColorpHast brand will give more accurate results. A pH meter is even more accurate and can come in handy for other projects, such as testing soil pH for gardening. For beer brewing purposes you need to take an accurate reading of the mash, so if using pH test paper, look for strips that measure a range of at least 4.6 to 6.2. A less accurate strip that can measure from at least 3 to 10 is also very useful for testing water and wine.

On to Practical Matters: How to Mash

When you brew beer from whole grains, you add a few steps, but after the mash is done, the basic process is unchanged: boiling the wort, adding hops, cooling, pitching yeast, fermentation, and packaging in bottles or kegs. If you have decided to start your hobby right out of the gate with whole grains and skip the extract brewing stage completely, you still need to learn all the other stages of the brewing process that are covered in chapter 3.

This chapter focuses on the process of extracting sugar from malted grains, from the mechanics to the chemistry. When brewing with extract, things such as mash pH and water chemistry are not critical to success, but they can be when brewing with all grains. Having a basic understanding of what goes on with enzymes, pH, and water mineral profiles is important if you want to brew quality beers consistently.

By now you probably have a good idea of the basic concept of mashing. There are three commonly used methods of mashing malt to make beer — single infusion, step infusion, and decoction mash.

Single infusion. The water is heated to a temperature slightly higher than the desired mash temperature before the grains are added. Because the grains are at room temperature, the water temperature drops to the target range when the grains are mixed in, and then it is held for 30 to 60 minutes until starch conversion is complete. This method is the most widely used today because most professionally malted grains contain a large quantity of enzymes and will complete the starch conversion with no more effort than this.

Step infusion. When brewing with a large percentage of unmalted grains such as flaked oats or precooked millet, or if you are working with under-modified malt (grains that have not developed to optimal enzyme and protein levels in the malting process — rare these days) or home-malted grains, the mash will need to be held at two or more temperature levels to break down additional proteins and beta-glucans that may be present. The mash routine is often specified in the recipe, but in general it is first held at a lower temperature for a while, and then more heat is added to bring the mash to the next stage. Heat can be added by turning on a burner or adding boiling water, or by straining out some of the wort, gently heating it up, then adding it back to the mash. Most step infusion mashes require a single temperature adjustment, but it is possible for a very complex recipe to have three or four stages.

Decoction mash. This type of mashing requires boiling a portion of the mash, grains and all, and returning it back to the mash tun. This process develops more caramel flavors by cooking the mash over several stages, and was developed to obtain better extraction rates from malt made from old-world barley that was difficult to malt properly. The extended cooking during the mash process breaks down the less soluble starches present in under-modified malts. If you grow and malt your own barley, this type of mash-ing might help you increase your extract yields. It is sometimes used when brewing German bock and Oktoberfest styles to develop the desired deep caramel flavors. If you want to try this method of mashing, see the recipe for Bawk-Bawk Bock on page 294.

A STEP-BY-STEP GUIDE TO MASHING

1. WEIGH AND CRUSH THE GRAINS

When brewing with large amounts of grains, the proper crush level is critical. When grains are properly crushed, each grain is split open so the starchy con-tents are exposed and can be dissolved in the mash. If the grains are ground too finely, the mash becomes too mushy and thick, and straining the wort from the grains is very difficult. A fine balance is needed — too coarse and the extract yield suffers; too fine and the lauter tun can get clogged. The milled grain mix is called *grist*.

A good roller mill is the preferred option; it cracks the grains without pulverizing the husks too badly. Plate mills, which have one or two disks that catch the grain and shred it, are widely available but are not ideal. If you have a choice between using a plate mill and having your grain milled on a roller mill when you purchase it, choose the milling service unless you will not be able to brew with the grains for over a week. A plate-style mill can be purchased for fifty or sixty dollars. Decent-quality roller mills are available starting at a hundred dollars.

If you are milling a combination of grains yourself, it is generally a good idea to weigh them and mix them together before milling. Different malts

DIY Mash/Lauter Tun

You can build your own stainless mash/lauter tun by converting a retired 15-gallon sanke keg or a stainless steel kettle. You can do this using a power drill and one of the widely available weld-free ball valves on the market, in combination with a pre-made false bottom or a mash filter you build yourself out of copper tubing. If you have the tools and the skill to weld stainless steel yourself, you can install a spigot fitting permanently, typically a half-inch coupler with a female pipe thread fitting, which can fit a stainless steel ball valve.

If you are not equipped to weld stainless steel yourself, it may be worth it to hire a local welding professional to do the job for you, which should cost less than fifty dollars. Sometimes a bottle or two of your finest homebrew will help you work out a better deal for the service! One of the weld-free kits generally works reasonably well but can become leaky if any of the metal parts or the area where it is installed on the pot become warped or dented. An expert weld job should serve you well for many years. I had a pot custom-modified when I first started brewing, and I still use it every time I brew, 18 years later!

have different sizes and hardness, and you can get a more consistent crush by milling them together. Set the mill for the optimum crush for the largest quantity of grain used, usually the base malt for the recipe. That way, you will not have to change the setting on your grain mill in midprocess. If this isn't possible, just do the best job you can milling the grains, and 99 times out of 100 all will be well. In some ways brewing can be very forgiving.

2. HEAT WATER AND START THE MASH

Use 1.5 to 2 quarts of brewing-quality water for each pound of grain. If you need to adjust minerals for a specific beer style, do so before adding the grains. For a single infusion mash, heat the water 10 to 15°F (6–8°C) higher than the desired mashing temperature. This starting temperature is usually referred to as the *strike temperature*.

If the ratio of water to malt is 1.5 to 1 and you want a starting mash temperature of 150°F (66°C), the strike temperature should be about 165°F (74°C). With a ratio of 2:1, the strike temperature should be a bit lower, or about 160°F (71°C). If your mash/lauter tun has a false bottom, you'll need to add extra water to account for the space underneath and drop the strike temperature a degree or two. After a few batches you will start to learn your system and will develop a good sense for how much temperature change will occur in your own particular setup.

When adding grain to the strike water, it is important to mix thoroughly to make sure all the grain particles are completely soaked. If you are heating the strike water in a separate pot from the mash tun, you can add a portion of the water, then a portion of the grains, and so on. Working in thirds usually

Brew Tip

IF YOU REALLY MISCALCULATE and your mash temperature exceeds 167°F (75°C), the enzymes that are needed to do the starch conversion will be denatured and your mash will not succeed. It's a harsh lesson but probably a mistake you'll only make once. (And if you keep chickens they may be pretty happy with the extrarich "spent" grain.)

works well. If you are heating up the water directly in your mash tun, it is fine to add your grain in batches, stirring after each addition, to the entire volume of mash water, and there is no need to dump some of the water out and then mix it back in. The point is to evenly mix the grains and water, so it doesn't matter whether you add the grains to the water or the water to the grains, so long as you mix them thoroughly.

(If math is fun for you, you can calculate precisely the exact strike temperature needed for x gallons of water mixed with y pounds of grain. You will need to know the starting temperature of the grain, the exact volume of water, and the exact weight of the grain. The basic formula is described in chapter 16 of *How to Brew* by John Palmer, or see Resources for an online calculator.)

Once you have done a few all-grain batches, you will start to develop an instinct for getting the balance of strike water temperature to grain right, and you will rarely need to correct it. It is always a good idea to start with a lower ratio of strike water to grist. That way if your temperature is too high or too low you can easily correct it by adding boiling water or cold water, a little at a time as needed, without skewing the water-to-grain ratio too badly. Keep adding water until the desired temperature is reached. Stir well after each water addition to make sure equilibrium is reached before adding more water.

3. TESTING FOR DONENESS (THE STARCH TEST)

When you first add the grains to hot water, the water is cloudy from all the pulverized bits of starchy grains. The wort becomes less and less cloudy as starches are transformed into sugars by the mash enzymes. The flavor also is transformed from being bready or grainy to syrupy and sweet. It can be tricky to figure out exactly when the process is complete; one way is to do a starch test. Some substances — one being iodine — produce a visible reaction when mixed with a solution containing starch. For this test you can use the same iodine solution you use for sanitizing.

A tincture of iodine will turn from red to a dark purplish black when mixed with a starchy liquid. To witness this reaction at its strongest level, pull a sample from the mash at the very beginning. Carefully tilt a spoon into the liquid to draw away some liquid without bits of grain in it. If you prefer, you can pull a sample, then strain it through a fine screen. Put several drops of iodine into the sample, swirl to mix, and observe the reaction. It should happen very quickly, and the change should be obvious.

When the mash water has cleared and becomes sweet, do another iodine test. If no color change occurs, the mash is done. Sometimes a slight reaction will occur even after the starches have converted as much as they possibly can. This is due to minute particles of grain husk and other proteins reacting with the iodine. This is why I suggest doing a reading at the beginning of the mash; it will give you a benchmark by which to gauge the extent of the change.

As you gain experience with mashing, you can learn to rely on your sense of taste to ascertain when a mash has finished. To this end, every time you brew you should frequently taste a small sample of the mash as it progresses so you can train your taste buds to detect subtle changes in the flavor. When just learning to mash or if tasting the mash does not work well for you, a starch test is very reliable and easy to perform.

4. LAUTERING, OR HOW TO SPARGE

Once the starch conversion is complete, it is time to lauter the grains. Lautering is the process of flushing or rinsing the grains with hot water to wash all the fermentable sugars into the wort for the boil. Technically, to sparge is to spray or sprinkle hot water over the grain bed. The terms "lauter" and "sparge" are often used interchangeably by homebrewers. Both mean to wash the sugars out of the mashed grains.

Heat the quantity of sparge water called for in your recipe to between 165 and 170°F (74 and 77°C). Take into account the amount of heat loss that occurs as the liquid travels between the sparge water tank and the top of the grain bed in the mash. Unless you're brewing in a very cold environment or the water has to travel an unusually long distance, the temperature drop is usually less than 10°F (6°C).

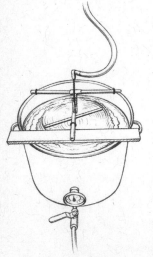

Lauter tun with built-in thermometer

Water temperature, volume of water, and flow rate are all very important in this process. Keep these tips in mind:

- The water must be hotter than the mash temperature, so the solution becomes more fluid and more sugars are dissolved and extracted, but not so hot as to leach tannins and other undesirable compounds from the grains.
- Calibrate the amount of water so the final total volume of liquid collected is the amount needed for the number of gallons being brewed.
- The water should flow gently and slowly in a solid sheet from the top down in the lauter tun. This flow works the most efficiently if the overall water level remains high and constant.
- Add fresh hot water at the top of the lauter tun at the same rate as it is removed by the spigot at the bottom. The grains in between act as a filter to keep most of the larger bits of grain and husk out of the wort. When it is flowing properly, only clear wort exits from the bottom.

The above method is known as *continuous sparging*. A less widely used technique is *batch sparging*. To batch-sparge, all the sweet wort is drained from the grains, and the mash tun (still filled with grains) is refilled with hot sparge water. The grains are steeped in this second batch of water for a short time — usually about 10 minutes — then drained again. If needed, a third batch of sparge water is used. Batch sparging is less efficient, resulting in yields up to 15 percent lower than continuous sparging, but it may be easier given available equipment.

5. ONWARD, TO THE BOIL!

Once the wort has been collected from the grains, the all-grain part of the process is basically done, and the rest of the brew works the same way as an extract or partial-mash brew does. The wort is boiled, hops are added, the wort is cooled, yeast is pitched, and so on. The only difference would occur if, as an extract brewer, you were used to doing partial-boil batches. When brewing all grain, you do not have the option to do a partial boil — in fact, it is usually the other way around. Often extra wort is collected and needs to be condensed slightly, which usually occurs in a 60-minute boil. In some circumstances it becomes necessary to extend the boil up to 90 or even 120 minutes to concentrate the wort down to the finished volume called for in the recipe.

Looking at Water Chemistry

To determine whether you need to adjust the mineral content or pH of your brewing water, you need to find out what your brewing water chemistry is like. Once you know your water chemistry, you can make adjustments for certain styles of beer. If the content of minerals other than bicarbonates is too high, the only way to reduce the parts per million (ppm) is by diluting with distilled or reverse osmosis (RO)–filtered water. If they are too low, you can add a measured amount of the right mineral to make adjustments.

If you are on a municipal water supply, in most areas you can request a basic analysis free of charge from the water department. If you have a well or rely on another source for your brewing water, you might want to have the water tested. A number of laboratories offer affordable water testing services; check agricultural testing companies that also do soil tests for farmers (see Resources). A basic household water mineral test should, at a minimum, give you the results listed below.

Bicarbonate (HCO$_3$). The best range for brewing is 0 to 250 ppm. Lower levels (0–50 ppm) are good for brewing lagers and light beers, and high levels (150–250 ppm) are good for strong and dark beers, with most other beer styles falling somewhere in between. Excess bicarbonate is easily removed by boiling; after 30 minutes most of the bicarbonate will precipitate out as a sediment or film at the bottom of the kettle. Then just carefully decant the water off the sediment. The drawback is that boiling also removes calcium, so if it would lower your calcium levels too much, diluting your brewing water with distilled or RO-filtered water may be a better option. Alternatively, after boiling to precipitate out the excess bicarbonate, you can add minerals to increase calcium levels.

Calcium (Ca). Best range for brewing is 5 to 150 ppm. Calcium is very important for enzyme function in the mash, protein reactions in the boil, and yeast metabolism. Calcium can be increased by the addition of calcium chloride, calcium sulfate (gypsum), or calcium carbonate.

Chlorine (Cl). Best range for brewing is 0 to 150 ppm. Within this range sodium helps to balance flavors and accentuate malt sweetness. Too high, and beer will taste salty. Adding calcium chloride or sodium chloride will increase chlorine levels, which might be appropriate for specialty beer styles — Gose, for instance.

Magnesium (Mg). Best range for brewing is 10 to 30 ppm. Levels over 50 ppm can cause a sour taste. Magnesium is important for yeast function, and some enzyme reactions rely on it. Add magnesium sulfate to increase levels.

Potassium (K). Best range for brewing is 0 to 10 ppm. Higher levels of potassium inhibit enzyme activity and are detrimental to yeast function. Additions of potassium are generally not needed. If your house uses a water softener, you should avoid using your tap water for brewing, as potassium levels are likely to be too high.

Sodium (Na). Best range for brewing is 0 to 150 ppm. As with chlorine too much sodium can lead to salty-tasting beer. Sodium at levels of 70 to 150 ppm can have a balancing effect on flavors in beer just as it does in food, but too much is never a good thing.

Other values given in a water report are:

pH value. This is often between 7 and 8. Remember that the pH value drops when malt is added to the water, so the important pH measurement is the one you take of the mash.

Total alkalinity. With this value and some fairly complex math you can estimate what the mash pH will be. I rarely find this to be necessary, but it can be a useful tool if you are experiencing problems with mash pH or having problems with full starch conversion. (See Resources for an online spreadsheet with these calculations, or consult chapter 15 of *How to Brew* by John Palmer.)

Although water hardness and pH can vary throughout the year, a single test should give you a ballpark snapshot of your water qualities and give you enough information to meet your homebrewing needs, unless you feel it is necessary to work with information of pinpoint accuracy. In that case a test during the driest season and one during the wettest season may serve you better.

WHY IS WATER IMPORTANT?

For many centuries brewers made perfectly fine beer without adjusting water chemistry. This is one of the reasons different styles of beer evolved that are unique to their brewing region. From an ecological perspective it makes sense to brew with local water and make beer styles that take advantage of the local flavor without adding imported minerals. Why not celebrate the natural advantages of your water to develop your own local flavor? If you have naturally hard water, you will do well with stouts, IPAs, and English-style IPAs. If your water is soft, pilsners and European ales are good candidates for becoming your signature local beer.

If you want to tailor your beer to a specific style, there are charts online to help you figure out the correct water profile (see Resources). To keep it simple for everyday brewing, though, you just want to keep the ppm of each mineral within the optimal brewing range described above. I find that as long as my water mineral levels are within the brewing "sweet spot," it is rarely necessary to change mineral levels or adjust the pH. My water is of average hardness, and when I am brewing styles that call for hard water, I find that adding a small amount of gypsum (calcium sulfate) gives the most pleasant-tasting result.

For most of us tweaking the water chemistry is important only if we are brewing for a competition or are correcting a problem that contributes an off-flavor to our beer. In competitions adherence to the style profile is important. If the water chemistry is markedly different from the standard for that style, it could cost you a few points, which could make the difference between a blue ribbon and no ribbon!

The Importance of Mash pH

The level of acidity or alkalinity of a solution, the pH, is measured on a scale of 1 to 14. One is considered extremely acidic, 7 is considered neutral, and 14 is extremely alkaline (or basic). Pure water usually has a pH of 7.0, but as the mineral content, or hardness, increases, the alkalinity goes up. This can sometimes be a problem for all-grain brewers. When working with mashing and wort, the ideal range for most mashes is 5.4 to 5.8 (measured at room temperature). In most cases simply mixing barley malt with water that is pH neutral or slightly alkaline will result in a pH within this range, because the acidity of the mash naturally lowers the pH. This is the range in which most of the desirable enzymatic activity happens at a lively pace.

In the mash, water temperature is the most important aspect to be precise about — as long as temperatures are within a few degrees of the optimum, everything will work out fine unless the pH is way out of balance. Many brewers mash without worrying too much about pH and make great beer without ever taking a pH reading. When brewing all grain it is sometimes necessary to make adjustments to the mash to achieve a balanced pH and produce a beer that meets your expectations.

If the pH is too high and the mash is too alkaline, too many tannins could be extracted from the grains and enzyme activity may be somewhat inhibited, slowing conversion rates and possibly reducing the yields. Too much tannin in the wort can cause a hint of bitterness or astringency in the finished beer. A pH that is too low will slow enzyme activity and may cause hints of acetone and excessive hop bitterness in finished beers. Darker malts tend to acidify the mash more than lighter malts, so a pH adjustment may be necessary when brewing one type of beer but not another.

During mashing the goal is usually to hit the sweet spot of 5.4 to 5.8 pH, but as long as you are within a few points of this range, your beer should turn out well. Most of the time you will be looking to lower the pH. It is very important to note that pH reading changes with temperature. By most accepted standards of measuring, the sample should be cooled to room temperature, or between 60 and 70°F (16 and 21°C), before the measurement is taken. The pH reading will be lower at mash temperatures of around 150°F (66°C).

If your reading is outside the range, it is good science to take a second reading before making any adjustments, just in case something went wrong the first time. A chunk of grain or a mash that was not adequately mixed could throw the reading off.

ADJUSTING PH LEVELS

If an adjustment is merited, there are several methods you can employ to adjust the mash pH. There are other substances available than those suggested here, but in my estimation some methods rely too much on chemical means and shouldn't be employed by eco-minded brewers.

Raising mash pH. If the mash is too acidic (pH is too low), add an alkaline substance such as calcium carbonate, or chalk ($CaCO_3$), or lime ($Ca(OH)_2$).

Lowering mash pH. It is more common to lower mash pH (make it more acidic) than to raise it, using common mineral salts such as gypsum ($CaSO_4$) or Epsom salts ($MgSO_4 \cdot 7H_2O$). Lactic acid or distilled white vinegar can also

continued on page 102

The Nitty-Gritty Details: How Mashing Works

Malted grains are basically seeds that have been modified by soaking and sprouting. If the sprouted grain is allowed to grow into a seedling, enzymes in the seed will convert starches into sugars to feed the seedling. Drying the grains at a peak point in the cycle, when both the starch and enzyme levels are high, stops that conversion process and preserves the enzymes and starches in a compact form with a good shelf life. The enzymes remain dormant in dry malt, even if heated; to become active they need to be dissolved in water. The activity level of malt enzymes is primarily affected by temperature of the liquid mash, although pH can influence their effectiveness as well.

It is useful to understand how the malting process works even though it is not necessary to malt your own grains to brew beer from whole-grain malt. Enzymes act as a catalyst that is like biological rocket fuel that speeds up reactions essential for life; without them the starch-to-sugar conversion would happen too slowly and the plant would starve and die. In malted grain several different types of enzymes work in concert to break down the complex starch and protein molecules into simpler, more digestible sugars and amino acids that yeast can eat. Some enzymes break the starches into sugars while others act on the proteins and cellulose in the grain.

Each of these specialized enzymes is most effective within a specific temperature range and pH level. Because we know which enzymes perform which functions at which temperature range, we can guide the outcome of our mash with precision, as long as the pH is not too far out of balance. Although all these different enzymes are working together in the mash to make it into wort, for most all-grain brewing we mainly need to concern ourselves with a few types of enzymes: alpha-amylases and beta-amylases, proteases, and beta-glucanases. Each has a slightly different job to do in the mash:

- **Alpha-amylase.** A fast-acting enzyme that works in the mash between 140 and 167°F (60 and 75°C) and most rapidly between 140 and 158°F (60 and 70°C). Alpha- or a-amylases break apart larger, more complex chains of starch molecules, producing maltose and other sugars. Amylase is present in human saliva, where it has been used by primitive cultures to start the mashing process by chewing whole grains (a last resort for homebrewing!).

- **Beta-amylase.** This enzyme produces only maltose; it is most active between 140 and 150°F (60 and 66°C), and performs optimally at 140 to 145°F (60–63°C). A somewhat fragile, plant-based enzyme, it becomes completely denatured within 10 to 20 minutes at temperatures over 155°F (68°C). To create a beer with a lighter body, hold the temperature around 145°F (63°C) for a short while to allow more of the enzymes to break down more of the complex carbohydrates that make a fuller beer.

- **Protease.** Barley malt contains a fair amount of protein that is too complex for yeast to eat. Protease enzymes break down proteins into amino acids, which aid in yeast metabolism and reproduction, essentially providing two valuable services to brewers for the price of one. Proteases are most active between 68° and 149°F (20 and 65°C) and perform best at 113 to 131°F (45–55°C). In modern malting processes many of the proteins are broken down; thus nothing special needs to be done by the brewer because the remaining proteins will be broken down sufficiently during a single temperature mash. If you are using a large proportion of unmalted grain (or grain that has been inexpertly malted at home), allowing a protein rest during the mash cycle or using a decoction mash may help reduce excess proteins that could cause *chill haze* in a finished beer. Be careful, though — a mash held at the protein-rest temperature range of 120 to 130°F (49–54°C) for longer than 30 minutes could result in a beer that is too thin.

- **Beta-glucanase.** Beta-glucans are nonstarch polysaccharides, basically plant cellulose and bran. Too many can be a problem in brewing, because if they are not broken down by beta-glucanases, the grains will have a thicker, gummy quality that can make it hard to rinse the fermentable sugars from the grains, thus lowering the yield. Allowing some beta-glucans to remain in the finished beer contributes a silky mouthfeel and body to beers such as oatmeal stout. B-glucanase is active between 68 and 122°F (20 and 50°C). A rest period during the mash in the optimal temperature range of 95 to 110°F (35–43°C) for 10 to 20 minutes will reduce the levels of beta-glucans and is suggested for grain bills that include a portion of unmalted grains that exceeds 20 percent.

be used, although they (as well as other liquid acids I don't recommend, such as hydrochloric acid or muriatic acids, often used by commercial brewers) can give a sour taste to the beer, which may be desirable in certain beer styles and definitely not wanted in others. Using one of the mineral salts will avoid this effect. Alternatively, a sour mash or acid malt can be used. See the recipe for Cultured Farm Girl (page 300), a Berliner Weisse, for a basic sour mash guide.

Making the adjustment. Whatever you use, add it slowly. The best method is to make a solution with the additive and add a small amount, stir well, wait a minute, then take a reading. For powdered minerals I suggest a solution of 1 teaspoon in 3 tablespoons of water, then add the mixture 1 tablespoon at a time until the desired pH is reached. For liquids such as lactic acid or vinegar, add 1 tablespoon at a time for a 5-gallon batch. Many compounds in the mash act as buffers, so a threshold will need to be reached before a change takes effect, and that change can be dramatic if too much is added all at once.

Here is an area where common sense should also prevail. You are adding stuff to beer that you will drink. Would you want to drink a glass of water mixed with some of that powder you are planning on adding to your brewing water? Adding minerals and acids can adversely affect the taste. You don't want your beer to taste like chalk or vinegar or something even nastier. By making small adjustments you will give yourself more fine-tuned control over the end result, and you will minimize your use of additives altogether. Take notes on what you are doing, so that if you like the results you can duplicate them or adjust them again if you aren't quite happy.

> ### Brew Tip
> *AS AN ECO-MINDED BREWER, I shy away from tweaking the chemistry of my mash and wort too much. Adding chemicals such as phosphoric acid or potassium hydroxide to balance pH runs counter to my sense of nature's balance. I only resort to adjustments if a problem is pronounced and will result in an unsatisfactory beer; then I use simpler ingredients such as gypsum or chalk whenever possible.*

Parameters for a Perfect Mash

A higher-temperature mash will produce a wort with more unfermentable sugars and a beer that is fuller bodied and sweeter. A lower-temperature mash will produce a thinner wort and a beer that is drier and more crisp. A short rest at a temperature range of 110 to 130°F (43–54°C) will reduce proteins and beta-glucans and is usually only necessary for beers with a percentage of unmalted grains higher than 20 percent.

The ideal environment for efficient mashing of most malt into wort for homebrewing purposes will consist of:

- *A temperature range of 150 to 155°F (65–68°C); higher temperatures for fuller beers and lower for lighter ones*

- *A pH range of 5.2 to 5.8*

- *A mash thickness of 1.5 to 2 quarts of water for each pound of grain (3–4 liters per kg)*

Aerate, Aerate, Aerate!

In the past dozen years or so, wort aeration has been given a lot more attention, as it rightly should be. Oxygen is a very important nutrient for the cellular reproduction of yeast. If there is not enough oxygen in the wort when the yeast is introduced, the yeast will still function, but in a diminished capacity, and the fermentation will not be as healthy as it should be.

The boiling process drives all the oxygen out of the wort, so it has to be added back in before fermentation begins. The higher the initial gravity of the wort, the higher the level of oxygen needs to be, because high-gravity beers require a larger population of yeast to do a proper job of fermenting. If you use the yeast pitching guide on page 58 and aerate the heck out of the really strong beers, you will be well on your way to master (home)brewer status!

Aeration isn't rocket science, although I am sure some rocket scientists have applied their considerable talents to the challenge of aerating their homebrew over the years. The object is to mix as much oxygen into the wort as possible without contaminating it, hopefully without making a huge mess. It is possible to achieve up to 8 ppm of dissolved oxygen by mixing air into the wort by one of the methods described below. Five ppm is the minimum required for healthy yeast growth.

Pouring/splashing. Pouring the beer into the carboy through a strainer or splashing it through a sanitized screen will partially aerate the wort. Using a siphon wort aeration device such as the Siphon Spray Wort Aerator made by Fermentap can enhance the process. For many beers a splash-as-you-transfer approach is all that is needed for adequate aeration. Note I said "adequate." If you aspire to greatness in your beers, you should always aerate well. This requires agitating, stirring, or using an oxygenation system after this step to enhance the aeration and propel your beer into the realm of greatness.

Agitating. If the beer is in a carboy, you can gently rock the vessel back and forth so the beer sloshes around inside. I find it helpful to put the stopper in so the airlock hole allows air in but no liquid escapes as long as you are careful. I put the carboy on a soft surface such as a thick rug or rubber mat while agitating it. A broken carboy full of homebrew is a real tragedy and in the worst-case scenario could cause a serious injury.

Stirring. If you are using a widemouthed fermenter, you can use a clean, sanitized stainless steel whisk to whip air into the wort. Choose one with a long handle to keep your hands away from the liquid. You could attach the whisk to a cordless drill to save your wrist, and homebrew shops sell aeration devices that attach to power drills. A strong word of caution about this: Never use a corded drill unless it is plugged into a ground-fault circuit interrupter (GFCI) outlet. If you drop an ungrounded drill into liquid, you could be electrocuted.

When it comes to aerating your wort, perserverance is more effective than brute force. Depending on the style of beer being made, agitate or stir for 1 to 5 minutes to ensure you have sufficiently aerated the wort. If you agitate really fast, the wort will foam up quickly, but it's likely that only the top third of the wort will be sufficiently aerated. A slow and steady agitation causes the oxygen to dissolve evenly throughout the fermenter from top to bottom.

Once several inches of foam have formed, the wort is usually sufficiently aerated — although strong beers can foam up quickly because of the higher density of the liquid. Since they need a higher level of aeration than an average- or low-gravity beer, a longer amount of time spent agitating the wort can really pay off with a more robust fermentation.

Maintain Accurate Temperatures

It's extremely important to keep track of the temperatures at which you are mashing and fermenting. A mash can be very forgiving, and the magic of starch conversion can happen over a fairly wide temperature range, but for consistent and predictable results, an accurate thermometer is essential (and make sure to keep it calibrated). I often use two thermometers when precision is required, just to make sure I am getting accurate results.

Doing every mash in the temperature range of 150 to 155°F (66–68°C) will always succeed in starch conversion and will usually make decent beer. To address potential flaws, reproduce the mash schedule of a classic beer style, or deal with excess proteins and beta-glucans in large amounts of unmalted grains, you may need more accurate target temperatures, and the process may require several temperature stages.

Using an Aeration Kit

Another way to aerate wort is by injecting air or even pure oxygen with an aeration stone. You can buy a kit that includes the stone, a filter, and either a small pump or a small regulator that attaches to the type of recyclable oxygen tanks sold for welding. If you often brew lagers or high-gravity beers, one of these devices may be worth the investment.

Aeration systems push air (or pure oxygen from a tank) via an aquarium pump through a stone that has hundreds of tiny holes. The holes create very small bubbles that dissolve into the wort much more quickly than normal air bubbles do. A higher concentration of dissolved oxygen can be achieved using an aeration stone and pure oxygen than any manual method of mixing air into the wort.

Most commercial breweries use pure-oxygen aeration systems for this reason. It is one thing they can do that will help ensure they produce good beer every time.

The subject of whether using pure oxygen makes better-tasting beer is one that experts disagree on. I don't think it's necessary; I have always found that my yeastie beasties thrive on plain old life-giving air.

In general, brewing beers with fuller body and sweetness calls for a higher mash temperature (153–158°F [67–70°C]), while beers that are lighter bodied and dry require a lower range (149–152°F [65–67°C]). To break down a larger amount of insoluble proteins, you can implement a protein rest by holding the mash at 120 to 130°F (49–54°C) for 10 to 20 minutes. To increase the activity of enzymes that break up the gummy beta-glucans, you can hold the mash in the optimal temperature range for beta-glucanases of 95 to 110°F (35–43°C) for 10 to 20 minutes. See The Nitty Gritty Details: How Mashing Works, page 100, for more details about enzyme reactions and what happens in the mash at different temperature ranges.

CONTROLLING FERMENTATION TEMPERATURES

This is an area where many homebrewers fail, despite being extra careful at every other stage of the brewing process. Maintaining the ideal fermentation temperature range can be a real challenge, especially when the weather is particularly hot or cold or the temperature in your fermentation area fluctuates quite a bit throughout the day. Professional breweries rely on refrigeration, glycol-cooled fermenter jackets, or heated fermentation rooms to maintain precise temperatures. Most homebrewers do not have budgets that allow for that kind of equipment, but there are many low-tech solutions, and some of them are very eco-friendly.

The first thing you should do when starting to brew is to find the best area of your house to store your fermenters while the yeast does its work. This may not always be the most convenient spot, but we brewers do what we must. An ideal location maintains a consistent temperature between 60 and 70°F (16 and 21°C). If you have such a spot in your house, count yourself lucky, because you will rarely need to do more than occasional monitoring to ensure successful ferments, except when brewing a lager (see Maintaining Lager Fermentation Temperatures, facing page). If not, you may have to modify an existing area or build a fermentation chamber. The eco-friendly option is always the one that does not require additional electricity.

Keeping Fermenters Warm

If the only fermentation area available to you is drafty and cold, your only option may be to install some type of heat source. For a single fermenter, heating pads and heating belts transfer heat directly to the fermenter, using less energy than heating a whole room. A seedling heating mat can serve double duty as a fermentation heater, though it usually warms to a set temperature that cannot be adjusted.

If you have more than one fermenter, heating the area around them might be a better option. If the area is very small and well insulated, it will not take much energy to control the ambient temperature. A small closet or cabinet often works, or you can build an insulated fermentation chamber. In a small enough space, the heat source can be a heating pad, an incandescent lightbulb, or a very small heater. If the chamber is well insulated, a no-power option might even be hot-water bottles or heated ceramic tiles. This is an excellent option if you have a woodstove or radiator where water bottles or stones can be heated without having to turn on an oven or heat water.

Whenever you are working with heating sources in small spaces, especially electric-powered ones, I strongly urge the highest level of caution to prevent the disaster of a fire. Always make sure that any flammable materials are kept away from heat sources. After setting up any kind of heating for your fermenting brew, check on it often, especially in the first 24 hours. Not only will this close monitoring give you peace of mind, it will also help you prevent overheating your fermenter, which could be as devastating to your beer as temperatures that are too cool.

Maintaining Lager Fermentation Temperatures

Maintaining the cooler temperatures required for crafting high-quality lagers can be more challenging than keeping fermenters warm. I grew up in Vermont, and during the winter our cellar was usually a chill 40 to 50°F (4–10°C). Alas, by the time I started brewing, I had moved to warmer climates. If you live in an area with a real winter and you have a basement, you can plan your lager fermentations to occur during the winter months so you never have to worry about artificial cooling methods.

Refrigerators and freezers. Many brewers have to resort to a temperature-controlled refrigerator, a fermentation chamber, or a lagering tub to maintain the necessary 40 to 50°F (4–10°C). (See Using Temperature Controllers, page 109.) A converted refrigerator is the most common solution, but running an extra refrigerator just to make beer might seem a little excessive. On the other hand, beer is food for mind, body, and soul, and, well, this is a choice each of us has to make. Whenever possible, it is best to utilize the resources already at hand. If there is a way to use existing refrigeration, it is usually preferable to maintaining a whole separate fridge.

If you do buy a dedicated homebrewing refrigerator, consider these factors:

- Choose the most energy-efficient model you can afford. If buying used, look for the energy usage data online if it is not available from the seller.
- Choose the smallest size that will fit your needs. Keep in mind that a separate freezer compartment usually cannot be turned completely off and if you use a temperature controller, it will be affected by the cycling on and off of the unit. It therefore may not be suitable for keeping items frozen.
- Consider how the new unit can be useful for other household or brewing needs, such as making extra ice for cooling wort, converting it to a kegerator (a refrigerator with taps for dispensing cold beer), or storing vegetables that do not need to be stored at cooler temperatures.
- Sometimes it makes sense to buy a smaller, more efficient fridge for the home and turn the old fridge into a brew fridge that you run as needed.
- A chest freezer with a temperature controller can be a more energy-efficient option, because less cold air is lost every time the lid is opened. Some sort of moisture control is necessary to prevent rust caused by moisture buildup, though, because most freezers do not have built-in fans.

Using a Fermentation Chamber

A small, well-insulated chamber makes it easier to maintain constant temperatures, using a small heating or cooling source as needed. A large cooler or discarded refrigerator can easily be converted, or use a small closet or cabinet and add additional insulation.

If well insulated, the chamber can be kept at temperatures in the 45 to 55°F range (7–13°C) simply by placing blocks or plastic bottles of ice inside regularly. If you are lucky enough to find an old-fashioned icebox still in good shape and at an affordable price, it could make a fabulous and fashionable fermentation chamber. All you need is enough room in your household freezer to freeze blocks of ice, which will not increase your energy consumption appreciably. In a pinch you can also buy block ice.

If you are not able to reach cold enough temperatures with ice alone, piping in air via a fan and ductwork over a pan of water can provide additional cooling by harnessing evaporative cooling principles. The fermentation chamber can be built to fit exactly into the opening of a small, low-energy-demand refrigerator, essentially extending the capacity of the unit.

Another method is to use a small air conditioner and port the cold air into the chamber via ducting. Crafty homebrewers have published many different plans online, but because these methods use a large amount of energy, they are not really appropriate for an eco-friendly homebrewing guide.

Using Temperature Controllers

External-thermostat temperature controllers are available in most home-brew supply stores in both analog and digital models. Johnson Controls and Ranco are two brands. Prices for most models range from fifty to one hundred dollars. The digital ones are more expensive but offer a wider temperature range. Some analog controllers work with either heating or cooling but not both. A dual-purpose controller may be worth the additional expense if you expect to need both capabilities.

> ## Brew Tip
> *IF YOU USE A SEEDLING HEATING MAT as a heat source, you can buy a thermostat to maintain the temperature of the mat between 65 and 110°F (18 and 43°C). I use a mat made by Hydrofarm (it cost about thirty dollars) for everything from heating seedlings to warming my yogurt cultures to brewing a Belgian-style beer that needs more heat than my fermenting area maintains.*

These controllers have a temperature-sensing probe that is run inside the fermentation chamber or that can be taped to the outside of the fermenter. The heating or cooling device is plugged into the controller, and the desired temperature is set. Once plugged in, the controller will turn the heating or cooling unit on when the temperature falls outside the specified temperature.

Because they override the power switch of the device, temperature controllers only work with appliances that turn on automatically when plugged in with the switch set to "on." Some units have a digital switch and will not turn on when being plugged in unless a user switches them on. Most quality controller units include a built-in differential or variance that prevents excessive switching on and off, which can cause unnecessary wear and tear on the appliance and shorten its service life.

Other thermostats perform a function similar to that of the remote-probe thermostats but lack the probe, which limits their usefulness if you need to regulate cooling temperatures in a refrigerator or chest freezer. They work great in small fermentation areas with a power source located inside the chamber, because the thermostat is on the unit itself. These are designed to be plugged into a wall outlet; prices range from thirty to sixty dollars. Most can be set within a temperature range of 45 to 90°F (7–32°C), which covers beer fermenting temperatures.

The Perfect Brew Closet

My brewing area takes up my side of the master bedroom closet. Instead of clothes (which I keep in a different room), it has wire racks with all my brewing gear and ingredients, and underneath is space enough to hold at least eight fermenters. It is all very neat and organized so I can find the brewing tools I need in a heartbeat. My husband's side of the closet is overflowing with clothes (organization is not his strong point), and we love the humor in it, but this is the best place in the house for my fermenters. It is not near an outside wall, and the temperature averages about 65°F (18°C). The floor is linoleum, and the back patio where I brew is right outside the bedroom door. It's perfect!

Lagering Efficiency

A lot of energy is used to maintain fermenters at lagering temperatures. If your fermenting area is too hot for brewing lagers, you have several low-tech options for lowering the fermentation temperature. Rigging an evaporative cooling system is the simplest and is effective if you need to lower the temperature by up to 25°F (14°C). This system works well in hot, arid climates where temperatures need to be lowered from over 85°F (29°C) to under 70°F (21°C).

A basic evaporative cooling system involves setting the fermenter in a tub of water and wrapping a towel around it so the towel wicks moisture from the tub. Setting a fan (a solar-powered one, preferably!) so it blows a steady breeze across the towel completes the effect. Instead of a fan you can place the fermenter near a window or door that has some natural airflow (but out of direct sunlight).

To achieve much lower lagering temperatures without refrigeration, further measures are usually required. It is not too difficult to maintain temperatures of 45 to 55°F (7–13°C) by keeping the fermenter in a cold-water bath and regularly adding ice. Freeze water in plastic bottles and simply rotate them as needed to maintain the temperature (twice a day is usually enough). You can take this concept one step further and build a fermentation chamber, which is basically an insulated cooler large enough to fit your whole fermenter in.

Finally, a root cellar is a great option if you have the land. At depths of 5 to 50 feet, underground temperatures generally stay at about the annual temperature average for the region, which in many areas is between 50 and 55°F (10 and 13°C). This happens to be a decent temperature for lagering as well as for serving ales, which are more flavorful at this temperature than they are at the 45°F (7°C) that most refrigerators maintain.

If you have the space to dig a small root cellar, it will be useful for lagering throughout the year as well as for storing not only homebrew but vegetables and preserves. A root cellar can greatly reduce your overall reliance on refrigeration.

PART 2

SUSTAINABLE BREWING in the KITCHEN and GARDEN

5

The HOMEBREWER'S KITCHEN

There are always ingredients left over from a batch of brew. Commercial breweries often have to pay to dispose of this "waste," so many of them have found ways to recycle it instead. As a homebrewer you have many options for repurposing your brewing leftovers. Spent grain, spent hops, and yeast slurry are all organic materials that can find a second life in your kitchen or garden. In addition to composting them, you can use these materials for baking bread, making dog biscuits, and making homemade yeast extract (similar to Marmite). An eco-friendly brewer recognizes the value of these leftovers and will never just throw them in the rubbish can!

Using Leftover Yeast

In most fermentations the volume of yeast increases up to 10 times its starting volume. Every batch of beer leaves a layer of goo on the

bottom of the fermenter, and most homebrewers simply dump this surplus down the drain. This sediment, called *trub* (pronounced "troob"), is composed of dormant or dead yeast cells, bits of proteins from the wort, and tiny bits of hops and grain. The trub, hop bits and all, can be added to compost, where it can help the composting process as well as add nutrients, but the yeast residue itself has great nutritional value. It is especially high in B vitamins, folic acid, and essential amino acids, including lysine and tryptophan.

Commercially, spent brewer's yeast is often made into nutritional flakes or a sandwich spread that is especially popular in the UK, Australia, and New Zealand. It can be made into a nutritional broth that is quite useful as a beef-broth substitute for vegetarians. Spent brewer's yeast is used in commercial animal feed for pigs and cows, and research has indicated that inactivated yeast fed to poultry can add selenium, folic acid, and biotin to the diet, which can increase egg production and fertility.

On the homebrew front, leftover yeast can be used for all these purposes and can even be used to bake bread, though because it usually takes longer to rise, it requires a little more patience. For most of my baking, I prefer to use a bread yeast sourdough starter, which is another way of reusing yeast. But when time permits and I want to branch out with new flavor characteristics, I enjoy making a batch of bread with brewer's yeast instead. Full disclaimer — I have only baked with brewer's yeast a few times, but there are plenty of bakers out there with a lot more experience, including a few microbreweries that use their yeast and spent grain to bake their own house bread.

Brew Tip

THE YEAST LEFT AT THE BOTTOM of the fermenter is very much alive and viable. It can be used to brew another batch of beer, as long as you keep everything it touches clean and sanitary when you transfer it to your next batch of beer. It is beneficial to wash the yeast first. Add a few quarts of boiled, cooled water to the spent yeast, agitate gently, then allow to settle for about 10 minutes. Decant the cloudy liquid into a sterile mason jar for storage — it contains mostly pure yeast still in suspension while the bits of protein, hops, and grain have dropped out. You can repeat this process if desired. Store in the fridge for several weeks.

Bread yeast has evolved over many centuries of bread baking to have strong characteristics favorable to bread baking: rapid activity at warm temperatures plus a resistance to acidic environments and compatibility with lactic acid–producing bacteria. This latter trait is especially important when you consider the health benefits of bread made from dough that has been allowed to ferment and develop over a longer period of time than modern, convenience-driven bread-baking strategies permit. Fermenting flours made of wheat and other grains helps to break down indigestible components,

Feeding Yeast to Animals

Feeding live yeast to animals can cause them gastric distress or other serious stomach problems. When I feed leftover brewing yeast to my chickens, I simply decant the slurry into a brew pot and bring it a boil to deactivate it. After cooling it down, I store the yeast in a mason jar in the refrigerator to add to the girls' daily chicken mash. The same technique can easily be used to feed other livestock.

For feeding yeast to dogs, however, it is critically important to completely remove the hops from the yeast. Use a fine-mesh strainer or hop bag to strain the hops out of the wort, then proceed with the primary fermentation. Rack the beer off the sediment after 3 or 4 days. This gives the hops and specks of grain time to settle to the bottom, but most of the yeast will still be in suspension. This will result in a yeast cake that is clean and almost completely free from hop particles. If feeding to hop-intolerant animals (dogs are the most sensitive, but it is prudent to avoid feeding to other pets and livestock), wash the harvested yeast to flush out remaining hop oils. See Making Yeast Broth and Yeast Extract, page 118, for more detailed instructions.

As when introducing any new food to your animal's diet, it is best to start with a small amount and observe the animal for 24 hours before feeding again. If there is no adverse reaction, you can increase the amount slightly at the next feeding, observe again, and repeat until you have reached a feeding level you and your animal are comfortable with.

notably phytic acids, the consumption of which in large amounts has been linked to digestive problems.

Incidentally, the large-scale manufacture of dehydrated baker's yeast does result in some environmental pollution and carries its own carbon footprint, so baking the occasional loaf of bread with your surplus brewer's yeast is an excellent way to have a positive impact on your personal ecosystem!

HARVESTING SPENT YEAST

Yeast slurry destined for the compost bin requires no prep — just rinse out the fermenter and dump the slurry. If you want to harvest yeast to use as a broth, for animal feed, or to make your own yeast extract, a few extra steps are required to ensure the results will be safe for consumption and will taste good. When harvesting yeast to use as a nutritional supplement for humans or animals, the most important thing is to remove all hop particles from the yeast slurry. The only practical way to do this is to siphon the beer into a secondary fermenter while primary fermentation is still under way and most of the yeast is still active and in suspension.

After 2 or 3 days in the primary fermenter, the proteins, bits of hops, and grain particles will settle to the bottom, while most of the yeast starts to settle after the fermentation slows down, usually after 5 to 7 days. Thus, the best time to rack the beer to a secondary fermenter is after 3 days of fermentation. Siphoning the beer off this undesirable trub while the yeast is still in suspension allows the yeast to form a clean layer of sediment that will be easy to harvest without any specialized equipment.

I have found that siphoning off at this point has the added benefit of improving the final brew. The trub can add slight off-flavors and prevent the yeast from settling in a clean, compact layer at the bottom of the fermenter. When racking early for the purpose of harvesting the yeast, I rarely find it necessary to transfer the beer again. Another advantage is that the beer is still so active that the large amounts of carbon dioxide being produced by the yeast scrub out any remaining oxygen in the fermenter, and any oxygen that is mixed into the beer at this stage can actually reinvigorate the yeast, resulting in a faster fermentation.

MAKING YEAST BROTH AND YEAST EXTRACT

Yeast has a unique savory flavor that can be described as meaty. This flavor, called "umami," comes from the naturally occurring glutamic acids. Although to some the idea of eating yeast just sounds gross, for many vegetarians around the world yeast is a very important source of vitamins not normally found in vegetable products, and the flavor can be downright addictive to some folks. Just ask any lover of Marmite!

During a 12-year stint as a vegetarian, I used both dried nutritional yeast and yeast extract in my cooking to add a savory flavor to such dishes as nut loaf, hearty soup, and gravy. Making a good-tasting, smooth-textured extract similar to Marmite or Vegemite or creating a clear, appetizing broth from yeast can take up to 5 days. There are several stages to the process:

1. Wash the yeast to remove beer flavors and bitterness from hops.
2. Add salt to cause yeast autolysis (cells die and rupture, releasing flavors into solution).
3. Heat slowly to further break down the yeast hulls.
4. Filter out the yeast hulls for a smooth texture.
5. Add vegetables to increase flavor, if desired. Cook into the broth and strain.
6. Use for soup stock or broth, or cook down to desired concentration.

SUPPLIES NEEDED

- 1 pint or more of fresh yeast slurry
- Filtered or distilled water, at least 2 quarts, for washing yeast
- Sea salt (4 teaspoons per cup of washed yeast)
- Enough 1-quart or ½-gallon mason jars to hold the volume of yeast being processed
- Slow cooker with warm setting, oven with pilot light or light that will maintain 100 to 125°F (38–52°C), or a small- to medium-size insulated cooler

- Fine-mesh straining bag or a large piece of fine cheesecloth (real cheese-making cloth, not the kind you buy in the grocery store, and preferably made of organic fibers)
- Large pot
- Colander that fits inside the pot
- Small, round, heavy object, such as a clean, flat stone or small jar full of water, to weigh down the straining bag

Step 1. Wash the Yeast

This process can take a few days, as the yeast must settle after each addition of water is made. A clear mason jar or Erlenmeyer flask doesn't take up too much room in the refrigerator and allows you to see the yeast layer more easily. If you have several batches of beer brewing within a week or so of each other, you can process more extract all at once. Once the yeast has been washed it will stay fresh for up to 2 weeks stored in the refrigerator with enough clean water to cover the yeast layer by at least an inch.

After removing the yeast layer from the fermenter, transfer the slurry to a clean jar. Rinse the fermenter with filtered water and pour that into the jar, too. Place the jar in a refrigerator or a cool place (40 to 55°F [4–13°C]) and allow to settle. It can take 2 to 8 hours for each rinse to fully settle, and the cool temperature slows the process of the yeast breaking down.

When the liquid at the top is clear, decant it off, leaving the yeast solids in the jar. Add enough fresh water to double the total volume, swirl the contents to mix well, and allow to settle. In commercial operations a centrifuge is typically employed to speed up this process.

Each rinse leaves a progressively cleaner yeast flavor as the beer residues are washed away. Three or four rinses are usually sufficient. Smell the yeast after each wash or taste a small dab, and let your own senses guide you. It should smell and taste yeasty, not like beer or hops. Even a slight hop bitterness can seriously detract from the flavor of the finished product, as it will be highly concentrated.

Washing the yeast

Once you have rinsed the yeast to your satisfaction, take note of the final volume of yeast. This is another good reason to use a mason jar or Erlenmeyer flask — with volume markings on the glass, you will not need to pour it into a measuring cup.

Step 2. Salt the Yeast

The amount of salt needed depends on the volume of yeast remaining after the washing stage. I prefer a quality iodine-free sea salt. Use 5 teaspoons of salt per cup of washed yeast. After measuring the yeast add enough water to double the liquid volume. For one cup of yeast, use one cup of water and so forth. Then add the salt and stir thoroughly to dissolve the salt completely.

Step 3. Heat the Yeast

After the salt is dissolved, the next step is to heat the mixture slowly, then maintain it at this temperature for 12 hours. To keep the yeast warm in an oven, gently heat the jar in a pan of water on the stove. When it reaches 100°F (38°C), place the jar in the oven with a pilot light or the oven light left on if that will maintain a temperature of 100 to 125°F (38–52°C). You can also use an insulated cooler large enough to hold the jar of yeast plus at least 2 quarts of water.

While heating the jar to 100°F on the stove, fill the cooler with hot water to warm the interior. Dump the water out, place the jar in the cooler, and fill the cooler to the liquid line of the jar with 130 to 140°F (54–60°C) water. Most tap water is hot enough for this purpose. Seal the cooler, and it will stay warm for hours, though it is a good idea to check it every 3 or 4 hours and refresh the hot water as needed.

If using a slow cooker, pour the salted yeast mixture into the pot, and turn the pot on low until the temperature reaches 100°F (38°C), then switch it to warm. Monitor the temperatures carefully, as some cookers become too hot even on the warm setting. I heat the salted yeast to 125°F (52°C), then unplug the cooker and wrap a towel around the whole thing, which keeps it warm for many hours. If the yeast cools below 100°F, heat it back up to 125°F again. It needs to be maintained at the 100 to 125°F temperature range for a full 12 hours.

Basically any method that will maintain a temperature between 100 and 125°F (38 and 52°C) for 12 hours will do the trick. Although the yeast dies pretty quickly when this much salt is added, the long temperature hold definitely increases the yield. In some of my trials, I shortened the time to 8 hours, and the yield was much lower. It is also important to keep the temperature below 125°F. Higher temperatures will cook the yeast and make it more difficult to filter out the hulls, which also lowers the yield.

Step 4. Filter the Yeast Extract

Yeast hulls have an unpleasant flavor and add a grainy texture that detracts from the final product. Filtering them out is a bit tedious, but it produces a higher-quality result. I find filtering to be absolutely necessary for making a condensed extract or a clear broth. Because the yeast slurry quickly becomes a paste that takes forever to filter by gravity alone, gentle pressure is needed to effectively separate the liquid from the yeast hulls.

I have found the following method to be the most effective. It takes at least 8 hours for the liquid to press out, and the yeast will spoil quickly if kept at room temperature for too long. Holding it under 55°F (13°C) is important; it's best to refrigerate the whole setup.

Line a colander with 2 or 3 layers of tightly woven cheesecloth. The cloth must be large enough to contain all the slurry and be tied into a bundle at the top. Put the colander in a large pot.

Pour the yeast slurry into the bag or cheesecloth, and tie it up tightly in a bundle. Leave the bag in the colander, and place a small, heavy object on it. Put the lid on the pot. If the lid doesn't fit, you can cover the whole setup with a large, clean plastic or paper bag. The objective is to collect all the liquid that is pressed out of the bag; this is your yeast extract.

Refrigerate the slurry. If there is no room in your refrigerator, set up the colander in a cooler with some ice packs. It is a good idea to check every few hours to adjust the position of the weight or to pour off excess liquid in the collection vessel. Store any excess liquid in a clean jar in the refrigerator until the extraction is complete.

This whole process can be done in minutes if you have a decent wine press available. You still need the fine filtration offered by the cheesecloth

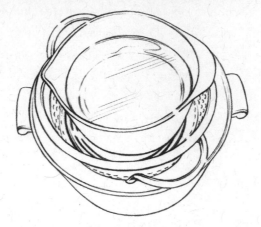

Filtering the yeast

or straining bags, but you can place these in the press, then press out the liquid following the normal procedure for your wine press. The mixture will be boiled after this step, so it is not necessary to sanitize anything, but do try to keep it clean!

Step 5. Prepare Broth or Spread

The exact ingredients for making Marmite and Vegemite are trade secrets, but I've developed the following recipe as a pretty close substitute. The first step is making broth, which you can use in all your regular recipes (and of course, if you are only making broth, not a concentrate, you can use whatever vegetables you like for flavoring).

To make broth, use the following vegetables for every 2 cups (500 ml) of filtered yeast extract.

- 1 small onion
- 1 carrot
- 1 stick celery
- 1 turnip

Chop the vegetables finely or process them in a food processor so they are finely diced but not puréed. Put them in a large saucepan or stockpot with the yeast extract and 1 cup of water for every 2 cups of yeast extract.

Bring to a boil, and simmer gently for 1 hour partially uncovered. Strain the vegetables out with a fine sieve or cheesecloth, pressing gently to extract all the liquid. Rinse with some fresh water to extract more flavor if you wish.

Note: If you prefer to make broth without vegetables, simply pour the filtered yeast extract in a saucepan or stockpot, bring to a boil, and boil for 15 minutes to sterilize. Add water to adjust the flavor to your liking (or you can add water when you cook with it), and pour into clean containers.

The broth will keep in the refrigerator for up to 2 weeks or in the freezer for up to 6 months. I use cup- and pint-size dairy containers for this purpose, so I have convenient recipe-ready amounts on hand. Either way, the broth is great for making Easy Vegetarian Gravy (page 124).

To make a flavored yeast spread, simply cook the broth down to spreading consistency over a long, slow boil. A wide pan will maximize the evaporation area. A heavy-bottom stainless steel pan is most effective. Depending on the volume of extract, it will take 1 to 4 hours to reduce to a thick consistency. Closely monitor the boil at the beginning, when it is prone to boiling over, and toward the end, when there is a danger of scorching. Reduce the heat toward the end so the mixture does not caramelize too much, and stir often, scraping the bottom of the pan to prevent it from sticking.

When it has reached the consistency of thick syrup, much like liquid malt extract, it is done. It will thicken further as it cools, so don't go too far and or it will become too thick to spread on buttered toast, which is the whole point! You can remove a small sample and cool it down to check the consistency.

Easy Vegetarian Gravy

If mashed potatoes and gravy are a favorite but vegetable broth does not quite give you the flavor you crave, this gravy may just be the thing. Based on a Marmite gravy recipe I learned from an English friend, this gravy is easy to make and usually gets rave reviews. Even the occasional scoffing from meat-loving, veggie-intolerant people usually turns to grudging praise after a taste.

2 cups gravy

4	tablespoons flour (may substitute gluten-free flour)
¼	cup water
2	tablespoons butter (may substitute margarine, palm shortening, or vegetable oil)
1	large onion, thinly sliced (optional)
½	cup sliced mushrooms (optional)
	Fresh or dried herbs to taste: savory, thyme, and sage work especially well (optional)
2	cups yeast broth or 2 tablespoons yeast extract plus 2 cups water
	Fresh-ground black pepper

1. Mix the flour with water in a small saucepan to make a roux (a runny paste). Add additional water if needed to give it a pourable consistency. Stir until lumps are dissolved, and set aside.

2. Heat the butter in a saucepan until melted. If adding onions or mushrooms, sauté them in the butter until softened and nicely browned. Toss in the herbs and stir.

3. Add the broth, and bring to a boil.

4. Pour the roux into the boiling broth in a steady stream, whisking constantly. Stir until the mixture thickens and lumps disappear.

5. Turn the heat to low, and simmer slowly for 5 to 10 minutes. Add freshly ground pepper to taste just before serving for the most pungent flavor. Serve piping hot over mashed potatoes, vegetarian meatloaf, your favorite veggies, or anything else you love gravy on.

Cooling Beer

This is an area where convenience may come at the cost of energy consumption. I consider refrigeration to fall under the homebrewing budget only if your brewing needs can't be met by your existing household refrigerator and you need a separate fridge for your homebrew. It is easy to make room in your existing fridge for a six-pack or two of the latest homebrew. If you have a cellar, the remaining bottles can stay cool there (they can be stored at room temperature, too; they just won't age quite as well). However, if you are thinking about upgrading to a more energy-efficient refrigerator, you might consider your homebrew requirements when choosing a replacement.

If you can get by with one refrigerator for all your homebrew needs plus your household food-storage needs, you will save a considerable amount of energy in the long haul, because one refrigeration unit is almost always better than two. If you must have a separate homebrew refrigerator dedicated to dispensing homebrew from kegs, be aware that it will have a negative impact on your personal ecosystem. Evaluate your needs carefully; you might be able to purchase a smaller model.

Using Spent Grain

Spent grain is one of the most valuable brewing by-products because it still has nutritional value suitable for both human and animal consumption, it is produced in large quantities by most brewers, and it can be used in many ways. Spent grain is a versatile cooking ingredient for breads and other baked goods. It is an excellent feed adjunct for livestock and can be used in ratios of up to 40 percent of an animal's diet.

Spent grain can also be used to make a growing medium for cultivating mushrooms, and it is an excellent green compost material that breaks down quickly and adds lots of organic matter to the soil (see chapter 6 for ways to use spent grain in your garden).

The Nutritional Content of Spent Grain

Spent grain, often called brewer's grain in the brewing, animal feed, and food industries, is an excellent source of grain-based nutrition. It has a higher protein and dietary fiber content than regular baking flour but contains about half the calories of most flours or whole grains. It is a good source of the minerals calcium, copper, iron, magnesium, selenium, and zinc. The starch and sugar content are relatively low because these elements are flushed out of the grains in the mashing process.

The malting process helps break down some of the more indigestible components in the grain and converts nutrients to a form more easily absorbed by the body. Some studies indicate that the gluten content is also dramatically lowered during malting, making the bread made from malt flour (often called sprouted grain flour) a healthier choice for gluten-intolerant folks.

Brewer's grain is an excellent source of dietary fiber of a type that is highly digestible, including the heart-healthy, soluble beta-glucan fiber. Spent grain is an excellent source of high-quality proteins and it contains many essential amino acids, including arginine, glycine, isoleucine, leucine, lysine, phenylalanine, proline, serine, tryptophan, tyrosine, and valine.

Here is a summary of the research I was able to gather, mostly from studies done for the animal feed industry, on the nutritional value of spent grain, with average ranges. It can serve as a guideline, whether you are feeding livestock or cooking for a family.

Calories: 200–240 per cup dry grains
Crude protein: 25–30%
Crude fiber: 12–19%
Dietary fiber: 50–60%
Nitrogen-free extract (sugars and carbohydrates): 40–50%

A COUPLE OF CAUTIONS

Wet grain can cause serious digestive problems if it goes sour, if it has not been mashed, or if you feed animals too much. Only feed animals fresh grain that has not gone moldy or fermented.

Also, hops are very toxic to dogs and some other animals, so never feed grains that have been steeped with hops to any animal without checking with your veterinarian.

IT MAKES GOOD ANIMAL FEED

The use of brewing grains to feed livestock is widespread, and the nutritional value for various livestock has been studied extensively. Of particular interest to eco-minded homebrewers who also have a small homestead are the nutritional benefits of feeding brewing grains to poultry, cattle, goats, sheep, and pigs. For poultry, spent grain provides selenium, which is important to breeding and egg laying, and feeding brewing grains has been shown to improve the quality of the egg yolk. Most sources advise keeping the total dietary proportion of spent grain to under 20 percent.

I regularly feed surplus spent grain to my chickens and geese. They love it more than just about anything else, especially the geese. There is nothing quite like a gaggle of hungry, excited geese bobbing their heads, flapping their wings, and honking when the fresh grain mash comes out!

Brewing grain is also widely used as a feed source for cattle. Combined with inexpensive nitrogen sources (like grass) and proper mineral supplements, it can make up 25 percent or more of a ruminant diet. Many farmers mix it 50/50 with dry grain and continue the normal amounts of fresh fodder and silage. It contains high-quality protein, and feeding fresh, wet brewing grain has been shown to increase milk production.

For pigs the grains primarily provide an added lean energy source and a good source of fiber, but the proteins and amino acid profiles are not ideally suited to their metabolism. For this reason it is advisable to keep the total feed proportion to under 20 percent for pigs. For horses, brewing grains are comparable to oats and soybean meal and can be fed in amounts up to 40 percent. Spent grain can also be a tasty treat and a source of protein for dogs and pet birds.

Storing Spent Grain

Grains go sour very quickly after brewing (in as little as 24 hours), so I pack them immediately in food-grade plastic tubs in meal-size portions and refrigerate or freeze them. Empty 1-quart yogurt containers are perfect. Grains will stay fresh for about a week in the refrigerator. Frozen, they will keep for up to 6 months. Or you can dry them thoroughly and store them in sealed containers, in which case they'll keep up to 3 months stored below 65°F (18°C).

Spent-Grain Poultry Feed Mixture

When feeding chickens spent grain, it is most economical to feed them wet grains unless you happen to have a solar dryer. If you do, by all means dry out the grains so they last longer. I feed my chickens a wet mash once a day to add additional nutrition to their diets. They love the mash so much they actually beg for it! When feeding a wet mash, it is best to mix just what they can eat in one feeding, as it will quickly grow rancid if left in the feeder for more than 12 hours.

Enough for about 12 adult hens

2 cups organic poultry feed (whatever you normally feed them)
1 cup spent brewing grains, drained
2 tablespoons flaxseed
2 tablespoons sunflower or sesame seeds (optional, but they love them!)
2 tablespoons plain yogurt (to provide probiotics)*
½ cup deactivated yeast slurry (optional)

*Milk itself is not very good for chickens, but live cultured yogurt is an excellent source of healthy intestinal bacteria and is rich in the calcium that laying hens need in large amounts.

Mix poultry feed, spent grain, flaxseed, sunflower seeds (if using), yogurt, and yeast slurry, if desired, and add water until mixture is the consistency of very thick oatmeal.

Spent-Grain Dog Biscuits

Spent grain can be fed to dogs in reasonably small amounts, but be aware that hops are toxic to dogs, so for these treats use only grains that have never been in contact with hops. I have tried dozens of online recipes for spent grain biscuits, but most recipes are not made to the nutrition standards I like to follow for our dog, Barley. I try not to feed wheat or soy products to my pets because most pet nutrition sources I trust advise a diet of meat and vegetables. If filler grains are used, then barley, oats, and rice are more digestible to most dogs than wheat, corn, or soy.

So after more than a bit of tinkering in the kitchen, I have settled on this recipe. Barley loves them, and they are quite easy to make!

About 2 dozen small biscuits

2	cups spent grain, pressed dry
½	cup instant potato flakes or 1 large potato, finely grated
½	cup quick-cooking oats
½	cup rice flour (more if needed to make a workable dough)
½	cup peanut butter
1	large egg

1. Preheat oven to 250°F (121°C).

2. Remove excess water from the grains by placing in a colander or grain bag and pressing or squeezing until liquid no longer comes out. Get them as dry as you can, as this will reduce the baking time considerably.

3. Mix spent grain, potato, oats, rice flour, peanut butter, and egg well to form a soft dough. If dough is too sticky, add as much rice flour and/or oats as needed to make the dough workable.

4. Roll the dough out about ½ inch thick, and cut into shapes with a cookie cutter. Or roll the dough into a 2-inch-diameter log and slice into ½-inch-thick disks.

5. Place on a lightly oiled cookie sheet at least ½ inch apart, and put in the oven for 1 to 2 hours, until completely dehydrated. If you have a moisture meter, the disks should be dried down to 5 to 10 percent moisture (the same as dry dog food). They should be completely dry to the touch and dry inside. These biscuits cook very well in the low heat of a solar oven, though it may take a few extra hours to dry them out.

6. Store in an airtight container for up to 2 weeks at room temperature or freeze for longer storage. When thawing, it is a good idea to toast them in the oven for about 10 minutes to dry off the residual dampness. For a softer, moister treat, store the biscuits in an airtight container in the refrigerator.

Cooking with Spent Grain

From an ecological perspective, the highest possible value from spent grain is obtained by using it for food. The recipes presented here have been gleaned from multiple sources and were developed over many years in my kitchen. These recipes all call for one of the following forms of spent grain.

Wet spent grain. Drain off excess liquid, and use grain as is. Some recipes call for pressing or squeezing the grain until no more liquid runs out.

Dried spent grain. Spread out to dry on cookie sheets in the oven, in a food dehydrator, or in a solar dryer until completely dry. The moisture level must be below 10 percent for the grain to be shelf stable. Before drying press out as much liquid as possible to lower drying time and reduce energy costs. If you have a small wine press, it may be worth the effort to use it to press out the excess liquid, especially if you are drying over 10 pounds of grain.

Spent grain flour. Grind dried grain into a fine flour with a food processor, blender, or flour mill.

The first thing you need to know is that spent grain is highly perishable! It smells tasty when freshly removed from the mash, but in just a few hours it will start to decompose, and within 24 hours it usually smells completely horrible. Refrigerate or freeze batches of spent grain as soon as they cool to room temperature. Most spent grain will remain fresh under refrigeration for about a week. Store in the freezer if you don't plan to use it within a week.

If you plan to make spent grain flour, dehydrate the grain soon after brewing. Once dried, store in airtight containers. The flour will keep at room temperature for several weeks or in the refrigerator for several months.

A second factor to take into account is that spent grain contains a large amount of husk material and is therefore very fibrous. Certain foods, such as a rustic bread or crunchy granola bars, are deeply satisfying with that extra crunch and chewiness. For other recipes the coarse grainy structure of the spent grain detracts from the expected result. When working with yeast or sourdough bread, for example, the sharp edges of the husks can prevent the bread from rising properly, as the bubbles that trap gas and give bread its loft are broken, creating a bread that is dense and chewy.

Third, spent grain adds the flavor of malt and the specialty grains from the brew to your recipe. Sometimes the type of beer lends itself to a certain recipe, but in other cases a batch of spent grain will be completely wrong. For example, a dark mash with a lot of caramel and chocolate malt probably won't work in a light sourdough recipe, but is absolutely delicious when used to make brownies. A wheat beer mash has a very different flavor that is great for breads but not quite so perfect for cookies, because it is just not as malty and sweet as a pale ale mash.

Double Chocolate Spent-Grain Brownies

These dense, rich brownies have multiple levels of chocolate flavor that add up to delicious decadence. One of my favorite recipes, it involves less guilt and more pleasure for knowing all the ingredients are high quality and fresh, and the grains add nutrition and fiber.

Approximately 12 large brownies

1	cup spent grain, measured after squeezing out as much liquid as possible*
2	large eggs
8	ounces butter or ½ cup coconut oil
2	ounces semisweet dark chocolate
1½	cups organic raw sugar
1	cup organic unbleached white flour
¾	cup unsweetened cocoa powder
½	teaspoon baking soda
½	teaspoon sea salt

Optional: 1 cup chocolate chips and/or ½ cup chopped nuts

*Use grains from a dark beer such as an oatmeal stout or Irish stout. The richly sweet chocolate and caramel malts make this brownie recipe so outstanding that everyone will beg you for more! It is worth the extra effort to steep the chocolate and caramel malts separately from other grains, and use only those, so that the caramel and chocolate flavors are more pronounced.

1. Preheat oven to 325°F (163°C).

2. Blend the spent grain with the eggs using a hand blender or food processor. Purée until smooth. The mixture should show specks and maintain a slight grainy texture.

3. Gently heat the butter and chocolate until just melted. Add to the egg and grain mixture, and mix well.

4. In a separate bowl combine the sugar, flour, cocoa powder, baking soda, and salt until mixed well.

5. Mix the liquid and dry ingredients together until all the dry ingredients are moistened. Try not to overmix, as this can make the brownies tough.

6. If adding chocolate chips, nuts, or other additional solid ingredients, do so now, and mix in gently.

7. Spread batter in a buttered 10-inch square or 7- by 11-inch pan.

8. Bake for 45 minutes to 1 hour. Brownies are done when they have risen fully and a knife or toothpick when inserted comes out clean.

Spent-Grain Chocolate Chip Cookies

What could be better than a rich, chewy chocolate chip cookie? A cookie made with spent grain, of course! These never last long. The barley malt sugar gives them a bit of a crunch on the outside, and they are moist and extra chewy on the inside. They contain less cane sugar than most standard cookies, making them a wee bit better for you.

About twenty 3-inch cookies

¼	pound butter (one stick) or ¼ cup coconut oil, softened
1	cup organic raw sugar
1	teaspoon vanilla extract
1½	cups spent grain, measured after squeezing out as much liquid as possible
1	egg
¾	cup organic unbleached white flour
½	cup spent grain flour
½	teaspoon baking soda
½	teaspoon sea salt
2	cups chocolate chips

Optional: 1 cup chopped nuts and/or dried fruit

1. Preheat oven to 350°F (177°C).

2. Mix the butter, sugar, and vanilla until creamy. Add the spent grain and egg, and mix well.

3. Mix the flours, baking soda, and salt in a separate bowl.

4. Add the creamed mixture to the dry ingredients, stirring until the dry ingredients are just moistened. Overmixing can lead to toughness.

5. Fold in the chocolate chips and any other additional solid ingredients.

6. Drop by spoonfuls onto an oiled or parchment-lined cookie sheet. Bake for 10 to 15 minutes, or until the centers are cooked through. Baking time will vary depending on the size of the cookie. Cool slightly before removing from sheet. These are a little stickier than most chocolate chip cookies.

Spent-Grain Oatmeal Raisin Cookies

I love making these with the grain left over from a batch of Belgian Wit. The flaked oats and wheat flakes add a touch more chewiness to this richly textured cookie. Most spent grains do well in this recipe, although for this particular cookie I personally shy away from the grains left from a dark beer.

About twenty 3-inch cookies

8	ounces butter or ½ cup coconut oil, softened
1¼	cups organic raw sugar
1	teaspoon vanilla extract
1½	cups spent grain, measured after squeezing out as much liquid as possible
2	eggs
¾	cup organic unbleached white flour
¾	cup spent grain flour
½	teaspoon ground cinnamon
½	teaspoon baking soda
½	teaspoon sea salt
1½	cups rolled oats
1	cup raisins

Optional: 1 cup chopped nuts (I like walnuts best)

1. Mix the butter with the sugar and vanilla until creamy. Add the spent grain and eggs, and mix well.

2. In a separate bowl combine the flours, cinnamon, baking soda, and salt until mixed well.

3. Mix the creamed and dry ingredients until the dry ingredients are moistened. Try not to overmix, as this can toughen the dough.

4. Add the oats, raisins, and nuts, if using. Mix gently until just combined.

5. The trick to producing thick and chewy cookies is to chill the dough before baking. You can either chill the dough for 30 minutes before baking or scoop the cookies onto the baking sheet and chill the whole sheet. Or shape the dough into a log, wrap in wax paper, store it in the refrigerator, and bake the cookies on demand. That way you can have fresh, warm-from-the-oven cookies whenever you want (need) them!

6. Drop by spoonfuls onto an oiled or parchment-lined cookie sheet. Bake for 8 to 12 minutes at 350°F (177°C) until the sides are slightly browned and the centers puff up but look slightly undercooked. Cool slightly, and remove from sheet after 10 minutes so they don't stick to the pan.

No-Bake Peanut-Honey Energy Bars

These grab-and-go treats are a tasty energy boost with all-natural ingredients. The bars hold together very well but are not overly sticky, and have a soft, chewy texture instead of being dry and crunchy. Even better, they are easy to make! The spent grain adds some crunch, a malty sweet flavor, and extra fiber. The basic recipe can be varied by adding fruits and nuts, chocolate chips, bits of candy, or puffed cereal. As long as you stick to the given proportion of grain, sweeteners, and oil or butter, the possibilities are almost endless.

1 dozen 6 × 3 inch bars

---

2 cups rolled oats (quick cooking or old-fashioned)
½–1 cup chopped nuts (optional)
2 cups dried spent grain
½–1 cup chopped dried fruit (optional)

½ cup honey

½ cup peanut butter*

¼ cup barley malt syrup

¼ cup butter

½ teaspoon salt

*If you wish to leave out the peanut butter, increase the butter by 2 tablespoons and the barley malt syrup by 1 tablespoon.

1. Toasting the oats (and nuts) brings out their flavor. If you are drying the grains right before using them, you can add the oats (and nuts) during the last 20 minutes of the drying process, increasing the heat to 325°F (163°C). The oats (and nuts) can also be lightly roasted to your preferred level of roast separately from the grains.

2. Combine the spent grain and oats, as well as the nuts and fruit, if using, in a mixing bowl, and set aside.

3. In a small saucepan slowly heat the honey, peanut butter, malt syrup, butter, and salt. Bring to a boil and simmer for 5 minutes. Pour this mixture over the dry ingredients while still hot. For best results add one-third of the hot syrup at a time, mixing well after each addition.

4. Line a large steep-sided pan or pans with wax paper. Spoon in the mixture, and press it firmly into the pan. Allow to cool for several hours at room temperature. Do not refrigerate.

5. When cool cut into bars. Individually wrap each bar in wax paper for portability, or keep in an airtight container. The bars will keep at room temperature for up to a week. They can be refrigerated or frozen for longer-term storage, but they are at their best eaten fresh!

Oatmeal-Stout Chocolate Cherry Pecan Bars

Another favorite around here. The process is similar to that for the Peanut-Honey Energy Bars, but the ingredients are quite different. To get the best flavor, use the grains from a batch of Oatmeal Stout (page 258) or another dark beer recipe that has a high concentration of chocolate and caramel malts.

About a dozen 6 × 3 inch bars

2 cups dried spent dark grain

2 cups rolled oats (quick cooking or old-fashioned), toasted

1 cup barley flakes, toasted

1 cup chopped pecans, toasted

1 cup dried cherries

½ cup dark chocolate chips (about 8 ounces of chocolate)

½ cup honey

¼ cup barley malt extract

¼ cup butter

½ teaspoon salt

1. Combine spent grain, oats, barley flakes, pecans, and cherries in a mixing bowl, and set aside.

2. Melt the chocolate chips, honey, barley malt extract, butter, and salt in a saucepan, and bring to a gentle boil. Allow to cool slightly, and mix thoroughly into the dry ingredients.

3. Press firmly into a wax paper–lined pan, and allow to cool for several hours before cutting into bars.

Spent-Grain Cranberry Date Pecan Muffins

This easy recipe can be quickly adapted to whatever grains and fresh fruit or vegetables you have on hand. A favorite on-the-go breakfast treat around our place, it only takes a few minutes to throw together. The grains provide interesting texture and flavor, not to mention the health benefits of the added protein and fiber!

You can also bake this in a loaf pan as a quick bread and slice it thick.

12 muffins or 1 large loaf

1½ cups wet spent grain

⅓ cup melted butter or vegetable oil

⅓ cup milk

1 large egg, beaten

2 tablespoons yogurt

1½ cups organic whole-wheat flour

⅓ cup chopped dried cranberries

⅓ cup chopped dried dates

⅓ cup chopped pecans

1 teaspoon baking powder

½ teaspoon baking soda

½ teaspoon sea salt

1. Preheat oven to 375°F (191°C).

2. Grease a 12-cup muffin tin or line with paper cups.

3. Mix the spent grain, butter, milk, egg, and yogurt in a small bowl, and set aside.

4. Combine flour, cranberries, dates, pecans, baking powder, baking soda, and salt in a large mixing bowl.

5. Gently stir the wet ingredients into the dry ingredients, using a rubber spatula to scrape the mixture up from the bottom and lightly combine.

6. Pour into the muffin pan, dividing evenly between the cups.

7. Bake for 20 to 25 minutes. If baking a loaf, bake for 40 to 45 minutes. Muffins (and loaf) are done when a knife or a toothpick inserted into the center comes out clean.

For variety try adding different combinations of dried fruit, nuts, or seeds, fresh chopped fruit or berries, or grated carrot, apple, or zucchini. Since these are a breakfast that fits in your fist, why not add things to give you a nutritional boost — to make a great start to your day — such as flaxseed or bran, or replace some of the milk or oil with mashed banana, applesauce, or mashed sweet potato.

Spent-Grain Granola

Once you start all-grain brewing you will be up to your ears in grains before you know it. If you are in the habit of splashing out five dollars or more per box of your favorite healthy breakfast cereal, you can cut that expense right in half by making your own granola! This easy recipe can be tweaked to incorporate your favorite ingredients. The grains are naturally sweet, but you can sneak in a little extra sweetening if your family won't eat it otherwise.

The grains really stick to the pan unless you oil it heavily or use parchment paper. Since I prefer my granola dry rather than oily, I use parchment paper, but either method will do.

Makes 12 cups (about 4 pounds)

¾–1¼ cups honey, maple syrup, or other liquid sweetener
¼ cup coconut oil, butter, or vegetable oil
1 teaspoon salt
8 cups wet spent grain
4 cups rolled oats or other flaked grain
1–2 cups raw sunflower seeds, poppy seeds, hulled pumpkin seeds, chia seeds, sesame seeds, flaxseed, or any combination
1 cup shredded coconut (optional)
1–2 cups chopped raw nuts (optional)
1–2 cups dried fruit (optional)

1. In a small saucepan heat the honey, coconut oil, and salt until hot but not bubbling (about 180°F [82°C]).

2. Combine spent grain, oats, sunflower seeds, and coconut and raw nuts, if using, in a large mixing bowl. (If you prefer to keep the seeds, nuts, and coconut raw, you can reserve them and add them after the baking stage.) Add the hot liquid mixture a little at a time, and stir well after each addition so the wet grains moisten the other ingredients. Set the mixing bowl aside. You will need it if adding dried fruit at the end.

3. Spread the mixture evenly over two large, well-oiled or parchment-lined cookie or baking sheets. Bake at 350°F (177°C) for 20 to 30 minutes. Stir every 10 minutes. The granola is done when it is fully dried and lightly browned. Make sure it has completely dried out — if the moisture content is too high, the granola will spoil quickly.

4. Add the dried fruit while the granola is still piping hot by tossing it all back in the large mixing bowl and stirring so the fruit softens and clumps up with the granola. To speed cooling, pour back onto the cookie sheets after mixing.

5. Store in an airtight container. It will keep for up to 4 weeks in airtight storage — if it lasts that long!

Spent-Grain Falafel

In the many years I spent eating a strictly vegetarian diet, I often made falafel. I enjoyed it prepared in the traditional manner: small patties stuffed into a pita pocket with lettuce and cucumber and drizzled with tahini-garlic or yogurt-cucumber sauce. I also enjoyed shaping the falafel into patties and serving it as veggie burgers with all the fixings.

The key to good falafel is a crispy crust and a moist, savory interior. This can be achieved by frying and by adding ingredients such as freshly grated carrots and chopped onions and parsley. Spent grain also works surprisingly well to add texture and to help keep the inside moist and the outside crunchy.

About 25 falafels or 6 good-size patties

1	cup dried whole chickpeas (or two 14-ounce cans, drained)
1½	cups wet spent grain
	Small bunch parsley, chopped (about ¼ cup)
2–4	cloves garlic
2	tablespoons chopped fresh mint
1	teaspoon ground coriander
1	teaspoon ground cumin
¼	cup chickpea flour
1	teaspoon baking soda
	Salt
	Cayenne pepper
1	small carrot, grated fine (about ½ cup)
1	small onion, finely chopped (about ½ cup)
	Juice from 1 small lemon
	Oil for frying: peanut or grapeseed works best

1. Rinse the dried chickpeas, place in a bowl, and add water to cover by about 3 inches. Soak overnight, or at least 12 hours. Drain, then rinse the chickpeas, and drain again. If using canned chickpeas, rinse and drain.

2. Coarsely chop the chickpeas, spent grain, parsley, garlic, mint, coriander, and cumin in a food processor until the texture resembles wet cornmeal. Add the chickpea flour, baking soda, salt, and cayenne pepper to taste, carrot, onion, and lemon juice, and pulse until just mixed.

3. Shape the mixture into balls for deep-frying or small patties for pan-frying. A melon baller or ice cream scoop can help to shape the balls.

4. Deep-fry in oil at 350°F (177°C) for about 5 minutes. Drain on paper towels or brown craft paper bags (the oil-soaked bags make great fire starters afterward).

5. Traditionally, falafel is deep-fried, but you can reduce the oil and panfry 2-inch-wide patties that are about ¾ inch thick. For burgers, shape into 5-inch patties about 1 inch thick and fry for about 10 minutes per side, or until fully cooked through and nicely browned.

Tahini Sauce

About 1 cup

1	teaspoon cayenne pepper
½	teaspoon ground coriander
½	teaspoon salt (use less if the tahini used has added salt)
½	cup tahini (sesame paste)
¼	cup water
2	cloves garlic
2	tablespoons lemon juice
2	tablespoons olive oil
2	teaspoons chopped fresh parsley (optional)

Blend cayenne pepper, coriander, salt (if using), tahini, water, garlic, lemon juice (more to taste if desired), and olive oil in a blender or with a hand mixer until smooth. If needed, add more water, a tablespoon at a time, until the sauce is thick but pourable. For the most appetizing appearance, add the parsley, if using, at the very end and pulse so there are flecks of parsley, instead of grinding it so fine that the sauce is uniformly green.

Quick Spent-Grain Veggie Burgers

In the summertime when friends come over to brew and the weather is fine, the urge to fire up the barbecue is overwhelming once the brewing is done and every-one has worked up a good appetite. This is a great recipe to whip up for the veg-etarians in the group, using a cup of the grain from that freshly brewed batch. The whole recipe mixes up in your food processor in minutes! If there is too much to eat that day, just shape the extra into patties and freeze. They can go right from the freezer to your grill or a frying pan.

About six 6-ounce burgers

1   small carrot
1   cup spent grain, measured after squeezing out as much liquid as possible
2   cloves garlic
    About ½ cup coarsely chopped red onion
½   fresh red bell pepper, coarsely chopped
1   teaspoon chopped fresh rosemary or thyme
¼   cup corn flour
2   tablespoons ground flaxseed
1   teaspoon chili powder or chipotle powder
½   teaspoon salt
    Black pepper
1   can (about 1½ cups) black beans, drained
1   egg
1   tablespoon soy sauce
1   tablespoon tomato paste
1   egg (for vegan burgers substitute a tablespoon of water)

1. Pulse the carrot in a food processor until coarsely chopped. Add the grains and garlic, and pulse again until finely chopped. Add the onion, bell pep-per, and rosemary, and pulse until mixed well and most particles are under ¼ inch in size.

2. Add the corn flour, flaxseed, chili powder, salt, black pepper to taste, black beans, egg, soy sauce, and tomato paste, and pulse so the beans are chopped but not puréed and everything is well mixed. To keep it from turning into mush, you might need to transfer to a bowl and finish mixing

it by hand. The patties should hold together fairly well. If needed, add a little more water or a little more flour to get a consistency that will hold its shape.

3. Grill on the barbecue or panfry in a small amount of oil for about 8 minutes per side, until nicely browned and cooked through. If they are crumbly and falling apart on the grill, try using an oiled grill pan or oiled sheets of foil. Adding more ground flaxseed or egg will help bind them together better. Sometimes I use two eggs instead of one when cooking on a grill.

Quick Brewer's Pizza Dough

I am completely crazy about pizza and have been handcrafting my own for over 20 years. It was a natural step to start incorporating leftover brewing grains into my pizza dough, and I think I have just about perfected the recipe. Quite a few pizza makers out there routinely add barley malt extract to the pizza dough because it contributes crunch and the malt sugar aids in rapid rising for a crisp yet light crust. Guess what? Because the spent grain still contains small amounts of malt sugar and plenty of malt flavor, you can get the benefits of adding malt to your pizza without having to shell out extra dough.

I suggest using grain from a lighter beer mash for most pizza dough. Amber, red, or dark beers usually have caramel and roasted malt flavors that might clash with the traditional pizza. But consider the toppings: in some cases a sweeter crust might be called for. A topping of thinly sliced apple and caramelized onion with Gruyère cheese could go quite nicely with a crust made from a Scottish ale or red ale. Let your creative instincts guide you, and the results could be memorable!

Two 12- to 14-inch pizza crusts, 1 large focaccia, or 4 to 6 calzones

2	cups wet spent grain
¾	cup water
1	packet dried brewer's yeast
3–4	cups of organic unbleached white flour
1	teaspoon salt
¼	cup olive oil

1. Purée the grain with ½ cup of the water using a food processor or blender until very smooth. It is okay to have small flecks of grain in the mixture, but all the large pieces should be gone.

2. Add the yeast to the remaining ¼ cup water in a large mixing bowl. Mix in about a tablespoon of the grain purée, which will cause some visible activity (bubbling and foaming) in the yeast within 30 minutes if it is viable. Ideally, the mixture should be within a temperature range of 90 to 110°F (32–43°C).

3. Once yeast is proofed, add 2 cups of the flour, the salt, and the oil. Mix well, then continue to add flour until the dough balls up and no longer sticks to the sides of the bowl. If you wish, use a stand mixer with a dough hook or a food processor to mix the dough.

4. Transfer the dough to an oiled bowl, and allow to rise for 1 to 2 hours, or until doubled in bulk. Punch the dough down, knead briefly until firm and no longer sticky, then divide into portions and shape as desired.

5. Top the pizza as desired, and bake in a hot oven — 400°F (204°C) is best for most ovens, but adjust according to your oven and preferences as needed. If you have a wood-fired brick oven, rejoice! For a smoky flavor try baking on a pizza stone on a grill.

Calzone or Focaccia

For calzones, fill rounds, squares, or triangles of dough with your favorite toppings and cheese, and bake until cooked hot and bubbly through to the center. The internal temperature should be 200°F (93°C), and the tops should be lightly browned.

For focaccia, lightly grease a large sheet pan with olive oil. Roll out the dough into a rectangular shape to fit the pan, and spread the dough into the oiled pan. Top with your favorite focaccia ingredients, such as olives, sun-dried tomatoes, or garlic and oil. Bake for 25 to 30 minutes.

Variation: Sourdough Pizza Dough

For a sourdough crust follow the instructions above but use the following ingredient proportions:

2 cups wet spent grain
½ cup water
1 cup sourdough starter
¼ cup olive oil
3–4 cups organic unbleached white flour
1 teaspoon salt

Blend the spent grain and water until smooth, add the starter and oil, then incorporate the flour and salt just as in the main recipe to form the pizza dough.

Spent-Grain Irish Soda Bread

This moist, chewy bread melts in your mouth. It still has that trademark soda bread flavor despite the addition of spent grain, which is not exactly traditional. I have perused dozens of cookbooks and websites and have made many different soda bread recipes because it happens to be a favorite accompaniment to Irish stew and corned beef. This recipe combines some traditional recipes, adding spent grain and refining the flour-to-liquid ratio to achieve a moist interior with a thick, crunchy crust.

1 large loaf (hand shaped or in a loaf pan)

1 cup spent grain, measured after squeezing out as much liquid as possible
¾ cup buttermilk, or milk with 2 teaspoons lemon juice added
⅓ cup beer — a low-hopped dark beer tastes the best
2 eggs, beaten
2½ cups organic unbleached all-purpose flour
½ cup organic whole wheat flour
¼ cup organic dry malt extract
1 teaspoon baking powder
½ teaspoon baking soda
½ teaspoon salt
½ cup (1 stick) butter
1 cup raisins

1. Preheat oven to 350°F (177°C).

2. Mix the spent grain, buttermilk, beer, and eggs in a small bowl, and set aside.

3. Combine the flours, malt extract, baking powder, baking soda, and salt in a large mixing bowl with a wire whisk so the flour is fluffed up and the baking powder and baking soda are thoroughly incorporated. Use a pastry cutter or two knives to cut the butter into the dough until the texture resembles coarse cornmeal.

4. Toss in the raisins so they are coated with flour. Mix in the wet ingredients using a sturdy spoon until dough forms a loose ball. Roll out onto a well-floured counter or board, and knead briefly. The dough should hold its shape and have a light coating of flour on it.

5. If baking as a rustic free-form round, butter a baking sheet, dust with flour, and drop the ball onto the sheet. Shape as desired with your hands. Cut an x across the top, and dust with a little more flour if desired. If using a loaf pan, butter the pan, dust with flour, and press the dough lightly into the pan.

6. Bake for 40 minutes to 1 hour. The large loaf will take the full hour or possibly a little longer. The loaf is done when a knife inserted into the center comes out clean.

Spent-Grain Sourdough Baguette

I have been doing quite a bit of baking ever since acquiring a wonderful San Francisco sourdough starter by mail order. This bread recipe uses a no-knead method I have found to be both easy and consistently successful.

If you do not wish to take care of a sourdough starter on a regular basis, you can use baker's yeast to make a small sour starter (see Yeast-Based Sour Starter, page 153). This bread works very well with grains from a light-colored beer recipe: pale ale, pilsner, Belgian Wit, or hefeweizen are good choices. You can make this with darker grains, but it will change the character of the loaf quite a bit.

This bread requires at least 3 hours to rise and then an overnight rest in the refrigerator. The dough can also be made in advance and stored in the refrigerator for up to 6 days. On the day you want fresh-baked bread, simply remove from the fridge, shape into loaves, and allow to warm up to room temperature while it slowly rises for a few hours. After it has risen, pop it in the oven, bake, and enjoy.

Two 20-inch loaves

2   cups spent grain, measured after squeezing out as much liquid as possible

1   cup water

6–7   cups organic unbleached bread flour

1–2   teaspoons salt (adjust to taste and dietary preference)

2   cups sourdough starter or sour starter (see Yeast-Based Sour Starter, page 153)

1. Combine the spent grain and water, and purée the mixture using a blender until it is smooth and most of the grain husks have been pulverized into small flecks. If needed, gently warm the blended grain-and-water mixture to just below lukewarm, or about 100°F (38°C).

2. Transfer to a large mixing bowl, and add 3 cups of the flour, the salt, and the sourdough starter, and mix well. Add 3 more cups of flour, a cup at a time, until the dough forms a loose ball. It will be very sticky. This is supposed to be a loose dough, with a higher moisture content than a traditional French bread dough. This allows the gluten strands, which contribute the springiness and air pockets in the finished bread, to develop naturally. The remaining flour is added on baking day if needed.

3. Cover with plastic wrap or oiled cloth. Allow the dough to rise in a warm place for 4 to 8 hours. When the dough has risen to double the original bulk, cover securely and refrigerate overnight. If temperatures are cool but not freezing, you can leave the dough outside or in an unheated room instead of refrigerating. Between 40 and 50°F (4 and 10°C) is best. You can hold the dough in the refrigerator for up to 1 week.

4. About 3 hours before baking time, remove the dough from the refrigerator and allow to warm for about 30 minutes before handling. If you are in a rush, you can skip the wait; it will be just fine, but your hands will feel the cold! Lightly knead the dough on a floured board for a few minutes, then shape it into two long baguettes (or any shape you prefer).

5. Slash each loaf across the top two or three times to allow gas to escape while rising. Place on a floured cookie sheet or on parchment lightly dusted with flour, and allow to rise for at least 1 hour and up to 2 hours before baking. Bread should be doubled in bulk before baking to ensure the lightest, spongiest texture. If the room temperature is cool or the sourdough is sluggish, the rising could take as much as 4 or 5 hours, but this is rare. If possible, give it all the time it needs. Sourdough breads take a little more time, but the flavors are worth the wait!

6. When the bread has almost doubled in bulk, preheat the oven to 400°F (204°C). If you are using a baking stone, preheat it for at least 40 minutes. Just before baking, place a pan of water (1 to 2 cups of water) on the bottom rack of the oven to create steam and develop a chewy crust. Place the loaves on the middle rack, directly on a baking stone if possible. If using parchment paper, simply hold the parchment on two edges and gently transfer the bread to the stone.

7. If you like a really thick, chewy crust, use a spray bottle to spritz the sides of the oven just after adding the bread to create a nice burst of steam. Spray again after 10 minutes.

8. Baking time will depend on the size of the loaves. When done, bread will have a firm, nicely browned crust and will have a hollow sound when tapped. For a foolproof doneness test, insert a probe thermometer into the bottom of the loaf. When the temperature reaches 185 to 195°F (85–91°C), the bread is done.

Grain-on-the-Brain Bread

Whenever I brew my multigrain Grain-on-the-Brain (page 283), I have double the anticipation because I always make this bread with some of the leftover grain. Thus I have a refreshing and complex ale on the way and a hearty, healthy loaf of bread to enjoy while I wait. The beer and the bread do go really well together, but the bread is usually long gone before the beer is ready.

2 large loaves, about 2 pounds each

¼ cup toasted buckwheat (kasha)

¼ cup whole amaranth

¼ cup whole millet

¼ cup whole quinoa

3 cups spent grain from Grain-on-the-Brain recipe*

2 cups whole-wheat flour

2–3 teaspoons salt

2 cups sourdough starter or yeast sponge (see below)

1 cup water, plus 4 cups for soaking and cooking the whole grains

2 tablespoons olive oil or vegetable oil

3–4 cups organic unbleached bread flour

2 tablespoons old-fashioned rolled oats to decorate loaves (optional)

¼–½ cup raw sunflower seeds, poppy seeds, pumpkin seeds, sesame seeds, or flaxseed (optional)

If you want to make the bread but did not brew the beer, use 2¼ cups spent grain plus ¼ cup rolled oats, ¼ cup flaked rye, and ¼ cup flaked wheat.

1. Make a sourdough sponge (see facing page).

2. Soak the buckwheat, amaranth, millet, and quinoa in 2 cups of spring water for 1 hour.

3. Drain and rinse the grains thoroughly, then soak again in 2 cups of water for 1 hour. This removes saponins on the quinoa and phytic acids on the grains that could contribute bitter flavors and reduce digestibility of the bread.

4. Place the drained and rinsed grains in a small saucepan with enough water to cover 1 inch and bring to a boil. Remove from heat and cool for 15 minutes, to allow the grains to soften, then drain and rinse with cold water.

5. Combine the spent brewing grains, precooked whole grains, whole-wheat flour, salt, sourdough starter, water, and oil in a large mixing bowl, and mix well. Continue to mix, and add 3 cups of the unbleached bread flour, a cup at a time, until the dough forms a ball. If you have an electric stand mixer with a dough hook, by all means use it! This dough can be a bit of a workout if done by hand. If needed, add more bread flour to make the dough firm enough to knead without sticking too much. Too much flour will make the bread too dry, so it is best to add flour a little at a time until the dough does not flatten out from its own weight when made into a ball.

6. Turn the dough out onto a floured board, and knead gently for about 5 minutes. If using the seeds, knead them into the bread so they are evenly distributed. Lightly coat the mixing bowl with oil, and place the dough in, turning over to coat with oil. Cover, and allow to rise in a warm place for 2 to 4 hours. The dough is ready to shape into loaves when doubled in bulk.

7. Punch the risen dough down, then turn back out onto the floured board and knead for a few minutes until dough is smooth and compact. Divide into two equal balls, and shape into oblong loaves to fit in standard bread loaf pans. Oil the bread pans, and fit the dough into each pan, coating the

dough evenly with oil. If desired, sprinkle rolled oats or dried spent grain over the loaves and press into the dough lightly just before putting in the pans. Set in a warm place to rise. Allow to rise for 1 to 4 hours, or until nearly doubled in bulk.

8. Bake in an oven preheated to 350°F (177°C) for 40 to 60 minutes. Loaves are done when the internal temperature reaches 190 to 200°F (88–93°C).

Making a Sourdough Sponge

The day before baking, or first thing in the morning if you will bake the bread in the evening, make a sponge if you will not be using sourdough starter. Mix together:

- 2 cups organic unbleached flour
- 1 packet active dry yeast or leftover brewer's yeast
- 2 cups lukewarm water

Cover and put in a warm place, and allow to ferment 4 to 12 hours. Making a sponge will proof the yeast and get it up to full activity, which will result in a better rise and more developed flavor in the finished bread.

Spent-Grain Rustic Rye Bread

This dense, crusty dark rye bread begs to be sliced thinly and served with rustic cheese, smoked fish with horseradish spread, or a fresh and pungent aioli. I am a huge fan of this style of bread, which I first tasted as a kid when it was given out for free at the Bread and Puppet Circus in Vermont when I was growing up. Bread and Puppet is a theater group founded by a German family in the '60s.

In addition to staging plays and street theater spiced with political satire and handcrafted puppets and stage props, it was the theater's tradition to make huge amounts of this bread in a giant outdoor mud oven and serve it freely to the thousands who came from far and wide to attend the annual circus, which was held for most of the '70s, '80s, and '90s. Although the circus is no longer, the theater still has regular summer performances in Glover, Vermont.

This recipe is an adaptation of the bread served by Bread and Puppet. It is built around spent grain, with whole rye kernels and rye flour, and is adjusted for baking in a home oven. Making this bread is a 2-day process but requires little hands-on time.

Two 9-inch round loaves

1	cup organic whole rye berries
½	cup water plus water for soaking rye berries
4–6	cups organic dark rye flour
2	cups sourdough starter or sour starter (see Yeast-Based Sour Starter, page 153)
2	cups wet spent grain — grains from a dark beer or a rye beer preferred
1–2	teaspoons salt

---

1. On day 1 put the rye berries in a bowl with enough filtered water to cover them. Cover the bowl and leave in a warm place for at least 12 hours.

2. Also on day 1, make a sourdough sponge by combining 3 cups of the rye flour, the water, the sourdough starter, and the spent grain in a bowl large enough to allow for expansion of up to double in size. Cover and let the sponge develop for 8 to 12 hours.

3. The next day, drain the rye berries into a sieve or colander, and rinse with fresh water. Partially grind the berries using a food processor or blender. A texture similar to the spent grain is what you are aiming for: most berries should be chopped in half, but it is okay if some are ground more finely while others are still whole.

4. Add the crushed rye berries to the sponge along with 2 cups of rye flour and the salt (adjust to taste and dietary preference).

5. The dough should be firm enough to work with your hands at this point. Turn the dough out onto a floured board, and knead gently for about 5 minutes until it is firm. It will be a sticky dough. Add more flour if needed to make the dough stiff enough to hold its shape.

6. Transfer the dough back to the bowl the sponge was in, cover, and allow to rise in a warm place for 2 to 4 hours. This dough is very dense and will not rise a lot, but you should see some increase in size before shaping into loaves.

7. Once the dough has risen, knead slightly on the floured board, then shape it into two round loaves. Slash the tops of the loaves, and place on floured pans or parchment to rise. Loaves will take 1 to 3 hours to rise depending on the ambient temperature. If bread starts to dry out during rising, mist it with plain water from a spray bottle so the surface does not crack.

8. Just before baking sprinkle the top of the loaf with some flour if you wish. This will help develop a nice crust.

9. Bake in an oven preheated to 400°F (204°C) for 15 minutes. After 15 minutes lower the heat to 350°F (177°C), and bake for 15 minutes. Then lower the heat to 300°F (149°C), and bake for 30 to 60 minutes longer, or until the bread is fully baked. The baking time will vary depending on the loaf size. Check the bread every 10 minutes once it has been in the oven for a total of 60 minutes. If you want an extra-chewy crust, you can use a pan of water and steam during baking (see Spent-Grain Sourdough Baguette, page 145).

Spent-Grain Sourdough Pretzels

Beer and pretzels — what's not to love? They go together so well that just the sight of a chewy, salty pretzel dripping with a favorite mustard can make a beer lover smile! Most pretzel recipes call for a bit of sugar or malt extract. This is totally unnecessary when using spent grain since it contributes enough sweetness to get the flavor right. This is one recipe where making a yeast starter with spent brewing yeast works really well and helps to further cement the pretzel's rightful place as a great partner with beer!

Although making pretzels might seem daunting, once you get the hang of it you will make them a favorite add-on to your brewing routine. Despite the steps that may seem unfamiliar, such as boiling in baking soda, pretzel making is forgiving of failure. Even a less-than-perfect-looking pretzel invariably comes out just right in the one area that does matter: taste. Make sure you have plenty of beer on hand to wash these delicious things down with. Prost!

About 18 large pretzels

2	cups wet spent grain
½	cup organic whole milk
3–4	cups organic unbleached wheat flour
1½	teaspoons kosher or sea salt
1	cup sourdough starter or sour starter (see Yeast-Based Sour Starter, page 153)
¼	cup baking soda (for water boil)
	Coarse sea salt for sprinkling on finished pretzels

1. Purée the spent grain and milk in a blender until smooth. How smooth is entirely up to you — larger chunks of spent grain can add a fun and interesting texture. For a more traditional texture, blend until the grain is just tiny flecks.

2. Gently warm the grain and milk mixture to lukewarm, or about 100°F (38°C).

3. Transfer to a large mixing bowl, and add 3 cups of the flour, the salt, and the sour starter, and mix well. Add the remaining flour while kneading (with a dough hook or by hand) a bit at a time until the dough forms a ball. It should be slightly tacky but smooth, and soft enough to slightly relax when rested on the kneading board.

4. Allow to rise in a covered bowl for 1 to 3 hours, until nearly doubled in bulk.

5. After the dough has risen, have fun working it into the shapes you desire. Place the shapes on a parchment-lined or flour-dusted baking sheet, and allow to rise for 30 to 60 minutes.

6. While pretzels are rising, add the baking soda to 4 to 6 cups of water in a large pot and bring to a boil. A wide stockpot works well, as it will give you more surface area for cooking the pretzels. It is very important to add the baking soda first — adding the soda to boiling water creates a spectacular boilover. Cook the pretzels in the boiling water, a few at a time, for 40 to 60 seconds, flip them over, and boil for another 40 to 60 seconds. Return the pretzels to the pan with tongs or a slotted spoon.

7. Sprinkle coarse salt over the pretzels, or for a different treat try brushing with garlic butter, then bake at 400°F (204°C) for 15 to 25 minutes. Baking time will vary depending on the size and shape of your pretzels and the desired final color.

Pumpernickel Pretzels

Substitute 2 cups of pumpernickel flour or dark rye flour for some of the wheat flour, and use spent grain from a dark beer batch. Add 1 teaspoon ground caraway to the dough, and sprinkle the tops with a mixture of salt and caraway seeds before baking. These are really freaking awesome!

Yeast-Based Sour Starter

If you do not maintain a sourdough starter on a regular basis, you will need to make a sour starter. For occasional use, a soured yeast dough that you make each time you make a sourdough bread is sufficient. If you bake on a regular basis, it may be worth your while to acquire a genuine sourdough starter from a gourmet cooking store or one of the many mail-order suppliers to be found on the Internet.

A quality sourdough starter can make the difference between a good bread and an exceptional, memorable one. As with brewing yeast there are a variety of sourdough strains available that have their origins in some of the famous bread-baking regions of the world.

San Francisco sourdough is world famous, and relatively easy to acquire, but if you are fond of a particular bread style, you can re-create that flavor by ordering the culture and growing that strain to use in your own baking.

Make the starter 3 days before you begin the bread recipe.

2   **cups filtered water at room temperature**

1   **package active dry yeast or leftover brewer's yeast**

2   **cups organic unbleached bread flour**

Pour 1 cup of the water into a wide-mouthed ceramic or glass jar, at least 1 quart in size. Sprinkle the yeast over the water, and let dissolve for 5 minutes. Stir in 1 cup of the flour. Cover with cheesecloth or a loose-fitting lid, and allow to ferment for 24 hours.

Add remaining 1 cup flour and 1 cup water, stir well, cover, and let sit for another 24 hours.

The starter should be ready for use on the third day. It should have bubbled and fermented and should have a clean, sour aroma and the consistency and appearance of pancake batter.

If it has a foul, rotten aroma and a dingy grey or pinkish color, discard it. This problem is rare if you keep everything reasonably clean and had a good-quality fresh yeast to begin with. Just as with brewing, cleanliness and treating the yeast with gentle respect help to ensure your success!

Making the Best of a Bad Batch (Vinegar!)

Sometimes things go wrong even in the best of circumstances, and you end up with a batch of beer that you consider undrinkable. It happens to even the most accomplished brewers, so don't be too hard on yourself. If you're willing to do some extra work, a "failure" can turn into a learning experience, and you will wind up with a fantastic batch of vinegar.

Mention the word *Acetobacter* around most homebrewers and you will probably witness an involuntary cringe. This bacteria is widely present and lives on fermentable fruits and vegetables. In the presence of oxygen, it metabolizes alcohol into acetic acid, more commonly known as vinegar. It is one of the main reasons brewers have to be so careful about cleaning and sanitizing, and why wort should be boiled. *Acetobacter* is one of the most common causes of beer that is either completely spoiled or just tastes "off."

As with yeast, there are different strains of *Acetobacter* that can produce different flavor profiles. Artisanal vinegar has many dimensions of flavor that shine in homemade dressings and marinades. Naturally fermented live vinegar also has many health benefits, including the ability to lower blood glucose levels and possibly cholesterol levels and blood pressure.

If *Acetobacter* gains a foothold in a batch, it is hard to get rid of, but you can easily encourage the process and turn your brew into malt vinegar, as brewers have done through the ages. Some infections are caused by bacteria other than *Acetobacter* and may smell and taste unpleasant. To help determine what has gone wrong, let taste and smell be your guide. *Acetobacter* infections smell and taste vinegary or sour. Some wild yeasts, such as *Lactobacilli*, also create a sour taste and smell, while others, such as *Brettanomyces*, can produce a leathery or barnyard smell.

This may be unpleasant to your senses yet still have the potential to evolve into a fantastic craft vinegar. Once the *Acetobacter* is thriving, the other bacteria and wild yeast will be suppressed as the liquid becomes more acidic, and those barnyard smells can age and blend with the developing vinegar tang to create a rustic and pleasing craft vinegar.

Some infections may be too severe to make into a palatable vinegar. If the spoiled beer has a strongly rotten or other extremely unpleasant smell, it has probably become too infected to be usable. There are still ways to recycle such a badly spoiled batch. You can make it into vinegar and then distill it into concentrated acetic acid to use for cleaning and sterilizing. Distilling is a bit outside the scope of this book, but there are plenty of books and guides available. If the batch is truly foul, it may be best used to water your compost pile.

SETTING UP

Although *Acetobacter* bacteria are everywhere, they are usually not present in large enough numbers to make vinegar efficiently. Adding some "mother of vinegar," or live vinegar, accelerates the process and ensures a quality product. Live, unpasteurized vinegar is available in health food or gourmet food stores; two brands are Bragg and Eden Foods. Look for vinegar that is labeled "live," "unpasteurized," or "raw"; it should have a layer of brown sediment at the bottom.

Vinegar starter culture is also sold in many homebrew supply stores, or you can order it online. These starter cultures are often specific to a certain type of vinegar, such as red wine, white wine, malt, cider, and so forth, but any vinegar culture can ultimately make any kind of vinegar, because the base beverage contributes most of the flavor.

If you get hooked on brewing your own vinegar, you can establish a healthy vinegar mother and keep using that. Unlike yeast, distinct strains of *Acetobacter* that contribute certain characteristics to vinegar have not been classified. If you are a vinegar connoisseur, seek out a raw vinegar that tastes really good (check out handcrafted vinegars at local farmers' markets or gourmet food stores).

The Mother of All Vinegar

The term "vinegar mother" is often used loosely, but it always refers to a culture containing living Acetobacter *that can be used to make vinegar. I refer to the solid mass that floats on the top of a vat of vinegar as the **vinegar mother**, and a liquid culture containing live* Acetobacter *but without a solid mother as a* **vinegar starter culture***.*

Vinegar is very acidic and must be stored in containers made from non-reactive material — traditionally, glass vessels, ceramic crocks, or oak barrels. Stainless steel can also be used, but over time the acetic acid could start to corrode the metal, especially if it is a lower grade of stainless steel. I strongly discourage the use of plastic because the vinegar could extract nasty compounds or flavors from it.

A container with a spigot is handy. The container should be wide to allow as much surface area as possible to be exposed to oxygen. A widemouthed glass demijohn, filled partway, works well. Many craft vinegar makers employ used oak wine barrels, set on their side and filled halfway. For small amounts of vinegar, a 1-gallon widemouthed jar or a large bowl is perfectly adequate.

In addition to a good vessel and a starter culture, other useful equipment for vinegar making includes pH test papers, an acid test kit, a hydrometer (the same one you use for brewing), and some good cheesecloth or unbleached cotton to screen the opening of your vinegar fermenter. An acid test kit and pH papers, available at most homebrew supply stores, will help you determine when the vinegar has reached the desired acid level. For aging and conditioning the vinegar, you may want oak chips to help develop flavor. Finished vinegar should be sealed in narrow-mouthed bottles to preserve the final flavor. Wine bottles work well, especially the 375 mL ones.

Just as with brewing, it is important to clean your vinegar-making equipment well. Clean with the homebrew cleaner you usually use or unscented dish detergent. Rinse well with hot water to remove all cleanser residue. I find it unnecessary to sanitize vinegar-making gear, but I usually give it a quick rinse with a little bit of distilled white vinegar. Sanitizing is perfectly fine if it makes you more confident.

HOW TO MAKE VINEGAR

The risk of the vinegar culture itself becoming spoiled is highest when you are first starting the batch. At this point the percentage of acetic acid is low enough that other bacteria can multiply, especially if they are already present in your beer. This is why it is important to keep the proportion of starter vinegar to fermented beer or wine fairly high. My own experience confirms the advice of most experts, who suggest a ratio of no more than two times beer or wine to starter culture. The safest bet is to use a 50:50 ratio of beer to starter. Before you mix the starter with the beer, however, the alcohol needs to be diluted.

Step 1. Dilute the Beer

To produce vinegar with an acid level that tastes as expected, use at least 5 percent alcohol by volume. This will produce a vinegar with an acetic acid level of over 5 percent, which is particularly important when vinegar is used for preserving food. It is okay to make a vinegar with an acid level as low as 4 percent to use in dressings and marinades, but under 5 percent is not safe for preserving and will not keep as well as a stronger batch. I like to stay on the safe side and always keep my vinegar acid level above 5 percent. I happen to like the sharper taste of the higher acid level. If the beer you are working with has an alcohol level lower than 5 percent, you could consider adding some barley malt or sugar to the fermenter and allow the extra sugar to ferment to increase the alcohol level before starting a batch of vinegar with it.

If the alcohol is stronger than 5 to 6 percent, dilute it with clean filtered water. To calculate the dilution rate, divide the known alcohol percentage of the beer by the percentage you want to end up with. For instance, if you want to dilute a 6.5 percent beer to 5 percent alcohol:

$$6.5 \div 5 = 1.3$$

Then multiply the volume of liquid to be diluted by this result to determine the finished volume. If starting with a pint of beer:

$$16 \text{ ounces} \times 1.3 = 20.8$$

To bring the total volume of liquid to 20.8 ounces, add 4.8 ounces of water to the beer.

During the conversion of beer or wine to vinegar, the *Acetobacter* consume alcohol and oxygen and produce acetic acid and water. In the end the percentage of alcohol consumed is nearly equal to the percentage of acetic acid produced. There are some fancy scientific equations you can do to calculate the exact conversion ratio of a wine or beer of a certain alcohol to a vinegar of a specific acid content. Because this calculation results in an acetic acid percentage almost identical to the alcohol percentage, it is really not necessary to do the calculations. Each molecule of alcohol is converted to a molecule of acetic acid, which has a slightly higher molecular weight. For the science geeks among us, this is the chemical formula:

$$2CH_3CH_2OH + O_2 = 2CH_3COOH + 2H_2O$$

Ethanol: 92 g/mol

Acetic acid: 120 g/mol

Step 2. Ferment the Vinegar

Once the alcohol level is adjusted, pour the base beverage into the vessel and add the vinegar starter (live vinegar or vinegar mother), keeping the proportion to within 2 parts base to 1 part starter. Mix well, and aerate to introduce plenty of oxygen. If using a demijohn or other narrow-necked vessel to ferment the vinegar, fill it only partway to leave as much surface area as possible exposed to air.

Cover the opening with clean cloth or other porous material, and secure it with a string or rubber band. The material should have a fine enough mesh to keep out vinegar flies (a.k.a. common fruit fly), which can ruin the vinegar. Most fabric sold as cheesecloth in grocery and hardware stores is not true cheesecloth, and fruit flies can get through it easily even if it is folded over several times. True cheesecloth or simple cotton muslin is a better choice.

Store the vessel away from light while fermenting and within a temperature range of 65 to 95°F (18–35°C) — 80°F (27°C) is ideal. Lower temperatures will slow the development time, while warmer temperatures will speed it up.

During the vinegar-making process, a solid mother will often form at the top of the liquid. This gelatinous, semitranslucent mass, made up of *Acetobacter* and cellulose, indicates healthy acetic acid conversion. You may also see long strands of gelatinous material, floating in the vinegar vat. These strands are also normal. They are sometimes referred to as vinegar eels, although that term is more accurately applied to a relatively harmless nematode that can sometimes infest vinegar before it reaches full acidity.

If you happen to find living vinegar eels (they are just barely visible, at 2mm in length) in your vinegar, strain the vinegar through a coffee filter and then pasteurize it before consumption. To ensure that the infestation is not present in the vinegar mother you are using, it is best to start with a fresh culture, and sterilize all equipment before beginning a new batch. Good sanitization practices and preventing flies from getting into your vinegar can help prevent the problem in the first place. The good news is, if you inadvertently consume vinegar containing these eels, there is little harm done; they are not parasitic and ingesting a few will simply add a minute bit of protein to your diet.

Step 3. Increase the Volume and Check for Completion

It can take up to 12 weeks for vinegar to develop to the 5 percent acetic acid level. Most of this conversion happens in the first 4 to 6 weeks. If you want to increase the size of your batch, you can add up to double the volume of base beverage every 4 weeks until the desired volume is reached. Thus, if you start with 1 quart of vinegar, in 4 weeks you can add another 2 quart of beverage, bringing the total volume to 3 quarts. Then, 4 weeks after that, add up to 6 quarts more, bringing the volume to just over 2 gallons. Make sure to dilute the base to 5 to 6 percent alcohol each time. Add more alcohol every 4 weeks until the desired volume is reached.

When it has been at least 4 weeks since the last addition, check for completion. If it smells like vinegar instead of alcohol and has the characteristic tang of vinegar, it is close to being done. Many home vinegar makers simply rely on their senses to assess doneness, but a wine acid test kit uses chemical titration to give you an accurate read of the acetic acid level. These kits cost between $10 and $20 and are found at most homebrew and wine-making supply shops. (See Using a Wine Acid Test Kit, page 162.)

Because the pH of vinegar ranges between 2.5 and 5, pH papers are not as accurate for determining the completion of a batch but are useful for comparing the pH of a current batch of vinegar with that of a previous batch of the same type.

Step 4. Pasteurize and Age

Once the vinegar has reached full strength, you need to halt the activity of the *Acetobacter*. This is usually done by pasteurization (heating to 150 to 160°F [66–71°C] and holding at that temperature for 30 minutes). If you prefer to use raw or live vinegar, pasteurization is not an option, but you can still force the *Acetobacter* to go dormant by removing its oxygen supply. If you don't halt this activity, certain strains of *Acetobacter* will start to convert acetic acid to carbon dioxide once all the alcohol is gone, gradually ruining your vinegar. Decant or siphon the vinegar into narrow-neck bottles or jars with tight-sealing lids to remove it from an aerobic environment.

Most gourmet vinegar is vastly improved by aging it for 6 weeks to a year. Some vinegars, notably balsamics, are aged for many years. Aging mellows the sharp bite of new vinegar and allows other flavors to develop. Often the flavor of the original beverage comes back in new and wonderful ways. I once produced a vinegar from a cider that was in a keg too long but when first tapped was lovely and tart with fresh apple aromas. It was sad to lose the cider, and at first the vinegar tasted like nail polish remover. I aged it in mason jars with some oak chips, and all but forgot about it in a dark corner of the garage. A year later I uncovered a treasure, one of the finest vinegars I have ever tasted, with a wonderful tang and distinct apple aromas.

Step 5. Bottling and Flavoring

When bottling vinegar, filter out any solids for appearance and enjoyment. A coffee-filter-lined funnel is an easy way to do this. Bottles should be cleaned and rinsed well with hot water. Sanitizing is not necessary because the acidity of the vinegar will prevent unwanted infection. Fill to within an inch of the top and cork, cap, or seal each bottle as you wish.

If you wish to flavor your vinegar with sprigs of fresh herbs, spices, or other flavors, add these to the bottles right before filling if you want the whole herbs or spices to remain in the bottles until use. When using fresh herbs, wash them carefully and dry before adding to the bottles. Sprigs of rosemary, thyme, mint, or basil are popular choices. Chile peppers, garlic, peppercorns, and citrus peel also work well.

Some spices, especially those with small bits, such as peppercorns or cloves, are a nuisance if left in the bottles. In this case you are better off adding the spices to the vinegar during the aging time and let them infuse for at least 2 weeks before bottling. The longer the herbs infuse, the stronger the flavors will become. Taste the vinegar every week or so until the flavor is right, then filter into the final bottles.

Support Your Mother

A large vinegar mother becomes quite heavy and tends to sink to the bottom of the vinegar vat, where it cannot take up oxygen as readily as it needs to, thus causing the *Acetobacter* to slow down or stall. A vinegar raft is a small piece of sterilized hardwood that has been inoculated with vinegar starter. It floats on the surface of the vinegar, holding the mother at the top of the vinegar vat, allowing the *Acetobacter* to more readily access oxygen.

You can buy a raft or make one yourself with a small piece of hardwood that has been sterilized for 20 minutes in boiling water. Oak is the most common wood used. The raft needs to be small enough to fit inside the opening of your vinegar-making vessel and large enough to float with the weight of a vinegar mother on it. Generally, a piece 4 inches square and ½ to 1 inch thick should suffice.

Place it in the vinegar vat along with the vinegar starter culture. If you are using a solid vinegar mother from a previous batch, use the raft to float the mother on the surface of the fermenting vinegar.

Using a Wine Acid Test Kit

It should be noted that wine acid test kits are designed for testing the percentage of tartaric acid, which is usually present at .55 to .75 percent in wine — much lower levels than the 4 to 6 percent acetic acid of most finished vinegars. Thus, testing vinegar using the formulas given with most wine acid test kits requires a large quantity of test chemicals.

To reduce the quantity of sodium hydroxide used, I reduce the amount of the vinegar sample by one half to one third, and then adjust the other ratios by the same amount. This reduces the accuracy of results somewhat, but when working with vinegar I am usually happy to have results accurate to the nearest tenth of a percent, while most wine tests rely on an accuracy of a hundredth of a percent.

When adjusting ratios and formulas, it is important not to stray from the basic formula for calculating the acetic acid percent in vinegar:

$$\text{mL sodium hydroxide (NaOH)} \times \text{n NaOH} \times 100 \times 0.060 \div \text{mL vinegar} = \% \text{ acetic acid}$$

The "n NaOH" refers to the solution strength of sodium hydroxide used, expressed as normality (n). In most home wine acid test kits, the sodium hydroxide included is .1 N.

Due to the difference in molecular weight between tartaric and acetic acid, a test kit designed for testing tartaric acid levels in wine will use a slightly different formula. Thus, your test results will be more accurate using the above formula rather than the one supplied by the kit.

6

THE HOMEBREWER'S GARDEN

In essence, beer is an agricultural product. There is a popular theory among beer lovers that at the dawn of civilization, humans settled down from a hunter-gatherer nomadic lifestyle into agrarian settlements not for the sake of growing food but for the love of beer! Whether or not you believe this, you may be interested in making your own production more self-sufficient by growing some of your own ingredients and using spent grain and other residue to improve your other crops.

Growing specialty crops such as hops and grain is a challenge, and processing your harvest into brew-ready ingredients is yet another undertaking. This chapter, which assumes a basic familiarity with food gardening, covers the key brewing crops of hops and barley, with a few other crops summarized in less detail.

Composting Spent Grain, Hops, and Yeast

All leftover brewing ingredients can be added to your compost pile to great effect. Brewing grains make excellent compost because the husk material breaks down slowly, adding organic matter to soil and helping to create well-aerated soil with good drainage. Spent hops and the trub left at the bottom of the brewing kettle also add fibrous material and nitrogen. Brewer's yeast is widely used in composting; some gardeners who don't brew add active brewer's yeast to compost to speed up the decomposition. Yeast will grow and ferment within the organic matter in the compost pile (especially the spent grain), which helps to break the cellulose down more rapidly.

The action of the yeast in the early stages of the decomposition process reduces the acidity of the organic waste. This drop in acidity helps provide the best environment for bacterial growth. Once the bacterial activity steps up the temperature in the compost pile, the yeast naturally subsides, allowing the bacteria to take over rapidly, speeding up the composting process. Although the benefits of adding yeast to the compost are debatable in some circles, it is certainly a convenient way to dispose of the yeast slurry without dumping it down the drain, where it might stress some sewage or septic systems.

Spent hops can start to smell and they are toxic to some animals, so when adding them to a compost pile, it is best to mix them in thoroughly. To use the yeast from the bottom of a fermenter, add some water to make a runny slurry, and pour it over the top of the pile so the yeast can drain through all layers of the pile.

Spent grain poses a bit of a composting challenge, especially if you have neighbors sensitive to smells right next door. The smell of decomposing grain can be nasty enough to compel a call to the health department and you surely don't want the smell near your own house either!

The trick is to drain as much excess liquid as you can from the grain before throwing it into the compost. I simply leave my grain in my mash tun overnight with the bottom valve open, and let gravity do the work. Even with good draining, the grain will smell nasty, so mix it well with the other compost materials, then cover the whole pile with leaves, hay, or other dry matter until the grains break down. I add a little wood ash to help cut the acidity of the grain. Some composting guides advise against using wood ash, but I haven't found that adding small quantities (less than 1 percent of the total mix) creates any problems.

Vermiculture

Vermiculture — composting with worms — is another way to use up spent brewing grains. If you have a worm bin already, you can start feeding spent grain to your worms. They love it, but you have to be careful because too high a concentration of spent grain can be too much for the little guys to handle all at once. I add no more than 50 percent spent grain to the total amount of compostable material I feed each week. If worm composting is your only method of composting, you might have too much grain after an all-grain batch to add all at once. You can divide up the grain to add in stages by freezing it in portions. Quart-size yogurt containers work well; thaw one portion per week and add to your worm bin.

Worm bins are a great way for urban dwellers to compost without concerning the neighbors, because they are small enough to use in a kitchen or mudroom or deck, they do not smell much when maintained properly, and they create a manageable amount of compost for container gardening. Some cities or municipal waste haulers even offer free or low-cost worm composting bins to local residents to encourage this wonderful method of recycling!

If a premade worm composter is out of your budget range, you can make one yourself out of two large plastic bins, the kind you get at a hardware or big box store, or even a series of nested plastic buckets. Plans are readily available online. And you can even order the worms online — digging up regular earthworms from your garden isn't recommended because they don't do as well in a composter as red wigglers (*Eisenia fetida*), which seem to thrive in the containers.

Making Mushroom Substrate with Spent Grain

In a sense, homebrewers already are mushroom farmers, because yeast is a form of fungi. For some of us the next logical step is to use our leftover brewing grain as a base to grow edible mushrooms. Nurturing mushroom spores requires some of the same attention to detail as beer brewing does: maintaining the right environmental conditions, preventing unwanted organisms by keeping things clean and pasteurizing the growth medium, and being patient as the natural miracle of growth unfolds to bring flavor, enjoyment, and nutrition to our diets.

Spent grain contains an ideal mix of biological nutrients for certain types of mushrooms, and it is not all that uncommon in the mushroom industry to use brewery grains for this purpose. Whole grains are often used to propagate mushroom spores that are later transferred to the growing medium, because they hold a powerhouse of nutrients that fuel rapid growth, and each grain kernel becomes an inoculation platform from which the mycelia can leap to the surrounding growth medium. Because of their high nitrogen content, brewing grains will perform better as a growing medium if they are mixed with a supplemental material such as chopped straw, newspaper, sawdust, or chipped wood.

Oyster mushrooms are some of the easiest to grow and will grow well on a substrate consisting of 3 parts basic substrate material mixed with 1 part spent grain. The easiest, most readily available material for most small-scale gardeners is wheat or rice straw. I buy it by the bale for nesting and bedding material for my chickens. According to Paul Stamets in his book *Growing Gourmet and Medicinal Mushrooms*, wheat straw is one of the most forgiving materials for beginning mushroom cultivators to use. If you are interested in cultivating your own mushrooms, I highly recommend this book, as it covers the topic extensively.

HOW TO START

Whatever materials you use, it is important to pasteurize the substrate before inoculating it with mushroom spores, to prevent the growth of unwanted mushrooms and bacteria. An easy way to do this is to immerse it in hot water in a large pot such as the brew pot. First, mix the grains and the straw or other growing medium together, then pack loosely into the kettle. If you have a metal false bottom, use it to keep the materials off the bottom of the pot while heating. A spigot on the pot provides a convenient way to drain the water after pasteurization.

Making Good Compost

A good recipe for making compost is 30 percent "green" material (kitchen scraps, grass clippings, chicken manure), 50 percent "brown" material (cardboard, newspaper, leaves, hay), and 20 percent soil and amendments. Spent grain has a high nitrogen content and is considered a green material.

Using 20 percent soil or compost greatly accelerates the rate of decomposition thanks to the natural microbes present in the soil and a composter's best friend, the humble earthworm. If you do not already have earthworms present in the soil, it is also a great idea to obtain composting worms if you can. If you regularly feed your compost pile with fresh brewing grains and kitchen scraps, the worms will be fruitful, multiply, and greatly improve the quality of your compost. For more on composting with worms, see Vermiculture, page 165.

The time it takes for your grain and other materials to break down into compost depends on how much work you want to do, the quantity of microbes and other critters at work in your pile, and the particle size of the ingredients. Smaller bits will decompose faster than larger bits, and the more compost-munching critters in the pile, the faster the process goes. The work part is entirely up to you. If you get out there every week or two with a pitchfork and mix the pile thoroughly, the matter will decompose more quickly and could be ready to apply to your garden in as little as 3 months.

If you are like me and have many other things keeping you busy, you will often skip the compost-turning chore, perhaps for weeks at a time, in which case it can take 6 months to a year for everything to break down. If you compost this way, it's a good strategy to have two compost piles: a full one that is covered and left to rot at nature's pace and another that you add organic waste to and stir every once in a while. Each time a fresh ingredient is added to the pile the decomposition process starts anew, which is why you want to have two piles — one to mature and one to build on.

Bring the liquid to just under a boil (180 to 200°F [82–93°C]), then turn the heat off and allow the substrate and water mixture to steep for at least 1 hour as it cools. After it has cooled to below 150°F (66°C), drain the water out. You can use this nutrient-rich water on the garden after it has cooled.

Recycle Sterilizing and Cooling Water

Most brewers run boiling hot water through their counterflow wort chiller for at least 15 minutes to sterilize it. This can easily mean 5 gallons of wasted water, even at slow flow rates. I use filtered water to sterilize my chiller, and after flushing through a few pints to rinse out any cleaning residue, I collect the rest into my lauter tun (sparge water tank). With all-grain brewing I am usually doing the mash while I sterilize the wort chiller, and the reserved water is usually still hot enough to sparge with. You could also use this hot water for the mash or to make a fresh batch of cleaning solution for cleaning fermenters and bottles.

Immediately reusing the hot water that exits your immersion chiller doubles your savings because you do not have to heat the water again. You can collect it for cleaning brew equipment, general household cleaning, or doing laundry (run the hot water from the wort chiller directly into your washing machine). Or think about irrigating your garden with cooling water. Here are two ways to do it:

1. Hook the outflow from your wort chiller directly to a water sprinkler or irrigation soaker hose and water your lawn or garden while you chill your wort. Usually the water is cool enough by the time it exits the chiller. If you use an immersion-style wort chiller, the first water that exits will be very hot, so collect this for cleaning before hooking the outflow to an irrigation system.

2. Collect it in a rain barrel or repurposed 50-gallon drum fitted with a spigot. If you store these tanks at a higher elevation than your garden, you can use gravity to irrigate with a hose or fill watering cans.

Once the substrate has cooled completely, you can inoculate it with the mushroom spores of your choice. If you purchased spores from a dealer, they should come with basic inoculation and growing instructions. Essentially, the spores are mixed into the growth medium and placed in a suitable container. You can use a plastic crate or bucket, a heavy cardboard or wooden box lined with plastic, or even a tubular plastic bag with holes cut out at regular intervals to allow aeration and a place for the mushrooms to sprout from. Stick with a modest size (under 4 cubic feet or 30 gallons) if using

The mushrooms grow on the outside of the container.

cardboard, because a large box filled with wet substrate and growing mushrooms could wind up bursting under its own weight. You can use a wooden container without a lining if you sterilize it first (steaming is a good option) or a nonrusting one made of stainless or galvanized steel.

Maintain a moisture level of 65 to 70 percent by misting the container at least daily and keeping it in an enclosed space. A small shaded greenhouse tented with plastic in a corner of a garage or shed serves this purpose well. Low light is fine, but most mushrooms do not do well in direct sunlight.

Typically, the growing area should stay within the temperature range of 60 to 90°F (16–32°C). More specific temperature ranges are somewhat dependent on the mushroom species being grown. Going into more detail here would take us too far from the main topic of this book, but I highly encourage you to dig deeper if you plan to start growing your own mushrooms. Just as in brewing, the basic concepts are simple to learn, but the craft of mushroom cultivation can take years to master.

Growing Hops

In a small backyard garden, creative homebrewers can grow a wide variety of herbs, fruit, and select vegetables that can be used as ingredients in beer. From dandelions to pumpkins, apples to quinoa, the variety of plants that can be grown for making beer or wine is astounding. The only limit to what you can grow is the available space you have and the amount of time you have to devote to it.

Of all the options, however, hops are surely the most popular feature of the homebrewer's garden. Hops, the classic spice of beer, are relatively easy to grow, pick, and dry on a home scale; also, they are attractive in the summertime and die back completely after harvest. Hop vines thrive on copious amounts of sun, fertilizer, and water and can climb up to 20 feet high when conditions are ideal. A well-established hop plant will reward you with many ounces or even pounds of fresh, sticky, aromatic hops at the end of the growing season.

Humulus lupulus, the species of hops cultivated for beer brewing, is a relative of nettles and hemp and is member of the Cannabaceae family. Contrary to popular belief, hops and *Cannabis* cannot be interbred, although both species have been valued by humans for centuries for their soothing medicinal properties. In addition to their value as a beer ingredient, hops are valued in herbal medicine, especially for promoting sleep and aiding in digestion. The latter benefit derives from the bitter oils of the flower, which are one of the most effective plant-based bitters available. The aftertaste of hop bitters is soft and much more pleasing than the taste associated with most other herb-derived bitters. Perhaps this is why a good hoppy beer pairs so well with a rich meal!

Hops are perennial plants that can live for up to 30 years and once established will propagate with ease. This could be considered a nuisance if growing space is limited, as you may have to dig up and cut back the rhizomes each year to prevent them from overtaking other parts of your garden. You can always give the excess rhizomes to friends who might be interested in growing their own. Hops thrive best in temperate zones that have long, hot summer days. Most commercial hop growth is concentrated between latitudes 30 and 50, in both the Northern and Southern hemispheres. Although hops do the best in temperate regions, they can be grown just about anywhere.

Even if your area does not have the ideal climate, you can successfully produce enough hops for homebrewing purposes if you provide the best growing conditions you can. For success choose a spot that receives at least 6 hours of direct sunlight a day; a south-facing location is the best. You will have to provide the plants with a strong trellis system to climb high and reach for even more sunlight, use generous amounts of good-quality organic compost or composted manure, and water regularly. A well-tended hop plant is strong and healthy, with the built-in ability to repel most pests and resist disease.

My own growing area on the central California coast has some drawbacks, but I have been able to keep my hop plants thriving, and each year they give me a slightly bigger harvest than the year before. The climate here is similar to the Mediterranean coast. We have a long growing season, but the summer days tend to be cool, often with a coastal fog that does not burn off until the afternoon. Adding to the challenge is that I live in a valley surrounded by oak, pine, and eucalyptus trees that provide additional shade, as well as forest insects and extra moisture that make pests and disease an ongoing concern. If hops can grow here, they can grow almost anywhere!

PLANTING HOPS

Because only female hop plants produce the seedless flower cones that are desirable for brewing, the best way to start a hop plant is by planting a healthy rhizome. Rhizomes are simply living root sections with budding sites that send up new shoots. Rhizomes can be obtained in the spring from many sources. Most homebrew suppliers offer rhizomes of varieties suitable for brewing. An often-overlooked source is other homebrewers who have established hop plants. A hop grower with an excess of rhizomes might be willing to give a few to you or trade them for some homebrew. Homebrew clubs and homebrew or gardening forums are good places to look for home hop growers willing to provide you with some cuttings.

Some plant nurseries sell hop rhizomes, but these are often ornamental hops of unknown variety, or they may even be the other hop family species, *Humulus japonicus*, which is often sold as an ornamental vine but does not produce hops adequate for brewing.

When planting hops for the first time, it is a really good idea to plant at least two of each variety. This will ensure that your efforts in establishing your hop garden are not wasted if one of your baby plants succumbs to a gopher or insect infestation, or never comes up at all. Most home gardeners choose two or three varieties rather than trying to grow a wide range. It makes sense to plant a few extra varieties in the first year, as you may find that one or two of the ones that you planted in the first year do not thrive. You can pull the weak varieties and focus your efforts on growing the types that really thrive.

Storing Rhizomes

If you can't plant your rhizomes right away, store them in a cool place until you are ready to plant. The vegetable drawer of your refrigerator is an ideal spot because it keeps them cool enough to mimic winter conditions so they will not start growing, and it maintains high enough humidity to keep them from drying out. Wrap the rhizomes in a damp newspaper or brown paper bag to help keep them moist. They should not be immersed in water or wrapped in very soggy material, as too much moisture could cause them to rot.

As soon as the soil is workable and the danger of heavy frost is past, you can plant the rhizomes. Hops prefer a mildly acidic soil with a pH in the range of 6.0 to 6.2. Soil should be loose, with enough biomass to stay moist, yet should drain well. The hop-growing area should be as weed-free as possible to minimize competition for nutrients and light while the plants are establishing their roots in the first growing season.

Growing hops organically means you want to give your hops plenty of nutrients in the form of compost, manure, and green manure. Chemical fertilizers can cause excess nitrogen in the soil, which can make the plants grow too rapidly at first, then weaken and become sickly as the nitrogen is depleted or flushed from the soil after repeated watering. Organic compost and green manure release nutrients slowly over time, leading to steady, healthy growth and plants that will thrive over their natural life span of 15 to 30 years.

Plant the hop rhizomes 2 to 4 inches deep. They can be planted horizontally, or vertically with buds pointing up — if roots have already started, they should be pointing down. Mound the soil over the planting slightly, and if you wish, mulch with clean hay or wood chips to keep the soil moist and to prevent weed growth. The first shoots should emerge in a week or two, though if temperatures remain cool, it can take up to 3 weeks.

Once the shoots appear they should grow quickly, and will climb (see Trellising for Hops, page 176). Although most of the first-year growth will happen underground as the young plant is developing its root system, if the plant gets a healthy start, you could see growth of 6 to 12 feet in the first year.

Because hops are a long-lived perennial, they do well when cared for in a manner similar to fruit trees or shrubs. Feed the vines annually by top dressing with good compost, or with an organic vegetable fertilizer of the slow-release variety. A periodic watering with compost tea throughout the season will help supplement this and encourage healthy, disease-resistant plants. Apply mulch over the root zone to discourage weeds and keep the soil moist. Avoid piling mulch over the crown and right up to the stem, as this can promote molds, diseases, and pests. Mulches that break down quickly, such as shredded paper or straw, are preferable, but wood chips can also be used.

HOP PESTS AND DISEASES

The first defense against disease and pests is to grow the healthiest plants possible, because healthy plants have a natural resistance. Trimming back the lower foliage and excess bines helps prevent diseases such as powdery mildew and downy mildew that spread in damp conditions. However, even healthy hops do attract a variety of pests and are prone to some serious diseases, which is why conventional hop crops are heavily sprayed. Fortunately, there are many ways to deal with pests and disease without resorting to chemical treatments.

Here are some basic guidelines for treating problems that might arise if you grow hops. Most good gardening or hop-growing guides have more detailed information about treating pests and diseases organically. I recommend *The New Organic Grower*, by Eliot Coleman, and *The Homebrewer's Garden* by Joe and Dennis Fisher.

Powdery mildew shows up early in the season as white powdery patches on the leaves. Infected cones turn a reddish color. Remove diseased vines immediately, and destroy them by burning or burying away from gardening areas. Keep remaining plants dry. Direct sunlight will inhibit further growth. Heavy fertilizer that is high in nitrogen encourages the spread of this disease, so slow-release nitrogen sources are best. Sulfur-based fungicides are effective at controlling the spread of powdery mildew, especially if applied early. Look for brands that comply with organic regulations (often indicated by the Organic Materials Review Institute's OMRI Listed Seal).

Downy mildew first affects bines or young shoots, appearing as a black or silvery mildew and stunting growth. If not treated early on, the leaves can develop black patches and the hop cones can become infected, making them unusable. The best treatment is to remove infected shoots as soon as they appear and prune the entire plant so plenty of air and light can reach all areas. Copper sulfate is an effective treatment if the mildew continues to spread after removal of infected bines.

Aphids love hops, especially when they are flowering, and can wreak havoc if not kept in check. Ladybugs, lacewings, and aphid midges are excellent natural predators. Insecticidal soap is effective at controlling aphids, but its use should be limited to heavy infestations as it can also hurt beneficial insects in the process. A good regimen is to encourage beneficial insects and use sprays on any sections of the plant that become heavily infested with aphids. Patches of aphids can also be blasted off with water, but be careful not to damage your hops in the process!

Spider mites can become a problem in hot, dry climates, as they build up large populations and suck the juices out of the leaves, making the plants prone to disease and reducing yields. These tiny insects can be detected by the fine silk webs they attach to the underside of leaves, which may also show signs of damage from these pests. Neem oil and pyrethrum spray are effective organic treatments. Removing excess bines and lower leaves can help prevent spider mites from becoming too populous.

HARVESTING HOPS

Determining the exact time to harvest your hops is a little tricky, but if you trust your sense of smell, you will get the hang of it. Picking fresh hops is the best part of the whole process — it is a rare brewer who doesn't love that smell! The hop cones are ripe when the green cones have just started to yellow and dry out and have fully developed lupulin, the little balls of aromatic oils that give hops their aroma and bittering qualities. The lupulin glands start out as a pale gold and develop into a deep yellow gold when fully ripe.

When a ripe hop cone is crushed between your fingers, the lupulin glands break open, releasing their aroma essence. Crush a cone and take a deep whiff, and you will know they are ripe by the strong heady smell that you can't wait to add to your next brew! When in doubt, it is better to err slightly on the side of less ripeness. If hops overripen, the oils can go rancid more quickly, and the hops will become too dried out and will crumble easily.

Depending on the size of your harvest, you have two options for picking the hops. If you just have a few plants, you can pick them by hand. The advantage to this is that you will have a larger harvest, as the cones do not all ripen at exactly the same time. Picking several times over a week or two allows you to select more hops at the perfect stage of ripeness, but it takes longer, especially if the hops are trellised really high. For larger harvests the faster method is to cut down the entire hop bine, twine and all. Then you can strip the hops off the bines at ground level, perhaps sharing the task with a friend or two with a few homebrews to help make the task a pleasant one.

However you harvest, pick on a clear day after several days without rain, if at all possible. Damp hops are harder to pick, and the cones will be harder to dry. Once the hops are picked, they need to be dried for long-term storage.

DRYING HOPS

The more quickly the hops are dried the better, because the delicate essential oils will be properly preserved, giving you the highest-quality hops possible. Home growers dealing with less than a pound of hops have many options that don't call for a large investment. Although solar-heated drying is the ideal method for eco-brewers, the actual area used for drying should be out of direct sunlight because UV light can damage the delicate lupulin glands.

On a hot, dry fall day, an attic or garage is an ideal location, especially if temperatures heat up to 100°F (38°C) or more. Whatever method you use, spread the hops in a shallow layer evenly over flat screens, burlap sacks, or, in a pinch, some brown paper shopping bags, cut open, and stir them a few times during the day. Ideally, the hops should have air circulation underneath to speed the drying time and prevent decay. The temperature should be kept below 140°F (60°C), ruling out most ovens.

continued on page 178

Trellising for Hops

Hop vines need a trellis system to climb on. Commercial growers typically have trellises that are 18 feet high for standard varieties. Dwarf varieties can have a shorter trellis system. Plan for your trellis to be at least 12 feet high, remembering that newly established plants will take a couple of years before attaining full growth each season.

There are many ways to build a trellis system. Hops like to grow up, and you will have the highest yields from your hop plants with a vertical trellis system, but if you do not have a suitable location, they can be trained to grow horizontally. A backyard arbor or pergola can be a lovely way to train the vines up and across a lattice system that provides a pleasant-smelling shady area for summertime relaxing.

Here is an inexpensive and easily installed system that works in a limited space: Plant the hops in a circle around a tall, well-anchored pole. The pole should be at least 3 inches in diameter if up to 10 feet long, and larger if over 10 feet. The diameter of the circle will depend on the number of plants, which should be spaced 2 to 3 feet apart. Plant different varieties at least 6 feet away from each other to keep them from commingling over the years. The pole is supported by diagonal lines — made from heavy twine, rope, or steel cable — anchored

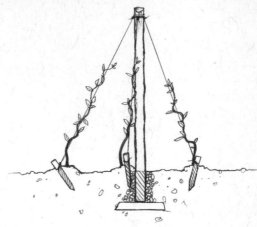

Tepee system

around the circle like a tepee. The drawback with a tepee-shaped trellis is that most hop flowers occur at the top where all the lines meet at the center, so it will become a tangled mess, and it will be difficult to keep different varieties separated.

A two-pole system is a good way to keep the hop plants separated, and it gives the vines more room to grow at the top. A full-size hop trellis system like this can cost hundreds of dollars to install, so for many home growers it is overkill, but if you love to grow things and you love hops, it may be worth the investment, especially when you consider you can count on at least 15 years of plentiful hops if you establish healthy plants in a good spot.

If you brew hoppy beers once a month, over 15 years you could easily save over $700 on hop purchases by growing your own. A two-pole system

will cost a fraction of this amount if you do the work yourself.

To build this trellis system, place two poles at each end of the row. For very long rows additional poles may be needed so that there is a pole every 20 feet or so. Anchor the poles with sturdy cables and buried anchors strong enough to bear the weight of the poles, the cables, and the fully mature hops.

Once the poles are strung and anchored cables are strung from pole to pole and winched tight, plant the hops every 4 to 5 feet, stringing twine from each plant up to the wires. A mature hop plant will produce lots of bines (the long stem of the plant that does the climbing), and you can maximize yield from each plant by running two lengths of twine from

each plant up to the overhead wire in a V shape.

Whatever system you use, it is important to establish the trellis system in the first season just before or after planting. Although the hops might not grow to full height in the first year as they are developing a root system, having the system in place when you plant prevents damage to established root systems and ensures your trellis is in place when the hops start to grow and climb.

In hot sunny weather it is not uncommon for the vines to grow more than 6 inches a day! You don't want to wind up scrambling to prop them up haphazardly while they are in full growth mode. Once the trellis is up and the rhizomes are planted, all you need to worry about are weeds and pests.

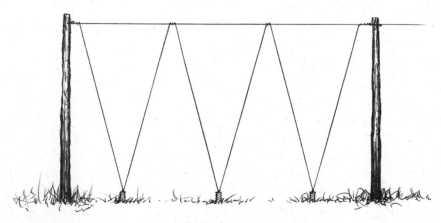

Two-pole system

A gas oven with a pilot light can work, as most of these maintain temperatures of 80 to 100°F (27–38°C). The electric light that comes with many ovens is also a slight heat source, thus an electric oven can be used as a warm drying area if the light is left on and the door closed.

Screens placed on top of sawhorses with a fan positioned underneath so air flows up from the bottom of the screen and through the hops will speed drying considerably. Another good option is a food dehydrator, if you have one. It is possible to use a clothes dryer, on a very low- or no-heat setting, if you have a rack that can be placed inside that does not rotate. Otherwise, the hops will be agitated too much and most of the lupulin glands (the good stuff!) will be broken up and lost.

A solar dryer can be used, but some degradation of quality may occur if the hops are exposed to direct sunlight. One design has racks for the food in an enclosed chimney, shielded from direct light, with the solar heat collector located below the chimney so the warm air is drawn up and through the collector by heat convection. It is a very efficient design that requires no fans or any kind of electricity, just a hot, sunny day. Perfect for drying hops!

Using Wet Hops

If you want to brew a wet-hopped beer with your fresh-picked hops, you should use them right away or seal them in airtight bags or jars and freeze them until brew day. When brewing with wet hops, you will need 4 to 6 times more wet hops by weight than dry hops called for in your recipe. If your recipe calls for 2 ounces of dry hops, you should use 8 ounces of wet.

Caution is advised, however, as using too many wet hops can impart a vegetable or grassy flavor to the beer. Most successful wet-hopped beers call for adding wet hops at the end of the boil and sticking to dried hops for bittering.

STORING HOPS

Hops must be stored away from light, heat, and oxygen to preserve maximum flavor. See details on page 35.

Growing Barley

Barley is a relatively easy crop to grow. It thrives in most temperate regions of the world. It was one of the first crops to be cultivated by humans, adding weight to the theory that early humanity abandoned its hunting and gathering lifestyle in favor of the agrarian way of life, all for the love of beer. Barley loves cool weather but can be grown in warmer regions as a winter crop. There are many varieties of barley; though only a few are typically grown for brewing, all varieties can be malted and used for brewing.

Barley is an excellent crop for a homebrewer's garden because it is easy to tend by hand, and barley that is malted for brewing does not need to be hulled. When choosing a variety, look for ones that grow well in your climate, especially those that have better resistance to local diseases. Local farm stores, farming forums, or the nearest USDA Cooperative Extension are good places to seek out information. A nearby university with an agricultural program can also be a valuable source of information. The USDA website has a locator tool that will help you find the Extension closest to you.

Seek out varieties that are easily hand threshed. Threshing is the process of removing the grains from the rest of the plant, which is usually done by machine in commercial settings but can be done by hand. If you are able to obtain a barley classified for malting, such as Harrington, Maris Otter, or two-row Klages, definitely do so! For the first few seasons, it is a good strategy to try a few different varieties so you can learn which does well in your plot. Save seeds from your first few successful crops for future plantings.

Why look for malting barley varieties instead of just growing a local feed variety? Good-quality malting barley is bred to have a low protein content, because high protein levels can cause problems with beer quality. Conversely, barley bred for food for humans and animals tends to have a high protein content. Malting barley also has naturally high enzyme activity, which is very desirable from a malting and mashing perspective. Many malting barley varieties also have low beta-glucan levels, which is preferred for better brewing mechanics and beer quality.

CHOOSING THE RIGHT BARLEY

It is helpful to understand a few of the differences between varieties of barley so you can choose the type that best suits your needs. There are three main classifications for barley. Each variety has a combination of the following characteristics; for instance, six-row, hull-less, and bearded.

Two-row or six-row. The number refers to the rows of kernels on each head of grain. Six-row is often favored for malting in the United States, while two-row is preferred in other parts of the world. Most two-row malts produce a slightly higher yield (1 or 2 percent) of malt sugar, although the differences between modern two- and six-row malting barley grown in the United States

Determining Alpha Acid Levels

Brewing with homegrown hops usually requires a little educated guesswork because the alpha acid levels are not known unless you have them tested. As long as the variety is known, you can look up the alpha acid range for that variety and work with an average of that number. The hop chart in chapter 9 lists most hop varieties and the typical alpha acid range for each.

After you have been brewing with homegrown hops for a few seasons, you will get the hang of brewing without the numbers — just as brewers did before laboratory analysis was an option. If using your own hops for bitterness, it is prudent to err on the low side, adding a small amount to the boil, then tasting halfway through the boil. If more bitterness is needed, a few more grams can be added. Adding bitterness is much easier than removing it, which can only really be done by dilution or blending with a very mild beer.

With homegrown hops, it is usually impractical to have them tested unless you grow a large quantity of a single variety. Most lab testing costs over $30 per sample, shipping not included. (See Resources.)

are so slight as to be almost negligible. Most six-row barley has a higher protein content, which can cause lower malt yields, erratic germination times, and increased soluble protein in the beer, which can cause haze problems. Six-row malts tend to have a higher enzyme level, which is a good thing when brewing with a large quantity of unmalted grains.

For home malting purposes the differences between the two types are slight enough to be almost unnoticeable, but two-row barley is arguably easier to work with, since the individual kernels tend to be larger and more uniform in size.

Hulled or hull-less. Most barley has a hull or thin husk that is tightly wrapped around each kernel. This hull is extremely difficult to remove. Most equipment that is used to remove the hull removes a significant portion of the nutrients as well. Although hull-less barley is easier for home growers to work with if growing barley for food, barley that is going to be malted should have a thin, tight-fitting husk. This husk protects the integrity of the kernel as it goes through the various stages of malting and helps to create a filter bed when lautering. A thinner husk is preferred because too much husk material can lead to astringent flavors in finished beer due to higher levels of polyphenols, or tannins, that are more concentrated in the husk than in the seed itself.

Bearded or beardless. Some varieties have 3-inch-long spikes called beards or awns that protrude from the top of each kernel on the seed head. These are the plant's defensive mechanism to poke a critter in the eye if it tries to eat the grain. Most malting barley varieties are bearded. The beards are removed before malting and do not play a significant role in the use of barley for malting purposes, but for a home grower they can be a nuisance when working closely with the plants before threshing. Beardless varieties of barley have been bred primarily as livestock fodder crops so livestock can eat the barley while it is growing in the pasture. These beardless varieties can certainly be malted but will probably not produce the highest quality malt.

PLANTING BARLEY

Barley grows well in reasonably fertile, well-drained soil on the alkaline side, with a pH of 7.0 to 8.0. It does not do well if pH levels are under 6.0. The soil

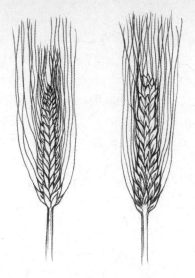

Two-row and six-row barley

should have a good amount of calcium, phosphorus, and potassium, which can be determined by a soil test. Soil that is deficient in these minerals can be amended before planting. Avoid adding excess nitrogen, which can cause very healthy bright green young plants that ultimately yield little grain.

Growing and malting barley require a significant time commitment. First-time grain growers should start with a modest 100-square-foot plot. By starting small you can keep the project fun and manageable while you learn the process. With 100 square feet you can expect a yield of 5 to 24 pounds of barley: enough for one or two batches of homebrewed (and homegrown) beer!

In cooler and temperate climates, plant barley in the spring after heavy frost danger has passed. If planting it as a winter crop in warmer areas, sow the seed at least 3 weeks before the first frost so the plants have time to become established before winter sets in. The soil should be lightly tilled before planting. Barley can be planted in rows or in solid blocks. Solid blocks help suppress weeds and can give higher yields but are difficult to weed without damaging the barley. A good compromise is to plant several rows 2 to 3 feet wide with enough space in between for you to work each bed.

Sow barley seeds by hand or with a hand-cranked spreader at a rate of about 4 ounces of seed per 100 square feet. Use a rake to lightly cover the seeds with soil, and water well. I have had good results by loosely covering the planting with seedless straw or hay to provide a little protection from birds and keep the soil moist until the seedlings are established. Once the seedlings are a few inches in height, thin them to 4 to 6 inches apart. While the barley is growing, pull weeds and water as needed. Once the plants reach their full height, the crop will block the light and keep new weeds from growing.

Most barley crops reach maturity in 90 to 100 days, although over-wintered crops can take several months longer, as the plants become dormant during the coldest, darkest months. Dormant plants start to show renewed bright green growth in the early spring and will be ready to harvest about 2 months after this renewed growth begins. As the barley reaches maturity, the plant dries out and the seed head starts to deepen in color.

As harvest time draws near, it is important to stop all irrigation. A good rule of thumb is to stop watering when at least 80 percent of the grain has turned golden. To test for harvest readiness, break open a seed head in your hand. The seeds should pop out from the husk easily, and individual kernels will harden to the point where they will remain dented when pressed by a fingernail, instead of springing back as they do when they are still too wet to harvest.

HARVESTING AND THRESHING

Harvest your barley by cutting the plants down at the base of the stalk. There are many methods of doing this. The traditional small-scale method is to cut the stalks with a scythe. A more modern approach is to use an electric weed trimmer. In a pinch a pair of gardening shears can be used, although this will take the most time. Whatever the method, the goal is to cut each plant at the base, leaving the stalks intact so they can be bundled into sheaves.

Gather the cut grain into bundles about 6 inches in diameter, and bind each one with cord about halfway up the stalk so the grain heads hang loose enough to allow air circulation to facilitate efficient drying. Prop the sheaves up in a circle against each other to form a shock. Cover the shock with burlap or other loosely woven cloth to prevent birds from eating the grain. Keeping the grains dry during this period is critical, so if rain is forecast, move the shocks into a shed or a garage to finish drying, or cover them with a water-proof tarp.

In most cases drying time for a barley crop is a few days, but in humid areas it can take a week. The grain must be adequately dried before it can be easily separated from the husks. Some varieties separate more easily than others, but most varieties will separate freely when crushed by hand if they are dry enough for threshing.

Threshing by hand is labor intensive. The basic procedure is to pound the grain with enough force to dislodge the individual kernels from the husks. This can be done by striking the sheaves with a flail or bat or broomstick, or by striking them against a wall or the side of a drum, or by stomping on them in a shallow box. Whatever method you choose, have a ground cloth, barrel, or box in place to capture the kernels as they are released from the husks.

Once all the grains have been threshed out of the sheaves, remove the straw — it makes great bedding for a chicken coop or mulch for hop plants. Winnow the chaff by pouring it from one container to another in a windy spot or in front of a fan so the heavy grains fall into the container and the lighter chaff and bits of straw are blown away.

Barley shocks drying

Malting Barley

Good malting barley is high in starch and relatively low in protein and is usually characterized by a large plump kernel. The barley must be modified, through the process of malting, to a form that is high in natural enzymes that can easily convert the starch into fermentable sugars. Malting is the process of sprouting grains to a point at which the natural enzymatic activity level is high and starts to convert complex starch stored in the seed to simple starches and sugars to feed the young seedlings. The sprouting is arrested at peak activity by drying out the grains. If the malt is dried at low temperatures, the enzymes remain viable and can be reactivated easily by rewetting the grains and holding them at optimal temperatures.

It is relatively easy to produce your own barley malt on a small scale, but creating world-class malt is a science that will challenge the limits of even the most ingenious homebrewer. From a sustainability point of view, the idea of making your own "estate"-produced homebrew is the ultimate way to reduce your eco-brewing environmental footprint in addition to the pure romance of the undertaking! Set your sights on a reasonable goal of producing a decent base malt with the understanding that the high-quality, evenly kilned malt available to most brewers today requires sophisticated equipment with precise temperature control, moisture meters, and rotating drums.

A STEP-BY-STEP GUIDE TO MALTING

If you approach your first malting project as a learning experience and work with a small quantity of grain, you will not have to worry so much about equipment and you will be able to focus on the process itself. Doing a test run of a pound or so will give you a better idea of what equipment you need if you decide to do it on a regular basis.

You can malt a pound or two of grain with a kitchen colander, mixing bowl, or steep-sided baking pan, and baker's sheet pans or cookie sheets for drying the grain. After a test run, you can step up to a scale you are comfortable working with. In my experience a 10- to 15-pound batch is manageable, yields enough for a batch of grain, and does not require a big investment of time and money in equipment to malt larger batches.

The system described here can be used to malt 5 to 15 pounds of barley or other grains. For more than that, you would need a larger system. Kilning larger batches is a challenge, because all the malt must be kilned at the same time to reach the proper level of modification. It is far easier to increase the capacity of the germination chambers or beds than it is to increase the capacity of the kiln. To make additional malt it might be more practical to run batches through the system in stages, or make two germination chambers and stagger the batches every 3 or 4 days until you have the amount of malt you want. This system can also be used to malt grains other than barley, an important feature for making gluten-free beer.

STEP 1. WEIGH THE GRAIN

The malting process takes 4 to 7 days. During this time the grains gain about twice their weight in water and lose it again when the malt is dried. If you don't have a moisture meter, you need to record the starting weight of the barley. When the final weight of the dried barley is the same as the starting weight or slightly less, you will know it is properly dried. With this method it is important to account for any losses due to spillage or the removal of chaff and debris.

Keeping a batch log allows you to duplicate successes, and the entries can help you identify anything that went wrong. Record each action and the corresponding environmental conditions; for instance, the length and temperature of soak time, the time the rootlets first emerge, and temperatures and duration of kilning.

STEP 2. CLEAN AND SOAK THE GRAIN

Place the grain in a clean 5-gallon bucket or any container large enough to hold it all with at least 2 inches of water covering it. It is not necessary to sterilize the container. Underdeveloped kernels, bits of chaff, stalks, and other foreign matter will float on the surface of the water, while the heavier grains will sink to the bottom. Agitate the grains with a long spoon to dislodge the debris, allow to settle briefly, then decant the water. Rinse this way several times until the water runs clear.

Brew Tip

YOU DON'T HAVE TO GROW YOUR OWN BARLEY, but you can buy unmalted barley and still malt your own. As long as the unmalted barley seeds are fresh enough to germinate, they can be malted. For best results use malting barley that is less than 1 year old.

If the volume of debris is significant and you are working with a large amount of grain, you might want to collect this debris, dry it, and weigh it, as the weight could be significant enough to influence the final ratio of raw barley to finished malt and thus could be a factor in determining if the malt has been dried sufficiently.

Once the water runs clear, drain off as much water as possible and refill the bucket so the barley is covered by at least 2 inches of water. This water should be unchlorinated if possible (it is okay to rinse with chlorinated water if more convenient). Soak the grains for several hours, then drain by pouring into a second bucket drilled with holes (the germinating chamber). Transfer the grain back to the solid bucket, and refill with fresh unchlorinated water.

This initial soak helps to remove excess impurities and refreshes oxygen levels, which can help early germination of the grains. After the initial rinse allow the grains to soak for an additional 6 to 12 hours. After a maximum of 12 hours total soaking time, rinse the grains one more time, then drain completely and keep them in the germinating chamber with the lid firmly sealed.

The soaking temperature is important. If temperatures are too low, the barley will not germinate or will grow too slowly. Temperatures that are too high will lead to rapid growth and will diminish the quality of the resulting malt. Overly warm temperatures can also encourage the rapid growth of molds and fungi. Keep the temperature as close to 50°F (10°C) as possible, avoiding temperatures that exceed 60°F (16°C).

STEP 3. GERMINATION AND RINSING

Keep the freshly rinsed barley in the germination chamber throughout the germination process. Barley prefers a germination temperature of about 50°F (10°C), so maintaining a temperature as close to this as possible will give you the best results. If you live in a really warm climate, you may need to use a temperature-controlled refrigerator, a cooler with ice, or a swamp-cooling arrangement. Warmer temperatures will dramatically increase the rate of germination, so if you must work at higher temperatures, monitor the sprouting progress carefully so you can stop the process at the right point.

Frequent rinsing and mixing will help ensure an even germination by maintaining the moisture level. Use a garden hose or sink faucet sprayer to

Germination chamber

thoroughly wet the grains each time you rinse them. Alternatively, you can dump the grains into a solid bucket, fill the bucket until the grains are just covered, then dump them back into the germination chamber to drain. Ideally, the grains should be rinsed and turned every four hours. This is impractical unless malting your own barley is important enough to make you get out of bed two or three times a night for a week! I have had good results with rinsing and turning right before going to bed, then again first thing in the morning. Try to rinse and turn the grains at least four times a day.

STEP 4. TEST FOR FULL MODIFICATION

The first sign of germination is the appearance of tiny rootlets (called *chits*) that emerge from the ends of the grains. This occurs just a day or two after the soaking period ends. Once the rootlets are visible, they grow quickly, and the development of the acrospire should be checked every four hours. The acrospire is the shoot that starts inside the grain and eventually becomes the first leaves of the barley plant. To check it, select a few kernels and slice them open lengthwise — you're looking for the greenish shoot that runs up the back side of the grain. As it develops, it grows towards the pointy end of the grain.

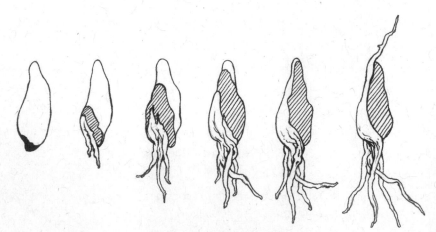

Grains sprouting over 4–5 days

Equipment Needed for Malting Small Batches

- **5-gallon food-grade plastic bucket** for soaking the grain

- **Germinating chamber:** a second 5-gallon bucket drilled with numerous small holes (1/16 inch or 3/32 inch in diameter, spaced 1/2 inch to 1 inch apart) to strain the grains after rinsing and to hold sprouting grain.

  This bucket must have a tight-fitting lid, also drilled with many small holes. This facilitates good aeration and allows for the chamber to be rotated frequently so the kernels are evenly mixed, ensuring equal temperature, moisture, and oxygen levels.

- **Good-quality thermometer**

- **Malt kiln:** This can be a food dehydrator, solar dryer, convection oven with low-heat setting, clothes dryer with a low-heat setting, or, if you get really serious, a homemade malt kiln capable of maintaining temperatures of 100 to 180°F (38–82°C).

  If you only plan to produce base malt, your malt kiln only needs to reach 120°F (49°C) maximum. You can finish crystallized malts (caramel through black) in a home oven.

- **Oasting boards:** An oast house is a traditional hops-drying kiln and these are drying screens made from aluminum or stainless steel screening on wire or metal frames. Wood frames can be used for low-temperature kilning of base malt but should not be used at temperatures higher than 125°F (52°C). The frames can be sized to fit inside the oven or drying chamber you will be using, or they can simply rest on oven or barbecue racks.

  Heavy-duty galvanized fencing can be used to reinforce the screens. Screen material on its own is too flimsy to support the weight of the malt.

- **Optional, but helpful:** a moisture meter capable of reading moisture content as a percentage of total moisture. Small digital meters for home use are available for thirty to fifty dollars from many online outlets.

Malt is considered fully modified when that shoot is between ⅔ and ⁹⁄₁₀ of the length of the kernel. The exact level of development will vary between individual grains, which is why you should test several kernels each time, then guesstimate the average development to determine the best point at which to stop the germination.

STEP 5. KILN THE MALT

Once the malt has reached full modification, the growing process must be stopped as quickly as possible by drying the malt out in a kiln. For most base malts the ideal drying temperature is between 100 and 120°F (38 and 49°C). Air circulation is critical to the drying process. If the malts are simply placed in a warm environment, they will dry too slowly and start to cook. This can result in lower enzyme levels, as well as further germination, which will lower the potential yield when mashing.

There are several options for kilning grain; the method you choose will depend on what equipment you have available or decide to purchase. You can use a convection oven if it is possible to turn on the convection feature without turning on the heat. The lowest setting on most home ovens (both electric and gas) is too high for kilning malt, but it might be possible to control the temperature of an electric oven with the type of digital temperature controller used for controlling fermentation temperatures. Some homebrewers kiln their malt by placing it in burlap or cotton sacks and running it in the clothes dryer with the low-heat setting. Before doing this, test the temperature of your dryer's low setting; if the temperature exceeds 125°F (52°C), it could destroy too many enzymes and produce a substandard malt.

If you are serious about producing your own malt and hops, a convection solar food dryer is a good investment. A well-designed solar food dryer has venting controls that allow you to adjust the airflow and thus the drying temperatures. Most solar food dryers achieve temperatures between 100 and 130°F (38 and 54°C), which is well suited to kilning base malt. Of course, a solar dehydrator requires a good sunny day to operate properly, and the weather does not always cooperate with your malting schedule. In a pinch a small electric heater can be placed near the intake vent of the solar dryer to push warm air into the dryer and ensure your malt dries on schedule.

If a solar food dehydrator is not an option, you can use an electric food dehydrator. Most home food dehydrators are quite small; thus, several drying sessions may be required to dry a batch of malt. It might be a good idea to match your malt batch size to the capacity of your food dehydrator. Otherwise, you will have fully modified malt that continues to grow while the first load is being dried. Most home dehydrators operate in a temperature range of 120 to 130°F (49–54°C). This is a little higher than the ideal, but it is acceptable, and most of the starch-converting enzymes will be preserved.

More elaborate options exist, from modifying smokers with heat elements and fans to converting a defunct refrigerator to a kiln by pumping hot air through it with a fan. Check online forums for discussions of various methods.

Whatever the drying method, the end result should be malt that has been dried to a level below 5 percent. Too much moisture in the finished malt can lead to a multitude of problems, from mold and mildew to too-rapid degradation of enzymes during storage. When the grain appears dry (this can take anywhere from a few hours to 48 hours depending on the temperature, airflow, and quantity of malt being dried), check the moisture level with the moisture meter. If it is too high, continue drying until the moisture level is firmly below 5 percent, checking the level every 30 minutes or so.

If you do not have a moisture meter, remove the grain when you think it is dry enough, and weigh it. If it weighs more than the starting weight, place it back on the drying screens and continue the kilning process until it is dried adequately. It is better to dry the malt too much than to stop the kilning before it is dry enough.

STEP 6. POLISH AND CONDITION THE MALT

After the malt is dry, rootlets and excess husk material are still attached to the grains. These should be removed because too much of this type of material can cause astringent flavors in your beer. If the malt was kilned in a clothes dryer, this debris was probably already dislodged and can simply be removed by winnowing, as you did with the threshed grains. If rootlets and loose husk bits are still clinging to the grains, gentle friction is the best way to remove them. You want to avoid hitting the dried malt with too much pressure, as this could cause the kernels to break open, which will reduce storage life and potential yields.

You can rub the grains together a handful at a time, but this is a tedious and potentially painful process. It's easier to put the grain in your thoroughly cleaned and dried germination chamber and vigorously agitate it for a few minutes to polish off the debris. Whatever your method, chances are the results won't be perfect. This is okay, as you just want to remove the majority of the excess material. Whatever does not fall through the holes of the germination chamber can be removed by winnowing.

Once the finished malt is polished, it should be stored in a dry place in a sack or airtight container for at least 2 weeks before you brew with it. This conditioning period is essential for the newly made malt to mellow. If you brew with it right away, the resulting beer is likely to be a bit harsh or "green" tasting. This is one situation where green is not necessarily a good thing!

The hobby of home malting has slowly gained popularity in the past few years. Some of the increase in interest has been inspired by a growing demand for gluten-free beer, spurring a desire to produce beer from uncommon ingredients like quinoa, buckwheat, and millet.

Kilning Specialty Malt

Specialty malts such as caramel or crystal malts and chocolate malts are processed differently from the lighter base malts. The wet malt is heated to starch-conversion temperatures before being dried in a kiln; then it is kilned at higher temperatures to develop the darker colors.

By the time barley has reached full modification, it has dried out too much for the starch conversion to be completely effective inside the grain. Consequently, once it reaches the kilning stage, it should first be soaked in clean filtered water for 4 to 8 hours before the grain is "mashed." After soaking, strain the grains and allow to drain for 15 to 20 minutes; then transfer them to a baking tray with high sides. A sheet-cake pan or casserole dish works well. The grains should be 2 to 3 inches deep, with enough room in the pan for occasional stirring.

Heat the oven to 160 to 170°F (71–77°C), and place a pan of water in the oven to create a moist environment during the starch-conversion stage. Cook the grains at this temperature for 60 to 90 minutes, or until starch conversion is complete. Stir the grains every 15 to 20 minutes to ensure the temperature is evenly distributed and the grains do not dry out too much at this stage. Use a good oven-safe thermometer to monitor the temperature in the grains, and adjust the oven temperature or stir more frequently if needed to maintain a temperature of 160 °F. A digital thermometer with a remote sensing probe and ovenproof cord is a great tool for this job. Make sure to maintain the water level in the pan of water in the oven throughout the starch-conversion stage.

It takes some practice and experience to know exactly when the starch conversion is complete, but you can check the progress by opening a few kernels every 15 minutes after the first hour has passed. The insides will go from a milky appearance to a more translucent one. They will taste very sweet instantly, instead of gradually sweetening in your mouth like malt does as the enzymes in your saliva convert the starch to sugar. If in doubt, it does not hurt to continue cooking the grains at a constant temperature of 160°F (71°C) for up to 2 hours. After 2 hours it is unlikely that any further starch conversion is going to happen.

LIGHT CRYSTAL MALTS

Once the grains have been converted, move them to a large shallow pan for kilning. The grains should be spread out in a layer about 1 inch deep. Remove the pan of water, and raise the oven temperature to 225°F (107°C). A convection oven speeds up the drying process considerably. Roast the grains, stirring every 20 to 30 minutes so they will dry out evenly.

The goal with this stage is to dry the malt without adding very much color. At this temperature you will have a light crystal malt after about 2 hours. This 2-hour kilning should be done for all color levels of crystal and chocolate malt and will result in a light crystal malt of 15 to 20 degrees Lovibond. If you want a crystal malt lighter than this, kiln the grains at a lower temperature (200 to 210°F [93–99°C]) for a bit longer than 2 hours. For darker crystal and chocolate malts, continue roasting past the 2-hour mark, as described below for each malt.

It is helpful to have a Lovibond color chart handy for monitoring the color. A digital version of the chart can be found online at many sites; I like the one published by the Screwy Brewer.

If you kiln your own specialty malts often, it might be worth buying a printed version or printing one out with a high-grade color printer so you can hold it up next to your sample. Keep in mind that the grains will continue roasting with the residual heat for a few minutes after removal from the oven, so it is best to pull the grains when they are slightly lighter than the desired finished color. You will develop a better sense of timing on this as you gain experience roasting your own specialty malts.

Crystal/caramel 40°L. Increase oven temperature to 300°F (149°C) and continue roasting for about an hour. Stir every 20 to 30 minutes to promote even roasting. Check the color each time you stir.

Crystal/caramel 60°L. After the initial 2-hour drying cycle, roast at 325°F (163°C) for about an hour, stirring and checking the color until the desired hue has been reached.

Crystal/caramel 80–100°L. After the initial 2-hour drying cycle, roast at 350°F (177°C) for 60 to 90 minutes, stirring and checking the color until the desired hue has been reached.

Crystal/caramel 120–140°L. After the initial 2-hour drying cycle, roast at 375°F (191°C) for 60 to 120 minutes, stirring and checking the color until the desired hue has been reached.

Special B malt. Use a multistage roasting process to develop the deep raisin and fig notes that special B malt is known for. After the starch-conversion stage, transfer to a flat pan and spread the grains about 1 inch deep. Roast at 225°F (107°C) for 1 hour, stirring every 20 to 30 minutes. After 1 hour raise the temperature to 250°F (121°C), and roast for another hour, stirring with the same frequency as before.

Increase the temperature to 300°F (149°C), and roast for 30 minutes, stir, then raise the temperature to 375°F (191°C), and continue roasting and stirring until the malt has reached 140 to 150 degrees Lovibond. This will take 45 minutes to an hour. During this final, hottest roast cycle, use a spray bottle to mist the grains every 15 to 20 minutes, and stir after each spritzing.

Chocolate and black malt. After the initial 2-hour drying cycle, roast at 400°F (204°C) for 90 to 120 minutes, stirring and checking the color until the desired hue has been reached. It can help with darker malts to spritz the surface with water occasionally so the exteriors of the grains do not scorch. When the color gets close to the desired target, check the malt frequently, and stir more often. The color deepens quickly toward the end, and it is all too easy to overshoot the mark. With black malt it is a fine line between "black" and "burnt to a crisp"!

If you kiln dark malts in your home oven, you will need to have an effective smoke-removal fan above your appliance, because roasting malts this dark creates a lot of smoke. If this becomes a problem, you can minimize the smoke by only roasting a pound or two at a time. If you have an electric toaster oven, another option is to take it outside. You can also pan roast over a camp stove or a barbecue. Pan roasting requires almost constant stirring, and it is more difficult to control temperatures, but you can roast much more quickly (and thus more energy-efficiently) this way.

TOASTED MALTS

These malts are roasted in the kiln to darker levels than base malts, just like crystal malts. The main difference in procedure is that the grains are kiln dried before roasting to darker levels. This means you can make your own toasted malts even if you do not malt your own grain from scratch simply by toasting organic pale ale malt. The trick with toasting these malts is to keep the temperatures low enough so the enzymes are not completely destroyed, yet the malt color deepens and flavors become richer.

Dry-roasted malts have fantastic toasty and biscuity notes, but none of the cloying sweetness of caramelized malts, and they are essential to building recipes for many styles of beer. The roasting process browns the starches and proteins in the grains; this is known as the Maillard reaction. The reaction can be enhanced with the addition of moisture. For toasted malts with deeper flavors, a periodic spritzing of the grains with water will add deeper and sweeter accents to the toasted flavors.

Vienna, Munich, and aromatic malt. Toast the dry malt at 250°F (121°C) for 1 to 2 hours, or until desired color is reached. The longer the malt is toasted, the higher the enzyme loss will be. This may not be important if you will be mashing the malt with a high percentage of base malt. Vienna malt should be toasted to 4 to 6 degrees Lovibond, and Munich should be toasted to 10 degrees Lovibond for light Munich and 20 degrees for dark Munich or aromatic malt. For the darker malt you can spritz with a small amount of water, which will enhance the Maillard reaction and deepen the toasted flavors.

Amber, biscuit, and Victory malt. These stronger and darker malts impart a distinct fresh-baked bread or biscuit flavor and more color and sweetness. Toast dry malt at 325°F (163°C) for 30 to 60 minutes, spritzing with water and stirring once or twice to enhance the color and flavor. Finish at 25 to 30 degrees Lovibond.

Brown malt. A warm brown color and a rich, dark bready flavor and aroma characterize brown malt. This malt was traditionally used in porter recipes but is now hard to find commercially. A good reason to make your own! Toast in a 375°F (191°C) oven for 30 to 60 minutes, spritzing a few times during the process. Roast until the color reaches 50 to 60 degrees Lovibond.

Ovens vary in heat levels and efficiency. If your results are different from what you expected, try adjusting the temperature up or down. The placement of the racks can also influence the quality. If grains are getting scorched, try placing the pan on a lower rack. Roasting malt to perfection is challenging, especially when working with home ovens.

Malt houses use rotating drum kilns to roast specialty malts, which results in a higher level of quality control and a uniformity of color that is almost impossible to achieve with home equipment. If you have a rotisserie oven or gas grill, it is possible to fabricate a drum that can be installed and used to roast malts. You can even purchase drums for this purpose made for roasting nuts or coffee, which can be modified easily to accommodate the small kernel size of malt by lining the drum with some stainless steel screen.

After you roast malt, a long rest period is highly desirable to allow the flavors, which can be somewhat sharp or harsh with freshly roasted malts, to mellow. This might seem counterintuitive, but trust me. The rest time ensures that the harsher aromatics will dissipate. Commercial malt is typically aged for 4 to 6 weeks before being sold.

SMOKED MALT

If you are dedicated to using eco-friendly organic ingredients but love a rich, smoky Rauchbier, your best option is to smoke your own malt, since organic smoked malts are not commercially available as of this writing. If you have a home charcoal barbecue or a home smoker, this is not too difficult. The wood you choose will greatly influence the final flavor. For a milder flavor try alder, maple, or birch. For a sweeter, fruity flavor, apple or cherry wood are great. Most fruit trees add hints of flavor reminiscent of the fruits they produce. How about a smoky apricot ale? For an intense, pungent smoke flavor, go for oak or hickory. Hickory gives a distinct bacon flavor, however, so be careful!

Here's how to smoke your own malt at home:

Prepare the malt. Start with whole kernel pale or pilsner malt. The malt must be moistened to allow the grain to absorb the smoke flavors. Soak the malt in water for 5 to 10 minutes, then drain. You can also simply spritz the grain liberally with water. Place the malt in a loosely woven cloth sack — a very large grain bag or an old pillowcase works well, or you can pin or roughly stitch together some burlap or cotton to serve as a roasting bag. The fabric will be impregnated with smoke aroma by the time you are done, so save it to smoke future batches with. It will be useless for anything else! Alternatively, you can fashion a tray out of some aluminum or stainless steel screen.

Set up the smoker. If using a smoker, set it up with enough coals to last about 2 hours. If using a barbecue, you will need to devise a rack to hold a pan of water above the bed of coals. You can build a platform with bricks or make a ring to stand it on with some sturdy galvanized wire fencing. The water will help keep the temperature of the malt between 200 and 225°F (93 and 107°C). Closing the dampers to keep the airflow low during the smoking process will help maintain cooler temperatures.

Smoke the malt. Once the desired temperature is reached, add wood chips on top the coals and place the malt on the top grate over the water pan. Smoke for 1 to 2 hours. The wood chips will generate the most smoke if they don't ignite, which can be accomplished by soaking them in water, then wrapping them in a foil packet with a few holes punched in the top to allow the smoke to escape. Seal up the smoker, and let the smoke do its work.

For a mildly smoked malt, smoke for about an hour. To increase smoky flavors add additional wood chips and spritz the grains with water several times during the smoking process, and smoke for up to 2 hours. If you want really intense flavor, go ahead and smoke the malt longer than 2 hours. How far you go is really up to you, but I do advise caution when brewing with it for the first time, so you don't overwhelm the beer!

Dry and condition the malt. Spread the malt on a cookie sheet, and dry in a low oven, food dehydrator, or solar dryer until it contains less than 5 percent moisture. Seal it in airtight containers, and allow it to rest for a few weeks before brewing with it so the flavor is no longer rough around the edges.

MALTING OTHER GRAINS

Growing and harvesting cereal grains such as wheat, rye, and oats is very similar to cultivating barley. You can follow the same basic procedures outlined for barley, although you will find each crop to have slight differences that will affect how you handle each stage. Crops like corn, millet, amaranth, and quinoa are easy to grow and are well suited to hand harvesting. With amaranth, harvesting is as simple as holding the bushy seed head over a bin and rubbing the seeds out by hand.

If you plan on growing and harvesting a variety of grains, I highly recommend the book *Homegrown Whole Grains* by Sara Pitzer. Each variety is covered in good detail and includes low-cost harvesting and threshing methods that can be done by hand.

This chart (pages 199–200) offers basic guidelines for growing and malting a variety of grains. The same basic principles can be used to malt almost any kind of grain, though there are a few variables, including specific grain varieties, temperature, and viability of the grain (most influenced by how long it has been stored). In most cases the grains should be sprouted until just before the acrospire emerges from the seed, and kilned at the same temperatures and to the same moisture levels as barley malt. When working with a new grain, observe the malting process particularly closely.

Grain	Notes for growing	Average days to plant maturity	Best germination temperature for malting	Special considerations for malting
Amaranth	Plants grow 5–10 feet tall and love warm weather.	90–120	60–70°F (16–21°C)	Seeds are very tiny. Use a large sprouting jar with a fine-mesh screen or pack seeds loosely in a fine-mesh bag inside the germination chamber.
Buckwheat	Grows fast in poor soil but is not frost tolerant.	65–90	50–60°F (10–16°C)	One of the most popular grains for gluten-free brewing. It can reach full modification in as little as 2 days.
Corn	Grows best in blocks for good pollination.	60–120 depending on variety	60–70°F (16–21°C)	Not all corn seeds will sprout, and unviable seeds should be picked out. Unlike other grains, with corn the green shoot (acrospire) should grow 1 to 2 inches outside the kernel for the malt to have good conversion power.
Kamut	Similar to wheat, grows well in poor soil.	100–140	50–60°F (10–16°C)	Said to be used by ancient brewers. Higher in protein than wheat, so may not be best for brewing and yields will be lower.
Millet	Easy to grow, thrives in poor soil. Choose seed intended for grain crops rather than forage for the best yield and quality.	60–120	70–80°F (21–27°C)	A good choice for gluten-free brewing and widely used to brew beers in Africa, including the traditional Bantu beer.
Oats	Plant hull-less oats, as hulls are very difficult to remove.	90–120	40–60°F (4–16°C)	Risky to malt, because of toxin-generating fungus that can develop.*

Grain	Notes for growing	Average days to plant maturity	Best germination temperature for malting	Special considerations for malting
Quinoa	Easy to grow and harvest. Cut stalks and dry indoors if there is any chance of rain.	90–120	50–60°F (10–16°C)	Gluten-free malt with a nutty flavor. Change initial soak water often to flush away the saponins, which can cause a soapy flavor.
Rice	Difficult to grow in most home settings, except in bins on a small scale, because of the need for swampy conditions.	90–180	70–80°F (21–27°C)	Rice malts easily, but to do it properly you need unhulled rice, which is difficult to find. Polished rice will not germinate at all, but brown rice will.
Rye	A cool weather crop that grows best when planted in the fall.	100–120	40–50°F (4–10°C)	Risky to malt, because of toxin-generating fungus that can develop.*
Sorghum	Loves warm weather. The stalks can also produce fermentable sugars.	90–120	70–80°F (21–27°C)	Widely used in gluten-free brewing. Acrospires should be allowed to grow 1 to 2 inches long before kilning.
Spelt	A relative of wheat; grow and harvest as you would wheat or barley. High yielding.	110–140	50–60°F (10–16°C)	Follow barley malting procedures, but allow acrospire to reach full length of the grain.
Wheat	Easy to grow and malt. Loves well-drained soil.	120–140	50–60°F (10–16°C)	Wheat hulls are removed before malting, and the grains will sprout quickly, so germination times are much shorter than barley.

*Oats and rye can develop dangerous infections, especially ergot if the grain becomes infected with the *Claviceps purpurea* fungus. If you wish to try malting these grains, keep everything very clean and rinse the grains in a sanitizer such as hydrogen peroxide or distilled vinegar to reduce the risk. With any malting process, insufficient rinsing of the grains increases the risk of infection. If any black mold or very unpleasant odors develop in your grain while it is germinating, throw it out. To prevent poisoning livestock or infecting your own grain crops, it is advisable to sterilize the infected batch by burning or boiling it before disposing of it.

Making Fruit Beers

Fruit has been used in alcoholic beverages for about as long as humans have known how to ferment. Fermented fruit turns into wine or cider, depending on the fruit being used. Fruit wines (as opposed to wines made from grapes) usually have added sugar, while ciders do not. Fruit beers are a fantastic merger of wine or cider and beer. Fruit can bring a tart, refreshing zing to an everyday ale and can impart its unique flavor to other styles.

ADDING FRUIT TO BEERS

In most cases you want to brew with fruit that is fully ripe and at peak flavor, but don't use overripe fruit that is starting to rot. Perfectly ripe fruit with fully developed sugars will contribute more fermentables and impart the strongest fruit flavor to the beer.

A fermentation is a complex biological process that creates many different flavors. Delicate fruit flavors can be drowned out by complex flavors of malt, hops, and yeast. Fruit flavors can also be changed by the fermentation process. The intense bubbling of carbon dioxide and other gases through the beer during the primary can actually scrub some of the more volatile and aromatic fruit flavors right out of the beer.

For these reasons and more, it is often preferable to add fruit to the secondary fermentation rather than adding it at the end of the boil. With some recipes that call for large amounts of fruit, another option is to divide the fruit, adding some in the primary and reserving some for the secondary fermentation. This is a good practice because adding all of it to the secondary will trigger a vigorous referment, causing many of the finer flavors and aromas to be lost.

Fruit should be washed, and peeled if necessary (see notes with individual fruits that follow). Some fruit skins contain high levels of tannin, which can add too much bitterness and astringency. Soft fruit can simply be crushed or puréed. Chop hard fruit such as apples into very small chunks or juice it before adding. A food processor is a great tool for this.

In most cases it is important to remove the seeds before adding fruit to any fermentation. Very tiny seeds such as the ones found in berries are usually okay, but many larger seeds contain toxins such as arsenic and cyanide.

Stone fruits such as plums and cherries have the highest levels of these toxins, and extra care should be taken to make sure all seeds are removed before fermenting.

Almost all fruit skins host lively colonies of wild yeast and *Acetobacter* (vinegar-causing bacteria). These organisms are attracted to the natural sugars, and the potential for natural fermentation increases as the fruit ripens and any openings appear in the skin from birds, insects, or through damage when the fruit falls from the bush or tree. To prevent wild fermentations that can cause unpredictable flavors, and to keep the brew from going sour from *Acetobacter*, unpeeled fruit should be pasteurized (see Pasteurizing Fruit, page 205) or treated with sulfites before adding to the fermenter.

Sulfites are added to the crushed fruit before fermentation in the form of sodium or potassium metabisulfite. Check the package for the correct dosage levels. The yeast is usually added 12 to 24 hours after the sulfites, as the sulfites will kill the yeast unless allowed to dissipate. Just be aware of the potential for sulfite allergies in the intended consumers of your fruit beer.

Some brewers like to celebrate the wild and allow the natural wild yeast to inhabit a fermentation. If the idea of letting nature take its course appeals to you, this is certainly an option. The results are unpredictable but can be amazing. It is a brave step, considering the cost of ingredients, so if you become a wild fermentation brewer, you have my admiration!

FRUITS AND BERRIES FOR BEERS

Some fruits are either too expensive or too acidic or do not contain enough fermentable sugars to be effectively fermented alone as a cider or wine, but almost any fruit can be fermented, either on its own or as a flavor or adjunct in beer or mead. For example, citrus and pineapple are too acidic to ferment on their own but can be used to complement beers such as IPA, wheat, saison, or Belgian Wit. This list that follows is by no means exhaustive, but I have seen all these fruits used successfully in beers, both homebrewed and commercially brewed. The wonderful thing about brewing with fruit is that it greatly increases the variety of ingredients you can grow yourself or source from a local farmer.

Apples

More often used for cider, apples can also contribute character to a beer. A green apple lambic is an exceptional treat, and apples combine well with cranberry and orange peel in holiday beers (see Wailing Wassail Spiced Beer, page 287). Apples can be added to the fermenter in the form of juice or purée. Peel and seed apples before puréeing them; strain juice if needed. Most 5-gallon recipes call for 3 to 15 pounds, or the equivalent amount of juice (1 to 3 quarts), depending on the level of apple character desired.

Apricots and Other Stone Fruits

Apricot is a popular flavor, especially for wheat beer. Unfortunately, most modern commercial examples use extract or artificial flavor instead of real fruit. If you have never tasted a brew made with fresh apricots, you are in for a real treat! I once made a yellow plum ale that ranks up there as one of my best beers ever.

Stone fruits are easy to work with. Blanch them for about 1 minute in boiling water, then dump into cold water to loosen the skins and make them easy to slip off. Peel, remove the seeds, and crush by hand or purée. As long as you use sanitized or steam-sterilized kitchen utensils to process the fruit, it is not necessary to pasteurize it, but you can pasteurize the purée if you wish. Use 2 to 6 pounds of fruit for 5 gallons.

Bananas

Bananas can make an interesting beer — it is a traditional favorite in Rwanda, brewed with millet or sorghum. Since banana is a common flavor associated with certain types of wheat beer and Belgian yeasts, adding real banana to the recipe can accentuate this character. In the world of homebrew, the only limit to what you can try is your own imagination. How about chocolate banana porter, or banana nut brown?

Choose soft, ripe bananas that have not turned brown. Mash and add to the secondary fermenter. Pasteurize if desired. Another option is to chop finely and steep in a neutral alcohol such as vodka for about a week, then add to the secondary. Use 1 to 3 pounds of fresh bananas for 5 gallons.

Blackberries, Raspberries, and Other Caneberries

There are many varieties of these berries, each with its own special flavor that could make your next homebrew a memorable one. Blackberry stout and raspberry wheat are popular choices, but these berries could grace a wide range of beer styles, except perhaps the most hoppy beers. Clean berries well, and crush before adding to the secondary. Unless you have ample berry bushes growing wild in your area, berries can be quite expensive, so adding a few pounds to a secondary fermentation is the best method for extracting the most flavor. Freezing the berries can help improve flavor extraction, as it ruptures the fruit cell walls, causing the juices to release when thawed. For good berry flavor use 1 to 4 pounds of berries for 5 gallons.

Cherries

Ahhh, cherries — their flavor pairs so well with certain beers. Cherry porter is my personal favorite — the chocolate flavors of dark malts combined with the fruit are reminiscent of chocolate-covered cherries. Cherry lambic, cherry wheat, or a wood-aged cherry beer are all great choices. Sour cherries do well in Belgian and wheat styles, whereas sweet bing cherries or black cherries are wonderful in porters and stouts. Try using dried cherry for a deeper, sweeter cherry flavor.

Remove all pits and crush or purée, and add to the secondary fermentation. You can leave the skins on for a stronger flavor, but in that case pasteurization is recommended, especially for lighter beers. Peeling is tedious, but it is a little easier if you immerse them in boiling water for 30 seconds, then dip them in ice water immediately; the skins should slip off more easily. Use 1 to 4 pounds of cherries for 5 gallons.

Citrus Fruits

Most citrus is very acidic, and the juice by itself can make your beer taste more like rocket fuel than beer, so proceed with caution. Citrus peel, on the other hand, is widely used in brewing, although dried peel is more commonly used than fresh, which is a pity! Fresh citrus peel contains delicate volatile oils, many of which are lost when the peel is dried. The best part of the peel is the zest, the very outer layer that contains the color; the white pith is extremely bitter. Using the zest imparts the citrus essence without the bitterness.

Some beer styles, such as Belgian Wit, benefit from some sharpness, so if brewing a witbier with fresh orange peel, use the whole peel instead of the zest. Fresh peel is best added at the very end of the boil or in the secondary fermenter. If you want to add fresh juice to a beer, keep the quantity low so the

Pasteurizing Fruit

Before adding fruit to the primary fermenter, pasteurize it by adding it directly to the brew kettle at the end of the boil. Do not add fruit directly to the boil. Boiling fruit activates the natural pectins and will cause problems with cloudiness.

After the heat has been turned off, allow the wort to rest for 10 to 15 minutes, or until the temperature drops to under 180°F (82°C), before adding the fruit. Stir the fruit in well, cover, and allow to stand for a full 20 minutes before chilling the wort.

Before adding fruit to the secondary fermentation, pasteurize it on the stovetop. You may need to add a small amount of water to the chopped fruit so it does not burn. To pasteurize, gently heat in a stainless steel pot until the temperature reaches 170°F (77°C). Place a lid on the pan, remove from the heat, and cover with a towel

so the temperature holds at about 160°F (71°C) for 20 minutes. Once pasteurization is done, cool it to 70 to 75°F (21–24°C), then add to the fermenter.

Adding fruit at this stage causes a referment when the yeast is exposed to the fruit sugars; this may require racking the beer off the additional sediment and fruit particles before bottling. After adding fruit allow it to ferment for 5 to 7 days, then rack to a clean fermenter. For the best clarity, you can allow the beer to settle and clear for a few days after racking it off the fruit sediment and then bottling it.

A note about freezing: not all organisms that can contaminate a beer are killed by freezing, so freezing is not as effective as pasteurization, but if the fruit is peeled or cleaned very well first, it is an adequate method for all but the lightest, low-alcohol beers. Thaw frozen fruit before adding it.

body and sweetness of the beer are not compromised by the thin, alcoholic, and highly acidic nature of fermented citrus juice. Citrus zest is quite powerful as a flavor. The zest from 3 to 5 fruits is usually sufficient for a 5-gallon batch.

Dates and Figs

Unlike most fruits, dates and figs contribute the sweetest and strongest flavor if the dried fruit is used. The fresh fruit can add a refreshing fig nuance to a lighter beer. For dried fruit, chop finely and add enough water in a saucepan so the water level is about 1 inch over the fruit. Heat slowly to 180°F (82°C), and turn the heat off, cover, and allow to cool naturally. Add to the secondary fermenter when cooled. Use 1 to 2 pounds of dried fruit for 5 gallons.

Grapes

Most of us consider grapes to reside squarely in the land of wine, but brewers can accomplish surprising and delightful things with grapes. A half wine and half beer beverage known as *pyment* was once popular, though it is practically unheard of today.

There are quite a few flavor possibilities. The choice of grape — from light and refreshing green grapes to dark, complex wine grapes — plus the base beer style used will each define the character of the resulting brew. A light grape, pressed and added without the skins, would add a mild light winey character to a beer that could make an impressive lager, pale ale, weissbier, or saison. On the other end of the spectrum, a red wine grape, crushed and added to the fermenter with the skins, would add a decidedly stronger wine character and would pair well, perhaps, with a richer beer such as a Belgian strong, a porter, an India Pale Ale, or a stout.

Grapes can add a significant amount of fermentable sugar, and most grape skins contain natural sulfites, which is a consideration for anyone who is allergic. Adding the skins to a ferment will add some tannins, which can increase the tart and dry mouthfeel but will also contribute astringency if overdone.

Keep in mind that most wines are aged over a much longer period of time than beers, which allows the tannins and other potentially harsh characteristics to mellow. A wine/beer hybrid can use the juice of up to 10 pounds of grapes per gallon (50 pounds for 5 gallons), while a mellower grape-flavored beer could use 4 to 8 pounds for a 5-gallon batch.

Kiwi

The tart and tangy essence of kiwi can add a nice touch to a crisp summer lager or wheat beer or, if you have the patience for a yearlong fermentation, a divine fruit lambic. This is definitely a fruit that must be peeled, so if you are very careful to keep everything clean during and after peeling, wild yeast and other bacteria are not a great concern. Chop finely or purée, and add to the secondary fermenter. Use 1 to 5 pounds of fresh kiwi per 5 gallons.

Melon

The refreshing taste of melon invites itself to be a part of a quaffable summer beer. Melons are so watery that using enough to infuse sufficient melon flavor into the beer without watering it down can be a problem. One solution is to brew a slightly concentrated beer, then add enough melon juice or purée to bring the liquid volume up to the desired level. Watermelons have so little pectin that the juice (strain out the pulp) can be added to the boil. Since cooking the melon changes the flavor, you may prefer to just add puréed melon to the secondary fermenter. Use 5 to 15 pounds of melon for a 5-gallon batch, and reduce the liquid volume of the beer accordingly. Because melon rind is so thick, the juice of unpasteurized melons is reasonably sanitary if care is taken.

Pears

Aside from making fantastic cider, pears have a tangy, earthy character that is an interesting pairing with such beers as saison or pale ale. The problem with pears is they create a mush that can be reluctant to settle to the bottom of the fermenter. Slightly underripe pears are much easier to work with than softer ones. Harder pears can be chopped in a food processor instead of puréed to help alleviate the mush problem. Most brewers opt to make pear cider instead, or add freshly pressed juice to the fermenter instead of purée. Use 3 to 15 pounds for 5 gallons, or the equivalent amount of juice (1 to 3 quarts).

Persimmons

Persimmons are a bit of an odd fruit, and these days not many people think to make beer with them. There is a widely shared recipe from the early 1900s for persimmon beer made with wheat bran mashed with persimmons, then fermented. Persimmons have a lot of tannins, so it is very important to use completely ripe fruit. On the verge of rotting is not only okay, it's desirable in this case! Otherwise the beer could be so astringent it would be undrinkable. Remove the skins and fibrous pulp, and strain out the seeds. Purée can be pasteurized or frozen (thaw before adding). Add to the secondary for the best flavor. Adding some persimmon pudding spices — cinnamon, nutmeg, and vanilla — and using a rich amber ale base can make a festive brew suitable for holiday dinners. Use 2 to 6 pounds of fruit for 5 gallons.

Quince

Quince is an ancient fruit similar to apples and pears but with a subtle flavor all its own. The taste is like a laid-back apple with a hint of spice and a dash of cherry. It is often used to enhance the flavor of dishes containing apples. Beers and ciders can be made by pressing out the juice, or the fruit can be chopped or puréed and added to the fermenter to be racked out later. Quince would not be out of place in a holiday beer, or a warm and complex Belgian ale. Use 3 to 10 pounds of fresh quince (or just the juice) per 5 gallons.

Strawberries

The delicate and distinctive flavor of strawberries is a delight in the right beer. A light strawberry ale is a fantastic springtime treat that whispers a promise of summertime fun to come. In my experience the flavor of organic strawberries is noticeably better. If you cannot find freshly picked berries, it may be better to buy frozen organic berries.

Puréed strawberries can create a thick sludge on the bottom of the fermenter that interferes with racking, so dicing the fruit is a better option. Dice, pasteurize (for beers with less than 7 percent alcohol), and cool, then add to the secondary fermenter for the best flavor. Use 2 to 5 pounds of fresh or frozen strawberries for 5 gallons. Frozen berries should be pasteurized unless they were pasteurized before freezing.

BREWING WITH VEGETABLES

Quite a few familiar vegetables (and some uncommon ones, too) can be thrown into the brew kettle, although certain flavors are not everyone's idea of a harmonious balance with beer. Pumpkins and hot peppers are used fairly commonly, but tomatoes or cucumbers may seem a tad adventurous. Then there are flavors that most of us would agree have little place in a brew kettle — broccoli and onions come to mind!

If you are prone to experimenting with unconventional flavors, there are no hard-and-fast rules, although common sense would dictate making very small test batches of your wildest ideas. Some vegetables add a considerable amount of fermentable sugars, while others, like hot peppers, are used simply for flavor. Here are some brief descriptions of vegetables that might find their way into one of your homebrews.

Arugula

The distinctive peppery flavor from these greens could add a lively note to a saison or wheat beer. For brewing purposes pick mature arugula, as the peppery flavor will be stronger. Add at the end of the boil so the spicy flavors are not lost. Four to 8 ounces of fresh arugula in a 5-gallon batch should add a hint of spiciness without flooding the taste buds with cooked spinach flavor.

Beets

Beets cooked in water and puréed with their own juices can be added directly to the boil to capture the earthy-sweet beet flavor and a hint of color, or can be added to the mash. For bolder, more daring flavor and color, you could add fresh beet juice to the secondary fermenter. Expect some fermentable sugars from beets. Use 1 to 5 pounds of beets or the juice from the same amount in 5 gallons of beer.

Carrots

You can expect to gain a small amount of fermentable sugars from carrots. Cook, purée, and add to the mash, or as with beets go wild and add some fresh carrot juice to the fermenter. Peel the carrots before cooking, if you want to reduce the earthy flavors the skins can impart. You should definitely peel raw carrots before juicing to reduce surface bacteria. You might also want to pasteurize the juice before adding to your beer, just to be on the safe side. Try a carrot IPA or ESB, or add enough to a Belgian Wit to give it a hint of orange. Use 1 to 5 pounds of carrots in 5 gallons.

Celery and Celeriac

Celery is mostly water, so a few whole bunches may be needed to infuse the flavor of celery into a beer. Celeriac root is starchy and will contribute some fermentable sugars to the beer, as well as a stronger flavor than does celery stalk. Celery seed has an almost salty flavor, and a small amount can add celery flavor to a beer. Use 1 to 3 bunches of celery, 8 ounces to 2 pounds of celeriac root, or up to 1 ounce of celery seed in a 5-gallon batch.

Chile Peppers

Chile beer has been around for a while, and I have tried some good ones, but the only one that I would personally brew again was an aji dulce–habanero amber ale. Aji dulce are similar to habanero peppers in flavor but not nearly as hot. Hot peppers can be added fresh, dried, or fire roasted. No matter how you prep them, a little goes a long way. My aji dulce–habanero beer was fiery hot with just two habanero peppers used in the boil. The milder aji dulce gave the beer a nice citrusy pepper flavor, while the sweet amber ale base balanced the heat of the peppers. For most peppers, 1 to 5 peppers in a 5-gallon batch should suffice. I heartily advise adding just a few, then tasting the wort before adding each additional pepper.

Cucumbers

The flavor of cucumber is so mild that it seems almost any beer would overpower it, yet a cucumber saison has been hitting the homebrew airwaves, and there are a few craft-brew versions of cucumber beer on the market. Cucumber is light and refreshing, so what better to pair it with than the lightest lagers or saisons? The delicate flavor can be destroyed by cooking, so add it as a purée or finely chopped to the secondary fermenter.

Keep everything very clean when processing the cucumbers. Wash them in a mild sulfite solution, or peel and use sanitized tools to process them. You can add Campden tablets to puréed cucumbers, to be on the safe side, if you are not opposed to adding sulfites to your homebrew. I recommend 1 to 3 pounds of cucumbers in a 5-gallon batch.

Horseradish

Bloody Marys aren't the only drink that can use this powerfully spicy root! Be cautious, however, as too much can ruin a beer. I tried one batch that had a kick not unlike the alcoholic warmth of a rich strong beer. It had little distinct horseradish flavor, but the heat of spice was quite nice. Grate a few ounces of peeled fresh horseradish root, and throw it in for the last 5 minutes of the boil to avoid the risk of contamination.

Leeks

It may seem odd, but these mild members of the onion family can be used to flavor beer. Raw leeks taste like a mild version of onion, and that is definitely not a flavor most consider compatible with beer, yet cooked they bring a whole different taste to the table. Leeks have a decent amount of sugar and develop an earthy, savory-sweet flavor once they have been sautéed until caramelized. Since throwing oil in the brew pot is a big no-no, use sugar to caramelize the leeks instead of oil, and leave out the green tops. The rich, creamy flavor of leeks does well with fennel and lemon peel. Use 1 to 3 pounds of leeks in a 5-gallon batch.

Parsnips

I love the earthy, rustic flavor of parsnips. When roasted they exhibit a nutty sweetness with hints of licorice just begging to journey outside the confines of a vegetable side dish. Why not make a beer with them! See the recipe on page 214 or try a parsnip ale or a stout. A parsnip saison is certainly not out of the question either. Oven-roast parsnip slices without any oil, purée, then add to the boil for the best flavor. Use 1 to 5 pounds in a 5-gallon batch.

Pumpkins and Squashes

A darling of the current craft beer renaissance, pumpkins have long been used to make beer, usually with an amber or a pale ale base that helps to accentuate the sweet earthy flavor of pumpkin. Many winter squashes have a very similar flavor; butternut and acorn squash are two of the densest and richest.

Pumpkin and squash should be cooked, then puréed and added to the mash or the boil. Cut in half, scoop out the seeds, and roast face down on a baking sheet at 350°F (177°C) for at least an hour. A long, slow roast caramelizes the sugars and develops the most pronounced pumpkin flavors. Adding the purée directly to the boil infuses the most pumpkin flavor into the beer. Most pumpkin or squash beers call for at least 3 pounds and as much as 6 pounds of cooked pumpkin or squash for a 5-gallon batch.

Most beer recipes also call for adding the traditional pumpkin pie spices — cinnamon, nutmeg, ginger, and cloves — to the beer, but this is often overdone. Most recipes call for up to a few tablespoons of each spice for a 5-gallon batch. Whole spices are the best because the flavors are not dulled by oxidation, and a full hour boil is plenty of time to extract the best flavor.

Rhubarb

The sourness of rhubarb can throw off a beer if it is not matched up with a good beer style, such as a pilsner, wheat beer, or saison. If you have a well-established rhubarb patch and are tired of strawberry rhubarb pie, a light, refreshing rhubarb witbier might make you wish you had a few more stalks to work with! Tart and sweet, rhubarb adds a unique flavor and a ton of fruit aroma. For a rhubarb witbier use about 12 stalks of fresh rhubarb for a 5-gallon batch. Add half of the finely chopped rhubarb to the wort just after flameout and allow to pasteurize. Pasteurize and add the other half to the secondary fermenter.

Sweet Potatoes

Sweet potato behaves a lot like pumpkin in beers, adding a hefty dose of sugar and rich, sweet flavor that does not overpower. An economical and gluten-free ingredient with a distinctive flavor, it has been generating quite a bit of interest in the craft beer scene in recent years. The slight earthy flavor goes really well with dark, full-bodied beers, porters and browns and stouts.

Bake the potatoes in their skins until soft, then remove the pulp and purée. The purée can be added to the mash or the boil. Incidentally, regular potatoes can be used to make beer as well. They are another cheap starch source, and with the skins removed, they don't actually add much flavor but will add plenty of fermentable sugars as long as they are mashed with high-enzyme malt. Use 1 to 5 pounds of either in a 5-gallon batch.

Tomatoes

At first it might seem insane to make beer with tomatoes, either because you are like me and you love vine-ripe tomatoes so much you wouldn't want to sacrifice them for anything other than fresh eating, or because the idea of a tomato beer just seems odd. Yet tomatoes have a high sugar content and a distinctive flavor that can work well if done right. At least one tomato beer, Short's Brewing Company's Bloody Beer (brewed with tomatoes, black pepper, dill, horseradish, and celery seed) can claim a medal in the prestigious Great American Beer Festival. See page 216 for a recipe that uses heirloom tomatoes.

Tomatoes can be puréed and added to the boil, or try chopped sun-dried tomatoes (hold the oil) for a stronger tomato flavor. Tomato is such an assertive flavor that it can do well in strong beers such as stout or IPA, but can lend a lot of character to a bland American lager as well. Use 1 to 5 pounds of fresh tomatoes or 8 ounces to 2 pounds of sun-dried tomatoes in 5 gallons. Plain tomato sauce can also be used (2 to 10 cups).

Roasted Parsnip & Fennel Brown Ale with Licorice & Ginger

A good roasted parsnip tastes earthy and sweet with hints of licorice, a bit like a mild turnip. Add fresh fennel, licorice, a little bit of anise, and some fresh ginger, and you have a remarkable beer. The trick is to not overdo any flavor. Adding just the right amount of each ingredient produces a beer that is nutty, earthy, and refreshingly drinkable. A kiss of flowery hops at the finish balances out the delicate flavors to complete this unusual but memorable brew.

I find better flavor extraction using chopped licorice root, but sticks are fine as well. Licorice root does not actually taste like licorice candy — that flavor comes from anise, and to a lesser degree, fennel.

Recipe for 5 US gallons

Original Gravity: 1.055–1.060	**Total AAUs:** 14
(gravity contributed by parsnips is hard to predict)	**Total IBUs:** 26
Final Gravity: 1.014–1.020	**Approximate ABV:** 5.5%

- 4 lbs raw parsnips
- 1 medium-size fresh fennel bulb (about 8 ounces)
- 1.5 lbs pale ale malt, crushed
- 8 oz Munich malt, crushed
- 12 oz crystal 60°L malt, crushed
- 6 oz chocolate malt, crushed
- 6 lbs pale liquid malt extract
- 2 oz dried licorice root (whole stick or chopped root) **Boil 60 minutes**
- 0.5 oz (6 AAU) American Simcoe pellet hops (21 IBU) **Boil 60 minutes**
- 1 oz (8 AAU) New Zealand Motueka hops (5 IBU) **Boil 15 minutes**
- 0.5 teaspoon Irish moss **Boil 15 minutes**
- 1 oz fresh gingerroot or ½ dried root, grated **Boil 5 minutes**
- 2 tablespoons fennel seeds, roasted for 2–3 minutes in a dry pan over heat
  Boil 5 minutes

Yeast: White Labs 023 Burton Ale or Wyeast 1968 London ESB
Priming Sugar: 4 oz corn sugar

PREPARE THE PARSNIPS

Peel the parsnips and cut into 2-inch cubes. Wash and cube the fennel bulb. Spread both vegetables evenly across a baking dish. To enhance caramelization, spritz with sugar water just before baking and again halfway through. Bake at 350°F (177°C) for 40 to 60 minutes. The parsnips and fennel bulb should be very soft, browned on the outside, but not blackened. Purée with some water until smooth.

STEEP

Add enough water to the purée to make 1.5 gallons. Mix in all the grains, and slowly heat the mixture to 150°F (66°C). Steep for 20 to 30 minutes.

Strain all the liquid from the grains. To extract more flavor, add another ½ gallon of water heated to 150°F (66°C) to the grains after straining, stir well, and strain again. Add enough water to the wort to fill the brew kettle; the total volume should be 5.25 to 5.5 gallons (adjust for your brewing system). Heat to just before boiling, add the extract, and dissolve completely.

BOIL AND COOL

Bring to a boil, and add the licorice and Simcoe hops. After 40 minutes of boiling, add the Motueka hops and the Irish moss, and boil for 15 minutes. Add the ginger and fennel seeds, boil 5 minutes, then stir well, and turn the heat off.

Cool to 65 to 70°F (18–21°C). Transfer to a sanitized fermenter and aerate well.

PITCH, FERMENT, AND BOTTLE

Add the yeast when cool, and aerate really well — strong beers require higher oxygen levels to ensure a healthy ferment. Ferment for 7 to 14 days at 65 to 70°F (18–21°C). Rack to a secondary fermenter after 5 to 7 days if desired. For a stronger licorice flavor, add 1 tablespoon of fennel seeds and 1 tablespoon of anise seeds to the secondary fermenter. Prime the beer, and bottle when fermentation is complete. Allow to condition for 12 to 21 days.

(See All-Grain Adaptation, next page.)

Omit the malt extract. Add:

6 more pounds pale ale malt, crushed
12 more ounces Munich malt, crushed
4 more ounces crystal 60°L malt, crushed

Instead of steeping as instructed above, do a full mash as follows:

Add enough water to the vegetable purée to make a total of 3.75 gallons of liquid. Heat to 170°F (77°C). Add all the grains, and mix well. Allow to rest for a few minutes, then adjust temperature to 151 to 153°F (66–67°C) if needed. Hold this temperature for 45 to 60 minutes, or until starch conversion is complete. If possible, just before lautering, heat the mash to 165°F (74°C). Sparge with 3.5 gallons of water at 168°F (76°C). Transfer the wort to the brew kettle, then proceed with the boil, fermentation, and bottling.

Fire-Roasted Heirloom Tomato–Chile Beer

I've had tomato beer spiced with classic Bloody Mary spices, and I've had chile beer. Both were pretty good, but I wanted the amazing flavors of sun-kissed heirloom tomatoes without drowning them in hops and spices. I was inspired to add a few Mexican chiles and the result was pure genius.

The beer is earthy with tart overtones from the tomatoes. A hint of tomato essence is there in the flavor, but it does not overpower. The subtle heat of the chiles comes in as the beer slides over your tongue, bringing with it dark cherry tang and warm earthy spiciness of the ancho and guajillo chiles. The hops add a hint of fruity citrus that complements the other flavors.

You have to use garden-fresh tomatoes (heirlooms are best but a mixture of heirlooms plus other varieties will do) and the right kind of chiles to duplicate this recipe. If you have your favorite dried chiles, go ahead and sub those if you prefer. A word of caution: using chipotle will make a fantastic beer, but the smokiness will overpower the tomato flavor.

Recipe for 5 US gallons

Original Gravity:	1.059	Total IBUs:	23
Final Gravity:	1.012–1.016	Approximate ABV:	5.9%
Total AAUs:	12		

- 8 lbs ripe heirloom tomatoes
- 1 oz dried ancho chile peppers (2–3 peppers)
- 1 oz dried guajillo chile peppers (4–5 peppers)
- 1.5 lbs pale ale malt, crushed
- 8 oz Vienna malt, crushed
- 8 oz crystal 40°L malt, crushed
- 4 oz crystal 120°L malt, crushed
- 2 oz chocolate malt, crushed
- 6 lbs pale liquid malt extract
- .5 oz (4 AAU) Wakatu (New Zealand Hallertaur) pellet hops (13 IBU) **Boil 60 minutes**
- 0.5 teaspoon Irish moss **Boil 20 minutes**
- 1 oz (6 AAU) American Cascade pellet hops (9 IBU) **Boil 15 minutes**
- .5 oz (2 AAU) German Saphir pellet hops (1 IBU) **Boil 5 minutes**

Yeast: White Labs 001 California Ale, Wyeast 1056 American Ale, or dry ale yeast

Priming Sugar: 4.5 oz corn sugar

PREPARE THE TOMATOES

Preheat the broiler of your oven. Wash the tomatoes, slice in half, and place cut side down on baking sheets in a single layer. Roast for 15 to 20 minutes, or until the skins are blackened and starting to shrivel up. Allow to rest until they are cool enough to handle, then slide the skins off, which is easier to do before the tomatoes cool completely.

While the tomatoes cool, broil the chiles for about 5 minutes, turning them halfway through. It is important that the chiles do not burn, but they should soften and they might inflate as they heat up. Allow to cool, then remove stems and seeds, crumble the peppers by hand and add to the tomatoes.

Purée the tomato and pepper mixture, then pass through a sieve to remove the seeds. Transfer to a saucepan, bring to a boil, simmer for 10 minutes, then turn the heat off.

Reserve 4 cups of this purée to be added to the secondary fermenter. You can store it in the refrigerator or freezer until needed, then boil for 15 minutes and cool before adding to the secondary fermenter. If you can the purée (add 1 tablespoon of lemon juice, pack in sterilized mason jar, and process in boiling water for 15 minutes), you can add it directly to the secondary fermenter without boiling.

STEEP

Add 1 gallon of water to the grains, and slowly heat the mixture to 150°F (66°C). Steep for 20 to 30 minutes.

Strain all the liquid from the grains. Add the tomato-pepper purée and enough water to fill the brew kettle; the total volume should be 5.25 to 5.5 gallons (adjust for your brewing system). Heat to just before boiling, add the extract, and dissolve completely.

BOIL AND COOL

Bring to a boil, and add the Wakatu hops. After 40 minutes of boiling, add the Irish moss, and boil for 5 minutes. Add the Cascade hops, and boil for 10 minutes. Add the Saphir hops, boil 5 minutes, then stir well, and turn the heat off.

Cool to 65 to 70°F (18–21°C). Transfer to a sanitized fermenter and aerate well.

PITCH, FERMENT, AND BOTTLE

Add the yeast when cool, and aerate really well — strong beers require higher oxygen levels than light ones to ensure a healthy ferment. Ferment for 7 to 10 days. The best fermenting temperature is 65 to 70°F (18–21°C). Once the beer has started to clear and the foam has died back, add the reserved tomato-pepper purée. Rack to a secondary fermenter if desired. Ferment for another 7 to 10 days. Prime the beer, and bottle when fermentation is complete. Allow to condition for 12 to 21 days.

Omit the malt extract. Add:

6.5 more pounds pale ale malt, crushed
8 more ounces Vienna malt, crushed
4 more ounces crystal 40°L malt, crushed

Instead of steeping as instructed above, do a full mash as follows:

Heat 3.75 gallons of water to 165°F (74°C). Add all the grains, and mix well. Allow to rest for a few minutes, then adjust temperature to 151 to 153°F (66–67°C) if needed. Hold this temperature for 45 to 60 minutes, or until starch conversion is complete. If possible, just before lautering, heat the mash to 165°F (74°C). Sparge with 3.5 gallons of water at 168°F (76°C). Transfer the wort to the brew kettle, add the tomato-pepper purée, then proceed with the boil, fermentation, and bottling.

Brewing with Herbs

Almost every beer brewed today is brewed with one herb: hops. In contrast, during the early recorded history of brewing, a wide range of herbs was used to brew beer, often whatever grew close to the brewery. Herbs helped to shape the regional flavor of local beers. Some traditional beers were made with a blend of herbs called *gruit* — the exact recipes were closely guarded secrets. The beer flavored with gruit was (and still is) often called gruit ale or just gruit.

Many perennial herbs are quite easy to grow. Once the plants are established in your homebrew garden, they require very little tending and can give you many years of fragrant, flavorful, and medicinal bounty. Because herbs and spices can quite easily be overdone, it is important, if following a recipe, to stick to the quantity specified in the recipe, at least the first time you brew it. When developing your own recipes with herbs, as with any unfamiliar flavor, less is better than more. Start with small amounts. If the flavor is not strong enough, use more the next time, or make a concentrated tea, boil after steeping to sterilize, cool, and add to the fermenter to increase the flavor of the current batch.

Most herbs are dried for long-term storage. The dried form concentrates the flavors and reduces vegetal matter, making them well suited for adding to beer. In many cases the dried form is vastly preferable, as many varieties of fresh herbs can contribute a cooked-vegetable character to a beer when a quantity sufficient to infuse the unique flavor and aromatics is used. Most herbs are relatively harmless unless used in excessive quantities, but some have powerful medicinal qualities and should be handled respectfully.

Dried herbs are typically added in small amounts, a few ounces or less for a 5-gallon batch. As with hops, many herbs can add their own bitterness. In some cases this bitterness can overpower a recipe. Wormwood is a good example. After a trip to Europe, where I had my first taste of absinthe, I enthusiastically decided to brew an absinthe beer. Just a few ounces of wormwood made that beer completely undrinkable, and the 5 gallons I brewed at a considerable cost became plant food.

Know Your Herbs

Please pay attention to the recommended amounts when working with herbs, especially if you are tempted to use a large quantity in a recipe. If you consider using a larger amount of an herb than recommended here, consult expert sources on herbal medicine before doing so. Some herbs are powerful medicines that can be harmful or even fatal in large doses!

Here are a few herbs that can be used in brewing and are reasonably easy to grow.

Alecost or Costmary

This herb has been used by brewers for centuries, hence the name "Alecost." It has a pleasant minty balsam aroma, which is retained for a long time when the leaves are dried. Although its use in herbal medicine and by brewers has declined drastically in modern times, the plant is still commonly found in herb gardens because of its pleasant smell and attractive appearance. Use 1 to 4 ounces of dried leaves in a 5-gallon batch.

Angelica

Angelica is perhaps more well-known for its use in spirits such as absinthe or Chartreuse than it is in brewing. It has a unique, sweet flavor and an aroma that is refined and delicate, more subtle than anise but similar. The root, leaves, stems, or seeds may be used. Each contributes unique flavor. Use up to 8 ounces of angelica root, 4 ounces of dried leaves, or 1 ounce of seeds in a 5-gallon batch of beer.

Anise

This powerful and familiar flavor, often thought of as licorice, has an established place in the world of fermented and alcoholic beverages. Although it does not fit well with many beer styles, it can be outstanding in specialty recipes, especially when the strong licorice-minty flavor is balanced with a full-bodied, sweet beer such as stout. There are two types: star anise, which is a tropical spice, and the milder herb that grows well wherever there is a frost-free growing season of at least 120 days, but it is not as commercially successful because of its mellower flavor. Both can be used in brewing.

Garden-variety anise (*Pimpinella anisum*), a relative of fennel, is grown for its small, fragrant seeds. It is not related to star anise, although the chemical compounds responsible for the aroma and flavor produced by the plant are quite similar. Anise seeds are used for flavor. Crush slightly in a mortar or food processor before adding to the end of the boil for the most pronounced flavor. Start with ¼ ounce of seed, and use up to 1 ounce for 5 gallons.

Basil

Until recently, basil, the common garden herb so essential to most Italian and Greek cuisine, was not widely considered in brewing recipes. A California brewery, Bison Brewing, changed all that with their Honey Basil Ale, which proved that a basil-flavored beer could be commercially successful. Just as in cooking the finest Italian dishes, brewing with fresh basil is worlds apart from using the dried herb. To maximize basil flavor use the leaves as well as the young flowers in the boil. The flavor balances well with honey, sage, chamomile, and lemon. Try lemon or lime basil paired with citrus peel for a refreshingly different Belgian Wit. One to 4 ounces of fresh basil or half as much dried basil should provide a prominent basil flavor.

Bay Leaves

Use a few fresh bay leaves in the boil to complement other flavors; they pair well with basil, coriander, fennel, lavender, lemon balm, oregano, sage, and yarrow. If purchasing bay leaves in a store, look for leaves that are well preserved, are structurally intact, and still have a vibrant green color. These will give you the best flavor. Fresh-picked leaves from a bay laurel tree will develop a more pleasant, rich, savory flavor after several weeks of drying time.

I am fortunate to be able to use California bay leaves, which when picked young and used fresh have a fantastic flavor that includes sage and cinnamon notes. I prefer them to stale, overdried Mediterranean bay leaves. In the end, fresh quality wins for better flavor. Use 2 to 12 dried bay leaves, added at the start of the boil for the most flavor extraction.

Betony

Betony is unfamiliar to most modern brewers, although it was commonly used in the dawning ages of brewing before hops became the predominant flavor. In most historical references its taste is often referred to as "agreeable." It has a slight astringency and a mild bitterness that make it a good substitute for hops, a characteristic worth noting if you or someone you are brewing for has an unfavorable reaction to hops (rare, but it can happen). It also shares with hops mild sedative and relaxation properties. The leaves have been historically used in brewing, but the roots are edible as well and can be used in beer to contribute starch and a hint of a peppery flavor similar to that of radish. Use 2 to 4 ounces of dried herb or 2 to 16 ounces of fresh root (1 to 8 ounces dried) in 5 gallons of beer.

Birch

Birch has been a popular flavor for fermented beverages and homemade sodas for many years. Most commercial examples use oil distilled from birch bark, but old-timers in New England and eastern Canada used to boil down the sap from birch trees to form the base of the beer. The flavor is similar to root beer. The best examples have an aromatic quality and a pleasant hint of woodiness. Birch sap does not have as much sugar as maple, but it will contribute an aromatic sweetness. The birch flavor can be enhanced by adding fresh young twigs from birch in the springtime.

Black birch was the most commonly used because it yields a sweeter, stronger-flavored sap. A birch tree can be tapped in the same manner as a maple tree in the spring. If you are fortunate to have access to birch trees in the spring, try a fresh birch porter or pale ale. Use fresh sap as a substitute for water plus up to 1 gallon by volume of fresh twigs for a 5-gallon batch. If you want to try brewing with birch but do not have access to the living trees, natural birch essential oil is available online.

Borage

Borage was widely used in brewing in earlier centuries but is virtually unknown today. It is an easy plant to grow and has a unique, refreshing cucumber-like flavor with a hint of sweetness. Borage is best used fresh, to take advantage of its delicate flavor and nutritive value. Try starting with a saison, a pale ale, a light brown ale, or a lager as a base style. Use 3 to 6 ounces of chopped fresh leaves and flowers in a 5-gallon batch, added late in the boil. If you have a bumper crop of borage and want a larger batch, consider macerating the borage in water, pressing out the resulting liquid, and brewing with that to reduce the vegetal matter in the brew.

Chamomile

One of the most surprisingly good beers I have tried was a homebrew made with chamomile that I sampled at a National Homebrewers Conference. Famous for making tea, chamomile (either German or Roman) produces a mild, smooth-tasting flavor with very little bitterness when steeped. The flowers are most commonly used, but for brewing, the entire plant can be used for enhanced flavor. The flavor and aromas of chamomile are excellent in witbiers, saisons, and summer wheat beers.

Chamomile blends well with other flavors, especially orange, lemon, pepper, and hops. Because the flavor is subtle and can easily be muted by other ingredients, heavily hopped or spiced beers could overwhelm it. Use 4 to 16 ounces of chamomile, fresh or dried, in 5 gallons of beer. Add at the very end of the boil, and allow to steep for 10 minutes before chilling the wort if using a large amount, to prevent any bitterness from being extracted by boiling.

Coriander

Coriander is a wonderful spice well known for its pivotal role in Belgian Wit. The seeds when crushed release a wonderful, warm, spicy character with hints of citrus. Coriander is remarkably easy to grow, reaching maturity in as little as 3 months and yielding heads of aromatic, easy-to-harvest seeds. The aromatics in coriander are quite volatile and diminish rapidly. For peak flavor and aroma, crush the seeds right before adding to the boil using a mortar and pestle, coffee mill, or spice grinder. In a pinch you can put the seeds in a small cloth bag and use a rolling pin or rubber mallet to crush them.

To heighten the coriander flavor, add some of the seeds to the secondary, as some of the essential oils are more soluble in alcohol than in water. They can be lightly toasted in a dry pan, which will cause them to pop, so crushing is not needed. This will also sanitize them, making it a cinch to add to a fermenter without the need for boiling or other sanitizing measures. Use ¼ to 1 ounce of seed or powder in 5 gallons. I recommend a late-boil addition and boiling for 15 minutes or less to retain most of the coriander flavor.

Dandelion

Both fresh dandelion leaves and flowers, dried leaves, and dried and sometimes roasted roots can be used for brewing. The leaves offer great bittering potential and can be used as a reasonable substitute for hops. Some recipes call for using the entire plant. Expect a tart, slightly floral and earthy flavor from dandelion, which will be more pronounced if larger amounts are used. Use 8 ounces to 2 pounds of fresh dandelion in a 5-gallon batch. When using more than 8 ounces of fresh dandelion, boil for no more than 15 minutes to prevent loss of flavor and excess bitterness.

The dried root can also be used. It adds a deeper bitterness and, if roasted first, a wonderful coffee or nutlike flavor. Roast in an oven on a cookie sheet until the root is a rich brown color. Toasted dandelion root in the boil plus flowers steeped at the end of the boil make a wonderful dandelion stout!

Elderflower

Brew with fresh elderflowers if you can, to capture more of the delicate floral aromas. The taste is a little hard to describe — herbal and flowery with a bit of tartness, not unlike lemon blossom. The flowers offer a slight sweetness of their own, but not enough to affect the alcohol content much unless you use more than a pound of fresh flowers. Try an elderflower Kölsch, wheat, or saison — or merge with orange peel and coriander for an outstanding Belgian Wit. The stems and leaves of the elder tree are toxic, so when harvesting make sure to leave those parts behind. Use 1 to 6 ounces of dried elderflowers, or 2 to 12 ounces of fresh-harvested flowers in 5 gallons of beer.

Fennel

Fennel is an easy plant to cultivate, and the seeds have a strong licorice flavor, though the fernlike leaves and sweet stalks can be used as well. Fennel is usually considered too strong for a lighter ale, but it works well in spiced holiday beers, Baltic porter, or stout. Pair with licorice root, anise, or star anise to achieve a strong licorice flavor. For a lighter style try using some of the bulb and the leaves as well as the seeds for a mellower flavor that would do well in a blond ale or a spicy wheat. Use the bulb, stems, leaves, and flowers (or seeds, depending on the maturity of the plant) from one fennel plant for a fresh fennel beer, or use ¼ to 2 ounces of dried fennel seeds for a 5-gallon batch. See page 214 for a recipe.

Ginger

Ginger is a versatile flavor long used in brewing, usually in accompaniment with other spices but highly regarded on its own for ginger beer — both the alcoholic and the nonalcoholic versions. Although not commonly grown by home gardeners, it is not too difficult to grow as a houseplant in cooler climates, or outside in warmer areas. Gingerroot is fantastic used fresh — powdered ginger is a poor substitute. If you must used dried ginger, the chopped root is a better choice, as more of the flavor is locked in. For an outstanding ginger beer, try a lager or very light ale as a base, and keep the hop level very low.

Most popular old-time recipes for alcoholic ginger beer were made with cane sugar or honey, lemon juice, and ginger. No hops or malt were used at all — but these days, with malt so readily available, malt-based ginger beers are becoming popular. Use 1 to 8 ounces of fresh ginger per 5 gallons, or one-third to one-half that amount of chopped dried ginger. Crystallized ginger contains a lot more sugar than dried ginger, so adjust your recipe to account for that if you use it.

Heather

Heather contributes a light herbal, slightly grassy flavor; hints of honey sweetness; and a unique woody aroma. The flowers plus the top few inches of the fronds are the best parts to use for brewing. Heather pairs well with stronger beers, from blonds to porters, and works very well in meads and beers made with honey. Traditional recipes, many of which are made without using hops, call for lightly pressing the tops, presumably to release the essential oils. Some heather beer recipes call for hops as well as the heather, but heather on its own can provide some bitterness. Some recipes also use yarrow, sweet gale, and other herbs for added flavor. Most heather ales call for 4 to 12 ounces of the fresh or dried tips and flowers.

Hyssop

A clean scent reminiscent of rosemary with hints of anise and mint makes hyssop an interesting brewing ingredient. It also contributes a distinctive minty-licorice flavor. Anise hyssop is preferred for brewing; it pairs remarkably well with beers with chocolate as a dominant flavor, such as porters, browns, and stouts. Or combine it with summer herbs such as nettle, yarrow, lavender, or lemon balm in a lighter-base beer for a refreshing, thirst-quenching beer. Use the leaves and young flowers of the plant, either fresh or dried, at a rate of ½ to 2 ounces of dried or fresh herb in 5 gallons.

Juniper

Juniper beer, or *sahti*, is a traditional beer of Scandinavia. The use of juniper in brewing is by no means limited to the traditional recipe — it is used in a wide array of today's commercial craft beers. Juniper berries can find their way into everything from stouts to saisons, and pale ales to dark lagers. The berries and the branches are both useful, although only the berries are sold by brew shops and bulk herb suppliers.

Juniper gives a fruity, piney aroma and pine-berry flavor with hints of herb and woodiness. When the branches are used, they are often boiled in water, then strained out, producing a juniper extract, which is used for making the beer. Juniper berries are a powerful flavor, and too much can be unpleasant. Most recipes call for using no more than 1 ounce in a 5-gallon batch.

Lavender

A powerful-smelling herb, lavender is starting to attract more interest in the brewing community for accentuating herbal notes in beers such as saisons, Belgian ales, witbiers, or even a light sour Berliner Weisse. To let the lavender stand out, try a malty and smooth base beer like a pale ale, or join it up with hops that lean toward citrus and floral aromas to make a bright and lively IPA. Decidedly floral and sagelike, the flavor of lavender also pairs well with chocolate and would do well in a porter or stout.

Use culinary lavender for brewing, as ornamental lavenders and some varieties cultivated for essential oils contain camphor. Just use the flowers, either fresh or dried. One-half to 2 ounces in 5 gallons is my recommendation. To enhance lavender flavors add up to an ounce, boiled in a small amount of water to sanitize, to the secondary fermenter.

Lemon Balm

Although almost unheard of today as a brewing ingredient, lemon balm was widely used as a brewing herb in the Middle Ages. It makes a great addition to wheat beer, witbier, and saison, and could complement the spiciness of a good Belgian blond. The flavors and aroma of lemon balm are delicate enough that it is best steeped like a tea at the end of the boil, and you need a large amount to really get a pronounced flavor. Between 1 and 2 pounds of fresh herb or 4 to 8 ounces of dried herb is called for in most recipes. This may be why I have not seen any commercial examples of lemon balm beer out there, even though the homebrew examples I have tried have been great.

Licorice

Licorice, which is widely used in brewing herbal or flavored beers, is not difficult to grow, so it can be a useful addition to your homebrew garden. In addition to its sweet, mildly herbal flavor, it is also well regarded as a natural additive to improve the foam and head retention, as well as adding body, a natural sweetness, and a deeper color, especially nice in stouts. The root, harvested after 2 or 3 years of growth, is the useful part of the plant. Typical recipes call for 1 to 6 ounces of dried root added at the start of the boil.

Mint

Mint has such a strong and distinct flavor it can overpower other flavors, so take care in its use to create a balanced and interesting beer. Mint pairs well with chocolate and will complement the rich character of dark, heavy beers. A mojito-style light-mint weissbier or a sweet ale aged with bourbon and oak, like a mint julep, are fascinating combinations. An interesting recipe for a Russian tribal beer calls for mint fermented with rye and barley. The crisp, dry character of rye could do well in a more modern interpretation. For a milder mint flavor, use fresh-picked mint steeped at the end of the boil. Make a concentrated mint tea, or steep fresh or dried mint in vodka or bourbon and add to the secondary fermenter for a stronger mint character. Use 1 to 8 ounces of fresh mint leaves or ½ to 4 ounces of dried mint, depending on the level of "mintyness" desired.

Nettles

It is hardly necessary to actually cultivate nettles, as they grow wild all over the place, but if there are none in your area, it can be handy to plant them for eating (they taste like spinach when cooked) and making nettle beer. Used in spring tonics and summer beers, often in combination with dandelions, nettles have a vegetable, bitter, earthy character that often needs something aromatic, such as hops or yarrow, and something flavorful, such as lemon or ginger, to balance it. The best part to use is the top 2 to 5 inches, or top few rows of leaves.

Traditional recipes for nettle beer use sugar as a fermentable base. A pleasant modern version is usually based on lighter, low-hop styles such as pilsner, weiss, witbier, or saison. The nettles will give a faint green color, an earthy vegetable flavor, and a slightly peppery herbal aspect to the beer. Most recipes call for 1 to 2 pounds of freshly harvested nettles. You could also use dried nettles, but these will not craft the same unique brew as fresh. Two to 6 ounces of dried nettles should be enough for a 5-gallon batch.

Roses and Rose Hips

The little fruits of the rose are high in vitamin C and have a tangy flavor with hints of floral rose that works well in Belgian ales, IPAs, saisons, witbiers, and wheat beers. Rose also pairs well with chocolate — a rose petal and rose hip chocolate stout could be a divine pairing for a special Valentine's Day dinner. Technically speaking, rose hips are a fruit, not an herb, but since the rose petals are also used as a flavoring ingredient, I have included them here. The rose hips should be crushed and added late in the boil or steeped at the end to retain the most flavor. Use 1 to 4 ounces of fresh or dried rose hips and/or rose petals in 5 gallons.

Sage

Sage gives a decidedly strong herbal flavor and aroma to beer: earthy, warm, and savory. It is a strong presence that works better in layers with other flavors. Mastering a balanced beer with sage as the dominant flavor is a feat any brewer should be proud of. It works well with heavy, complex beers, especially Belgian, amber, and nut brown ales, and pairs nicely with citrus peel, hops, and honey. Culinary sage is normally called for, but if you live in an area where wild sage grows, it can add an unusual flavor. Use 2 to 8 ounces of fresh sage, or half as much of dried sage, for 5 gallons.

Spruce

The flavor of spruce is pleasant and uplifting, described by some as being rather like cola, with its citrusy and resinous flavor notes. The pale green tips of black or red spruce in the Northeast or Sitka spruce in the Northwest offer the best flavor and vitamin content. The natural vitamin C provides an energizing effect and acts as a natural preservative and counterbalance to the malty sweet wort of barley-based beers. For a typical 5-gallon batch, use 4 to 12 ounces of freshly harvested spruce tips.

Concentrated spruce essence is available from most homebrew retailers; however, most commercially prepared spruce essence contains the preservative sodium benzoate. While most health officials claim small amounts of sodium benzoate are safe for human consumption, there is concern about using it in conjunction with vitamin C. When sodium benzoate combines with vitamin C, benzene can form, which is a known carcinogen. If you do not live near a good source of spruce, you might be able to harvest a large amount while on a trip so you can store it in your freezer until brew day. Spruce will survive a journey of several days without refrigeration, so another option is to find a friend or relative to harvest some and mail it to you.

Wintergreen

This low-growing shrub can be difficult to grow in some areas, but where it does thrive it can supply you with plenty of its leaves and berries, which have the spearmintlike flavor so distinctive of modern root beer. Its pungent, aromatic aroma can overpower a beer, which is fine if you are going for an alcoholic root beer flavor but will probably be too much if you are aiming for something more subtle. Combine with sassafras or sarsaparilla, cloves, and licorice for a brewed-from-scratch root beer character.

On its own, wintergreen can provide a more subtle aroma and minty flavor that is quite nice in light, spicy beer styles such as weissbier or saison. Use 1 to 3 ounces of fresh or dried wintergreen leaves in 5 gallons. The berries can also be used. Add at the end of the boil, and steep before cooling. If a strong wintergreen flavor is desired, allow to steep in the primary fermenter, and rack the beer off the leaves after 2 to 5 days. Or you can dry hop with wintergreen in the secondary fermenter.

Wormwood

This powerfully bitter medicinal herb has been used in brewing for millennia. Its bittering power is so strong that it is a very economical substitute for hops when they are scarce or too expensive. It does not offer much in the way of flavor, but can be used in a wide range of beer styles as a bittering agent that will also give the beer a slight herbal quality. I have never enjoyed the flavor, but don't let my opinion sway you from trying a little wormwood in a batch if it intrigues you. Play it safe: start with very small quantities of ¼ to ½ ounce in 5 gallons and gradually increase in subsequent batches if you want a stronger wormwood presence.

Yarrow

At one time yarrow enjoyed a favored role in brewing, with its presence in a brew believed by many to increase the intensity of intoxication. It grows almost anywhere and is one of the most widely used medicinal herbs in the world. With its pleasing aroma — herbal with hints of anise and lemon — it does well in rustic European styles such as saison or porter, Belgian ale, or IPA. Yarrow has good bittering properties, giving a complementary bitterness without a harsh aftertaste. Its aromatics dissipate quickly in a boil, so adding some yarrow at the end of the boil or as an infusion in the fermenter will help to impart more yarrow flavor. Use 2 to 4 ounces of dried yarrow or 4 to 8 ounces of fresh-picked yarrow for 5 gallons. For a balanced bittering use 1 to 2 ounces of dried yarrow during the boil, and use the remainder as a late addition or dry hop if desired.

PART 3

BREWING
ORGANIC
BEER

7

EASIER RECIPES for BEGINNING BREWERS

All the recipes in this book are formatted in the same way, so once you know how to "read" this recipe, you should not have any trouble understanding the other recipes that are included. When you start exploring recipes from other sources, you will notice there are some similarities in formatting, because most homebrewers who create recipes to share use many of the same guidelines. This is one of the great things about homebrewing: folks who brew love to share recipes, brewing tips, and ideas.

Pale Rider Ale

This style of beer was made famous by Sierra Nevada Pale Ale, and has become one of the signature beers of the United States. This beer helped to spark the craft brew renaissance, from which we enjoy wonderful benefits today. At the time it was a beer with a lot more flavor and character than most beer drinkers were used to, and this helped propel it toward success. The beer is slightly sweet and malty, with a hint of caramel and toasted bread. The hop nose is distinctively citrus, with hints of pine and spice. For many homebrewers a good pale ale is a great go-to beer. When in doubt brew this one, and tweak the recipe just a little each time to perfectly suit your own taste to make it your own!

Recipe for 5 US gallons

Original Gravity:	1.054	**Total IBUs:**	39
Final Gravity:	1.010–1.014	**ABV:**	5.4%
Total AAUs:	24		

- 8 oz crystal 20°L malt, crushed
- 4 oz crystal 40°L malt, crushed
- 6 pounds pale dry malt extract
- 1 oz (8 AAU) Perle pellet hops (26 IBU) **Boil 60 minutes**
- 1 oz (8 AAU) Cascade pellet hops (13 IBU) **Boil 15 minutes**
- 0.5 teaspoon Irish moss **Boil 15 minutes**
- 1 oz (8 AAU) Cascade pellet hops **Add at flameout**

Yeast: White Labs 001 California Ale or Wyeast 1056 American Ale

Priming Sugar: 4 oz corn sugar

STEEP

Mix the grains with at least 2 quarts of water, or fill a grain bag and place it in your brew pot filled with water. Gently heat to 150°F (66°C), and steep for 15 to 20 minutes.

Strain all the liquid from the grains. Add enough water to the wort to fill the brew kettle; the total volume should be 5.25 to 5.5 gallons (adjust for your brewing system). Heat to just before boiling, add the extract, and dissolve completely.

BOIL AND COOL

Bring to a full rolling boil, then add the Perle hops. Boil for 45 minutes. Add 1 ounce of Cascade hops and the Irish moss. Boil for 15 minutes. At the very end of the boil, add the rest of the Cascade hops, stir well, then turn the heat off.

Cool to 65 to 70°F (18–21°C). Transfer to a sanitized fermenter, and aerate well.

PITCH, FERMENT, AND BOTTLE

Add the yeast. Ferment for 10 to 14 days.

Rack to a secondary fermenter after 5 to 7 days, once fermentation has slowed, if desired.

Boil the priming sugar in 1 cup of water, and cool to 70°F (21°C). Stir the sugar gently into the beer, then bottle it. Let the beer condition in the bottles for 14 to 21 days.

All-Grain Adaptation: Pale Rider Ale

Omit the malt extract. Add:

9 pounds pale 2-row malt, crushed
4 more ounces crystal 20°L malt, crushed
4 more ounces crystal 40°L malt, crushed

Instead of steeping, do a full mash as follows:

Heat 3.75 gallons of water to 170°F (73°C). Add all the grains, and mix well. Allow to rest for a few minutes, then adjust the temperature to 151 to 153°F (67–68°C) if needed. Hold this temperature for 45 to 60 minutes, or until starch conversion is complete. If possible, just before lautering, heat the mash to 165°F (74°C). Sparge with 3.5 gallons of water at 168°F (76°C). Transfer the wort to the brew kettle, then proceed with the boil, fermentation, and bottling.

Redwood Summer Ale

A good red ale is a celebration of fine malts and the fruitier side of hops. A liberal dose of caramel malts gives the beer a malty sweetness, and the Vienna malt adds a bit of toast flavor. Combined with hops that exhibit a fruity and citrus character, this beer is a real thirst quencher that comes across as "wetter" than most beers. This recipe highlights some of the newest organic hops that have become available. If you are unable to obtain them, see chapter 9 for a guide to substituting hops.

Recipe for 5 US gallons

Original Gravity:	1.052	Total IBUs:	35
Final Gravity:	1.010–1.014	ABV:	5.3%
Total AAUs:	23		

- 8 oz Vienna malt, crushed
- 6 oz crystal 60°L malt, crushed
- 3 oz Cara-Munich malt, crushed
- 3 oz crystal 120°L malt, crushed
- 2 oz Carafa II malt, crushed
- 7 lbs pale malt extract syrup
- 0.5 oz (7 AAU) American Bravo whole hops (20 IBU) **Boil 60 minutes**
- 0.5 teaspoon Irish moss **Boil 15 minutes**
- 0.75 oz (6 AAU) English Challenger whole hops (9 IBU) **Boil 15 minutes**
- 0.5 oz (5 AAU) American Citra pellet hops (6 IBU) **Boil 10 minutes**
- 0.5 oz (5 AAU) American Citra pellet hops **Add at flameout**

Yeast: White Labs 001 California Ale or Wyeast 1056 American Ale

Priming Sugar: 4 oz corn sugar

STEEP

Mix the grains with at least 2 quarts of water, or fill a grain bag and place it in your brew pot filled with water. Gently heat to 150°F (66°C), and steep for 20 to 30 minutes.

Strain all the liquid from the grains. Add enough water to the wort to fill the brew kettle; the total volume should be 5.25 to 5.5 gallons (adjust for your brewing system). Heat to just before boiling, add the extract, and dissolve completely.

BOIL AND COOL

Bring to a boil, and add the Bravo hops. Boil for 45 minutes. Add the Irish moss and the English Challenger hops, and boil for 5 minutes. Add 0.5 ounce of American Citra hops, and boil 10 minutes. At the very end of the boil, add the remaining 0.5 ounce of American Citra hops, stir well, and turn the heat off.

Cool to 65 to 70°F (18–21°C). Transfer to a sanitized fermenter, and aerate well.

PITCH, FERMENT, AND BOTTLE

Add the yeast, then ferment for 10 to 14 days. Rack to a secondary fermenter after 5 to 7 days if desired. Prime the beer, and bottle when fermentation is complete. Allow to condition for 14 to 21 days.

All-Grain Adaptation: Redwood Summer Ale

Omit the malt extract. Add:

8 lbs pale 2-row malt, crushed
2 more oz crystal 60°L malt, crushed
Instead of steeping, do a full mash as follows:
Heat 3.75 gallons of water to 172°F (74°C). Add all the grains, and mix well. Allow to rest for a few minutes, then adjust the temperature to 151 to 153°F (67–68°C) if needed. Hold this temperature for 45 to 60 minutes, or until starch conversion is complete. If possible, just before lautering, heat the mash to 165°F (74°C). Sparge with 3.5 gallons of water at 168°F (76°C). Transfer the wort to the brew kettle, then proceed with the boil, fermentation, and bottling.

Variation — Irish Red Ale

If you prefer a taste from the Emerald Isle, this recipe can be easily adapted to an Irish-style red ale with three very simple changes.

Remove the Cara-Munich, and increase the crystal 60°L to 8 ounces and the crystal 120°L to 4 ounces.

Omit the Citra hops, and reduce the Challenger hops to 0.5 oz (4 AAU).

Use Irish Ale yeast instead of American Ale yeast.

Since the Irish Red style is drier and less hoppy, the reduction of caramel malts and hops will bring this into the right style range, and of course Irish Ale yeast is a must.

Extra Special Bitter (ESB)

This happens to be one of my favorite beers. ESBs were more popular before IPAs started to dominate the craft beer scene. This beer has a ton of hop character, a floral hoppy nose, and hints of fruit in the taste. The bitterness is less intense than the tang of most IPAs, which is why I like it so much. This beer ferments quickly and is really at its best when served fresh. It is possible to have a drinkable beer ready in 2 weeks, but the best flavors will develop if you allow a full month from brew day to the day you crack the first bottle.

Recipe for 5 US gallons

Original Gravity:	1.055	**Total IBUs:**	41
Final Gravity:	1.014–1.018	**ABV:**	5.1%
Total AAUs:	24.5		

- 4 oz barley flakes
- 8 oz crystal 20°L malt, crushed
- 8 oz crystal 60°L malt, crushed
- 8 oz Munich malt, crushed
- 7 lbs pale liquid malt extract
- 1 oz (6.5 AAU) Kent Goldings pellet hops (22 IBU) **Boil 60 minutes**
- 0.5 teaspoon Irish moss **Boil 15 minutes**
- 1 oz (6 AAU) Whitbread Goldings pellet hops (10 IBU) **Boil 15 minutes**
- 0.5 oz (6 AAU) New Zealand Rakau pellet hops (9 IBU) **Boil 15 minutes**
- 0.5 oz (6 AAU) New Zealand Rakau pellet hops **Add at flameout**
- *Yeast:* White Labs 023 Burton Ale, Wyeast 1099 Whitbread Ale, or dry ale yeast
- *Priming Sugar:* 4 oz corn sugar

STEEP

Mix the barley flakes with 1 quart of water, and bring to a boil. Remove from heat, and allow to stand for 10 minutes, then add at least 4 quarts of water. Add the rest of the grain, gently heat to 150°F (66°C), and steep for 20 to 30 minutes.

Strain all the liquid from the grains. Add enough water to the wort to fill the brew kettle; the total volume should be 5.25 to 5.5 gallons (adjust for your brewing system). Heat to just before boiling, add the extract, and dissolve completely.

BOIL AND COOL

Bring to a boil, and add the Kent Goldings hops. Boil for 45 minutes. Add the Irish moss, the Whitbread Goldings, and 0.5 ounce of New Zealand Rakau hops, and boil for 15 minutes. At the very end of the boil, add the remaining 0.5 ounce of New Zealand Rakau hops, stir well, and turn the heat off.

Cool to 65 to 70°F (18–21°C). Transfer to a sanitized fermenter, and aerate well.

PITCH, FERMENT, AND BOTTLE

Add the yeast, and ferment for 10 to 14 days. Rack to a secondary fermenter after 5 to 7 days if desired. Prime the beer, and bottle when fermentation is complete. Allow to condition for 14 to 21 days.

All-Grain Adaptation: Extra Special Bitter

Omit the malt extract. Add:

8.5 pounds pale 2-row malt, crushed
Instead of steeping, do a full mash as follows:
Heat 3.8 gallons of water to 172°F (78°C). Add all the grains, and mix well. Allow to rest for a few minutes, then adjust the temperature to 151 to 153°F (66–67°C) if needed. Hold this temperature for 45 to 60 minutes, or until starch conversion is complete. If possible, just before lautering, heat the mash to 165°F (74°C). Sparge with 3.5 gallons of water at 168°F (76°C). Transfer the wort to the brew kettle, then proceed with the boil, fermentation, and bottling.

Variation — Oaked ESB

If you love the complexity of oak flavor, adding oak works really well with this beer. I like to use oak chips saved from wood harvested at my homestead and cured in the garage. If you do this, remove all of the bark, which could add too many tannins. If you do not have your own oak trees, most homebrew shops sell oak chips or cubes. I recommend starting with 1 or 2 ounces of oak for a

5-gallon batch. It is all too easy to overdo oak, so add it with a light hand. You can always add more, but the only practical way to reduce the oak effect once a beer has too strong an oak flavor is to blend it with another batch.

Sterilize the oak chips before adding to the fermenter by boiling them in a small amount of water or putting them in a vegetable steamer for 15 minutes. If you want a heightened toasted oak character, spread them out on a small baking pan and toast them in an oven at 325°F (163°C) for 15 minutes. Cool to room temperature before tossing them into the fermenter about halfway through the fermentation, or after 6 to 8 days.

Classic India Pale Ale

You have no doubt noticed the dizzying array of IPAs available today. With the recent hop explosion in the American craft beer scene, many interpretations of the India Pale Ale style have almost gone off the deep end with hoppiness and alcohol levels. Sometimes you want a more civilized IPA, one with a structured balance of hops and malt that features the refined and mellow English-style hops.

This classic IPA fits that bill nicely and goes down quite well with a hearty British pub meal or a fiery Indian curry. It allows you to slip back through time and revisit the humble beginnings of the original IPA style, which was brewed with higher alcohol levels and hop bitterness than beer styles of the day to withstand the long voyage from Britain to India.

Recipe for 5 US gallons

Original Gravity:	1.060	Total IBUs:	46
Final Gravity:	1.014–1.018	ABV:	5.7%
Total AAUs:	26.3		

- 8 oz crystal 40°L malt, crushed
- 8 oz Munich malt, crushed
- 4 oz crystal 60°L malt, crushed
- 2 oz crystal 120°L malt, crushed
- 8 lbs pale liquid malt extract
- 1 oz (10 AAU) Pilgrim pellet hops (32 IBU) **Boil 60 minutes**
- 0.5 teaspoon Irish moss **Boil 20 minutes**

1 oz (7 AAU) Kent Goldings pellet hops (13 IBU) **Boil 20 minutes**

0.5 oz (2.3 AAU) Fuggles whole hops (1 IBU) **Boil 5 minutes**

1 oz (7 AAU) Kent Goldings pellet hops **Dry hop**

Yeast: White Labs 023 Burton Ale, Wyeast 1099 Whitbread Ale, or dry ale yeast

Priming Sugar: 4 oz corn sugar

STEEP

Mix the grains with at least 3 quarts of water, or fill a grain bag and place it in your brew pot filled with water. Gently heat to 150°F (66°C), and steep for 20 to 30 minutes.

Strain all the liquid from the grains. Add enough water to the wort to fill the brew kettle; the total volume should be 5.25 to 5.5 gallons (adjust for your brewing system). Heat to just before boiling, add the extract, and dissolve completely.

BOIL AND COOL

Bring to a boil, and add the Pilgrim hops. Boil for 40 minutes. Add the Irish moss and Kent Goldings hops, then boil for 15 minutes. Add the Fuggles hops, and boil for 5 minutes, then stir well, and turn the heat off.

Cool to 65 to 70°F (18–21°C). Transfer to a sanitized fermenter, and aerate well.

PITCH, FERMENT, AND BOTTLE

Add the yeast, then ferment for 10 to 14 days. Rack to a secondary fermenter after 5 to 7 days if desired. Add the Kent Goldings dry hops after racking, or 7 days after the start of primary fermentation. Prime the beer, and bottle when fermentation is complete. Allow to condition for 14 to 21 days. This beer is at its best 1 to 3 months after bottling, so if you can be patient, it is worth the wait!

All-Grain Adaptation: Classic India Pale Ale

Omit the malt extract. Add:

9.5 pounds English pale 2-row malt, crushed

4 more ounces crystal 60°L malt, crushed

2 more ounces crystal 120°L malt, crushed

Instead of steeping, do a full mash as follows:

Heat 4.2 gallons of water to 171°F (77°C). Add all the grains, and mix well. Allow to rest for a few minutes, then adjust the temperature to 151 to 153°F (66–67°C) if needed. Hold this temperature for 45 to 60 minutes, or until starch conversion is complete. If possible, just before lautering, heat the mash to 165°F (74°C). Sparge with 3.25 gallons of water at 168°F (76°C). Transfer the wort to the brew kettle, then proceed with the boil, fermentation, and bottling.

Tip for greatness: This beer celebrates classic English-style hops, so it is worth it to use good-quality hops. If you have a hard time obtaining the hops specified in the recipe, make sure that the ones you do use are fresh and have a good aroma. This is especially important for the dry hopping and the last boil addition. Good substitutions for fresh Fuggles or Kent Goldings are Target, Challenger, Willamette, or US Goldings.

Global Village Imperial India Pale Ale

If you just can't get enough hops and you really like strong beer, this one packs over 7 ounces of hops into a beer that is sure to be memorable. This huge beer takes the best the world has to offer of citrusy, floral, fruity organic hops and blends them in a concert of hop flavors delivered with a mouth-smacking hop bite.

The key to a good strong beer is balance. This one delivers a balance of alcohol warmth to malt structure, with enough hop bitterness to counter the back notes of sweetness and a bright hop aroma. This beer is just exploding with hops, so if you love the scent and flavor of hops with an extra helping of bitterness, this one is for you!

Recipe for 5 US gallons

Original Gravity:	1.091	Total IBUs:	75
Final Gravity:	1.018–1.022	ABV:	9.2%
Total AAUs:	68.5		

    1 lb American pale 2-row malt, crushed
    8 oz crystal 20°L malt, crushed
    8 oz crystal 40°L malt, crushed
    8 oz Munich malt, crushed

8	oz white wheat malt, crushed
4	oz crystal 60°L malt, crushed
10	lbs pale liquid malt extract
1	lb corn sugar
0.5	oz (5 AAU) Pilgrim pellet hops (12 IBU) **Boil 60 minutes**
0.5	oz (7.5 AAU) American Summit pellet hops (18 IBU) **Boil 60 minutes**
0.5	oz (5 AAU) Pilgrim pellet hops (9 IBU) **Boil 30 minutes**
0.75	oz (11.2 AAU) American Summit pellet hops (21 IBU) **Boil 30 minutes**
0.5	teaspoon Irish moss **Boil 15 minutes**
1	oz (8.5 AAU) German Smaragd pellet hops (10 IBU) **Boil 15 minutes**
1	oz (10 AAU) New Zealand Rakau pellet hops (5 IBU) **Boil 5 minutes**
1	oz (8.5 AAU) Cascade pellet hops **Add at flameout**
0.5	oz (4.3 AAU) German Smaragd pellet hops **Dry hop 7 days**
1	oz (8.5 AAU) Cascade* pellet hops **Dry hop 7 days**

Yeast: White Labs 001 California Ale, Wyeast 1056 American Ale, or dry ale yeast

Priming Sugar: 4 oz corn sugar

*Use New Zealand or American Cascade, whichever you prefer.

STEEP

Mix the grains with at least 2 to 2.5 gallons of water, or fill a grain bag and place it in your brew pot with 2.5 gallons of water. Gently heat to 150°F (66°C), and steep for 30 to 40 minutes.

Strain all the liquid from the grains. Rinse the grains with an additional 0.5 to 1 gallon of water, and collect all the liquid. Add enough water to the wort to fill the brew kettle; the total volume should be 5.25 to 5.5 gallons (adjust for your brewing system). Heat to just before boiling, add the extract and corn sugar, and dissolve completely.

BOIL AND COOL

Bring to a boil, and add 0.5 ounce Pilgrim hops and 0.5 ounce American Summit hops. Boil for 30 minutes. Add second 0.5 ounce Pilgrim hops and 0.75 ounce Summit hops, and boil for 15 minutes. Add the Irish moss and 1 ounce Smaragd hops, and boil for 10 minutes. Add the Rakau hops, and boil for 5 minutes. Add the Cascade hops, stir well, and turn the heat off.

Cool to 65 to 70°F (18–21°C). Transfer to a sanitized fermenter, and aerate well.

PITCH, FERMENT, AND BOTTLE

Add the yeast, then ferment for 12 to 14 days. Rack to a secondary fermenter after 7 to 9 days if desired. Add dry hops after racking, or 7 to 9 days after the start of primary fermentation. Prime the beer, and bottle when fermentation is complete. Allow to condition for at least 14 to 21 days.

All-Grain Adaptation: Global Village Imperial Pale Ale

Omit the malt extract. Add:

11.25 more pounds American pale 2-row malt, crushed
4 more ounces crystal 40°L malt, crushed
8 more ounces Munich malt, crushed
4 more ounces crystal 60°L malt, crushed

Keep the corn sugar, or substitute 1.5 pounds flaked or ground corn added to the mash and increase the volume of strike water by 2 quarts.

Instead of steeping, do a full mash as follows:

Heat 5.75 gallons of water to 171°F (77°C). Add all the grains, and mix well. Allow to rest for a few minutes, then adjust the temperature to 149 to 151°F (65–66°C) if needed. Hold this temperature for 45 to 60 minutes, or until starch conversion is complete. If possible, just before lautering, heat the mash to 165°F (74°C). Sparge with 2.25 gallons of water at 168°F (76°C). Transfer the wort to the brew kettle, then proceed with the boil, fermentation, and bottling.

Tips for greatness: Give the yeast the extra attention it needs to do a great job fermenting this high-alcohol, highly hopped beer. For a 5-gallon batch I recommend a 3-quart or 1.5-liter starter. Hops have antibacterial properties and in high amounts can slightly inhibit yeast activity. The fairly high alcohol content of this beer will also cause the yeast to struggle harder, so introduce as much oxygen to the wort as you can at yeast-pitching time. Prevent shocking the yeast by having both the yeast and the wort as close to 70°F (21°C) as possible when pitching.

(See Variations, next page.)

Because some love hop bitterness more than others, I have toned down the hop bitterness levels of this beer a wee bit. It is very hoppy — don't get me wrong — but it is not quite the level of some Imperial IPAs out there. One of the most famous examples is Pliny the Elder, which clocks in at a whopping 100 IBU. I have found recipes that go even higher. If you are the daredevil type and really like hops, you could crank it up by increasing the boiling hops by 0.5 to 1 ounce.

I like a citrus flavor in this beer. If the hops themselves do not add enough citrus, a little bit of orange or lemon zest added at the end of the boil can add just enough extra citrus zing to accent the lovely hop aromas. Add it carefully, though — with over 7 ounces of expensive organic hops in this beer, the last thing you want to do is overshadow them!

Barley's Bark Brown Dog Ale

This hearty brown ale is richer in malt and hop flavor than the milder British-style nut brown ale. I named it after my dog, Barley, a Lab whose rich brown coat is the same color as this beer. Barley likes to steal a few slurps of the wort when I am brewing, if given a chance!

This full-bodied, creamy brown ale has flavors of toasty malts, nuttiness, and hints of coffee. It goes well with harvest season salads, such as spicy greens and cranberry salad with roasted nuts; earthy and nutty cheeses such as Camembert; a rich mushroom gravy; or a hearty beef stew. The recipe is great for a quick brew, because it tastes good as little as 3 weeks after fermentation starts.

Recipe for 5 US gallons

Original Gravity:	1.056	Total IBUs:	30
Final Gravity:	1.012–1.014	ABV:	5.3%
Total AAUs:	15		

- 8 oz chocolate malt, crushed
- 8 oz crystal 40°L malt, crushed
- 8 oz crystal 60°L malt, crushed
- 8 oz Vienna malt, crushed
- 7 lbs pale malt extract syrup

0.5   oz (4 AAU) American Bravo pellet hops (12 IBU) **Boil 60 minutes**
0.5   teaspoon Irish moss **Boil 20 minutes**
1   oz (7 AAU) Kent Goldings pellet hops (14 IBU) **Boil 20 minutes**
0.5   oz (4 AAU) New Zealand Hallertaur whole hops (4 IBU) **Boil 10 minutes**
Yeast: White Labs 023 Burton Ale or Wyeast 1968 London ESB
Priming Sugar: 4 oz corn sugar

STEEP

Mix the grains with at least 2 quarts of water, or fill a grain bag and place it in your brew pot filled with water. Gently heat to 150°F (66°C), and steep for 15 to 20 minutes.

Strain all the liquid from the grains. Add enough water to the wort to fill the brew kettle; the total volume should be 5.25 to 5.5 gallons (adjust for your brewing system). Heat to just before boiling, add the extract, and dissolve completely.

BOIL AND COOL

Bring to a boil, and add the Bravo hops. Boil for 40 minutes. Add the Irish moss and the Kent Goldings hops, and boil for 10 minutes. Add the New Zealand Hallertaur hops, boil for 10 minutes, stir well, and turn the heat off.

Cool to 65 to 70°F (18–21°C). Transfer to a sanitized fermenter, and aerate well.

PITCH, FERMENT, AND BOTTLE

Add the yeast, then ferment for 7 to 14 days. Rack to a secondary fermenter after 5 to 7 days if desired. Prime the beer, and bottle when fermentation is complete. Allow to condition for 12 to 21 days.

All-Grain Adaptation: Barley's Bark Brown Dog Ale

Omit the malt extract. Add:

8 pounds pale 2-row malt, crushed
8 more ounces Vienna malt, crushed
Instead of steeping, do a full mash as follows:
Heat 3.9 gallons of water to 164°F (73°C). Add all the grains, and mix well. Allow to rest for a few minutes, then adjust the temperature to 151 to 153°F (66–67°C) if

needed. Hold this temperature for 45 to 60 minutes, or until starch conversion is complete. If possible, just before lautering, heat the mash to 165°F (74°C). Sparge with 3.5 gallons of water at 168°F (76°C). Transfer the wort to the brew kettle, then proceed with the boil, fermentation, and bottling.

Variation — Buck-Nut Brown

If nutty is your thing, add some buckwheat to really step up the flavor. The key is to use toasted buckwheat, often called kasha, which is sold at most health food stores. Use 1 pound for a 5-gallon batch. To enhance the nuttiness, right before brewing toast the buckwheat again on a cookie sheet at 325°F (163°C) for 10 minutes. After toasting it, add 3 cups of water, and bring to a boil. You can use a grain bag and slightly more water if you want.

Turn the heat down and simmer for 10 minutes so the grains are fully cooked. Allow to cool slightly so it can be safely handled if you will be adding other grains to the grain bag. Add the 2 gallons of water first, to bring the temperature down. Otherwise the specialty malts will get too hot. Add all the specialty grains, and follow the regular instructions for this recipe to complete the batch. Because the buckwheat is not mashed, only a little fermentable sugar will be extracted, so the strength of the beer will not change much.

Rustic and Rugged Porter

There is nothing quite like a well-crafted porter. It is a basic and unassuming beer of humble origins, a day laborer's beer, and it can be a great comfort after a long day, especially as the season shifts from summer to fall. This beer is a hearty dark brown color, booming with roasted malt and dark malt character, with hints of coffee and chocolate. Although a hearty dark beer, it is not quite as thick or as dry as a stout, and it remains quite quaffable in moderate amounts. The hops are present, but they definitely don't dominate. Rather, they let the malty, roasted flavors come through, resulting in a balanced and satisfying drink.

Recipe for 5 US gallons

Original Gravity:	1.058	Total IBUs:	32
Final Gravity:	1.016–1.020	ABV:	5.1%
Total AAUs:	22.2		

- 1 lb crystal 60°L malt, crushed
- 12 oz crystal 15°L malt, crushed
- 4 oz black malt, crushed
- 4 oz Cara-Munich malt, crushed
- 4 oz chocolate malt, crushed
- 7 lbs pale malt extract syrup
- 0.5 oz (8.2 AAU) New Zealand Pacific Gem pellet hops (26 IBU) **Boil 60 minutes**
- 0.5 teaspoon Irish moss **Boil 20 minutes**
- 1 oz (5 AAU) Fuggles pellet hops (5 IBU) **Boil 20 minutes**
- 0.5 oz (9 AAU) German Opal pellet hops (1 IBU) **Boil 1 minute**

Yeast: White Labs 002 English Ale, Wyeast 1098 Whitbread Ale, or dry ale yeast

Priming Sugar: 3.5 oz corn sugar

STEEP

Mix the grains with at least 3 quarts of water, or fill a grain bag and place it in your brew pot filled with water. Gently heat to 150°F (66°C), and steep for 20 to 30 minutes.

Strain all the liquid from the grains. Add enough water to the wort to fill the brew kettle; the total volume should be 5.25 to 5.5 gallons (adjust for your brewing system). Heat to just before boiling, add the extract, and dissolve completely.

BOIL AND COOL

Bring to a boil, and add the Pacific Gem hops. Boil for 40 minutes. Add the Irish moss and the Fuggles hops and boil for 19 minutes. Add the Opal hops, boil for 1 minute, then stir well and turn the heat off.

Cool to 65 to 70°F (18–21°C). Transfer to a sanitized fermenter, and aerate well.

PITCH, FERMENT, AND BOTTLE

Add the yeast, then ferment for 7 to 14 days. Rack to a secondary fermenter after 5 to 7 days if desired. Prime the beer, and bottle when fermentation is complete. Allow to condition for 12 to 21 days.

All-Grain Adaptation: Rustic and Rugged Porter

Omit the malt extract. Add:

8.25 pounds pale 2-row malt, crushed
4 more ounces Cara-Munich malt, crushed
Instead of steeping, do a full mash as follows:
Heat 4.1 gallons of water to 171°F (77°C). Add all the grains, and mix well. Allow to rest for a few minutes, then adjust the temperature to 151 to 153°F (66–67°C) if needed. Hold this temperature for 45 to 60 minutes, or until starch conversion is complete. If possible, just before lautering, heat the mash to 165°F (74°C). Sparge with 3.3 gallons of water at 168°F (76°C). Transfer the wort to the brew kettle, then proceed with the boil, fermentation, and bottling.

Flavor Variations

Porter lends itself well to the addition of flavors. Cherry, raspberry, vanilla, coffee, and chocolate are all common favorites. You can add fresh fruit to the secondary (see page 201 for directions on adding fruit to your beer), or drop two or three vanilla beans into the boil for the last 20 minutes. Add 4 to 6 ounces of unsweetened cocoa powder or the same amount of cocoa nibs for the last 20 minutes of the boil for a chocolate porter. Make it a Mexican chocolate porter by adding two or three high-quality cinnamon sticks to the boil with the chocolate.

Mocha Madness: Chocolate Coffee Porter

I love coffee about as much as I love beer, and I roast my own beans, so I always use a freshly roasted coffee on brew day. This beer really shines if you use the best-quality coffee you can get your hands on. I recommend going with a lighter roast because the dark roast flavors can come across as too burnt. Done right, this beer emits an enticing fresh-roasted-coffee aroma and has bittersweet coffee, chocolate, and toasted malt flavors, with hops playing second fiddle. There are just enough hops to balance the malt sweetness, plus a nice dash of floral citrus hop nose that complements the coffee flavors nicely. This beer evokes that old saying: "Beer — it's not just for breakfast anymore!"

You might be thinking that a whole pound of coffee will overcaffeinate this beer. It does provide a decent caffeine kick, but diluting a pound of coffee in 5 gallons of water actually makes for a pretty weak cup of coffee.

Recipe for 5 US gallons

Original Gravity:	1.064	**Total IBUs:**	30
Final Gravity:	1.014–1.018	**ABV:**	6.5%
Total AAUs:	25.4		

1	lb	Munich malt, crushed
8	oz	crystal 20°L malt, crushed
6	oz	chocolate malt, crushed
6	oz	crystal 40°L malt, crushed
6	oz	crystal 60°L malt, crushed
4	oz	Carafa II malt, crushed
4	oz	roasted barley, crushed
7	lbs	pale malt extract syrup
0.5	oz	(4.2 AAU) German Smaragd pellet hops (13 IBU) **Boil 60 minutes**
4	oz	unsweetened cocoa powder **Boil 60 minutes**
0.5	teaspoon	Irish moss **Boil 20 minutes**
0.5	oz	(4.2 AAU) German Smaragd pellet hops (8 IBU) **Boil 20 minutes**
1	oz	(9 AAU) New Zealand Cascade whole hops (9 IBU) **Boil 9 minutes**
1	oz	(8 AAU) New Zealand Saaz whole hops **Boil 1 minute**
1	lb	fresh-roasted coffee (coarsely ground just before brewing) **Steep 10 minutes after boil**

Yeast: White Labs 001 California Ale, Wyeast 1056 American Ale, or dry ale yeast

Priming Sugar: 4 oz corn sugar

STEEP

While you are steeping the grains and boiling the wort, sterilize a cloth straining bag by boiling it in a small amount of water in a covered saucepan for 10 minutes. Pour off all the water, and allow to cool with the lid firmly on the pot. When the bag and pot are completely cool, carefully put the coffee grounds in the bag, and pull the drawstring tight. Keep the bag of coffee grounds in the pot with the lid in place so it will stay clean until needed.

Mix the grains with at least 2 to 2.5 gallons of water, or fill a grain bag and place it in your brew pot with 2.5 gallons of water. Gently heat to 150°F (66°C), and steep for 30 to 40 minutes. Strain all the liquid from the grains. Rinse the grains with an additional 0.5 to 1 gallon of water, and collect all the liquid. Add enough water to the wort to fill the brew kettle; the total volume should be 5.25 to 5.5 gallons (adjust for your brewing system). Heat to just before boiling, add the extract, and dissolve completely.

BOIL AND COOL

Bring to a boil, and add 0.5 ounce Smaragd hops and the cocoa powder. Boil for 40 minutes. Add the Irish moss and the remaining 0.5 ounce Smaragd hops, and boil for 10 minutes. Add the Cascade hops, and boil for 9 minutes. Add the Saaz hops, boil for 1 minute, stir well, and turn the heat off.

Now for the important part: Do not cool the beer yet! After the heat has been turned off, allow the wort to rest for a few minutes so it cools to 195 to 205°F (91–96°C) and all boiling activity has ceased. Place the bag of coffee grounds into the hot wort, stir gently, and allow to steep undisturbed for 10 minutes. This "brews" the coffee right in the wort at the proper temperature.

Give the bag of coffee and wort one final stir, then cool to 65 to 70°F (18–21°C). Transfer to a sanitized fermenter, and aerate well. It is okay to leave the coffee in the wort while cooling.

PITCH, FERMENT, AND BOTTLE

Add the yeast, then ferment for 7 to 14 days. Rack to a secondary fermenter after 5 to 7 days if desired. Prime the beer, and bottle when fermentation is complete. Allow to condition for 12 to 21 days.

Omit the malt extract. Add:

8.5 pounds pale 2-row malt, crushed
2 more ounces crystal 60°L malt, crushed
Instead of steeping, do a full mash as follows:
Heat 4.6 gallons of water to 171°F (77°C). Add all the grains, and mix well. Allow to rest for a few minutes, then adjust the temperature to 151 to 153°F (66–67°C) if needed. Hold this temperature for 45 to 60 minutes, or until starch conversion is complete. If possible, just before lautering, heat the mash to 165°F (74°C). Sparge with 3 gallons of water at 168°F (76°C). Transfer the wort to the brew kettle, then proceed with the boil, fermentation, and bottling.

Tips for greatness: For even stronger coffee flavor, add some freshly brewed coffee right before bottling. Use 1 quart of water to boil the priming sugar, then use this liquid to brew the coffee. Add 4 ounces of coffee directly to the boiled priming solution after the boiling has completely stopped, and steep for 10 minutes. Pour through a coffee filter into a sterilized mason jar, and cool to room temperature. This solution can be made the night before bottling and stored in the refrigerator overnight. Add the cooled solution to the fermenter or bottling bucket, then proceed with bottling.

Log Tosser Scottish Ale

I think I may have discovered how Scotsmen get the strength to engage in caber tossing, that strange sport of flinging 8-foot-long logs in the air — it must be the beer. This "wee-heavy" (strong) Scottish ale always disappears from my home tap way too quickly. Perhaps it is the rich malty character followed by a cozy alcohol warmth that just seems perfect after a long day when the evenings are cool.

It has a rich, grainy, caramel taste that follows with hints of caramel apple and plum sauce. It is very mellow on hops, but there is a hint of bitterness to help balance the sweet maltiness, and a slight herbal hop character comes through when you take a whiff of this beer in the glass.

Recipe for 5 US gallons

Original Gravity:	1.072	Total IBUs:	29
Final Gravity:	1.016–1.020	ABV:	6.8%
Total AAUs:	21		

1   lb crystal 40°L malt, crushed

8   oz Cara-Munich malt, crushed

8   oz crystal 15°L malt, crushed

2.5 oz roasted barley, crushed

9   lbs pale liquid malt extract

0.75 oz (8 AAU) Perle pellet hops (16 IBU) **Boil 60 minutes**

1   oz (5 AAU) American Palisades pellet hops (11 IBU) **Boil 30 minutes**

0.5 teaspoon Irish moss **Boil 15 minutes**

1   oz (8 AAU) Hallertaur pellet hops (2 IBU) **Boil 5 minutes**

Yeast: White Labs 028 Edinburgh Scottish Ale, Wyeast 1728 Scottish Ale, or dry ale yeast

Priming Sugar: 4 oz corn sugar

STEEP

Mix all the grains, and steep in at least 6 quarts of water. Heat to 150°F (66°C), and steep for 15 to 20 minutes.

Strain all the liquid from the grains. Add enough water to fill the brew kettle; the total volume should be 5.25 to 5.5 gallons (adjust for your brewing system). Heat to just before boiling, add the extract, and dissolve completely.

BOIL AND COOL

Bring to a boil, and add the Perle hops. Boil 30 minutes, add the Palisades hops, and boil for 15 minutes. Add the Irish moss, and boil another 10 minutes. Add the Hallertaur hops, and boil 5 minutes, stir well, and turn the heat off.

Cool to 65 to 70°F (18–21°C). Transfer to a sanitized fermenter and aerate well.

PITCH, FERMENT, AND BOTTLE

Add the yeast when cool, and aerate really well — strong beers require higher oxygen levels than light ones to ensure a healthy ferment. Ferment for 12 to 21 days. The best fermenting temperature is 65 to 70°F (18–21°C). Rack to a secondary fermenter after 5 to 7 days if desired. Prime the beer, and bottle when fermentation is complete. Allow to condition for 12 to 21 days.

All-Grain Adaptation: Log Tosser Scottish Ale

Omit the malt extract. Add:

10.1 pounds pale ale malt, crushed
1 pound pale Munich malt, crushed
Instead of steeping, do a full mash as follows:
Heat 5 gallons of water to 162°F (72°C). Add all the grains, and mix well. Allow to rest for a few minutes, then adjust the temperature to 151 to 153°F (66–67°C) if needed. Hold this temperature for 45 to 60 minutes, or until starch conversion is complete. If possible, just before lautering, heat the mash to 165°F (74°C). Sparge with 2.75 gallons of water at 168°F (76°C). Transfer the wort to the brew kettle, then proceed with the boil, fermentation, and bottling.

Variation — Scottish Heather Ale

Traditional Scottish heather ale was brewed during a time when heather was plentiful and cheap in Scotland while hops were not. Some folks developed a liking for this unique beer, so the style is still brewed by a few craft breweries today. If the idea of a woody herbal taste with hints of lavender and cinnamon appeals to you, a heather ale is bound to be a real treat.

To brew this as a heather ale, omit the Palisade and Hallertaur hops. When 20 minutes of boiling time remains, add 4 to 8 ounces of heather tips to the boil. Strain out with the hops before fermenting. To heighten the heather flavor, try dry hopping with an additional ounce of heather during the final 5 to 7 days of fermentation.

Dark and Foamy Irish Stout

Irish-style stout is dry rather than sweet, and most versions are lower in alcohol, which means you can enjoy a few in one sitting without feeling the alcohol too much. Earthy and bittersweet dry-roasted coffee flavors dominate. This sturdy beer has so much body that you can practically float a spoon on the thick, creamy head. It will pour an even thicker head if you are able to dispense it from a keg with a beer gas (nitrogen and carbon dioxide).

Most recipes for Irish stout do not call for as much chocolate and black malt as this one does; at the time of this writing, the only organic roasted barley available is lighter than the roasted barley usually used in this beer. The addition of some black and chocolate malts make this beer as dark as a true-to-style Irish stout should be.

Recipe for 5 US gallons

Original Gravity:	1.050	Total IBUs:	32
Final Gravity:	1.010–1.014	ABV:	4.6%
Total AAUs:	15		

8   oz barley flakes

8   oz black malt, crushed

8   oz Carafa II malt, crushed

8   oz roasted barley, crushed

4.5   pounds dry malt extract

0.75   oz (7 AAU) Kent Goldings pellet hops (18 IBU) **Boil 60 minutes**

1   oz (8 AAU) Challenger pellet hops (14 IBU) **Boil 15 minutes**

0.5   teaspoon Irish moss **Boil 15 minutes**

Yeast: White Labs 004 Irish Ale, Wyeast 1084 Irish Ale, or dry ale yeast

Priming Sugar: 3.5 oz corn sugar

STEEP

Mix the barley flakes with 1 quart of water, and bring to a boil. Remove from heat and allow to stand for 10 minutes, then add 3 to 4 quarts of cold water. Add the rest of the grain, gently heat to 150°F (66°C), and steep for 20 to 30 minutes.

Strain all the liquid from the grains. Add enough water to fill the brew kettle; the total volume should be 5.25 to 5.5 gallons (adjust for your brewing system). Heat to just before boiling, add the extract, and dissolve completely.

Note: The flaked barley absorbs a lot of water, making it difficult to filter all the liquid out. To extract more flavor and color when brewing with a grain bag, set the bag of grains in a colander over a pot after removing from the steeping liquid. Allow the grains to drain for an additional 30 to 45 minutes, and add the extra liquid collected to the wort as it boils.

BOIL AND COOL

Bring to a boil, add the Kent Goldings hops, and boil for 45 minutes. Add the Challenger hops and Irish moss, boil for 15 minutes more, stir well, and turn the heat off.

Cool to 65 to 70°F (18–21°C). Transfer to a sanitized fermenter and aerate well.

PITCH, FERMENT, AND BOTTLE

Add the yeast when cool, and ferment for 10 to 14 days. Rack to a secondary fermenter after 5 to 7 days if desired. Prime the beer, and bottle when fermentation is complete. Allow to condition for 12 to 21 days.

All-Grain Adaptation: Dark and Foamy Irish Stout

Omit the malt extract. Add:

6.5 pounds 2-row pale malt, crushed
1 more pound barley flakes
Instead of steeping, do a full mash as follows:
Heat 3.6 gallons of water to 160°F (71°C). Add all the grains, and mix well. Allow to rest for a few minutes, then adjust the temperature to 149 to 151°F (65–66°C) if needed. Hold this temperature for 45 to 60 minutes, or until starch conversion is complete. If possible, just before lautering, heat the mash to 165°F (74°C). Sparge with 2.75 gallons of water at 168°F (76°C). Transfer the wort to the brew kettle, then proceed with the boil, fermentation, and bottling.

Tips for greatness: If you are a fan of Guinness Stout, you can add a little sourness to this beer to get closer to that authentic imported flavor. Here is how: Remove about 1 pint of the beer just after adding the yeast. Strain a few ounces of plain yogurt through a coffee filter, and add the clear whey to the beer. Or you can add a pure strain of *Lactobacillus* bacteria (available at home fermentation shops, usually in a single-dose package). Leave the jar in a relatively dark place draped with a cheesecloth cover to keep insects out while allowing wild bacteria to make the sample more sour and funky.

A day or two before bottling or kegging, decant the soured beer into a clean saucepan (leave the sediment behind), and bring to a boil. Boil for 15 minutes to sterilize, cool, and pour into the fermenter. Allow to settle for at least 24 hours, then bottle or keg the beer.

Of course, you could skip all the extra work of souring a portion of the beer by buying lactic acid and just pouring it into the finished or fermenting beer. Add small amounts at a time, and taste a sample after each addition till you have the exact flavor you desire.

Velvet Midnight Oatmeal Stout

This is a roasted malt beer, almost black in color, with hints of molasses-caramel sweetness and roasted coffee. When fully carbonated, it pours with a thick brown head that lingers as you sip. Oatmeal stout is a beer often described as "chewy." The oats contribute to a thick body, creamy mouthfeel, and silky texture.

These are desirable characteristics, but be warned that oats can make a hot, sticky mess. They expand and become gelatinous when cooked, so straining them is a bit of a challenge. This recipe also has more whole grains than most of the other recipes in this chapter. For this reason I recommend you brew a few simpler homebrewed recipes before attempting this beer. If you are a fan of full-bodied, rich-tasting beers, the extra effort really is worth it!

Recipe for 5 US gallons

Original Gravity:	1.056	Total IBUs:	31
Final Gravity:	1.014–1.018	ABV:	5.3%
Total AAUs:	11.5		

- 12 oz quick-cooking oat flakes
- 8 oz black malt, crushed
- 8 oz Carafa II malt, crushed
- 8 oz crystal 60°L malt, crushed
- 8 oz Munich malt, crushed
- 4 oz crystal 120°L malt, crushed
- 4 oz roasted barley, crushed
- 6 pounds liquid malt extract
- 1 oz (7 AAU) Kent Goldings pellet hops (23 IBU) **Boil 60 minutes**

1 oz (4.5 AAU) Fuggles pellet hops (8 IBU) **Boil 15 minutes**

0.5 teaspoon Irish moss **Boil 15 minutes**

Yeast: White Labs 001 California Ale, Wyeast 1056 American Ale, or dry ale yeast

Priming Sugar: 3.5 oz corn sugar

STEEP

Mix all the grains, and immerse in at least 2.5 to 3 gallons of water. Gently heat to 150°F (66°C), and steep for 30 to 45 minutes. Try to keep the temperature constant, and stir occasionally.

Strain all the liquid from the grains. If steeped in less than 3 gallons of water, rinse the grains with an additional 0.5 to 1 gallon of water, and collect all the liquid. Add enough water to fill the brew kettle — the total liquid collected should be 5.25 gallons. Heat to just before boiling, add the extract, and dissolve completely.

BOIL AND COOL

Bring to a boil, add the Kent Goldings hops, and boil for 45 minutes. Add the Fuggles hops and Irish moss, boil for 15 minutes, stir well, and turn the heat off.

Cool to 65 to 70°F (18–21°C). Transfer to a sanitized fermenter and aerate well.

PITCH, FERMENT, AND BOTTLE

Add the yeast when cool, and aerate really well — strong beers require higher oxygen levels than light ones to ensure a healthy ferment. Ferment for 12 to 21 days. The best fermenting temperature is 68 to 73°F (20–23°C). Rack to a secondary fermenter after 5 to 7 days if desired. Prime the beer, and bottle when fermentation is complete. Allow to condition for 12 to 21 days.

All-Grain Adaptation: Velvet Midnight Oatmeal Stout

Omit the malt extract. Add:

7 pounds 2-row pale malt, crushed

8 more ounces oat flakes (quick-cooking or regular)

Instead of steeping, do a full mash as follows:

Heat 3.9 gallons of water to 171°F (77°C). Add all the grains, and mix well. Allow to rest for a few minutes, then adjust the temperature to 151 to 153°F (66–67°C) if needed. Hold this temperature for 45 to 60 minutes, or until starch conversion is complete. If possible, just before lautering, heat the mash to 165°F (74°C). Sparge with 3.5 gallons of water at 168°F (76°C). Transfer the wort to the brew kettle, then proceed with the boil, fermentation, and bottling.

Steamer Lane Lager

Northern California is widely recognized as the birthplace of the California Common beer, a style preserved by Anchor Brewing in San Francisco with its flagship Anchor Steam lager. I named this recipe for the local surf culture in Santa Cruz — Steamer Lane is renowned for its regular powerful waves. Uncommon Brewers, a local organic brewery, has a tasty take on this style called Steamers Lane, flavored with lavender.

This refreshing lager hits the spot after a hard day of work or a full day of outdoor fun in the sun. It is a rich amber malty brew with a citrus balsam accent and a lively carbonation level. The key to making this beer right is the yeast. The California Lager yeast ferments beautifully at 60°F (16°C) while retaining crisp, quaffable lager characteristics. It's an easy-to-brew lager for those who do not have access to a winter cellar or refrigerated fermenting space.

Recipe for 5 US gallons

Original Gravity:	1.048	Total IBUs:	30
Final Gravity:	1.010–1.014	ABV:	4.5%
Total AAUs:	24		

- 8 oz Carahell malt, crushed
- 8 oz Vienna malt, crushed
- 4 oz crystal 40°L malt, crushed
- 5.7 lbs pale malt extract syrup
- 8 oz corn sugar
- 0.5 oz (4 AAU) German Perle pellet hops (14 IBU) **Boil 60 minutes**
- 0.5 teaspoon Irish moss **Boil 15 minutes**
- 1 oz (8 AAU) California Ivanhoe whole hops (12 IBU) **Boil 15 minutes**

0.5 oz (4 AAU) German Perle pellet hops (4 IBU) **Boil 5 minutes**
  1 oz (8 AAU) American Cascade pellet hops **Add at flameout**
Yeast: White Labs 810 San Francisco Lager or Wyeast 2112 California Lager
Priming Sugar: 4.5 oz corn sugar

STEEP

Mix the grains with at least 2 quarts of water, or fill a grain bag and place it in your brew pot filled with water. Gently heat to 150°F (66°C), and steep for 20 to 30 minutes.

Strain all the liquid from the grains. Add enough water to the wort to fill the brew kettle; the total volume should be 5.25 to 5.5 gallons (adjust for your brewing system). Heat to just before boiling, add the extract and corn sugar, and dissolve completely.

BOIL AND COOL

Bring to a boil, and add 0.5 ounce of Perle hops. Boil for 45 minutes. Add the Irish moss and Ivanhoe hops, and boil for 10 minutes. Add the remaining 0.5 ounce of Perle hops, and boil for 5 minutes. At the very end of the boil, add the Cascade hops, stir well, and turn the heat off.

Cool to 60 to 65°F (16–18 °C). Transfer to a sanitized fermenter, and aerate well.

PITCH, FERMENT, AND BOTTLE

Add the yeast, then ferment for 10 to 14 days, keeping the temperature between 55 and 65°F (13 and 18°C). Rack to a secondary fermenter after 5 to 7 days if desired. Prime the beer, and bottle when fermentation is complete. Allow to condition for 14 to 21 days.

All-Grain Adaptation: Steamer Lane Lager

Omit the malt extract. Add:

6.5 pounds 2-row pale malt, crushed
4 more ounces Vienna malt, crushed
4 more ounces crystal 40°L malt, crushed

Instead of steeping, do a full mash as follows:

Heat 3.1 gallons of water to 170°F (77°C). Add all the grains, and mix well. Allow to rest for a few minutes, then adjust the temperature to 149 to 151°F (65–66°C) if needed. Hold this temperature for 45 to 60 minutes, or until starch conversion is complete. If possible, just before lautering, heat the mash to 165°F (74°C). Sparge with 4 gallons of water at 168°F (76°C). Transfer the wort to the brew kettle, then proceed with the boil, fermentation, and bottling.

Cerveza Negra Buena

This simple lager is similar to the popular Mexican dark beer Negra Modelo. It is mellow, smooth, and slightly sweet with a crisp lager finish. It goes great with Mexican food, especially spicy tacos. This is a lager, so if you do not have a cool fermenting area such as a basement in the winter, I recommend using a California Common lager yeast instead of the Mexican lager yeast to prevent excess off-flavors (such as banana and fruit) commonly produced by most lager yeasts at higher temperatures.

Recipe for 5 US gallons

Original Gravity:	1.058	**Total IBUs:**	26
Final Gravity:	1.012–1.016	**ABV:**	5.5%
Total AAUs:	8		

- 8 oz Cara-Munich malt, crushed
- 8 oz Vienna malt, crushed
- 4 oz Crystal 20°L malt, crushed
- 4 oz Crystal 40°L malt, crushed
- 2.5 oz Carafa II chocolate malt, crushed
- 5 lbs dry malt extract (DME)
- 1 lb corn sugar
- 1 oz (4.5 AAU) German Hersbrucker pellet hops (15 IBU) **Boil 60 minutes**
- 0.5 oz (3.5 AAU) German Hallertaur Tradition pellet hops (11 IBU) **Boil 20 minutes**
- 0.5 teaspoon Irish moss **Boil 20 minutes**
- *Yeast:* White Labs 940 Mexican Lager, or Wyeast 2035 American Lager*
- *Priming Sugar:* 4 oz corn sugar

*Use California Common Lager yeast (Wyeast 2112 or White Labs 810) if you cannot hold fermenting temperatures between 50 and 60°F (10 and 16°C). Use a dry lager yeast if you cannot obtain liquid yeast.

STEEP

Mix all the grains, and immerse in at least 5 quarts of water. Gently heat to 150°F (66°C), and steep for 15 to 20 minutes. Strain all the liquid from the grains. Add enough water to fill the brew kettle; the total liquid collected should be 5.25 gallons. Heat to just before boiling, add the extract and corn sugar, and dissolve completely.

BOIL AND COOL

Bring to a boil, add the German Hersbrucker hops, and boil for 40 minutes. Add the Hallertaur Tradition hops and the Irish moss; boil for 20 minutes, stir well, and turn the heat off.

Cool to 60 to 65°F (16–18°C). Transfer to a sanitized fermenter and aerate well.

PITCH, FERMENT, AND BOTTLE

Add the yeast when cool, and aerate really well — lagers require higher oxygen levels than ales of the same strength to ensure a healthy ferment. Ferment for 10 to 14 days. The best fermenting temperature is 50 to 60°F (10–16°C). Rack to a secondary fermenter after 5 to 7 days if desired. A 3-week fermentation is recommended for this beer, but it may need longer to fully clear. Prime the beer, and bottle when fermentation is complete. Allow to condition for 12 to 21 days.

All-Grain Adaptation: Cerveza Negra Buena

Omit the malt extract. Add:

7 pounds 2-row pale malt, crushed
8 more ounces Vienna malt, crushed
3 more ounces crystal 40°L malt, crushed
Instead of steeping, do a full mash as follows:
Heat 3.5 gallons of water to 170°F (77°C). Add all the grains, and mix well. Allow to rest for a few minutes, then adjust the temperature to 149 to 151°F (65–66°C) if needed. Hold this temperature for 45 to 60 minutes, or until starch conversion is complete. If possible, just before lautering, heat the mash to 165°F (74°C). Sparge

with 3.75 gallons of water at 168°F (76°C). Transfer the wort to the brew kettle, then proceed with the boil, fermentation, and bottling.

Tips for greatness: Keeping the temperatures within the recommended range will really make a difference in the quality of this beer. The final beer will improve further with a cold aging stage, a process called lagering. Read more about maintaining lager fermentation temperatures in chapter 4.

Oktoberville Festbier

Oktoberfest was one of those beers that got me excited about brewing when I first tasted it. When properly aged, this is a real treat that evokes all the best things of autumn: the fall harvest; warm fires; rich fall dishes such as apple pie, sausages, and hearty stew. It is a smooth, malty beer with a mellow dose of refined German hops that gives the beer a subtle spicy aroma.

This beer needs to ferment cold, so you will need room in a refrigerator or a cold cellar. If you do not have access to a temperature-controlled fermenting environment, there are a few options. You can use California Common yeast to ferment it instead of traditional lager yeast, or you can place the fermenter in an ice-water bath. If you fill plastic bottles with water, freeze them, and float them in the bath, then change them each day, it is possible to achieve the required fermenting temperatures, as long as you are diligent.

Recipe for 5 US gallons

Original Gravity:	1.052	**Total IBUs:**	22
Final Gravity:	1.012–1.014	**ABV:**	5.1%
Total AAUs:	13.5		

- 1 lb Carahell malt, crushed
- 1 lb Munich malt, crushed
- 8 oz Crystal 60°L malt, crushed
- 4 oz Cara-Munich malt, crushed
- 4 oz rye flakes*
- 5.5 lbs pale malt extract syrup
- 0.5 oz (3.5 AAU) German Hallertaur Tradition pellet hops (11 IBU) **Boil 60 minutes**
- 0.5 oz (4.5 AAU) German Opal pellet hops (10 IBU) **Boil 20 minutes**

| 0.5 | teaspoon Irish moss **Boil 20 minutes** |
| 1 | oz (5.5 AAU) German Spalt Select pellet hops (1 IBU) **Boil 1 minute** |

Yeast: White Labs 830 German Lager, or Wyeast 2124 Bohemian Lager**

Priming Sugar: 4 oz corn sugar

*A tiny dash of rye helps give this beer a slightly tart finish. If you are a purist and want to brew this in the true German tradition, with only barley and hops, by all means skip the rye and use four more ounces of Munich malt instead.

**Use California Common Lager yeast (Wyeast 2112 or White Labs 810) if you cannot hold fermenting temperatures below 50°F (10°C). Use a dry lager yeast if liquid yeast is not available.

STEEP

Mix all the grains, and immerse in at least 5 quarts of water. Gently heat to 150°F (66°C), and steep for 20 to 30 minutes. Strain all the liquid from the grains. Add enough water to fill the brew kettle; the total liquid collected should be 5.25 gallons. Heat to just before boiling, add the extract, and dissolve completely.

BOIL AND COOL

Bring to a boil, add the Hallertaur Tradition hops, and boil for 40 minutes. Add the Opal hops and Irish moss, then boil for 19 minutes. Add the Spalt Select hops, boil for 1 minute, stir well, and turn the heat off.

Cool to 60 to 65°F (16–18°C). Transfer to a sanitized fermenter, and aerate well.

PITCH, FERMENT, AND BOTTLE

Add the yeast when cool, and aerate really well — lagers require higher oxygen levels than ales of the same strength to ensure a healthy ferment. Once fermentation activity starts, slowly drop the temperature by about 8°F (4°C) per day so that it reaches 44°F (7°C) in 2 days. Ferment at this temperature for 14 to 28 days. Racking to a secondary fermenter after 7 to 10 days is recommended. A 3-week fermentation is recommended for this beer, but it may need up to a week longer to fully clear. Prime the beer, and bottle when fermentation is complete. Allow to condition for 12 to 21 days.

Omit the malt extract. Add:

5.5 pounds pilsner malt, crushed
1.5 pounds pale Munich malt, crushed
2 more ounces Cara-Munich malt, crushed

Instead of steeping, do a full mash as follows:

Heat 3.8 gallons of water to 172°F (78°C). Add all the grains, and mix well. Allow to rest for a few minutes, then adjust the temperature to 151 to 153°F (66–67°C) if needed. Hold this temperature for 45 to 60 minutes, or until starch conversion is complete. If possible, just before lautering, heat the mash to 165°F (74°C). Sparge with 3.5 gallons of water at 168°F (76°C). Transfer the wort to the brew kettle, then proceed with the boil, fermentation, and bottling.

Tips for greatness: Keeping the temperatures within the recommended range will really make a difference in the quality of this beer. Additionally, the final beer will improve further with lagering. Read more about maintaining lager fermentation temperatures in chapter 4.

Summer of Lovenweizen

This is a tart, refreshing wheat beer in the clean American style, perfect for a hot summer day and a wonderful complement to grilled veggies, chicken, or fish. Unlike a German-style wheat beer, which typically exhibits clove and banana, this beer has a refreshing flavor with hints of citrus and apricot. The light body and clean flavor make it ideal for adding fruit or spices (see Variation).

Extract recipes for wheat beers typically call for wheat malt extract. Because wheat extract is not available in organic form, this is a partial-mash recipe calling for more precise temperature control than some of the other recipes in this chapter. Although you could certainly tackle this recipe for your very first brew, you might have better results if you brew a few simpler recipes before taking on the added detail of doing a mini mash brew. This beer really depends on the yeast to achieve the desired hefeweizen characteristics. If you substitute a different yeast, the flavor profile will not quite match what is described here.

Recipe for 5 US gallons

Original Gravity:	1.050	Total IBUs:	25
Final Gravity:	1.010–1.014	ABV:	4.6%
Total AAUs:	9.5		

3 lbs white wheat malt, crushed

8 oz Vienna malt, crushed

4 lbs dry malt extract

0.75 oz (5.5 AAU) New Zealand Motueka whole hops (17 IBU) **Boil 60 minutes**

1 oz (4 AAU) German Saphir pellet hops (8 IBU) **Boil 20 minutes**

Yeast: White Labs 380 Hefeweizen IV, Wyeast 1010 American Wheat, or dry wheat beer yeast

Priming Sugar: 3.5 oz corn sugar

STEEP

Mix the grains, and immerse in at least 2.5 to 3 gallons of water. Gently heat to 150°F (66°C), and steep for 30 to 45 minutes. Try to keep the temperature constant, and stir occasionally. Strain all the liquid from the grains. If steeped in less than 3 gallons of water, rinse the grains with an additional 0.5 to 1 gallon of hot water (170°F [77°C]), and collect all the liquid. Add enough water to fill the brew kettle; the total liquid should be 5.25 gallons. Heat to just before boiling, add the extract, and dissolve completely.

BOIL AND COOL

Bring to a boil, add the Motueka hops, and boil for 40 minutes. Add the Saphir hops, boil for 20 minutes, stir well, and turn the heat off.

Cool to 70 to 75°F (21–24°C). Transfer to a sanitized fermenter, and aerate well.

PITCH, FERMENT, AND BOTTLE

Add the yeast when cool, and aerate well. Ferment for 12 to 21 days. The best fermenting temperature is 65 to 72°F (18–22°C). Rack to a secondary fermenter after 5 to 7 days if desired. Prime the beer, and bottle when fermentation is complete. Allow to condition for 12 to 21 days.

All-Grain Adaptation: Summer of Lovenweizen

Omit the malt extract. Add:

4.25 pounds 2-row malt, crushed
1 more pound white wheat malt, crushed
8 more ounces Vienna malt, crushed

Instead of steeping, do a full mash as follows:

Heat 3.5 gallons of water to 170°F (77°C). Add all the grains, and mix well. Allow to rest for a few minutes, then adjust the temperature to 149 to 151°F (65–66°C) if needed. Hold this temperature for 45 to 60 minutes, or until starch conversion is complete. If possible, just before lautering, heat the mash to 165°F (74°C). Sparge with 3.75 gallons of water at 168°F (76°C). Transfer the wort to the brew kettle, then proceed with the boil, fermentation, and bottling.

Tips for greatness: The white wheat malt in this brew becomes quite sticky in the mashing process, making it difficult to filter all the liquid out. Sparging the grains with hot water will aid in the extraction of more fermentable sugars (see Lautering, or How to Sparge, page 94). If brewing with a grain bag, set the bag of grains in a colander over a pot after removing from the steeping liquid. Allow the grains to drain for an additional 30 to 45 minutes, and add the extra liquid collected to the wort as it boils.

Variation — Apricot Wheat

Apricots complement the flavors of this hefeweizen very well, and the fruit adds a refreshing tartness that really quenches your thirst on a hot summer day. It goes great with barbecued pork ribs, summer salads, or fruit desserts. Fresh apricots really make this beer. If you add apricots or other fruit to this beer, use slightly less water when you brew it so there is room in the fermenter for the fruit.

To infuse the most fruit flavor, it is best to add the fruit during secondary fermentation. By waiting for the most vigorous part of the fermentation to pass, more of the aromas and flavors of the fruit will remain in the beer instead of being driven off by the rapid off-gassing that occurs during primary fermentation. The best time to add the fruit is after the foam has almost completely disappeared from the top of the beer, and the bubbling through the airlock or blowoff tube has slowed to a crawl. Five to 7 days is usually right.

Use at least 2 pounds and up to 6 pounds of fruit for this recipe. The more fruit you add, the more intense the flavor. More fruit will also add alcohol to the beer, though, so don't overdo it, because a strong alcohol flavor could overwhelm the delicate fresh fruit flavors. See page 201 for directions on adding fruit to your beer.

Jalapeño Loco Saison

This beer contains a riotous mix of flavors that work surprisingly well together: the saison style that evolved in Wallonia, Belgium, with the added spice of the taco houses that abound in the area I live in, plus a dash of pulque-fermented agave. The jalapeños lend an earthy, fresh-cut pepper flavor that tingles the mouth without being overpowering. The agave gives a distinct cactus dryness, and the citrus nose of the hops adds a nice counterpart.

The saison beer style was truly the homebrew of farmers in their small artisanal breweries, made as a quaffing beer for thirsty farmworkers. Although most beer styles have a distinct profile, saisons vary quite a bit in recipe. Some have added spice, and the hops and malts used vary widely from recipe to recipe, yet the saison style as a whole offers a distinctive complexity. The saison yeast is very important to this particular beer, as it contributes the unique spicy characteristics, fruit undertones, and hint of acidic sourness that define the style.

Recipe for 5 US gallons

Original Gravity:	1.076	**Total IBUs:**	27
Final Gravity:	1.018–1.021	**ABV:**	7.1%
Total AAUs:	24.5		

- 2 lbs Gambrinus white wheat malt, crushed
- 1 lb Gambrinus pilsner malt, crushed
- 8 oz Gambrinus Munich malt, crushed
- 6 lbs dry malt extract
- 1 lb light agave syrup
- 0.5 oz (7.5 AAU) American Summit pellet hops (20 IBU) **Boil 60 minutes**
- 0.4 oz (4.5 AAU) New Zealand Nelson Sauvin pellet hops (6 IBU) **Boil 15 minutes**

0.4 oz (4.5 AAU) New Zealand Nelson Sauvin pellet hops (1 IBU)
   Boil 5 minutes

1–5 fresh jalapeño peppers, seeds and stems removed, diced
   Boil 5 minutes

0.7 oz (8 AAU) New Zealand Nelson Sauvin pellet hops **Add at flameout**

Yeast: White Labs 565 Belgian Saison I, or Wyeast 3724 Belgian Saison

Priming Sugar: 4 oz corn sugar

STEEP

Mix all the grains, and immerse in at least 2.5 to 3 gallons of water. Gently heat to 150°F (66°C), and steep for 30 to 45 minutes. Keep the temperature constant, and stir occasionally.

Strain all the liquid from the grains. If steeped in less than 2.5 gallons of water, rinse the grains with an additional 0.5 to 1 gallon of hot water (170°F [77°C]), and collect all the liquid. Add enough water to fill the brew kettle; the total liquid collected should be 5.25 gallons. Heat to just before boiling, add the extract and agave syrup, and dissolve completely.

BOIL AND COOL

Bring to a boil, add the Summit hops, and boil for 45 minutes. Add the 0.4 oz. Nelson Sauvin hops, and boil for 10 minutes. Add another 0.4 oz. Nelson Sauvin hops and the jalapeños (adjust to your liking — caution advised!), and boil for 5 minutes. Add the last of the Nelson Sauvin hops, stir well, and turn the heat off.

Cool to 70 to 75°F (21–24°C). Transfer to a sanitized fermenter, and aerate well.

PITCH, FERMENT, AND BOTTLE

Add the yeast when cool, and aerate well. Ferment for 14 to 30 days. The best fermenting temperature is 75 to 85°F (24–29°C), as the saison yeast really likes a warmer fermentation temperature. Rack to a secondary fermenter after 5 to 7 days if desired. Prime the beer, and bottle when fermentation is complete. Allow to condition for 12 to 21 days.

Tips for greatness: Maintain a warmer fermentation for this beer. Saison yeast starts out quite vigorous but tapers off quickly, and if the temperature is too low, you may wind up with an incomplete fermentation. Try not to go overboard on the jalapeños: Use more if the peppers are small, or if you like a lot of heat. Use fewer to keep the heat down or if they are large. Taste a small bit of the pepper to gauge the hotness of the pepper, and adjust accordingly. The trick is to add enough jalapeño to be noticeable but not so much that it overpowers the subtle pepper flavors imparted by the yeast.

Early summer is a great time to brew this beer so that it will be at its peak goodness in the fall, perfect to enjoy with fall harvest vegetable dishes, such as warm squash soup, roasted heirloom tomatoes, or corn on the cob. This beer improves with some aging, so set those bottles in a dark pantry or closet that stays between 60 and 70°F (16 and 21°C), and let them age for 2 to 6 months.

All-Grain Adaptation: Jalapeño Loco Saison

Omit the malt extract. Add:

9 more pounds pilsner malt, crushed
8 more ounces Munich malt, crushed
Instead of steeping, do a full mash as follows:
Heat 4.5 gallons of water to 170°F (77°C). Add all the grains, and mix well. Allow to rest for a few minutes, then adjust the temperature to 148 to 150°F (64.5–65.5°C) if needed. Hold this temperature for 45 to 60 minutes, or until starch conversion is complete. If possible, just before lautering, heat the mash to 165°F (74°C). Sparge with 3.25 gallons of water at 168°F (76°C). Transfer the wort to the brew kettle, then proceed with the boil, fermentation, and bottling.

8

ADVANCED all-grain RECIPES

These recipes are gleaned from my collection of all-grain organic homebrew recipes that has been almost 20 years in the making. I have chosen a few favorites and tried to include a wide range of styles. This is only the tip of the iceberg — I am only one brewer in a community of thousands who are interested in brewing beer made with organic and/or locally grown and seasonal ingredients. I invite you to dabble in recipe creation (covered in the next chapter) and to contribute your successful recipes to the growing library of sustainably brewed recipes (see Resources and check out my website, www.amelialoftus.com).

Hop Goddess Bitter (English Pale Ale)

This is an English-style session beer, the kind you expect when you walk into a pub in London and order a pint of bitter to quench your thirst. Not too strong and not too light, with just the right level of hops. It isn't "in your face" hoppy like an American pale ale, but it still has a good whiff of hops. The hops don't explode with pine and citrus, either. In true European fashion they are more refined and mellow, with herbal hints and a slight kiss of fruit. It all adds up to a well-balanced ale perfect for relaxing after a long day on the job. Better yet, it is a very easy all-grain recipe to brew, and a great choice for your first all-grain batch.

Recipe for 5 US gallons

Original Gravity:	1.052	Total IBUs:	34
Final Gravity:	1.012–1.016	ABV:	4.9%
Total AAUs:	19		

- 8.5 lbs English pale ale malt, crushed*
- 8 oz crystal 20°L malt, crushed
- 8 oz Victory or Biscuit malt, crushed
- 4 oz crystal 90°L malt, crushed
- 1 oz (7 AAU) Kent Goldings pellet hops (24 IBU) **Boil 60 minutes**
- 1 oz (5 AAU) Fuggles pellet hops (10 IBU) **Boil 20 minutes**
- 0.5 teaspoon Irish moss **Boil 20 minutes**
- 1 oz (7 AAU) Kent Goldings pellet hops **Add at flameout**

Yeast: White Labs 023 Burton Ale, Wyeast 1275 Thames Valley Ale, or dry ale yeast

Priming Sugar: 3.5 oz corn sugar

*At this writing, organic Crisp English malt is available in the United States, and other brands are available from time to time. If you cannot find English malt, Gambrinus pale malt is a good alternative.

STEEP

Heat 3.75 gallons of water to 165°F (74°C). Add all the grains, and mix well. Allow to rest for a few minutes, then adjust the temperature to 152 to 154°F (67–68°C) if needed. Hold this temperature for 45 to 60 minutes, or until starch conversion is complete. If possible, just before lautering, heat the mash to 165°F (74°C). Sparge with 3.5 gallons of water at 168°F (76°C). Transfer the wort to the brew kettle, and bring to a boil.

BOIL AND COOL

Once the wort has reached a full boil, start your timer, and add 1 ounce of the Kent Goldings hops. Boil for 40 minutes. Add the Fuggles hops and the Irish moss, and boil for 20 minutes. Add the second ounce of Kent Goldings hops, then turn the heat off.

Cool the wort to 65 to 70°F (18–21°C). Transfer to a sanitized fermenter and aerate well.

PITCH, FERMENT, AND BOTTLE

Add the yeast, then ferment for 5 to 7 days. Rack to a secondary fermenter if desired. Ferment for an additional 7 to 10 days. Prime the beer, and bottle when fermentation is complete. Allow to condition for at least 14 to 21 days.

Grateful Summer Ale

Summer ales are the top fermenter's answer to "lawn mower beers" — those highly quaffable but usually flavorless national brand lagers that many American beer drinkers were raised on. This light, refreshing, and oh-so-civilized beer really hits the spot when temperatures soar. The grapefruit and lemon zest pair nicely with the citrus hops to give this beer an exciting yet lighthearted zing that's perfect with lighter summer fare, such as salads, cold sandwiches, quiche, or grilled chicken and fish. If maintaining cooler fermentation temperatures is a challenge but you want a light and refreshing beer, this just might be your answer.

Recipe for 5 US gallons

Original Gravity:	1.055	Total IBUs:	29
Final Gravity:	1.010–1.015	ABV:	5.2%
Total AAUs:	16		

- 4 lbs pilsner malt, crushed
- 4 lbs 2-row malt, crushed
- 1 lb white wheat malt, crushed
- 1 lb light honey
- 0.75 oz (6 AAU) Sterling pellet hops (20 IBU) **Boil 60 minutes**
- 1 oz (4 AAU) German Saphir pellet hops (8 IBU) **Boil 20 minutes**

0.5	teaspoon Irish moss **Boil 20 minutes**
1	oz (6 AAU) American Cascade pellet hops (1 IBU) **Boil 1 minute**
1–2	oz fresh zest from 1 or 2 grapefruits *and* 2 to 4 lemons **Add at flameout**

Yeast: White Labs 002 English Ale, or 001 California Ale, or Wyeast 1968 London ESB Ale, or 1056 American Ale, or dry ale yeast

Priming Sugar: 4 oz corn sugar

STEEP

Heat 3.5 gallons of water to 165°F (74°C). Add all the grains, and mix well. Allow to rest for a few minutes, then adjust the temperature to 149 to 151°F (65–66°C) if needed. Hold this temperature for 45 to 60 minutes, or until starch conversion is complete. If possible, just before lautering, heat the mash to 165°F. Sparge with 3.75 gallons of water at 168°F (76°C). Transfer the wort to the brew kettle, add the honey, and stir to dissolve completely, then bring to a boil.

BOIL AND COOL

Once the wort has reached a full boil, start your timer and add the Sterling hops. Boil for 40 minutes. Add the Saphir hops and the Irish moss, and boil for 19 minutes. Add the Cascade hops, boil 1 minute then turn the heat off. As soon as the heat has been turned off, add the citrus zest and stir well.

Cool the wort to 65 to 70°F (18–21°C). Transfer to a sanitized fermenter, and aerate well.

PITCH, FERMENT, AND BOTTLE

Add the yeast, then ferment for 5 to 7 days. Rack to a secondary fermenter if desired. Ferment for an additional 7 to 10 days. Prime the beer, and bottle when fermentation is complete. Allow to condition for at least 14 to 21 days.

Flavor Variations

The clean, crisp, palate-cleansing base of this recipe provides an excellent springboard to showcase the complementary flavors of fruits, herbs, and spices. Along with citrus zest, some flavors to try include chamomile, coriander, ginger, grains of paradise, kiwi, lavender, lemongrass, sage, white grapes, or white pepper. Most of these flavors should be added right after the heat is turned off or in the secondary fermenter.

My, Oh Rye (Red Rye Ale)

Rye tends to bring up the spiciness of whatever hops and other flavors might be added to a beer. This is a full-bodied, deep copper–colored ale with the right mix of herbal spicy hops to accentuate the rye and caramel flavors. Hints of clove and caraway meld with a touch of citrus and a definitive hop bite that verges on bitter. With just a bit of breadiness, this beer evokes visions of fresh-baked caraway rye crackers.

Organic rye malt is difficult to find, so flaked rye is used instead. It does not take much rye to give a beer its signature flavor. The dry, crisp character of this beer is wonderful with rich, spicy food, especially Indian and Caribbean dishes.

Recipe for 5 US gallons

Original Gravity:	1.063	**Total IBUs:**	49
Final Gravity:	1.015–1.020	**ABV:**	6.0%
Total AAUs:	30.5		

- 7.5 lbs 2-row malt, crushed
- 2 lbs rye flakes
- 12 oz Cara-Munich malt, crushed
- 12 oz Munich malt, crushed
- 8 oz Cara-Pils malt, crushed
- 8 oz crystal 40°L malt, crushed
- 6 oz crystal 90°L malt, crushed
- 2 oz roasted barley, crushed
- 1 oz (8 AAU) German Perle pellet hops (24 IBU) **Boil 60 minutes**
- 1 oz (8.5 AAU) German Smaragd pellet hops (16 IBU) **Boil 20 minutes**
- 0.5 teaspoon Irish moss **Boil 20 minutes**
- 1 oz (8 AAU) New Zealand Hallertaur pellet hops (9 IBU) **Boil 10 minutes**
- 1 oz (6 AAU) American Cascade pellet hops **Add at flameout**

Yeast: White Labs 002 English Ale, or 001 California Ale, or Wyeast 1968 London ESB Ale or 1056 American Ale, or dry ale yeast

Priming Sugar: 4 oz corn sugar

STEEP

Heat 3.75 gallons of water to 140°F (60°C). Add all the grains, and mix well. Allow to rest for a few minutes, then adjust the temperature to 119 to 121°F (48–49°C), if needed. Hold this temperature for 30 minutes. Meanwhile, bring 2 gallons of water to a boil. Add this boiling water to the mash at the 30-minute mark. This should bring the temperature up to 149 to 151°F (65–66°C). Steep for another 30 minutes, or until starch conversion is complete. If possible, just before lautering, heat the mash to 165°F (74°C). Sparge with 2 gallons of water at 168°F (76°C). Transfer the wort to the brew kettle, and bring to a boil.

BOIL AND COOL

Once the wort has reached a full boil, start your timer and add 1 ounce of Perle hops. Boil for 40 minutes. Add the Smaragd hops and the Irish moss, and boil for 10 minutes. Add the New Zealand Hallertaur hops, and boil for another 10 minutes. Add the Cascade hops, stir well, and turn the heat off.

Cool the wort to 65 to 70°F (18–21°C). Transfer to a sanitized fermenter, and aerate well.

PITCH, FERMENT, AND BOTTLE

Add the yeast, then ferment for 5 to 7 days. Rack to a secondary fermenter if desired. Ferment for an additional 7 to 10 days. Prime the beer, and bottle when fermentation is complete. Allow to condition for at least 14 to 21 days.

Hop Variations

The base style of this beer is an IPA, so if you like your IPAs really hoppy, go ahead and add a bit more bittering hops. A 30-minute hop addition works well. Use another ounce or two of Cascade or Hallertaur to dry hop in the secondary for an added hoppy nose. You can also accentuate the spiciness imparted by the rye by adding a bit of clove or caraway. Both of these spices are very strong; just a few teaspoons added in the last 10 minutes of the boil will impart a distinct flavor.

Born in the IPA

This big, malty, and slightly sloppy beer bursts with a vibrant hoppy nose and a nice hop bite that balances out the sturdy malt backbone. It's a true celebration of American hops utilizing three wonderful all-American varieties: Chinook, Sterling, and Simcoe. Since availability of organic hops changes from year to year, you may need to substitute hops. Choose ones with piney and citrus characteristics to stay true to the style of this beer. (See the hop chart starting on page 317 for ideas.)

The hops in this brazen beer are loud and proud, making English IPA seem tame and refined in comparison! With its boldly assertive hop flavor and hefty alcohol content, this is a great beer to serve with your best barbecue or just a simple and delicious burger — if you are vegetarian, try it with a Quick Spent-Grain Veggie Burger (page 141).

Recipe for 5 US gallons

Original Gravity:	1.073	**Total IBUs:**	64
Final Gravity:	1.015–1.020	**ABV:**	7.4%
Total AAUs:	62		

11 lbs American 2-row malt, crushed

1 lb crystal 20°L malt, crushed

12 oz Cara-Pils malt, crushed

12 oz Munich malt, crushed

4 oz wheat malt, crushed

2 oz crystal 60°L malt, crushed

1 oz (10 AAU) American Chinook whole hops (26 IBU) **Boil 60 minutes**

2 oz (16 AAU) American Sterling pellet hops (27 IBU) **Boil 20 minutes**

.5 teaspoon Irish moss **Boil 20 minutes**

1 oz (12 AAU) American Simcoe pellet hops (11 IBU) **Boil 10 minutes**

1 oz (12 AAU) American Simcoe pellet hops **Add at flameout**

1 oz (12 AAU) American Simcoe pellet hops **Dry hop in secondary fermenter**

Yeast: White Labs 001 California Ale or 051 California V, Wyeast 1056 American Ale, or dry ale yeast

Priming Sugar: 4 oz corn sugar

STEEP

Heat 5 gallons of water to 160°F (71°C). Add all the grains, and mix well. Allow to rest for a few minutes, then adjust the temperature to 148 to 150°F (64–66°C) if needed. Hold this temperature for 60 to 90 minutes, or until starch conversion is complete. If possible, just before lautering, heat the mash to 165°F (74°C). Sparge with 3 gallons of water at 168°F (76°C). Transfer the wort to the brew kettle, and bring to a boil.

BOIL AND COOL

Once the wort has reached a full boil, start your timer, and add the Chinook hops. Boil for 40 minutes. Add the Sterling hops and the Irish moss, and boil for 10 minutes. Add 1 ounce of Simcoe hops, and boil for another 10 minutes. Add the second ounce of Simcoe hops, stir well, and turn the heat off.

Cool the wort to 65 to 70°F (18–21°C). Transfer to a sanitized fermenter, and aerate well.

PITCH, FERMENT, AND BOTTLE

Add the yeast, then ferment for 5 to 7 days. Rack to a secondary fermenter if desired. Ferment this beer for a total of 12 to 21 days. Add the third ounce of Simcoe hops to the secondary fermenter when the beer has nearly completed fermentation, so that they remain in the beer for the last 5 to 7 days. Leaving them in the beer for too long can cause the beer to taste fruity and exhibit a heightened bitterness. Prime the beer, and bottle when fermentation is complete. Allow to condition for 12 to 21 days.

Variation — Black IPA

For a beer that is just as delicious but decadently dark, add 8 ounces of Weyermann Carafa II and 4 ounces of black malt. Reduce the crystal 20°L from 16 to 12 ounces and the 2-row to 10.5 pounds. Follow the same brew schedule as the above recipe.

Irie in a Jar (Irish Red Ale)

A good Irish ale does not have to be jet-black and thick enough to float a coaster! This sturdy beer is surprisingly refreshing and just what you need to keep up a lively pace when dancing to your favorite pub band. The beer is a deep ruby red with a decent head that lingers in the glass. Roasted malt and caramel flavors are balanced with mild earthy and woodsy hop flavors and the clean finish that will make you want a second glass. It is just perfect with Irish dishes, such as potato and leek soup or corned beef, or try it with some Spent-Grain Irish Soda Bread (page 144).

Recipe for 5 US gallons

Original Gravity:	1.050	Total IBUs:	22
Final Gravity:	1.012–1.016	ABV:	4.8%
Total AAUs:	11		

- 8 lbs English pale ale malt, crushed
- 8 oz barley flakes
- 8 oz crystal 60°L malt, crushed
- 4 oz Special B malt, crushed (or use dark caramel 120–140°L)
- 2 oz chocolate malt, crushed
- 2 oz roasted barley, crushed
- 0.5 oz (4 AAU) English Challenger pellet hops (14 IBU) **Boil 60 minutes**
- 0.5 teaspoon Irish moss **Boil 20 minutes**
- 0.5 oz (3.5 AAU) Kent Goldings pellet hops (6 IBU) **Boil 15 minutes**
- 0.5 oz (3.5 AAU) Kent Goldings pellet hops (2 IBU) **Boil 5 minutes**

Yeast: White Labs 004 Irish Ale, Wyeast 1084 Irish Ale, or dry ale yeast
Priming Sugar: 4 oz corn sugar

STEEP

Heat 3.5 gallons of water to 172°F (78°C). Add all the grains, and mix well. Allow to rest for a few minutes, then adjust the temperature to 151 to 153°F (66–67°C) if needed. Hold this temperature for 45 to 60 minutes, or until starch conversion is complete. If possible, just before lautering, heat the mash to 165°F (74°C). Sparge with 3.75 gallons of water at 168°F (76°C). Transfer the wort to the brew kettle, and bring to a boil.

BOIL AND COOL

Once the wort has reached a full boil, start your timer, and add the Challenger hops. Boil for 40 minutes. Add the Irish moss, and boil for 5 minutes. Add 0.5 ounce of Kent Goldings hops, and boil for 10 minutes. Add the second 0.5 ounce of Kent Goldings hops, boil for 5 minutes, then turn the heat off.

Cool the wort to 65 to 70°F (18–21°C). Transfer to a sanitized fermenter, and aerate well.

PITCH, FERMENT, AND BOTTLE

Add the yeast, then ferment for 5 to 7 days. Rack to a secondary fermenter if desired. Ferment for an additional 5 to 7 days. Prime the beer, and bottle when fermentation is complete. Allow to condition for 10 to 21 days.

Nutty Moo (English Brown Ale)

A classic brown ale like this is a favorite, because it's a quick brew that almost everybody likes. This mild, civilized beer is a great session beer for cooler days or nights. A hearty mouthfeel that is not too thick complements the nutty, toffee caramel flavors and subtle and pleasant hops. This beer is just about perfect on a misty California afternoon after the chores are done!

A great accompaniment to a simple snack such as sliced apples and pears with some cheese and crackers, it also pairs well with chocolate for those days when you just have to bust out the cookies (or try the Double Chocolate Spent-Grain Brownies on page 131). It's also a good one to brew for your first all-grain batch, because it's quite simple.

Recipe for 5 US gallons

Original Gravity:	1.045	Total IBUs:	24
Final Gravity:	1.011–1.015	ABV:	4.2%
Total AAUs:	7.5		

7 lbs English pale ale malt, crushed

8 oz crystal 60°L malt, crushed

8 oz Victory or Biscuit malt, crushed

6 oz chocolate malt, crushed

2 oz Carafa II malt, crushed

0.75 oz (5 AAU) Kent Goldings pellet hops (19 IBU) **Boil 60 minutes**

0.5 oz (2.5 AAU) Fuggles pellet hops (5 IBU) **Boil 20 minutes**

0.5 teaspoon Irish moss **Boil 20 minutes**

Yeast: White Labs 005 British Ale, Wyeast 1098 British Ale, or dry ale yeast

Priming Sugar: 3.5 oz corn sugar

STEEP

Heat 3.25 gallons of water to 168°F (76°C). Add all the grains, and mix well. Allow to rest for a few minutes, then adjust the temperature to 150 to 152°F (66–67°C) if needed. Hold this temperature for 45 to 60 minutes, or until starch conversion is complete. If possible, just before lautering, heat the mash to 165°F (74°C). Sparge with 3.75 gallons of water at 168°F (76°C). Transfer the wort to the brew kettle and bring to a boil.

BOIL AND COOL

Once the wort has reached a full boil, start your timer, and add the Kent Goldings hops. Boil for 40 minutes. Add the Fuggles hops and the Irish moss, and boil for 20 minutes, then turn the heat off.

Cool the wort to 65 to 70°F (18–21°C). Transfer to a sanitized fermenter, and aerate well.

PITCH, FERMENT, AND BOTTLE

Add the yeast, then ferment for 5 to 7 days. Rack to a secondary fermenter if desired. Ferment for an additional 5 to 7 days. Prime the beer, and bottle when fermentation is complete. Allow to condition for 10 to 21 days.

Grain-on-the-Brain

This recipe has always been a personal favorite. I like to think it has a higher nutritional value than your average beer because of all the different grains in it, but what really matters is that it is a tasty beer with some unique nuances that will intrigue your friends: nutty, malty, and slightly spicy. These are accentuated rather than overpowered by some noble German hops and a dash of fresh American hops for a hint of citrus. I love this beer with fresh-baked spent-grain bread, still hot from the oven and slathered with fresh creamery butter (see Grain-on-the-Brain Bread, page 147). It is worth freezing some of the grains so you can bake the bread when the beer is ready.

Feel free to tweak the recipe to use local grains or what you like the most. Because of a high concentration of adjuncts, a step mash is essential to achieve a decent mash efficiency. Because of the various grains in this recipe, some extra preparation is required.

Recipe for 5 US gallons

Original Gravity:	1.063	**Total IBUs:**	32
Final Gravity:	1.015–1.020	**ABV:**	6.0%
Total AAUs:	18.5		

- 8 oz brown or basmati rice
- 8 oz quinoa
- 8 oz toasted buckwheat
- 7 lbs pale ale malt, crushed
- 1 lb Vienna malt, crushed
- 1 lb wheat malt, crushed
- 8 oz crystal 40°L malt, crushed
- 8 oz oat flakes
- 8 oz rye flakes
- 2 oz Carafa II malt, crushed
- 0.75 oz (6 AAU) German Perle pellet hops (24 IBU) **Boil 60 minutes**
- 1 oz (4.5 AAU) German Mittelfrüh pellet hops (8 IBU) **Boil 20 minutes**
- 0.5 teaspoon Irish moss **Boil 20 minutes**
- 1 oz (8 AAU) American Sterling pellet hops **Add at flameout**

Yeast: White Labs 002 English Ale, or 001 California Ale, or Wyeast 1968 London ESB Ale or 1056 American Ale, or dry ale yeast

Priming Sugar: 4 oz corn sugar

STEEP

At least 3 hours before starting the mash, soak the rice, quinoa, and buckwheat in filtered water. During that time, rinse and drain the quinoa several times to remove compounds that can cause bitterness and inhibit fermentation. After 3 hours, rinse and drain the rice and buckwheat, and add with the quinoa to a large stockpot along with 1 gallon of water.

BOIL AND COOL

Bring to a boil, then simmer for 30 minutes. Allow to cool slightly, then use a hand blender or blend in batches until the grains are puréed. Return the mixture to the stockpot, and add enough water to make a total of 2 gallons. Bring to a boil, timing this so that it is boiling right when the mash has reached the 30-minute mark.

Heat 3.25 gallons of water to 140°F (60°C) in your brew pot. Add all the malted and flaked grains, and mix well. Allow to rest for a few minutes, then adjust the temperature to 119 to 121°F (48–49°C) if needed. Hold this temperature for 30 minutes. At the 30-minute mark, add the 2 gallons of boiling puréed grain mixture to the mash. This should bring the temperature up to 149 to 151°F (65–66°C). If needed, add just enough boiling water or cold water to reach the correct temperature. Steep for another 30 minutes, or until starch conversion is complete. If possible, just before lautering, heat the mash to 165°F (74°C). Sparge with 2 gallons of water at 168°F (76°C). Transfer the wort to the brew kettle, and bring to a boil.

Once the wort has reached a full boil, start your timer and add the Perle hops. Boil for 40 minutes. Add the Mittelfrüh hops and the Irish moss, and boil for 20 minutes. Add the Sterling hops, stir well, and turn the heat off.

Cool the wort to 65 to 70°F (18–21°C). Transfer to a sanitized fermenter, and aerate well.

PITCH, FERMENT, AND BOTTLE

Add the yeast, then ferment for 5 to 7 days. Rack to a secondary fermenter if desired. Ferment for an additional 7 to 10 days. Prime the beer, and bottle when fermentation is complete. Allow to condition for at least 14 to 21 days.

Bootlegger's Bourbon Vanilla Porter

Some of my friends consider this my signature beer. Even though it contains bourbon, which I have yet to find an organic version of, I just had to include this recipe because I have been asked for it so many times! This huge beer can be enjoyed like a sippin' whisky; it's meant to be savored while the complex flavors roll slowly across the tongue. The full-bodied malty base with a mellow hop profile is the perfect showcase for the rich vanilla, oak, and bourbon flavors that distinguish this beer.

Plan for a long aging period with this beer, and you won't be disappointed. It is at its best when it is fully mature, which takes at least 6 weeks. This is the perfect after-dinner beer, great with something chocolate or vanilla if you have room, but I usually find it suffices as dessert all on its own.

Recipe for 5 US gallons

Original Gravity:	1.061	**Total IBUs:**	29
Final Gravity:	1.012–1.016	**ABV:**	7.1%
Total AAUs:	12	*(the bourbon adds roughly 1% ABV)*	

500ml   80–90 proof bourbon (40–45% ABV)

1   oz whole vanilla beans (manufacturing grade or gourmet)

2   oz American oak chips, lightly toasted

5   lbs pale ale malt, crushed

2   pounds Munich malt, crushed

1   lb crystal 60°L malt, crushed

12   oz crystal 40°L malt, crushed

12   oz flaked corn or grits*

8   oz Carafa II malt, crushed

8   oz chocolate malt, crushed

8   oz Victory or Biscuit malt, crushed

0.5   oz (7 AAU) Magnum pellet hops (22 IBU) **Boil 60 minutes**

1   oz (5 AAU) Palisades pellet hops (7 IBU) **Boil 15 minutes**

0.5   teaspoon Irish moss **Boil 15 minutes**

Yeast: White Labs 001 California Ale, Wyeast 1056 American Ale, or dry ale yeast

Priming Sugar: 4 oz corn sugar

*If you cannot find flaked corn or grits, you can substitute 8 ounces corn sugar, added to the boil.

STEEP

On brew day put the bourbon and vanilla beans in a 1-quart or 1-liter wide-mouthed glass jar with a tight-sealing lid. Toast the oak chips at 350°F (177°C) for 10 minutes to bring out the oak fragrance. Cool, and add to the bourbon and vanilla bean mixture. Set aside to steep for 7 to 10 days while the beer is in the primary fermenter.

Heat 4.25 gallons of water to 162°F (72°C). Add all the grains, and mix well. Allow to rest for a few minutes, then adjust the temperature to 151 to 153°F (66–67°C) if needed. Hold this temperature for 45 to 60 minutes, or until starch conversion is complete. If possible, just before lautering, heat the mash to 165°F (74°C). Sparge with 3.25 gallons of water at 168°F (76°C). Transfer the wort to the brew kettle, and bring to a boil.

BOIL AND COOL

Once the wort has reached a full boil, start your timer, and add the Magnum hops. Boil for 45 minutes. Add the Palisades hops and the Irish moss, and boil for 15 minutes, then turn the heat off.

Cool the wort to 65 to 70°F (18–21°C). Transfer to a sanitized fermenter and aerate well.

PITCH, FERMENT, AND BOTTLE

Add the yeast, then ferment for 7 to 10 days. The long primary stage ensures that most of the yeast and solids will settle to the bottom before racking. This beer has to be racked so off-flavors do not develop during the secondary fermentation. Pour the bourbon-oak-vanilla mixture into a clean fermenter, then rack the beer into it. Ferment for an additional 7 to 14 days. If desired, pull a sample and taste it after 7 days. If the vanilla-oak flavor is not strong enough, leave it in the fermenter for another week. Prime the beer, and bottle when fermentation is complete. Allow to condition for at least 21 days.

Wailing Wassail Spiced Beer

The idea for this recipe came from The Homebrewer's Garden, *by Joe and Dennis Fisher. A friend discovered the recipe and decided it had to be her first foray into homebrewing in 20 years. Undaunted by my suggestion that this is a particularly challenging recipe because of the amount of whole fruit that must be added to the fermenter, we proceeded to brew it. Despite many frustrations with transferring the beer off the fruit, the final result was exceptional and has since become a favorite. Six pounds of fresh cranberry and apple give the beer a ciderlike tartness, and the fresh spices add a festive, spicy nose that begs to be celebrated.*

Recipe for 5 US gallons

Original Gravity:	1.070	**Total IBUs:**	28
Final Gravity:	1.016–1.020	**ABV:**	6.6%
Total AAUs:	12.5		

8.5	lbs pale ale malt, crushed
12	oz Munich malt, crushed
8	oz crystal 60°L malt, crushed
6	oz crystal 40°L malt, crushed
3	oz chocolate malt, crushed
2	lbs light honey
1	oz (5.5 AAU) German Spalt Select pellet hops (16 IBU) **Boil 60 minutes**
0.25	oz crushed whole coriander **Boil 20 minutes**
0.5	teaspoon Irish moss **Boil 20 minutes**
1	oz (7 AAU) New Zealand Saaz (Motueka) pellet hops (12 IBU) **Boil 20 minutes**
0.25	oz crushed whole coriander **Boil 10 minutes**
2	cinnamon sticks (3 inches long) **Boil 10 minutes**
1	oz dried orange peel or zest from 4 oranges **Boil 10 minutes**
4	lbs fresh or frozen cranberries, crushed **Steep 15–20 minutes**
2	lbs tart apples or crab apples, crushed **Steep 15–20 minutes**

Yeast: White Labs 002 English Ale, Wyeast 1028 London Ale, or dry ale yeast

Priming Sugar: 4 oz corn sugar

STEEP

Heat 4 gallons of water to 168°F (76°C). Add all the grains, and mix well. Allow to rest for a few minutes, then adjust the temperature to 152°F (67°C) if needed. Hold this temperature for 45 to 60 minutes, or until starch conversion is complete. Just before lautering, heat the mash to 165°F (74°C). Sparge with 3.5 gallons of water at 168°F (76°C). In the brew kettle add the honey to the wort collected, stir to dissolve, then bring to a boil.

While the wort is boiling, wash all the fruit and drain in a colander. Coarsely chop the cranberries in a food processor or blender. Peel, core, and chop the apples. The fruit will start to oxidize immediately, so do this step within 1 hour of adding to the brew pot. Or you can prepare the fruit ahead of time, then freeze it in clean containers. Added frozen, the fruit will help speed up the cooling process.

BOIL AND COOL

Once the wort has reached a full boil, start your timer, and add the Spalt Select hops. Boil for 40 minutes. Add half the coriander, the Irish moss, and the Saaz (Motueka) hops and boil for 10 minutes. Add the rest of the coriander and the rest of the spices, and boil for 10 minutes. Turn the heat off, and let the wort rest for 1 minute so the boil completely stops.

Add all of the chopped fruit, and steep in the hot wort for 15 to 20 minutes. Steeping the fruit at high temperatures will pasteurize it.

Cool to 65 to 70°F (18–21°C). Transfer the wort, fruit and all, to a sanitized fermenter, and aerate well. Doing the primary fermentation in a widemouthed fermenter with a spigot makes racking the beer off the fruit much easier. If your widemouthed fermenter does not have a spigot, placing the fruit in a sterilized straining bag before adding it to the brew kettle will facilitate the straining process.

PITCH, FERMENT, AND BOTTLE

Add the yeast, then ferment for 5 to 7 days. Rack to a secondary fermenter, leaving the fruit pieces behind, within 7 days to prevent excess tannins from being extracted, which could cause an astringent taste. After racking, allow to ferment in the secondary fermenter for 7 to 14 days. Prime the beer, and bottle when fermentation is complete. Allow to condition for 12 to 21 days.

Truffle Snuffler Baltic Porter

The unlikely combination of a strong, dark, and full-bodied beer with a crisp finish and full mouthfeel that is not heavy on the tongue is strangely compelling and simply delicious. Baltic Porter is a style that evolved in Northern Europe through the seventeenth and eighteenth centuries to become what it is today: a strong porter made with a bottom-fermenting lager yeast that exhibits very little hop character and a hint of anise flavor.

This is a very smooth brew with an almost winelike sophistication when properly aged, exhibiting such flavors as dark plum and raisin, along with a mature alcohol warmth that helps the flavors linger as you savor each sip. Truly a brew to serve with a rich feast, or to be enjoyed as a liquid feast in its own right!

Recipe for 5 US gallons

Original Gravity:	1.088	**Total IBUs:**	28
Final Gravity:	1.020–1.024	**ABV:**	8.7%
Total AAUs:	15		

9 lbs pilsner malt, crushed

6 lbs Munich malt, crushed

6 oz Carafa II malt, crushed

6 oz Cara-Munich malt, crushed

6 oz chocolate malt, crushed

6 oz crystal 40°L malt, crushed

6 oz crystal 90°L malt, crushed

4 oz Special B malt, crushed

1 oz (8 AAU) German Perle pellet hops (20 IBU) **Boil 60 minutes**

1–6 pieces star anise* **Boil 60 minutes**

0.5 oz licorice root or licorice stick **Boil 60 minutes**

1 oz (7 AAU) New Zealand Saaz (Motueka) pellet hops (8 IBU) **Boil 20 minutes**

0.5 teaspoon Irish moss **Boil 20 minutes**

Yeast: White Labs 820 German Lager, Wyeast 2124 Bohemian Lager, or dry lager yeast

Priming Sugar: 4.5 oz corn sugar

*Choose the quantity to suit your desired flavor profile. One or two anise stars will add a barely perceptible anise flavor. The more you add, the stronger the flavor will be. Larger amounts will also contribute a licorice/anise aroma.

STEEP

Heat 5.5 gallons of water to 165°F (74°C). Add all the grains, and mix well. Allow to rest for a few minutes, then adjust the temperature to 150 to 152°F (66–67°C) if needed. Hold this temperature for 60 to 90 minutes, or until starch conversion is complete. If possible, just before lautering, heat the mash to 165°F (74°C). Sparge with 2.75 gallons of water at 168°F (76°C). Transfer the wort to the brew kettle, and bring to a boil.

BOIL AND COOL

Once the wort has reached a full boil, add the German Perle hops, anise, and licorice. Boil for 40 minutes. Add the Saaz (Motueka) hops and the Irish moss, and boil for 20 minutes, stir well, and turn the heat off.

Cool the wort to 65 to 70°F (18–21°C). Transfer to a sanitized fermenter, and aerate well.

PITCH, FERMENT, AND BOTTLE

Add the yeast, then ferment for 7 to 9 days at 55 to 60°F (13–16°C). This beer should be racked to a secondary fermenter for the longer lagering stage. Ferment in the secondary for 3 to 6 weeks at 35 to 45°F (2–7°C), or until the target final gravity is reached and the beer is very clear. Prime the beer, and bottle when fermentation is complete. Allow to condition for 12 to 21 days.

Flavor Variations

This beer does well with added spices and flavors. Try vanilla beans, cacao nibs, fennel, or even chiles. I think a mole porter — combining chipotle and adobe pepper, chocolate, and cinnamon— is completely divine!

Vienna Twist Lager

This is my take on the Mexican version of the Old World German-style Vienna lager. As with the historical recipe, it is a clean and smooth beer with a light toasted malt aroma and a mellow hop flavor with just a hint of spicy and floral aroma from the noble hops. This beer is full-bodied but not too sweet and has a dry, clean finish that is decidedly thirst quenching. The twist in this recipe is the addition of a slight amount of cinnamon — just enough to add a hint of spice flavor and warmth without detracting from the style. This is a great beer to accompany a spicy feast, such as a chicken mole, or try it with a couple of Spent-Grain Sourdough Pretzels (page 151).

Recipe for 5 US gallons

Original Gravity:	1.052	**Total IBUs:**	20
Final Gravity:	1.012–1.016	**ABV:**	4.9%
Total AAUs:	12.5		

- 5.5 lbs Vienna malt, crushed
- 2.5 lbs pilsner malt, crushed
- 1 lb corn grits or cornmeal
- 8 oz light Munich malt, crushed
- 4 oz Cara-Munich malt, crushed
- 4 oz crystal 40 °L malt, crushed
- 2 oz Carafa II malt, crushed
- 1–2 cinnamon sticks (3 inches long) **Boil 60 minutes**
- 0.5 oz (3.5 AAU) German Hallertaur Tradition pellet hops (11 IBU) **Boil 60 minutes**
- 1 oz (4.5 AAU) German Mittelfrüh pellet hops (9 IBU) **Boil 20 minutes**
- 0.5 teaspoon Irish moss **Boil 20 minutes**
- 1 oz (4.5 AAU) German Mittelfrüh pellet hops **Add at flameout**

Yeast: White Labs 838 Southern German Lager, Wyeast 2308 Munich Lager, or dry lager yeast

Priming Sugar: 4 oz corn sugar

STEEP

Heat 3.75 gallons of water to 165°F (74°C). Add all the grains, and mix well. Allow to rest for a few minutes, then adjust the temperature to 152 to 154°F (67–68°C) if needed. Hold this temperature for 60 to 90 minutes, or until starch conversion is complete. If possible, just before lautering, heat the mash to 165°F (74°C). Sparge with 3.5 gallons of water at 168°F (76°C). Transfer the wort to the brew kettle, and bring to a boil.

BOIL AND COOL

Once the wort has reached a full boil, add the cinnamon stick and the Hallertaur Tradition hops. Boil for 40 minutes. Add 1 ounce Mittelfrüh hops and the Irish moss, and boil for 20 minutes. Add the second ounce of Mittelfrüh hops, stir well, then turn the heat off.

Cool the wort to 55 to 60°F (13–16°C). Transfer to a sanitized fermenter, and aerate well.

PITCH, FERMENT, AND BOTTLE

Add the yeast, then ferment for 7 to 9 days at 50 to 55°F (13–16°C). Rack to a secondary fermenter for the lagering stage. Ferment in the secondary for 3 to 6 weeks at 35 to 45°F (2–7°C), or until target final gravity is reached and the beer is very clear. Prime the beer, and bottle when fermentation is complete. Allow to condition for 12 to 21 days.

Saphira Pils

A wonderfully clean, soft pilsner is such an enjoyment, especially with lighter fare and warm weather. Although pilsner is arguably the most popular beer style in the world, most examples are watered down, practically flavorless examples that are often loaded with additives and preservatives. A fresh, properly brewed pilsner is like drinking the finest Arabica coffee, fresh roasted and brewed, rather than cheap instant coffee. This version celebrates the finest noble organic hops and is named for our Angora kitty, as well as the Saphir hops that add to the flavor profile of this beer.

This is a reasonably easy recipe to brew. The only tricky part is maintaining cooler temperatures for lagering, but if you love lagers and brew often, you have probably set up a system to help you ferment them properly. If you have hard water, it is worth the effort to use at least 50 percent distilled water or find a local source of soft water to achieve the proper mineral profile for this beer style.

Recipe for 5 US gallons

Original Gravity:	1.050	Total IBUs:	31
Final Gravity:	1.010–1.014	ABV:	5.0%
Total AAUs:	16		

9	lbs pilsner malt, crushed
8	oz Cara-Pils malt, crushed
0.75	oz (5 AAU) German Hallertaur Tradition pellet hops (18 IBU) **Boil 60 minutes**
1	oz (4 AAU) German Saphir pellet hops (8 IBU) **Boil 20 minutes**
0.5	teaspoon Irish moss **Boil 20 minutes**
1	oz (7 AAU) New Zealand Saaz (Motueka) pellet hops (5 IBU) **Boil 5 minutes**

Yeast: White Labs 830 German Lager, Wyeast 2124 Bohemian Lager, or dry lager yeast

Priming Sugar: 4 oz corn sugar

STEEP

Heat 3.5 gallons of water to 170°F (77°C). Add the grains, and mix well. Allow to rest for a few minutes, then adjust the temperature to 152 to 154°F (67–68°C) if needed. Hold this temperature for 60 to 90 minutes, or until starch conversion is complete. If possible, just before lautering, heat the mash to 165°F (74°C). Sparge with 3.75 gallons of water at 168°F (76°C). Transfer the wort to the brew kettle, and bring to a boil.

BOIL AND COOL

Once the wort has reached a full boil, add the Hallertaur Tradition hops. Boil for 40 minutes. Add the Saphir hops and the Irish moss, and boil for 15 minutes. Add the Saaz hops, boil for 5 minutes, then stir well, and turn the heat off.

Cool the wort to 55 to 60°F (13–16°C). Transfer to a sanitized fermenter, and aerate well.

PITCH, FERMENT, AND BOTTLE

Add the yeast, then ferment for 7 to 9 days at 50 to 55°F (10–13°C). Rack to a secondary fermenter for the lagering stage. Ferment in the secondary for 3 to 6 weeks at 35 to 45°F (2–7°C), or until target final gravity is reached and the beer is very clear. Prime the beer, and bottle when fermentation is complete. Allow to condition for 12 to 21 days.

Bawk-Bawk Bock

Our chickens love the spent grain from this recipe, so I named it for the happy cluck-ing they make when they see their favorite treat! If you like strong beer but don't like it dark, this is a wonderful style. A deep gold color and clean, full-malt body are graced with a thick, foamy head and a balanced and refined hop character.

This recipe does an outstanding job of bringing through the fine malt charac-ter in the finished beer. A batch of this was one of my best brews ever; it was memo-rable for the slight peppery spicy notes from the hops that enhanced the excitement on the tongue added by the high carbonation level. Give this beer some time to mature at lagering temperatures and you will not be disappointed.

Recipe for 5 US gallons

Original Gravity:	1.071	**Total IBUs:**	28
Final Gravity:	1.016–1.020	**ABV:**	7.0%
Total AAUs:	16.5		

    7   lbs Vienna malt, crushed
  5.5   lbs German Pilsner malt, crushed
    1   lb light German Munich malt, crushed
    4   oz Biscuit malt, crushed
  0.5   oz (4.5 AAU) German Opal pellet hops (13 IBU) **Boil 60 minutes**
 0.75   oz (7 AAU) German Opal pellet hops (12 IBU) **Boil 20 minutes**
  0.5   teaspoon Irish moss **Boil 20 minutes**
    1   oz (5 AAU) American Liberty pellet hops (3 IBU) **Boil 5 minutes**

Yeast: White Labs 830 German Lager or 833 German Bock, Wyeast 2206 Bavarian
         Lager, or dry lager yeast

Priming Sugar: 4 oz corn sugar

STEEP

Traditionally, this beer style is mashed with the decoction method (see page 90), which increases efficiency and develops malt flavors, resulting in more malt complexity in the finished beer. This recipe calls for a double-decoction mash. Heat 5 gallons of water to 140°F (60°C), add all the grains, and mix well. Allow to rest for 20 minutes. Remove about 2 gallons of the mash, and place in a stockpot. Try to keep the ratio of grains to liquid in the portion you remove about the same as the rest of the mash.

Alternatively, you can use a single infusion mash by mashing in 5 gallons of water at a mash temperature of 151 to 152°F (66–67°C).

BOIL AND COOL

Slowly bring the portion in the stock pot to a boil, stirring frequently to keep from scorching. Once it reaches boiling temperature (212°F [100°C]), return this decoction to the main mash, a third at a time, and stir after each addition. The temperature should be 148 to 150°F (64–66°C). Allow to rest for 30 minutes. For the second decoction remove 0.75 gallon, bring to a boil, then slowly mix the 0.75 gallon back into the mash to bring the temperature to 153 to 155°F (67–68°C). Let rest for 30 minutes, then continue to the lautering stage.

Sparge with 3.75 gallons of water at 168°F (76°C). Transfer the wort to the brew kettle, and bring to a boil.

Once the wort has reached a full boil, start your timer, and add 0.5 ounce Opal hops. Boil for 40 minutes. Add 0.75 ounce Opal hops and the Irish moss, and boil for 15 minutes. Add the Liberty hops, boil for 5 minutes, stir well, and turn the heat off.

Cool the wort to 55 to 60°F (13–16°C). Transfer to a sanitized fermenter, and aerate well.

PITCH, FERMENT, AND BOTTLE

Add the yeast, then ferment for 7 to 9 days at 50 to 55°F (10–13°C). Rack to a secondary fermenter for the lagering stage. Ferment in the secondary for 3 to 6 weeks at 35 to 45°F (2–7°C), or until target final gravity is reached and the beer is very clear. Prime the beer and bottle. Allow to condition for 12 to 21 days.

Wit Have I Got Toulouse (Belgian Witbier)

Witbier is complex and refreshing and bursting with fresh citrus and bready spiciness. It has a ton of character, as does my Toulouse goose, who really starts honking when I bring her some spent grain! Most recipes call for dried citrus peel, but fresh is so much better. Orange peel is traditional, but you can use just about any type, although lime can be overly bitter. Use key lime if you love lime; it's much less bitter. It really depends on what you like.

This is a quick brew, and quite drinkable within 10 days of pitching the yeast if you serve it from a keg. If bottling, it will need at least another week to carbonate naturally. It likes hotter fermentation temperatures, so it is a good choice if summer weather has put the brakes on your regular brew routine. This recipe calls for nearly 3 pounds of flaked grains. This should not cause problems when sparging, as long as you keep the water level up, if continuously sparging, until you are ready to drain. If batch sparging, you might want to use a pound of rice hulls to prevent a stuck runoff.

Recipe for 5 US gallons

Original Gravity: 1.054   Total IBUs: 15

Final Gravity: 1.012–1.014   ABV: 5.4%

Total AAUs: 11

5	lbs pilsner malt, crushed
2.5	lbs white wheat malt, crushed
2	lbs wheat flakes
0.75	lb rolled oats
1	oz (4 AAU) German Saphir pellet hops (10 IBU) **Boil 30 minutes**
1	oz (7 AAU) New Zealand Saaz pellet hops (5 IBU) **Boil 10 minutes**
1	oz citrus peel (to taste)* **Boil 10 minutes**
0.75	oz whole organic coriander, cracked **Boil 10 minutes**

Yeast: White Labs 400 Belgian Wit, Wyeast 3944 Belgian Witbier, or dry ale yeast

Priming Sugar: 5 oz corn sugar

---

*Use a sharp vegetable peeler to peel the outer layer from clean organic fruits. Avoid the white pithy layer as much as possible, as it can contribute an unpleasant bitterness.

STEEP

Heat 4 gallons of water to 170°F (77°C). Add all the grains, and mix well. Allow to rest for a few minutes, then adjust the temperature to 149 to 151°F (65–66°C) if needed. Hold this temperature for 60 to 90 minutes, or until starch conversion is complete. If possible, just before lautering, heat the mash to 165°F (74°C). Sparge with 3.25 gallons of water at 168°F (76°C). Transfer the wort to the brew kettle, and bring to a boil.

BOIL AND COOL

Once the wort has reached a full boil, start your timer, and boil for 30 minutes. After 30 minutes add the Saphir hops. Boil for 20 minutes. Add the Saaz hops, citrus peel, and coriander. Boil for 10 minutes, stir well, and turn the heat off.

Cool the wort to 70 to 75°F (21–24°C). Transfer to a sanitized fermenter, and aerate well.

PITCH, FERMENT, AND BOTTLE

Add the yeast, then ferment for 5 to 7 days at 70 to 75°F (21–24°C). Rack to a secondary fermenter if desired. Ferment for an additional 4 to 10 days. Prime the beer, and bottle when fermentation is complete. Allow to condition for 7 to 14 days.

Will o' Weiss

This is a classic summer wheat beer, refreshing, complex with clove and spice notes, crisp and slightly tart, with nuances of banana and bubblegum, finishing with a vanilla smoothness. A whisper of fresh-baked wheat bread character is balanced with subtle citrus and spice character from the yeast and hops. A light beer, it works well as a session beer that is especially appealing on a hot summer day. It pairs well with cold soups, quiches, salads, and sandwiches.

The low mash temperature of this recipe helps to develop ferulic acid, which contributes to the tartness, and develops a high level of fermentable sugars to create a very light-bodied beer.

Recipe for 5 US gallons

Original Gravity:	1.047	Total IBUs:	13
Final Gravity:	1.010–1.012	ABV:	4.5%
Total AAUs:	7		

5 lbs pale wheat malt (preferably German wheat), crushed

3.5 lbs German Pilsner malt, crushed

4 oz wheat flakes

0.5 oz (3 AAU) German Spalt Select pellet hops (8 IBU) **Boil 30 minutes**

1 oz (4 AAU) Mittelfrüh hops (5 IBU) **Boil 10 minutes**

Yeast: White Labs 380 Hefeweizen IV, Wyeast 3333 German wheat, or dry wheat beer yeast

Priming Sugar: 6 oz corn sugar

STEEP

This recipe call for a triple-infusion mash:

1. Infusion 1: Add all the grains to 2.25 gallons of water heated to 118°F (48°C) and mix well. Rest for 30 minutes at 98 to 100°F (37–38°C). The mash will be very thick.

2. Infusion 2: Add 0.75 gallon of boiling water, and stir well. Rest for 30 minutes at 120 to 122°F (49–50°C).

3. Infusion 3: Add 1.1 gallons of boiling water, and stir well. Rest for 45 to 60 minutes at 144 to 146°F (62–63°C).

   Sparge with 3 gallons of water at 168°F (76°C). Transfer the wort to the brew kettle, and bring to a boil.

BOIL AND COOL

Once the wort has reached a full boil, let it boil for 30 minutes without adding anything. At the 30-minute mark, add the Spalt Select hops. Boil for 20 minutes. Add the Mittelfrüh hops. Boil for 10 minutes, stir well, and turn the heat off.

   Cool the wort to 65 to 70°F (18–21°C). Transfer to a sanitized fermenter, and aerate well.

PITCH, FERMENT, AND BOTTLE

Add the yeast, then ferment for 3 to 5 days. Rack to a secondary fermenter if desired. Ferment for an additional 3 to 5 days. Prime the beer, and bottle when fermentation is complete. Allow to condition for 7 to 14 days.

Black Ninja Abbey

This is a sneaky twist on a classic beer style, hence the name. If you prefer the classic version, it is easy enough to drop the chocolate and black malt to make this a more traditional amber brown Belgian Dubbel. No matter the color, this beer is malty, rich and complex, with hints of fruit and spice in the flavor. A slight tingle of alcohol warmth hits your throat on the way down, but it definitely does not overpower the lovely flavor of this beer. Notes of dark plums, chocolate, and bread pudding find their way into this beer, making it a great choice for pairing with desserts — especially dark chocolate!

Recipe for 5 US gallons

Original Gravity:	1.082	**Total IBUs:**	25
Final Gravity:	1.014–1.018	**ABV:**	8.8%
Total AAUs:	11		

10	lbs pale ale malt, crushed
1	lb Biscuit malt, crushed
1	lb light Munich malt, crushed
8	oz caramel 60°L malt, crushed
8	oz Special B malt, crushed
8	oz wheat malt, crushed
6	oz Carafa II malt, crushed
4	oz black malt, crushed
1	pint dark candi syrup (see page 333)
1	oz (7 AAU) Kent Goldings pellet hops (19 IBU) **Boil 60 minutes**
1	oz (4 AAU) German Mittelfrüh pellet hops (6 IBU) **Boil 20 minutes**
0.5	teaspoon Irish moss **Boil 20 minutes**

Yeast: White Labs 550 Belgian Ale, Wyeast 1214 Belgian Ale, or dry Belgian yeast
Priming Sugar: 5 oz corn sugar

STEEP

Heat 5.25 gallons of water to 162°F (72°C). Add all the grains and mix well. Allow to rest for a few minutes, then adjust the temperature to 149 to 151°F (65-66°C) if needed. Hold this temperature for 60 to 90 minutes, or until starch conversion is complete. If possible, just before lautering, heat the mash to 165°F (74°C). Sparge with 2.75 gallons of water at 168°F (76°C). Transfer the wort to the brew kettle. Add the dark candi syrup, stir well to dissolve completely, then bring to a boil.

BOIL AND COOL

Once the wort has reached a full boil, start your timer, and add the Kent Goldings hops. Boil for 40 minutes. Add the Mittelfrüh hops and the Irish moss. Boil for 20 minutes more, stir well, and turn the heat off.

Cool the wort to 70 to 75°F (21–24°C). Transfer to a sanitized fermenter, and aerate well.

PITCH, FERMENT, AND BOTTLE

Add the yeast, then ferment for 7 to 9 days at 70 to 75°F (21–24°C). Rack to a secondary fermenter if desired. Ferment for an additional 7 to 21 days. Prime the beer, and bottle when fermentation is complete. Allow to condition for 14 to 30 days. This beer ages well, so put some bottles away for at least 6 months to savor when they have fully developed.

Cultured Farm Girl (Berliner Weisse)

This is a very tart, sour beer that is refreshing like a good lemonade. I love this recipe because it is so simple to make, requires just a few ingredients, and can use one of the most health-friendly microbes around — the humble Lactobacillus. *The trick is using* Lactobacillus — *the same critters that make yogurt — to create the sour flavor the Berliner Weisse style is known for.*

Lactobacillus *thrives at higher temperatures than yeast normally likes, so the most reliable method I have found calls for making a warm-temperature sour mash a few days before brewing the main recipe. If you make your own yogurt, the process should be familiar. If not, it is really quite easy if you follow the procedures described* below. The exact variety of hops for this recipe are not important, although hops with a citrus character seem to work best. The predominant flavor is sour with hints of citrus. The hops should be barely present.

It is traditional to serve this beer with a flavored syrup, such as raspberry or woodruff. This is a great vehicle to showcase a homemade syrup made from fresh fruits or berries. If you like really sour beers, there is no need to add a thing — this is quite delicious all by itself.

Recipe for 5 US gallons

Original Gravity:	1.033	**Total IBUs:**	7
Final Gravity:	1.008–1.010	**ABV:**	3.6%
Total AAUs:	7		

- 1.5 lbs pilsner malt, crushed (for sour mash)
- 1 lb wheat malt, crushed (for sour mash)
- 3.5 lbs pilsner malt, crushed
- 2 lbs wheat malt, crushed
- 1 oz (7 AAU) German Hallertaur Tradition pellet hops (7 IBU) **Boil 15 minutes**

Yeast and cultures: Any clean-fermenting ale yeast or wheat beer yeast, plus yogurt whey or a pure *Lactobacillus* culture such as Wyeast Strain 5335 *Lactobacillus*

Priming Sugar: 5 oz corn sugar

MAKE THE SOUR MASH

Make a sour mash 2 to 4 days before brewing the main recipe: To keep things sterile I recommend doing the mash in a small stockpot with a tight-fitting lid that you can keep the mash in for the duration of the souring stage. Sterilize the container by boiling a few cups of water in it. Although you want a spontaneous fermentation to happen with naturally occurring *Lactobacillus*, sanitizing the vessel will minimize the activity of unwanted microorganisms. To prevent *Acetobacter* from turning your mash into vinegar, it is important to avoid mixing oxygen into the mash. Floating a piece of plastic wrap or aluminum foil directly on top of the mash can reduce the risk; I rarely find it necessary as long as my container is clean and has a lid that fits well.

Heat 1 gallon of water to 162°F (72°C). Add 1.5 pounds pilsner and 1 pound of wheat malt, stir well, and allow to steep for 30 to 40 minutes. Once starch conversion is complete, gently and slowly raise the temperature to 170°F (77°C), then remove from the heat and allow to cool naturally to 120°F (49°C) before inoculating with *Lactobacillus*. You can use the whey produced by straining yogurt through a coffee filter, use a pure *Lactobacillus* strain, or add a few grams of whole malt — the husks contain naturally occurring *Lactobacillus* bacteria. I have had the most consistent results with yogurt whey or a pure culture.

During the sour mash you need to maintain a temperature of 110 to 115°F (43–46°C). I use my oven with the light turned on. You can also use a cooler that can hold the stockpot containing your sour mash plus hot water. The water level should be about the same as the level of the sour mash. Change the water as needed to maintain the desired temperature range. Allow the mash to sour for 2 to 4 days. The longer it incubates, the more sour the results will be.

Smell and taste it after 2 days, and continue until it is at the level you want. I must warn you that before the mash truly sours it can produce some rather unpleasant odors — something to keep in mind when choosing a location for the incubation! If it sours properly, the taste will be distinctly sour, although the odor may still seem unpleasant. If you find mold growing on the top, the batch should be discarded.

Once the sour mash is ready, continue with the rest of the brew.

STEEP

Heat 2.25 gallons of water to 162°F (72°C). Add 3.5 pounds of pilsner malt and 2 pounds of wheat malt, and mix well. Adjust the temperature to 149°F (65°C) if needed. Meanwhile, gently heat the sour mash up to 149°F, and add it to the new mash 20 to 30 minutes into the mash cycle. The delay is necessary because, once the sour mash is introduced, the very low pH will inhibit enzyme activity. Continue the combined mash for another 30 to 40 minutes, or until starch conversion is complete.

Sparge with 3 gallons of water at 165°F (74°C). Transfer the wort to the brew kettle, and bring to a boil.

BOIL AND COOL

Once the wort has reached a full boil, add the Hallertaur Tradition hops, and boil for 15 minutes. Stir well, then turn the heat off.

Cool the wort to 65 to 70°F (18–21°C). Transfer to a sanitized fermenter, and aerate well. Add more *Lactobacillus* culture — you can strain about half a cup from the sour mash before heating it if you like, but I prefer to use one-quarter cup of fresh yogurt whey at this stage.

PITCH, FERMENT, AND BOTTLE

Add the yeast, then ferment for 5 to 7 days. Rack to a secondary fermenter if desired. Ferment for an additional 7 to 21 days. The longer the beer ferments, the more sour it will be. I find it reaches a decent level in 2 to 3 weeks. Prime the beer, and bottle when fermentation is complete. Allow to condition for 7 to 14 days.

Basic Buckwheat Gluten-Free Ale

Most of the gluten-free beer recipes I have come across over the years call for sorghum syrup. I have a few issues with this. First is the bitter aftertaste that I have detected in every sorghum syrup–based beer I have tried. The other issue is that I have never been able to find organic sorghum syrup.

A very nice gluten-free ale can be made with rice syrup as the base. Including buckwheat adds a pleasing nutty, grainy flavor that makes the finished drink more beerlike. The buckwheat is not malted, and thus does not contribute much fermentable sugar, but adding it contributes significantly to the flavor and character of the beer. This is a light golden ale with a clean flavor accented by hints of nuttiness from the buckwheat, balanced with clean earthy and floral hop accents.

This beer makes a great base for fruit or spice beer, which greatly increases the potential flavor variations using this recipe it is possible to add a variety of flavors to create different styles of beer. Try other gluten-free sugars or grains, cocoa, coffee, or molasses.

Recipe for 5 US gallons

Original Gravity:	1.052	**Total IBUs:**	24
Final Gravity:	1.014–1.018	**Approximate ABV:**	4.6%
Total AAUs:	10		

1.5	lbs toasted buckwheat, crushed
6	lbs rice syrup
1	lb corn sugar
8	oz maltodextrin
.5	oz (3 AAU) Spalt Select pellet hops (10 IBU) **Boil 60 minutes**
1	oz (7 AAU) New Zealand Motueka pellet hops (14 IBU) **Boil 20 minutes**
0.5	teaspoon Irish moss **Boil 20 minutes**

Yeast: White Labs 002 English Ale, Wyeast 1968 London ESB, or dry ale yeast

Priming Sugar: 4.5 oz corn sugar

PREPARE THE BUCKWHEAT

Toasted buckwheat is also sold under the name kasha. If the buckwheat is raw, spread evenly on a cookie sheet and toast at 350°F (177°C) for 10 to 15 minutes, or until the color and aroma are at the stage you want. If you purchase buckwheat that was already toasted, you can skip this step, unless you want a stronger roasted grain character.

Add the toasted buckwheat to 1 gallon of water and gently bring to a boil. Boil for 20 minutes, then strain the liquid into the brew pot and discard the grains. Alternatively, you can put the buckwheat in a grain bag and boil it in the full volume of brewing water in your brew pot for 20 minutes and then remove before adding the rice syrup. The spent buckwheat is tasty as breakfast cereal or as a baking ingredient.

Add enough water to fill the brew kettle; the total volume should be 5.25 to 5.5 gallons (adjust for your brewing system). Heat to just before boiling, add the rice syrup, corn sugar, and maltodextrin, and dissolve completely.

BOIL AND COOL

Bring to a boil, and add the Spalt Select hops. After 40 minutes of boiling, add the Motueka hops and Irish moss, and boil for 20 minutes. At the end of the boil stir well, then turn the heat off.

Cool to 65 to 70°F (18–21°C). Transfer to a sanitized fermenter and aerate well.

PITCH, FERMENT, AND BOTTLE

Add the yeast when cool, and aerate well. Ferment for 8 to 14 days. The best fermenting temperature is 65 to 70°F (18–21°C). Rack to a secondary fermenter after 5 to 7 days if desired. Prime the beer, and bottle when fermentation is complete. Allow to condition for 12 to 21 days.

Gluten-Free Buckwheat Millet Ale

In Africa millet beer has been brewed for millennia. It has a very light body and mouthfeel, and is a bit delicate in taste. This makes for a wonderful beer that is quite refreshing in the hot climate of Africa but may seem a bit lacking to the palates of American craft beer drinkers. Blending millet and buckwheat malt, some of it toasted, adds depth to the flavor without adding significantly to the cost. Organic buckwheat typically costs three times as much as millet, so brewing a beer from buckwheat alone is quite expensive! Blending the two results in an enjoyable, eminently quaffable beer that most budgets can accommodate.

This recipe calls for malted buckwheat and millet; they are relatively easy to malt yourself but the process does require some advance planning. Due to the rapidly growing interest in gluten-free ingredients, there are some gluten-free malts being made in the United States, but I haven't yet to discover any that are also organic. Colorado Malting Company has a line of millet, buckwheat, and other gluten-free malts, and these may be worth seeking out if you want to brew gluten-free beer but do not have the time or space to malt your own grains.

Just like the previous gluten-free recipe, this recipe creates a simple, clean beer that can be a canvas for adding your own creative embellishments. Once you have brewed the basic recipe to your liking, the options for adding flavor and color are limited only by your imagination and dietary requirements.

Recipe for 5 US gallons

Original Gravity:	1.052	**Total IBUs:**	25
Final Gravity:	1.010–1.016	**Approximate ABV:**	4.8%
Total AAUs:	15		

2	lbs malted buckwheat
8	lbs malted millet
1	lb malted buckwheat (toast at 350°F [177°C] for 10 to 15 minutes)
0.5	oz (3 AAU) Spalt Select pellet hops (10 IBU) **Boil 60 minutes**
1	oz (5 AAU) Palisades pellet hops (10 IBU) **Boil 20 minutes**
0.5	teaspoon Irish moss **Boil 20 minutes**
1	oz (7 AAU) New Zealand Motueka pellet hops (5 IBU) **Boil 5 minutes**

Yeast: White Labs 002 English Ale, Wyeast 1968 London ESB, or dry ale yeast

Priming Sugar: 4.5 oz corn sugar

MALTING THE GRAINS

Malt each grain separately, as they have different germination times and temperature ranges. Kiln them according to the instructions on page 190.

For the millet, soak for 20 hours at 75 to 80°F (24–27°C), draining completely and refilling with fresh water every 4 to 8 hours. During germination, try to keep the temperature between 75 and 85°F (24 and 30°C). Stir and rinse the grains at least every 8 hours. The total germination time is 45 to 50 hours.

For the buckwheat, soak for 20 hours at 65 to 70°F (18–21°C), draining completely and refilling with fresh water every 4 to 8 hours. During germination, try to keep the temperature between 65 and 75°F (18 and 24°C). Stir and rinse the grains at least every 8 hours. The total germination time is 55 to 65 hours.

STEEP

Heat 3.5 gallons of water to 140°F (60°C). Add all the grains, and mix well. Allow to rest for a few minutes, then adjust the temperature to 119 to 121°F (48–49°C) if needed. Hold this temperature for 30 minutes. Add 1.75 gallons of boiling water to raise the temperature to 149 to 151°F (65–66°C). You may need to add a bit more water or add a small amount of cold water to achieve the correct temperature. Mash for an additional 30 minutes, or until starch conversion is complete. If possible, just before lautering, heat the mash to 165°F (74°C). Sparge with 3.5 gallons of water at 168°F (76°C). Transfer the wort to the brew kettle, and bring to a boil.

BOIL AND COOL

Once the wort has reached a full boil, start your timer, and add the Spalt Select hops. Boil for 40 minutes. Add the Palisades hops and the Irish moss, and boil for 15 minutes. Add the Motueka hops, boil for 5 more minutes, then turn the heat off.

Cool the wort to 65 to 70°F (18–21°C). Transfer to a sanitized fermenter and aerate well.

PITCH, FERMENT, AND BOTTLE

Add the yeast, then ferment for 5 to 7 days. Rack to a secondary fermenter if desired. Ferment for an additional 7 to 10 days. Prime the beer, and bottle when fermentation is complete. Allow to condition for at least 14 to 21 days.

9

CREATING YOUR OWN Organic BEER RECIPES

If you are interested in eco-friendly brewing, you've probably noticed that most beer recipes call for ingredients that aren't organic or locally available. This can be very frustrating, but it does not have to be. These days there is a wide enough range of organic ingredients available that you should be able to craft almost any style of beer imaginable. If you are willing to work with the palette of ingredients available without lamenting the lack of this or that, the array of beers you can make is simply dazzling. Where there is a will, there is a way!

Instead of thinking about substituting malts or hops as compromising, think of it as adapting. It can lead to outstanding beers that are packed with local character and flavor — even if they are slightly different from the standard profile. Over the years my organic beers have won many awards, even though I was competing against entries brewed with the full range of conventionally grown malts and hops.

Converting Existing Recipes to Organic

The charts in this chapter will help you tweak conventional recipes into organic recipes, and to use your homegrown ingredients in place of what a recipe calls for. Substituting organic ingredients for conventional ingredients is just a matter of understanding the characteristics of those ingredients. You can develop that understanding by reading about them, tasting and smelling them, and by studying these charts. In most cases you can simply substitute organic ingredients for nonorganic ones, pound for pound or ounce for ounce.

To develop your own recipes, you have to train your senses to aid in the quest of crafting great, individual beers that are exclusively organic. This takes a little more finesse and skill than simply substituting ingredients while following the basic blueprint of a recipe. And it takes time and hands-on experience to fine-tune your brewing taste buds. Each time you brew with a new ingredient, you should smell and taste it and observe how those flavors and smells work when combined with the rest of the ingredients and fermented into beer.

Brewing is as much art as it is science. Most homebrewers enjoy both aspects and tend to hang out in the safer middle ground where art and science converge. This is not only safe, it is practical, sensible, and usually cost-effective, because either extreme poses risks that can lead to an expensive waste of ingredients. Some brewers tend to veer toward one or the other. I love the science of brewing, but I often drift to the arty side of the equation. Instead of precise measuring, I am prone to adding a dash of this or a dash of that. Usually it works out, but I have brewed many not-so-great beers, too. Even after 20 years, every batch I make is a learning journey that helps me refine my brewing senses.

Most great beers are born by successfully adhering to the highest standards in three areas: use good ingredients, practice excellence in brewing techniques, and follow a great recipe. If you're reading this chapter, you should already have a good grasp of the first two criteria. If you are committed to using organic ingredients to create your beers while following your favorite great recipes, read on.

Organic Malt Extracts and Fermentable Sugars

When converting a conventional recipe to organic, the easiest thing to convert is malt extract, because you don't have a lot of choices. As a general rule of thumb, you can substitute pound for pound the total amount of liquid or dry malt extract that the recipe calls for with organic liquid or dry malt extract. Typically, dry malt extract is lighter in color than liquid, so for recipes that call for the lightest-color extract, choose dry.

Dry malt extract is more highly concentrated, and liquid malt extract is about 20 percent water weight. When using dry malt extract in place of liquid malt extract, use 20 percent less, and when using liquid malt extract in place of dry, use 20 percent more. So if a recipe calls for 5 pounds of dry malt extract, you need 20 percent more liquid malt extract, or 6 pounds.

The only organic malt extract currently available in the United States as of this writing is pale malt extract, which can replace light, golden, or pilsner extract (see Resources). To replace light or pilsner, use light or pale dry malt extract if you can, and if possible choose a recipe that calls for a mini mash or partial mash with at least 3 pounds of whole barley malt. This will help you achieve the lighter color of these beers. The grains add little color themselves and dilute the color contributed by the extract.

Most modern homebrew recipes do not call for dark extract, and few call for amber extract, because darker extract can be a bit of a mystery. What dark grains were used in the manufacture of the dark extract, and how much? The exact contents do not need to be included on the label when extract is packaged for the homebrewing market, so it is entirely possible that a caramel color was added instead of actual malt. You will brew better-tasting beer by using fresh specialty grains to add color and flavor to your amber to dark beers.

Amber extract substitutions. Use pale malt extract plus ½ pound of caramel 60°L malt. Use ¼ pound less extract than the recipe calls for.

Dark extract substitutions. Use pale malt extract plus ½ pound of chocolate malt and ¼ pound caramel 120°L malt. Use ⅓ pound less extract than the recipe calls for.

Organic Malts and Adjunct Grains

A decent variety of organically grown malts is available to homebrewers. There are a few gaps in the selection, and the more exact your recipe and standards are, the more difficult it will be to find the right substitution. In general, it is easier to substitute malts in darker beers and beers with strong hop or spice flavors than it is in very light beers that derive a lot of their flavor from the malts used.

It may be more of a challenge to create a pilsner that tastes exactly like Pilsner Urquell, for instance, although crafting a great-tasting, excellent-quality pilsner-style beer with organic pilsner malt is very doable. To a particularly sensitive palate, the difference might be noticeable, but most beer drinkers are not that picky, and most well-trained beer judges will not lower scores unless the beer falls outside the style range.

MALT AND FERMENTABLE ADJUNCTS

This chart (pages 311–314) will help you choose malts, adjunct grains, and fermentable sugars for an established recipe, make substitutions as needed, or build a recipe from scratch. The extract potential data is used to estimate the specific gravity of a new recipe (see page 322). If you are simply substituting a malt in a recipe, you do not really need this information; it is included here for reference when building a new recipe from scratch.

Malt Type	Flavor/ Characteristics	Mash Required?	Color Range Lovibond or SRM[†]	Extract Potential Range in PPG
Acid malt	Sour taste from lactic acid; can use to adjust mash pH	Yes	3	25–30
Amber malt	Adds color and strong biscuit flavor	Yes	20–25	30–35
Aromatic malt	Adds very strong malty flavor	Yes*	22–28	30–35
Biscuit malt	Strong biscuit flavor and maltiness	Yes*	20–25	30–35

Malt Type	Flavor/Characteristics	Mash Required?	Color Range Lovibond or SRM†	Extract Potential Range in PPG
Black malt	Also referred to as black patent malt; adds deep roasty flavors and dark color	No	450–500	20–25
Brown malt	Gives dry, roasted biscuity flavor and brown color	Yes*	60–70	28–32
Caramel/crystal 25–40	Adds body and amber color, sweet caramel flavor	No	23–45	29–34
Caramel/crystal 60–75	Adds body and reddish amber color, sweet caramel toffee flavor	No	55–80	29–34
Caramel/crystal 90–120	Adds body and reddish brown color; deep, slightly burnt caramel flavor	No	85–125	28–33
Cara-Munich malt	Adds body and copper-amber color; sweet toasted caramel flavor	No	30–60	27–32
Cara-Pils/Carafoam/dextrin malt	Adds body and foam retention without adding color	Yes	1–3	28–32
Chocolate malt	Adds reddish to chocolate-brown color, roasted and cocoa flavors	No	340–360	24–28
Munich malt	Adds malty sweet and light toasted flavor, orange-amber color	Yes*	10–20	30–35
Pale malt (2-row)	Base malt, little to no color, and clean malt flavor	Yes	2–4	32–38
Pale malt (6-row)	Base malt, slightly higher enzyme level than 2-row	Yes	2–4	30–35
Pilsner malt	Base malt for lagers	Yes	1–3	31–37

Malt Type	Flavor/ Characteristics	Mash Required?	Color Range Lovibond or SRM†	Extract Potential Range in PPG
Roasted barley	Unmalted for adding rich, dry, roasted-coffee-like flavor and dark brown color	Yes*	290–310	22–25
Rye malt	Adds crisp rye flavor	Yes	3–6	25–29
Smoked/peat malt	Adds smoky flavor	Yes*	3–10	31–36
Special B malt	Adds strong caramel flavor with nuances of raisin and plum	No	140–160	27–31
Victory malt	Adds toasted flavor and light amber color	Yes*	25–30	29–34
Vienna malt	Adds warm malt flavor, golden orange color	Yes*	4–7	30–35
Wheat malt	Base malt for wheat beers	Yes	1–3	31–37

†SRM stands for Standard Reference Method, which is one of the systems brewers use to measure the color of beer. Although there are slight differences between this and the Lovibond (°L) scale, the scales are close enough to use the numbers interchangeably for homebrewing purposes.

*Although mashing is required to extract fermentable sugars from these grains, small amounts may be steeped to add flavor.

Grain Type	Flavor/ Characteristics	Mash Required?	Color Range Lovibond or SRM†	Extract Potential Range in PPG
Amaranth (pre-cooked or malted)	Gluten free; can be malted and used as a base malt	Yes	1–3	31–37
Barley (flaked)	Adds body and aids in head retention	Yes	1–3	28–32
Buckwheat (pre-cooked or malted)	Gluten free; can be malted and used as a base malt. Nutty flavor	Yes*	1–3	18–24
Corn (flaked or grits)	Gluten free; can be malted and used as a base malt	Yes	1–3	33–39

Grain Type	Flavor/ Characteristics	Mash Required?	Color Range Lovibond or SRM[†]	Extract Potential Range in PPG
Millet (precooked or malted)	Gluten free; can be malted and used as a base malt	Yes	1–3	26–30
Oats (flaked)	Gluten free if processed in gluten-free facility; adds silky texture	Yes*	1–3	28–32
Quinoa (pre-cooked or malted)	Gluten free; can be malted and used as a base malt	Yes	1–3	31–37
Rice (flaked or precooked/ ground)	Gluten free; use to lighten body while adding fermentables	Yes	1–3	32–38
Rye (flaked)	Adds dry, crisp rye flavor	Yes	1–3	30–36
Sorghum (pre-cooked or malted)	Gluten free; can be malted and used as a base malt	Yes	1–3	30–39
Wheat (flaked)	Adds haziness desired in wits and wheat beers	Yes	1–3	30–36

†SRM stands for Standard Reference Method, which is one of the systems brewers use to measure the color of beer. Although there are slight differences between this and the Lovibond (°L) scale, the scales are close enough to use the numbers interchangeably for homebrewing purposes.

*Although mashing is required to extract fermentable sugars from these grains, small amounts may be steeped to add flavor.

EXTRACT AND FERMENTABLE SUGARS

Using extracts and sugars in brewing is very straightforward, and substitutions of different extracts can be made as long as the total points per pound per gallon (PPG) for the batch remains constant and the item substituted is reasonably close in character and type of sugar. It does not benefit the finished flavor of most beers to replace all or part of the malt extract with table sugar, but it would result in the same starting gravity and alcohol content as long as the total PPG remained constant. (See pages 332 to 335 for information on making your own candi, or invert, sugar.)

Malt or Sugar	Flavor/ Characteristics	Type of Sugar	Lovibond or SRM†	Average Extract Potential in PPG
Liquid malt extract	Malty, slight caramel	Maltose and others	6–12	36
Dry malt extract	Malty, sweet	Maltose and others	4–8	42
Agave syrup	Gluten free; can impart a tequila or pulque flavor. Be sure to use pure agave; some cheaper brands contain cane sugar	Fructose, sucrose, and other sugars. Quality agave is 90% fructose or higher	1–5	32–38
Brown sugar	Gluten free; adds brown sugar flavor; best used in small quantities	Sucrose and other complex sugars (some unfermentable)	8–10 (light) 30–40 (dark)	46
Cane sugar	Gluten free; lightens body, increases alcohol; can add dry, cidery flavor if too much is used	Sucrose	0–2	46
Corn sugar	Gluten free; lightens body, increases alcohol; little to no flavor	Dextrose	0	46
Honey	Gluten free; honey flavor, sweetness; can contribute dryness. Some honeys have strong flavors from source flowers	Glucose and fructose with smaller amounts of other sugars and unfermentables	1–10	35
Maple syrup	Gluten free; distinct flavor. Be sure to use pure maple and not corn syrup or maple-flavored syrup!	Sucrose and other complex sugars (some unfermentable)	5–20	30
Molasses	Gluten free; adds strong distinct flavor, body, and color.	Sucrose and other complex sugars (at least 25% unfermentable)		36
Rice syrup	Adds fermentable sugar with little body or color. Gluten free. Some manufacturers use enzymes derived from barley to produce	Glucose with smaller amounts of maltose and fructose	5–10	32

Malt or Sugar	Flavor/ Characteristics	Type of Sugar	Lovibond or SRM[†]	Average Extract Potential in PPG
Maltodextrin	Gluten free; unfermentable sugar used to add body but low sweetness; adds to finished gravity	D-glucose and other complex sugars	0–1	40
Sorghum syrup	Gluten free; can contribute a bitter aftertaste in beers. Processed from the plant stalks, the syrup is different from sorghum malt extract, which is processed from sorghum grains.	Sucrose, with smaller amounts of glucose and fructose, plus unfermentable sugars	5–10	34–36
Sorghum malt extract	Gluten free; grainy, slightly sour. Made from malted sorghum grains	Maltose and others	2–10	36–38

†SRM stands for Standard Reference Method, which is one of the systems brewers use to measure the color of beer. Although there are slight differences between this and the Lovibond (°L) scale, the scales are close enough to use the numbers interchangeably for homebrewing purposes.

Organic Hops

Until recently, obtaining organic hops was the biggest challenge for brewers because certain varieties were simply not available. This is rapidly changing as American hop growers have gotten into the business of growing organic hops. Not all of this bounty trickles down to the homebrewer's marketplace, however, and some of these are not available in other countries, so homebrewers still have a limited selection.

One way around this is to grow some of your own hops, and another is to mail-order hops even if it means shipping them a great distance. The average weight of hops in a typical batch of homebrew is about two ounces, or about 0.5 percent of the weight of the finished beer. That represents a relatively small carbon cost, especially if you buy a year's supply in one shipment that can be stored in your freezer.

With hops, whether you are substituting varieties or not, you must be careful to adjust for the alpha acid level, which varies from crop to crop. Often organic hops have higher alpha acid levels, so it is important to check this. The reason organic hops have higher alpha acid levels than conventionally grown ones is not entirely clear, but some speculate that the natural fertilizers and absence of inhibiting chemicals have something to do with it.

HOP VARIETY

This chart (pages 318–321) lists most of the conventionally grown hop varieties available as of this writing and offers suggestions for substituting organic hops. It also includes the typical alpha and beta acid ranges to help you choose appropriate hops when formulating your own recipes. The alpha acid should always be made available to you when buying hops from a dealer — usually it is printed right on the package. If it isn't, inquire before purchasing. Beta acid is not always as easy to determine, but each hop variety has a typical range that stays consistent from season to season. Beta levels are not as critical to a beer style as the alpha levels.

Hop variety name	Flavor/aroma characteristics	Alpha acid range (%)	Beta acid range (%)	Organic available?	Suggested substitutions
Admiral	Herbal, woody, some citrus	13–16	4.8–6	Sometimes	Challenger, Chinook, Target
Ahtanum	Citrus, floral, slight spice	5–7	5–6.5	No	Cascade, Simcoe
Amarillo	Tropical fruit and floral; citrus (grapefruit/orange)	8–11	6–7	No	Cascade, NZ Rakau
B Saaz (Motueka)	Earthy, mild spice, citrus (lemon-lime)	7–8	5–5.5	Yes	Hallertau, Wakatu
Bravo	Fruit (apple, apricot, pear), floral	13–17	3–4	Yes	Rakau, Smaragd
Brewer's Gold	Spicy, hints of fruit (black currant)	6–10	3–4.5	No	Chinook, Perle
Cascade	Floral, citrus, grapefruit	4.5–7	4.5–7	Yes	NZ Cascade, Centennial
Centennial	Floral, mild citrus, clean bitterness	9.5–11.5	3.5–5	Sometimes	Cascade, Chinook, Simcoe
Challenger	Floral, sweet citrus, mild spice	5–9	3–4.5	Yes	Perle, Saphir
Chinook	Spicy, piney, mild citrus/grapefruit	12–14	3–4	Yes	Admiral, Centennial, Perle
Citra	Strong citrus & tropical fruit, gooseberry notes	10–13	3.5–4.5	Sometimes	Nelson Sauvin, Rakau, Simcoe
Cluster	Floral, earthy, sweet fruit	5.5–8.5	4.5–5.5	No	Challenger, Wakatu
Columbus	Herbal, earthy, mild citrus	12–18	4.5–5.5	Sometimes	Chinook, Magnum, Target
Crystal	Woody, floral, herbal, slight spice	3.5–6	4.5–6.7	No	Hersbrucker, Hallertau, Liberty
East Kent Goldings	Delicate spice, sweet citrus	4–7	2–2.8	No	Fuggles, WGV
First Gold	Smooth flowery-herbal, mild spice, slight woodiness	6.5–8.5	3–4	No	Kent Goldings, WGV

Hop variety name	Flavor/aroma characteristics	Alpha acid range (%)	Beta acid range (%)	Organic available?	Suggested substitutions
Fuggles	Herbal, woody, mild floral	3–6	2–3	Yes	Kent Goldings, WGV
Galena	Woody, clean bittering, fruit (peaches/grapes)	12–14	7–9	No	Bravo, Rakau, Smaragd
Glacier	Pleasant, balanced, fruit/citrus, mild herbal	4–9.5	5.5–9.5	No	Palisade, Fuggles
Goldings	Delicate floral, refined spicy	4–6	2–3	Yes (Kent Goldings)	Fuggles, WGV
Hallertau	Mild flowery, spicy	3.5–5.5	3–4	Yes	Hallertaur Tradition, Liberty, Wakatu
Hallertaur Tradition	Earthy, spicy, sweet fruit, floral	5–7	4–5	Yes	Hallertau, Liberty, Wakatu
Hersbrucker	Spice and fruit, pleasant floral	2–5	3–6	Yes	Liberty, Mittelfrüh
Horizon	Floral, citrus fruit	10.5–16	6.5–8.5	Sometimes	Magnum, Wakatu
Liberty	Earthy spice, fruit (grapes, peaches)	3–6	3–4	Yes	Hallertau, Wakatu, Mittelfrüh
Magnum	Very clean bittering with little aroma	10–14	4.5–8	Yes	Columbus, Bravo
Mittelfrüh	Mild flowery, spicy, hints of citrus	3–5.5	3–5	Yes	Hallertau, Hallertaur Tradition, Liberty, Wakatu
Mt. Hood	Warm, pungent, slightly spicy	4–8	5–8	No	Hallertau, Liberty, Wakatu
Nelson Sauvin	Earthy, white-wine fruitiness, gooseberry	12–13	6–8	Yes	Citra, Rakau
Northdown	Clean bitterness, delicate hoppy aroma	6–10	4.5–6	No	Admiral, Challenger, Perle
Northern Brewer	Woody, minty, evergreen flavor	8–10	3–5	No	Chinook, Perle

Hop variety name	Flavor/aroma characteristics	Alpha acid range (%)	Beta acid range (%)	Organic available?	Suggested substitutions
Nugget	Woodsy, herbal, mild, marked bitterness	9.5–14	4–6	No	Columbus, Magnum, Wakatu
Opal	Very flowery, fruity with citrus, spicy with pepper, herbal	6–10	3.5–5.5	Yes	Goldings, Tettnanger
Pacific Gem	Oak-woody, fruit with blackberry, floral	13–18	7–9	Yes	Admiral, Columbus
Palisade	Floral, herbal, earthy, sweet nectar fruit	5.5–9.5	6–8	Yes	Fuggles, Tettnanger
Perle	Spicy, mild aroma, slight minty herbal	6–10	3–5	Yes	Hallertau
Pilgrim	Hoppy, floral citrus/lemon	9–13	4–5	Sometimes	Challenger, Goldings, Target
Rakau	Clean mineral bitterness, tropical fruit	11–13	5–6	Yes	Admiral, Simcoe, Summit
Saaz	Floral, earthy, mild pleasing hoppy	2–6	3–8	No	Motueka, Sterling
Santiam	Flowery aroma, spicy/peppery, herbal	5–8	5–8	No	Tettnanger, Opal
Saphir	Floral, fruity, sweet citrus/tangerine	2–4.5	4–7	Yes	Liberty, Mittelfrüh
Simcoe	Earthy, fruity, hints of pine	12–14	4–5	Yes	Chinook, Summit, Magnum
Smaragd	Fruity, floral, hoppy	4–6	3.5–5.5	Yes	Admiral, Rakau, Summit
Sorachi Ace	Predominant lemon, woody, herbal, dill, ginger	10–16	6–7	No	Opal, Pilgrim

Hop variety name	Flavor/aroma characteristics	Alpha acid range (%)	Beta acid range (%)	Organic available?	Suggested substitutions
Spalt Select	Mild flowery, light fruitiness, hint of spice	3.5–6.5	3–4.5	Yes	Motueka, Tettnanger, Hersbrucker
Sterling	Slight spice, herbal, floral, slight citrus	6–9	4–6	Yes	Motueka
Strisselspalt (French)	Mild hoppy bouquet, hint of spice, fruit, mild citrus	3–5	3–5.5	No	Hersbrucker, Hallertau, Liberty, Motueka
Styrian Goldings	delicate hints of spice, floral	3–6	2–4	No	Fuggles, Palisade
Summit	Spicy onion/garlic, citrus/orange/grapefruit	14–18	3–6	Sometimes	Cascade, Columbus, Simcoe
Target	Smooth floral, woody, herbal, pungent aroma	8–13	4.5–6	Sometimes	Admiral, Challenger, Fuggles
Tettnanger	Floral spice, refined and pleasant	3–6	3–5	Sometimes	Hersbrucker, Opal, Spalt Select
Vanguard	Woody, herbal, spicy, hint of citrus	5–6	5–7	No	Hallertau, Liberty, Mittelfrüh, Wakatu
Wakatu (NZ Hallertaur)	Strong, floral, citrus, hint of lime	6.5–8.5	8–9	Yes	Hallertau, Sterling
Warrior	Strong, clean bittering, mild flavor	15–17	4.5–5.5	No	Bravo, Magnum, Summit
Willamette	Delicate floral, herbal, mild peppery spice	4–6	3–4.5	No	Opal, Palisade, Tettnanger
WGV (Whitbread Goldings Variety)	Slight sweet fruit, mild floral and herbal, rustic earthy	5–8	2–3	Yes	Challenger, Goldings

Developing Recipes from Scratch

To develop a new beer recipe, you need to figure out the starting gravity (original gravity), hop bitterness (measured in IBU), and color (measured in degrees Lovibond) to make sure the beer comes out the way you want. In addition to the measurable statistics of a new recipe, the aromas and flavors from the hops, malts, and other ingredients need to be taken into account. Aroma and flavor cannot truly be measured, but as you gain experience working with various ingredients, you will learn to apply your senses to the development of your homebrew recipes.

MALT YIELDS

The first thing to figure out in a new recipe is how strong the beer will be by calculating the starting specific gravity. To do this you need to know how much sugar or specific gravity points will be contributed by each ingredient. For ingredients such as malt extract, sugar, or honey, this is a reasonably straightforward calculation, because you are simply dissolving the sugar in water and looking up that ingredient's yield in points per pound per gallon (PPG). Each gravity point equals 0.001 specific gravity. The charts in the preceding section list common brewing ingredients and the typical PPG for each ingredient.

To arrive at a starting gravity for a recipe, first multiply the weight of each ingredient by the PPG, and add the totals together. This gives you the total gravity if you dissolved all that extract in 1 gallon of water, which would be an insanely concentrated brew! To deduce the starting gravity of your recipe, divide the total PPG by the number of gallons of finished beer, multiply by 0.001, then add 1. Since most hydrometers are only accurate to 0.001, it doesn't hurt to round off the finished result.

For example, here are the ingredients in a simple recipe for a 5-gallon batch of pale ale brewed with extract:

$$7 \text{ pounds liquid malt extract} \times 36\text{PPG} = 252$$

$$1 \text{ pound corn sugar} \times 46\text{PPG} = 46$$

$$298 \text{ total PPG} \div 5 \text{ gallons} = 59.6 \times .001 + 1 = 1.060 \text{ SG}$$

The PPG listed in the Extract and Fermentable Sugars and the Malt and Fermentable Adjuncts charts on pages 311 to 316 is the simplified typical PPG, rather than the more detailed maximum PPG listed in some brewing references. For small-scale brewing volumes of under 20 gallons the typical PPG is accurate enough, and saves you from having to work out the projected gravity point yields from the %Extract figures provided on a typical malt analysis sheet. You can do the longer math by hand for each recipe, if you wish, but many of us would rather use a simple reference guide and get on with the brewing!

That being said, it is good to know how to do the math and understand how the PPG numbers are arrived at. If you have a malt that is not on this chart and you cannot find the PPG, or if you malt your own grain and want to know how much you will need to brew a beer with a predetermined starting gravity, you need to determine the %Extract.

Converting %Extract to PPG

The %Extract is the maximum percentage of the total weight of the malt that can yield sugars (both fermentable and nonfermentable) that will be converted in the mash, then dissolved into the liquid and extracted by the lauter. The portion that can be dissolved in solution is referred to as soluble extract. Most malts have husk material and proteins that never dissolve and are left behind when the soluble extract is flushed from the grains.

For most base malts such as pale malt, the %Extract is determined in a laboratory, where a carefully measured amount of malt is ground into a powder, mashed precisely, and strained completely. The remaining ground-up material is thoroughly dried to zero percent moisture, then weighed. The weight difference is listed as the %Extract (see The Congress Mash, page 336.)

If the %Extract of a malt is known but the PPG is not, calculating the PPG is a snap. Simply multiply the %Extract by the PPG of table sugar, 46, which is the standard of measure. For a grain with a %Extract of 80, the PPG is calculated just so:

$$\text{PPG: } 80\% \times 46 = 36.8$$

Potential Extract and Extract Efficiency

With barley malt you have to consider the starch conversion rate. Most homebrewing environments do not have laboratory precision — nor do they need it to brew great beer. Although determining the %Extract is possible in a lab with a finely ground sample, brewing with finely ground malt is completely impractical on a homebrewing scale. The extract efficiency takes into account the difference between the maximum possible yield and the everyday yield you get with your all-grain brewing system at home. For most homebrewers this efficiency rating is between 70 and 80 percent of the maximum yield.

The extract efficiency must be factored into the equation to secure a good estimate of the actual yield. When using PPG to calculate the estimated gravity for whole grains and malts that are steeped or mashed, you have to multiply the PPG by the extract efficiency to arrive at a realistic estimate of starting gravity.

For example, here is how to calculate the estimated starting gravity for an all-grain version of the pale ale recipe I used as an example earlier (see page 322). I'll assume an average extract efficiency of 75 percent:

9.25 pounds pale ale malt × 36 PPG = 333 × 75% extract efficiency = 249.75

1 pound corn sugar × 46PPG = 46

295.75 total PPG ÷ 5 gallons = 59.15 × .001 + 1 = 1.059 SG

Note that the extract efficiency is not applied to the corn sugar because the corn sugar does not need to be mashed or extracted — it dissolves 100 percent in solutions, as do all the sugars listed in the Extract and Fermentable Sugars chart on page 315 and 316.

HOP UTILIZATION AND IBUS

In chapter 3 I covered using hops by making sure the AAUs are the same each time you make a certain recipe, even if the alpha acid levels are different from the hops used in the original recipe. This is an easy and perfectly suitable method for achieving consistency from batch to batch when brewing from an existing recipe. To build your own recipe from scratch, you need a slightly more sophisticated method to ensure the beer will have the balance of hop bitterness to malt body and sweetness that you are striving for. International bitterness units (IBUs) are the standard for measuring hop bitterness.

When hops are boiled in wort, the bittering acids are extracted slowly. The extraction of bitterness is affected by the density, or specific gravity, of the wort; the length of time the hops are boiled; and the form of hop used: whole or pellet. The hop resins that contribute bitterness are not water soluble, and it takes the heat and motion of a boil to change the alpha acid compounds enough to dissolve in water. Even with optimal conditions, it is rare to achieve an extraction of more than 30 percent. This rate of extraction is known as the hop utilization rate, and this value is required to calculate the IBUs for a given recipe.

Hop pellets, because they are made from hops ground into small pieces, have a larger surface area that contacts the wort; thus bitterness is extracted at a higher rate than with whole hops. The density of wort influences utilization rates, because a higher-gravity wort contains more sugar molecules, which reduces the solubility of the alpha acids, while a lower-gravity wort allows a higher percentage of alpha acids to dissolve.

Other variables, such as the total volume of the boil and the gradual increase in specific gravity as water evaporates during the boil, also have an effect on hop utilization, but these factors are more difficult to measure and thus are not usually calculated for small-scale brewing. The variables that affect hop utilization are many, and not all of them are easily measured or even understood. Greater minds than mine have studied this very carefully, and results from these studies provide brewers with data we can use to determine the hop utilization value for our recipes.

Before you calculate IBUs, it is a good idea to evaluate the malt-to-hop balance of your recipe to make sure it fits the style of beer you are brewing. The great beers of the world are usually balanced, although there are some extreme styles out there! In the beginning it is a good idea to keep within generally accepted guidelines until you develop a more refined instinct for what levels suit your own tastes the best. Beers with a lower specific gravity are lighter in flavor and malt sweetness, and the hop bitterness comes through strong even at lower IBU levels.

Most low-gravity beers have a correspondingly low IBU — otherwise, they would taste unpleasantly bitter. Higher-gravity beers have more malt body and residual sweetness; thus, a higher IBU level is needed to balance out the sweetness. I use the following guidelines for balancing hop bitterness in my recipes, unless I am aiming to target a specific style, in which case I use the IBU range specified for that style.

The Beer Judge Certification Program (BJCP) beer-style guidelines offer a good resource for targeting the IBU level of certain beer styles. If you are brewing one of these styles, or a beer that is similar, matching the starting gravity and IBU levels of the style is highly recommended. The complete beer-style guidelines can be found at the BJCP website. Apps are available for most devices as well.

STARTING GRAVITY RANGE	IBU BITTERNESS RANGE
1.030–1.040	8–15
1.041–1.050	10–25
1.051–1.060	15–35
1.061–1.070	25–40
1.071–1.090	30–50
1.091 and up	40–60

Using the Hop Utilization Table on page 330, along with the alpha acid numbers for the hops, the starting gravity of your beer, and the desired bitterness level, you can now calculate the IBUs for your recipe. To be accurate, one IBU is 1 milligram of iso-alpha acid per liter of beer. English units are used universally, so the basic equation includes a conversion factor of 1.34 to allow us to do the math with ounces and gallons and still arrive at the correct IBU figure. For this formula to work properly, the percentages for alpha acid and hop utilization are expressed as whole numbers rather than decimals. Thus an alpha acid of 10 percent is recorded as the number 10, and a utilization value of 25 percent is recorded as the number 25.

IBU = weight of hops (ounces) × alpha acid% × %Utilization (from chart)
÷ total gallons of finished beer × 1.34

This example is for a 5-gallon brew with 1 ounce of pellet hops with an alpha acid of 10 percent boiled for 60 minutes in a wort with a specific gravity of 1.060. From the Hop Utilization Table the utilization rate for a 60-minute boil in a 1.060 SG wort is 0.211. The math looks like this:

$$(1 \text{ oz} \times 10 \times .211) \div (5 \times 1.34) = 31.5 \text{ IBUs}$$

Often it is more desirable to work the formula backwards, because we already know our target IBU but need to determine the weight of hops needed to reach the target IBU. The pale ale recipe we have been using as an example is a beer with a midrange starting gravity of 1.060, so we are looking for an IBU of about 30 for a balanced beer. This recipe calls for Summit hops (14% AA) for bittering and Cascade hops (7% AA) for flavor. Most of the IBUs will be coming from the Summit hops because they have a higher alpha acid content and they will be boiled for 60 minutes. We also have to allow for some bitterness to come from the Cascade hops, since they will be boiled for 20 minutes.

For starters I'll aim for 24 IBU from the bittering hops. The utilization for a 1.60 wort and a 60-minute boil is 21.1, as before. The remaining 6 IBUs will come from the flavor hops. The utilization for a 1.60 wort and a 20-minute boil is 10.7. First, the formula:

$$\text{ounces of hops} = \text{IBUs} \times \text{total gallons of finished beer}$$
$$\div \text{ alpha acid\%} \times \text{\%Utilization}$$

Then, plug in the numbers:

$$\text{Summit hops: } 24 \times 5 \div 14 \times 21.1 = 0.41 \text{ ounce}$$

$$\text{Cascade hops: } 6 \times 5 \div 7 \times 10.7 = 0.4 \text{ ounce}$$

Depending on the accuracy of your scale, you may need to round the numbers down further or convert to grams. Convert to grams by multiplying ounces by 28.3. Doing this, I have figured the hop schedule for this beer as follows:

0.4 oz (11 grams) Summit hops (14% AA) – 24 IBU

0.4 oz (11 grams) Cascade hops (7% AA) – 6 IBU

The pale ale recipe also uses a late hop addition for the last 1 minute of boiling time to give it the hoppy nose so characteristic of the style. As you can see from the Hop Utilization Table, the utilization rate is so low for boil times of under 5 minutes that it does not contribute a noticeable amount of bitterness; thus, it is perfectly acceptable to leave this hop out of the calculations. The recipe also calls for a dry hop addition added to the secondary fermenter. Because dry hops are not boiled at all, they are not factored into the IBU equations.

Adjustments for Hop Flavor and Aroma

When I look at the above recipe with an experienced eye, I immediately notice a flaw. The math is correct, and the bitterness level will be accurate, but what is missing is additional flavor, which can only come from flavor hop additions. Flavor is not a quality that is easily measured. There are many essential oils and volatile compounds that are not fully understood, yet they add a desirable finish to a beer that lets it stand apart from scientifically correct beers. This is where art and instinct come in.

My instincts tell me that my American-style pale ale will not have the hoppy flavor I am looking for if I use just 0.4 ounce of Cascade hops for the flavor addition. For the sake of great beer, it is worth reworking my calculations to account for that citrus hop character I am looking for. Based on past experience, I want to use at least 1 ounce of hops. Therefore, I will calculate the IBUs that are contributed by boiling 1 ounce of Cascade in my 1.060 wort for 20 minutes:

$$1 \text{ oz} \times 7 \times 10.7 \div 5 \times 1.34 = 11.2 \text{ IBUs}$$

After this adjustment I will need an additional 18.8 IBUs to achieve the target of 30 IBUs:

$$\text{Summit hops: } 18.8 \times 5 \div 14 \times 21.1 = 0.32 \text{ ounce or 9 grams}$$

Thus with some simple math plus an instinct for beer flavor and style, art and science can work in concert to design a wonderful beer!

Correction for Boiling Gravity

If the boiling gravity of the wort is significantly different from the final gravity of the finished beer, it is important to take this into account when calculating the IBUs. For example, if you can only boil 3 gallons of a beer with a final gravity of 1.060, the actual specific gravity during the boil will be much higher than the finishing gravity, and this will affect the hop utilization. If accuracy is important, you must adjust the hopping rates to account for the difference in wort gravity. A partial boil is only truly possible with an extract or partial mash brew. To determine your boiling gravity, just quickly redo the starting gravity calculations for Pale Rider Ale that we started with at the beginning of the chapter:

$$7 \text{ pounds liquid malt extract} \times 36PPG = 252$$

$$1 \text{ pound corn sugar} \times 46PPG = 46$$

$$298 \text{ total PPG} \div 3 \text{ gallons} = 99.3 \times 0.001 + 1 = 1.099 \text{ SG}$$

With a higher gravity we have a different utilization rate of 14.7. With this, the formula for bittering hops can be redone:

$$\text{Summit hops: } 18.8 \times 5 \div 14 \times 14.7 = 0.46 \text{ ounce or 13 grams}$$

Because the change in utilization rate is much lower with the shorter boil time for the flavor hops, recalculating the IBUs for the later hop additions is rarely necessary.

Correction for Whole Hops

The jury is still out on this, but many trusted sources suggest that whole hops have a lower utilization rate than pellet hops. In whole hops the lupulin glands that contain the bittering acids are intact, and the time it takes for them to burst when added to the boil results in a slightly lower utilization rate. The lupulin glands are broken during the pelletizing process; thus, the acids are more immediately available for isomerization in the boil.

All of the formulas for IBU calculation in this book assume the use of pellet hops. To adjust for the difference between whole hops, calculate the IBUs and hop weights as described above, then add 10 percent to the weight to adjust for the lower utilization levels of whole hops.

So for our pale ale recipe, our new hop schedule will be this:

$$0.4 \text{ oz (11 grams) Summit hops} \times 1.1 = 0.44 \text{ oz (12 grams)}$$

$$0.4 \text{ oz (11 grams) Cascade hops} \times 1.1 = 0.44 \text{ oz (12 grams)}$$

HOP UTILIZATION TABLE

Decimal Alpha Acid Utilization vs. Boil Time and Wort Original Gravity

Boil Time (min)	Original Gravity:										
	1.030	1.040	1.050	1.060	1.070	1.080	1.090	1.100	1.110	1.120	1.130
0	0.000	0.000	0.000	0.000	0.000	0.000	0.000	0.000	0.000	0.000	0.000
3	0.034	0.031	0.029	0.026	0.024	0.022	0.020	0.018	0.017	0.015	0.014
6	0.065	0.059	0.054	0.049	0.045	0.041	0.038	0.035	0.032	0.029	0.026
9	0.092	0.084	0.077	0.070	0.064	0.059	0.054	0.049	0.045	0.041	0.037
12	0.116	0.106	0.097	0.088	0.081	0.074	0.068	0.062	0.056	0.052	0.047
15	0.137	0.125	0.114	0.105	0.096	0.087	0.080	0.073	0.067	0.061	0.056
18	0.156	0.142	0.130	0.119	0.109	0.099	0.091	0.083	0.076	0.069	0.063
21	0.173	0.158	0.144	0.132	0.120	0.110	0.101	0.092	0.084	0.077	0.070
24	0.187	0.171	0.157	0.143	0.131	0.120	0.109	0.100	0.091	0.083	0.076
27	0.201	0.183	0.168	0.153	0.140	0.128	0.117	0.107	0.098	0.089	0.082
30	0.212	0.194	0.177	0.162	0.148	0.135	0.124	0.113	0.103	0.094	0.086
33	0.223	0.203	0.186	0.170	0.155	0.142	0.130	0.119	0.108	0.099	0.091
36	0.232	0.212	0.194	0.177	0.162	0.148	0.135	0.124	0.113	0.103	0.094
39	0.240	0.219	0.200	0.183	0.167	0.153	0.140	0.128	0.117	0.107	0.098
42	0.247	0.226	0.206	0.189	0.172	0.158	0.144	0.132	0.120	0.110	0.101
45	0.253	0.232	0.212	0.194	0.177	0.162	0.148	0.135	0.123	0.113	0.103
48	0.259	0.237	0.216	0.198	0.181	0.165	0.151	0.138	0.126	0.115	0.105
51	0.264	0.241	0.221	0.202	0.184	0.169	0.154	0.141	0.129	0.118	0.108
54	0.269	0.246	0.224	0.205	0.188	0.171	0.157	0.143	0.131	0.120	0.109
57	0.273	0.249	0.228	0.208	0.190	0.174	0.159	0.145	0.133	0.121	0.111
60	0.276	0.252	0.231	0.211	0.193	0.176	0.161	0.147	0.135	0.123	0.112
70	0.285	0.261	0.238	0.218	0.199	0.182	0.166	0.152	0.139	0.127	0.116
80	0.291	0.266	0.243	0.222	0.203	0.186	0.170	0.155	0.142	0.130	0.119
90	0.295	0.270	0.247	0.226	0.206	0.188	0.172	0.157	0.144	0.132	0.120
120	0.301	0.275	0.252	0.230	0.210	0.192	0.176	0.161	0.147	0.134	0.123

Chart courtesy of Glenn Tinseth (www.realbeer.com/hops)

Homebrew Recipe Development Software

To be honest, most homebrewers today use some sort of recipe development software, instead of doing the math by hand. Recipe development software can really speed up the process of calculating the vital statistics of a new recipe. However, even if you use software on a regular basis, it helps to understand how the calculations work.

If you know how to determine malt yields and calculate hop bitterness, and you have a good grasp of the typical profiles of common ingredients, you will be able to spot an error if it occurs when using software. Inputting an incorrect number or being off by a decimal point can really mess up a brew, until you have brewed enough to realize that a 30-pound malt bill for a 5-gallon batch is not going to give you a starting gravity of 1.040.

There is a myriad of homebrew recipe development applications available to homebrewers. Most programs will calculate the estimated specific gravity, bitterness (usually in IBUs), color range, and alcohol percentage. A good application can also save recipes and allow you to print out a copy to use on brew day. Most can help you compare your recipe to the style guidelines and can help you track the progress through fermentation, bottling, and evaluation.

Some of the more sophisticated programs can even manage your inventory of brewing ingredients and provide you with a shopping list of ingredients you need to purchase to complete your recipe. See Resources for some applications I feel comfortable recommending.

Using Candi Sugar

Many recipes, especially Belgian-style recipes, call for candi sugar or invert sugar, which increases alcohol without adding too much body. Some of the darker candi sugars also contribute subtle caramel flavors plus a hint of color. Most true Belgian breweries use invert sugar, which is sometimes called candi sugar syrup.

The crystallized rock candy that is sold in homebrew stores as candi sugar is not the same as invert syrup and will basically contribute the same flavors to beer as plain old table sugar. You could simply use the same weight of organic cane sugar in recipes that call for the rock candy type. Boiling it for a full hour with the rest of the ingredients results in the best flavor, as the heat and acidity of the wort will cause the sugar to invert, at least to some degree. If you want to brew a more authentic Belgian-style beer, you need to make some candi syrup, which is fairly simple and quite a bit like canning.

Sugar in its granulated form is sucrose, a complex sugar that is hard for yeast to digest. This accounts for the development of less-desirable flavors, usually described as thin or cidery. Invert sugar has undergone a simple chemical reaction that converts the sucrose into glucose and fructose, both of which are more highly fermentable by yeast than sucrose. Invert sugar tastes sweeter and is less prone to crystallization; it is prized by bakers for this reason.

Sucrose inverts to glucose and fructose when it is dissolved in water and heated. The process can be accelerated by the addition of a small amount of acid, such as lemon juice or cream of tartar. An acid-accelerated conversion does not allow enough time for caramel colors and flavors to develop, and the common acids do not yield the rich flavors that the best candi syrups are renowned for. It takes a nitrogen source to develop complex caramel and fruit flavors and the deepest caramel colors. Diammonium phosphate (DAP), a chemical sold in homebrew shops, is commonly used, but ammonium carbonate (baker's leavening or baker's ammonia, sold in specialty shops) may also be used. I have used both, but prefer the flavor of candi syrup made with ammonium carbonate.

Adding the nitrogen to the sugar solution speeds up the Maillard reaction, causing a browning effect similar to the caramelization used in the baking and confectionary world. The more DAP or baker's leavening added, the darker the final color. The final cooking temperature is also important — a higher temperature results in a darker syrup with a stronger flavor.

The cooking process should take at least 30 minutes, and up to 90 minutes for large amounts of dark syrup. The long cooking process is important when using DAP or baker's ammonia, because it enables the ammonia portion to evaporate. Residual ammonia can contribute an unpleasant flavor to the final product.

Making Organic Candi Syrup

The process for candi syrup is basically the same for each of the following recipes. A longer cook time is required for darker syrup, and more water must be added during and at the end of the cooking process to replace the liquid that evaporates away. Each recipe produces 1 pint (16 fl oz) of syrup, which weighs 24 ounces or 1.5 pounds. As long as you observe the ratio of 1 pound of sugar to 1 pint of syrup, the final PPG per pound will be between 30 and 32.

The following recipes may be increased by a factor of up to 6 without changing procedure much, except for a longer cook time and possibly a larger pot. If your vessel is too small, you are likely to have a miserable boilover and a nasty cleaning job on your hands. Use a cooking pot that is at least three times the volume of the amount of sugar being made.

Choose the highest-quality pot you have. A heavy-bottom stainless steel pot with straight sides is best. Steep sides allow crystals to wash back into solution more readily, and boilover is less likely.

STEP-BY-STEP PROCEDURES

1. Combine the sugar, the first amount of water, and the DAP or ammonium carbonate in a heavy saucepan. Bring to a boil, stirring gently just until the solids completely dissolve. Do not stir after this, as stirring can cause crystals to form, which you do not want. Simmer at medium heat for the first 10 to 20 minutes, or until the mixture reaches 240°F (116°C).

2. Once the temperature reaches 240°F, reduce heat to low and simmer slowly. If crystals start to form on the sides of the pan, use a clean pastry brush dipped in water to wash down the sides of the pan. Placing a lid partially over the pan will allow steam to perform a similar function.

3. Cook until desired temperature and color are reached. For darker syrups, the color can change rapidly at the end. You can add a small amount of water to slow the reaction time down. This prolongs the overall cooking time, allowing more complex flavors to develop and reducing the risk of burnt flavors.

4. Once the desired color is reached, remove from heat and gently pour in the final addition of water. Stir after all the water has been added to help avoid spattering.

5. Return the pan to the stove and heat the mixture back to 240°F (116°C).

6. If needed, add enough water to make 1 pint (16 fl oz) for each pound of sugar used. Diluting the syrup can be a little tricky, since you are dealing with very hot liquids. A saucepan with volume measurements makes things easier, because you simply add water to the desired level after the boiling stops. Otherwise, cool the liquid to below 200°F (93°C) before pouring it into a large heatproof measuring cup or bowl. Or pour into a heated pint-size mason jar (or as many as you need for your batch). Fill each jar equally with syrup, top up with hot water to the pint line, and stir to blend thoroughly.

7. You can use the syrup immediately or can it to use later. To can, after you pour the hot syrup into heated canning jars, place the lids on the jars and process the jars in boiling water for 15 minutes. The syrup will keep indefinitely at room temperature if properly canned.

LIGHT CANDI SYRUP (SRM 5–20)

A very mellow syrup with light vanilla flavors and hints of apricot; it will be light amber in color if unbleached sugar is used. Makes 1 pint.

1	pound organic cane sugar
½	cup water
½	teaspoon DAP or ammonium carbonate

Heat above mixture to 260°F (127°C), then add

¾	cup cold water

Bring temperature back up to 240°F (116°C), then remove from heat immediately.

AMBER CANDI SYRUP (SRM 40–50)

This sweet syrup has flavors of vanilla, caramel, and warm bread. Makes 1 pint.

- 1 pound organic cane sugar
- ½ cup water
- 1 teaspoon DAP or ammonium carbonate

Heat above mixture to 280°F (138°C), then add

- ¾ cup cold water

Bring temperature back up to 240°F (116°C), then remove from heat immediately.

DARK AMBER CANDI SYRUP (SRM 80–100)

This rich, deep red-amber syrup adds chocolate and toffee notes, plus nuances of dried cherries or plums. Makes 1 pint.

- 1 pound organic cane sugar
- ½ cup water
- 1¼ teaspoons DAP or ammonium carbonate

Heat above mixture to 290°F (143°C), then add

- ¾ cup cold water

Bring temperature back up to 240°F (116°C), then remove from heat immediately.

EXTRA DARK AMBER CANDI SYRUP (SRM 150–180)

This syrup has a rich mahogany color; it lends intense bittersweet coffee and dark chocolate flavors, and hints of fig and anise. Makes 1 pint.

- 1 pound organic cane sugar
- ½ cup water
- 1½ teaspoons DAP or ammonium carbonate

Heat above mixture to 300°F (149°C), then add

- ¾ cup cold water

Bring temperature back up to 240°F (116°C), then remove from heat immediately.

The Congress Mash

No, this is not several different malt parties with enzymes that cannot agree to work together on anything! The Congress Mash is a brewing industry standard method of determining the %Extract. It is a procedure that always uses the same time, temperature, and water proportions so that results can be compared against a standard of measure. Pure crystallized sugar is used as the standard of measure because it completely dissolves in solution, thus resulting in a %Extract of 100. One pound of pure sugar dissolved in 1 gallon of water results in a specific gravity of 1.046, or 46 PPG. Comparing this standard to soluble extracts from different types of malt can provide meaningful information to the brewer.

Although a laboratory is not available to most of us homebrewers, it is not too difficult to do this type of test on your own malt samples at home. An accurate scale and thermometer, a food processor or coffee mill to grind the malt finely, a fine mesh strainer, and filter paper or paper towels are all that are required. The results may not be as accurate as those a laboratory can produce, but they will give you a good ballpark figure to work with when formulating recipes with your own homegrown grain or unusual malt that does not have a PPG listed for it.

Step-by-Step DIY Congress Mash

1. Weigh out a 1-pound sample of the malt to be tested and grind it into a powder with a food processor, coffee mill, or flour mill.

2. Heat 2 quarts of distilled water to 120°F (49°C), add the grain, and mix thoroughly. The temperature should be 113°F (45°C). Hold at this temperature for 30 minutes.

3. Slowly increase the temperature to 158°F (70°C). In the lab this temperature is increased 1.8°F (1°C) per minute, which is tricky to do on a kitchen stove; just do the best you can to make the increase happen slowly over a 35-minute period, and don't worry too much about increments. Hold the mash at 158°F for 1 hour.

4. Line a strainer with paper towels or filter paper. Weigh the paper towels or filter paper, and record this weight. Strain the mash, collecting all the solids in the filter paper. It may take some time to completely drain, so it is a good time to go enjoy a homebrew.

5. Once the liquid is drained, you can cook it down and add it to your next brew, or boil it to make a yeast starter if you wish.

6. Dry out the solids collected on the filter paper, paper and all. You can use a food dehydrator, an oven set to 200°F (93°C), or set it outside on a hot sunny day. If you are setting it outside, be very careful that it is in a spot well protected from wind so you do not lose any of the grain residue while it dries. It should be as dry as possible — realistically, in your home "laboratory" the sample will have a moisture content of 5 percent or less.

7. Once the malt solids have dried completely, weigh them. Subtract the weight of the paper towels or filter paper. This will give you the total amount of undissolved solids. Subtract the undissolved solid weight from the original weight of malt used, 1 pound. This will give you the weight of the soluble extract that was removed.

8. Calculate the %Extract:

weight of soluble extract ÷ weight of original sample = %Extract

This gives you what is known as %Extract As-Is Basis. In the laboratory the malt sample can be dried to 0 percent moisture, which is almost impossible to do in a home setting without starting a fire. When the malt sample being tested is dried to 0 percent moisture, it gives a %Extract Dry Basis, which is usually listed on a malt analysis sheet.

LIST OF BEER RECIPES

METRIC CONVERSION CHART

Unless you have finely calibrated measuring equipment, conversions between U.S. and metric measurements will be somewhat inexact. It's important to convert the measurements for all of the ingredients in a recipe to maintain the same proportions as the original.

GENERAL FORMULAS	
Ounces to grams	multiply ounces by 28.35
Grams to ounces	multiply grams by 0.035
Pounds to grams	multiply pounds by 453.5
Pounds to kilograms	multiply pounds by 0.45
Cups to liters	multiply cups by 0.24
Fahrenheit to Celsius	subtract 32 from Fahrenheit temperature, multiply by 5, then divide by 9
Celsius to Fahrenheit	multiply Celsius temperature by 9, divide by 5, then add 32

APPROXIMATE EQUIVALENTS BY WEIGHT	
U.S.	**Metric**
¼ ounce	7 grams
½ ounce	14 grams
1 ounce	28 grams
1¼ ounces	35 grams
1½ ounces	40 grams
2½ ounces	70 grams
4 ounces	112 grams
5 ounces	140 grams
8 ounces	228 grams
10 ounces	280 grams
15 ounces	425 grams
16 ounces (1 pound)	454 grams
0.035 ounces	1 gram
1.75 ounces	50 grams
3.5 ounces	100 grams
8.75 ounces	250 grams
1.1 pounds	500 grams
2.2 pounds	1 kilogram

APPROXIMATE EQUIVALENTS BY VOLUME	
U.S.	**Metric**
1 teaspoon	5 milliliters
1 tablespoon	15 milliliters
¼ cup	60 milliliters
½ cup	120 milliliters
1 cup	230 milliliters
1¼ cups	300 milliliters
1½ cups	360 milliliters
2 cups	460 milliliters
2½ cups	600 milliliters
3 cups	700 milliliters
4 cups (1 quart)	0.95 liter
1.06 quarts	1 liter
4 quarts (1 gallon)	3.8 liters

Recipes, Recipe Calculators, Brewing Apps

Below are some apps I have found to be useful and worthwhile. This is by no means an exhaustive list. Most paid applications have a free trial version.

The Beer Recipator

http://hbd.org/cgi-bin/recipator/recipator
A free Web-based spreadsheet-type program. It has a bit of a learning curve and some quirks, but it allows you to format the finished recipe into one page for printing. Includes a massive recipe database generated by users (over 9,000 recipes so far).

BeerSmith Home Brewing Software

http://beersmith.com
This sophisticated software program is reasonably priced, has a generous free trial period, and offers a useful companion smartphone app. Support is good and updates are frequent. The database of recipes and articles is huge. The program features built-in ingredients, adjustments for efficiency, and style guides. The interface works like a Web browser with tabbed pages and form-based input menus and fields. Recipes can be formatted and printed in a variety of ways, including a great format for submitting contest entries. It has an inventory tracking feature and even allows you to adjust the program to work with your own homebrewing equipment.

Brew Pal
DJP SOFTWARE

www.djpsoftware.com/brewpal
This program was designed for the smartphone user, and I have found it incredibly easy to use. It includes all the essential tools, plus has a flavor and aroma wheel that is handy when tasting and evaluating the results of your latest brewing efforts. I often use it to cross-check the results for a recipe I have been working on in another program.

Editing Recipe
BREWER'S FRIEND

www.brewersfriend.com/homebrew
A subscription, cloud-based program, free for limited use. It is very user-friendly with drop-down menus, simple input fields, and an easy-to-understand, single-page-view organization. It supports all brewing levels, covers technical aspects such as mash method and water chemistry, and works in metric or US units of measure. Recipes can be exported to your local drive or printed in a format for brew day. The help docs and the ability to use all the features with a smartphone make this one of my favorites.

Homebrewopeida
AMERICAN HOMEBREWERS ASSOCIATION
http://wiki.homebrewersassociation.org
This is a great database of award-winning homebrew recipes, organized by style.

Mash Infusion and Rest Schedule Calculator
BREWER'S FRIEND
www.brewersfriend.com/mash
Strike water temperature calculator

Testing Laboratories

BrewLaboratory
Holt, Missouri
www.brewlaboratory.com
Hop analysis

KAR Laboratories, Inc.
Kalamazoo, Michigan
269-381-9666
http://karlabs.com
Hop and water analysis

Siebel Institute of Technology Laboratories
Chicago, Illinois
312-255-0705
www.siebelinstitute.com/services
Wide range of testing services including alcohol content; hop, nutritional, and water analysis; and sources of beer off-flavors

Ward Laboratories, Inc.
Kearney, Nebraska
800-887-7645
http://producers.wardlab.com
Brewer's water testing package

Homebrewing Resources

Amelia Loftus
www.amelialoftus.com
Links to articles about plastics, avoiding GMO ingredients, and other sustainability issues.

Seven Bridges Cooperative
800-768-4409
www.breworganic.com
This is a cooperatively owned brewing supply store that specializes in organic brewing ingredients. They have the best selection of organic brewing ingredients in the home brewing market. Full disclosure: I helped found Seven Bridges in 1997 and am still an active voting member.

INTERNATIONAL SUPPLIERS

Australia
Brewers Choice
Multiple locations
www.brewerschoice.com.au

Europe
Hop & Grape
Darlington, United Kingdom
+44-0-1325-380-780
www.hopandgrape.co.uk
Good selection of items including liquid
yeast. They ship all over the British Isles
and to mainland Europe.

NORTH AMERICAN SUPPLIERS

Canada
Canadian Home Brew Supplies
Brampton, Ontario
905-450-0191
www.homebrewsupplies.ca

USA
Austin Homebrew Supply LLC
Austin, Texas
800-890-2739
www.austinhomebrew.com

Blichmann Engineering
www.blichmannengineering.com
Quality stainless kettles, fermenters, and
accessories available through retailers
worldwide

Eco-Bags Products, Inc.
800-720-2247
www.ecobags.com
Cotton gauze produce bags that work
well as straining bags

Five Star Chemicals & Supplies, Inc.
Commerce City, Colorado
800-782-7019
www.fivestarchemicals.com
Manufacturer of PBW and Star San

Keystone Homebrew Supply
Montgomeryville, Pennsylvania
215-855-0100
www.keystonehomebrew.com

MoreBeer
Concord, California
800-600-0033
http://morebeer.com

Polar Ware Company
Kiel, Wisconsin
800-319-9493
www.polarware.com
Quality stainless pots and accessories,
including funnels; most items made in
the USA

Sierra Chemical Co.
West Sacramento, California
916-371-5943
www.sierrachemicalcompany.com
An industrial supplier of technical grade
hydrogen peroxide and 99% acetic acid

U.S. Plastics Corp.
Lima, Ohio
800-809-4217
www.usplastic.com
Offers many alternatives to PVC tubing;
lists which tubing contains plasticizers

Organic Brewing Ingredients

Northern Brewer Homebrew Supply
Roseville, Minnesota
800-681-2739
www.northernbrewer.com

Rebel Brewer
Goodlettsville, Tennessee
615-859-2188
www.rebelbrewer.com
A few organic items; some hops from
New Zealand may not be USDA certified
organic

HOP SOURCES
Hippie Chicks Organic Hops
Palisade, Colorado
970-250-9987
www.hippiechicksorganichops.com
Whole hops only, in 2 oz. and 6 oz.
packages

Hops Direct LLC
Mabton, Washington
888-972-3616
www.hopsdirect.com
A small hop broker offering a
few imported organic hops;
minimum 1-lb packages

Hops-Meister, LLC
Clearlake, California
415-828-3086
www.hopsmeister.com
Small growers that cultivate Ivanhoe, a
revival of the California Cluster variety

Michigan Organic Hops LLC
Mendon, Michigan
513-232-9977
www.michiganorganichops.com
Small-scale growers with a decent
selection of varieties

Palisade Organic Hops Farm
Palisade, Colorado
info@palisadeorganichops.com
www.palisadeorganichops.com
Small-scale growers who offer a few
varieties and sell rhizomes

Roots Down Organic Farm

Gananoque, Ontario
613-382-9568
www.rootsdownorganichops.ca
Small-scale grower offering several popular varieties

MALT PRODUCERS

Rebel Malting Co.

Reno, Nevada
775-997-6411
http://rebelmalting.com
Small-scale operation that offers a simple organic all-grain kit for homebrewers

Riverbend Malt House

Asheville, North Carolina
855-962-6258
http://riverbendmalt.com
A new operation of this writing; not currently offering malt for online purchase but as distribution grows, they may sell to a supplier that does

Valley Malt LLC

Hadley, Massachusetts
413-349-9098
http://valleymalt.com
A few organic malts available

ADJUNCT GRAINS

Bob's Red Mill Natural Foods

Milwaukie, Oregon
800-349-2173
www.bobsredmill.com
A wide selection of organic grains and flaked grains, including hard-to-find spelt and triticale, plus good gluten-free options

Eden Foods, Inc.

Clinton, Michigan
888-424-3336
www.edenfoods.com
A decent selection of organic flaked grains including flaked rice and kamut; ships from both coasts so shipping costs are relatively reasonable

Great River Organic Milling

Fountain City, Wisconsin
608-687-9580
www.greatrivermilling.com
Unmilled wheat, barley, rye, oats, spelt, buckwheat, corn, and millet, all of which can be home malted; sold in 25- and 50-lb bags

Pleasant Hill Grain

Hampton, Nebraska
800-321-1073
www.pleasanthillgrain.com
Whole grains packed in 6-gallon nitrogen-sealed pails with Mylar lining and oxygen absorbers. Each pail is packed full, which means the weight will vary from 35 to 48 pounds, depending on the type of grain. Good selection of grain mills too.

Sun Organic Farm

San Marcos, California
888-269-9888
www.sunorganicfarm.com
A wide selection of whole grains, including sprouting-quality grains good for malting; sold in 1-pound, 3-pound, or 25-pound bags

SUGARS
Sun Organic Farm

San Marcos, California
888-269-9888
www.sunorganicfarm.com
Agave syrup, granulated date and maple sugar, and unrefined sugar

BREWING HERBS AND SPICES
Frontier Natural Products Co-op

Norway, Iowa
800-669-3275
www.frontiercoop.com
High-quality organic herbs, spices, available in bulk or in small quantities

Mountain Rose Herbs

Eugene, Oregon
800-879-3337
www.mountainroseherbs.com
Excellent selection of herbs and spices, including unusual items like heather flowers; extensive website with lots of information about each ingredient

---

Recommended Reading and Other Resources

BOOKS

Beach, David R. *Homegrown Hops*, 2nd ed. D. R. Beach, 2000.

Coleman, Eliot. *The New Organic Grower*, 2nd ed. Chelsea Green Publishing, 1995.

Daniels, Ray. *Designing Great Beers*. Brewers Publications, 1996.

Diggs, Lawrence J. *Vinegar: The User Friendly Standard Text Reference and Guide to Appreciating, Making, and Enjoying Vinegar*. Authors Choice Press, 2000.

Fisher, Joe, and Dennis Fisher. *The Homebrewer's Garden*. Storey Publishing, 1998.

Fodor, Eben. *The Solar Food Dryer*. New Society Publishers, 2005.

Hartung, Tammi. *Homegrown Herbs*. Storey Publishing, 2011.

Markham, Brett L. *The Mini Farming Guide to Fermenting*. Skyhorse Publishing, 2012. See esp. chapters 11 and 12.

Palmer, John J. *How to Brew*. Brewers Publications, 2006.

Peragine, John. *The Complete Guide to Growing Your Own Hops, Malts, and Brewing Herbs*. Atlantic Publishing Group, 2011.

Pitzer, Sara. *Homegrown Whole Grains*. Storey Publishing, 2009.

White, Chris, and Jamil Zainasheff. *Yeast: The Practical Guide to Beer Fermentation*. Brewers Publications, 2010.

OTHER RESOURCES

Build a Solar Dehydrator
www.rootsimple.com/2008/10/build-a-solar-dehydrator
A simple overview of a self-convecting solar dryer that could easily be used to dry hops

Center for Food Safety
www.centerforfoodsafety.org
Guide for avoiding GMO foods and other fact sheets

Ecology Center
http://ecologycenter.org
Information on "the problems with plastics"

GMO Education
INSTITUTE FOR RESPONSIBLE TECHNOLOGY
www.responsibletechnology.org/gmo-education

Non-GMO Project
www.nongmoproject.org

Small-Scale and Organic Hops Manual
www.crannogales.com/site/manual.php
A free download about growing organic hops, either at home or as a small-scale commercial venture, offered by Crannog Ales, a small on-farm brewery in British Columbia (Canada)

YEAST TUTORIALS

Brewing Articles and Technical Gadgets
MALTOSE FALCONS
http://archive.maltosefalcons.com/tech
Look for the very technical yet accessible guide "Yeast Propagation and Maintenance: Principles and Practices," by M. B. Raines-Casselman

"Yeast Culturing from Bottles: Techniques"
BREW YOUR OWN MAGAZINE
http://byo.com/stories/item/1661-yeast-culturing-from-bottles-techniques
An article by Chris Colby in the September 2005 edition

INDEX

Page numbers in *italic* indicate illustrations; those in **bold** indicate charts.

R

racking cane, 11–12, *11*
racking the beer, 74–76
recipe(s). *See also specific recipe*
    importance of proven, 46–47
    software for, 331
recipe creation
    adjunct grains, 311, **313–14**
    candi sugar and, 332–35
    converting recipes, 309
    eco-friendly brewing, 308
    extracts and, 314, **315–16**
    fermentable sugars and, 310, 314, **315–16**
    hops and, 317, **318–321**
    hop utilization/IBUs, 324–29, **330**
    malt extracts and, 310
    malts, 311, **311–13**
    malt-to-hop balance, 325
    malt yields and, 322–24
recycling, sterilizing and cooling water, 168
refrigerators, 108, 109
reverse osmosis (RO) filtered water, 40, 96
root cellar, 111
Rye Bread, Spent-Grain Rustic, 149–151

S

salmonella, 19
sanitizers. *See* cleansers and sanitizers
sanitizing with heat
    about, 23–24
    dry heat sterilization, 24, **24**, *24*
    wet heat, 8, 25
scales, for brewing, 11
secondary fermenter, 10, 44
sediment. *See* trub
siphoning
    brew tip, 80
    racking beer and, 75
    transfer gear and, 11–12, *11*
    trub and, 117
smoked malt, 197–98
soda ash, 18–19

sodium percarbonate, 18–19
software, recipe development and, 331
solar heat, brew water and, 63
sources, brewing ingredients, 44, 342–44
Sourdough Baguette, Spent-Grain, 143–47
Sourdough Pizza Dough, 143–44
Sourdough Pretzels, Spent-Grain, 151–52
Sourdough Sponge, 149
Sour Starter, Yeast-Based, 153
space requirements, brewing beer, 47
sparging, *88*
    batch, 88, 95
    objective of, 88
    process, 85, 94–95
    sparge arm, *86*, 88
    water tank for, 87–88
Special B malt, 194
specialty malts, 29–30. *See also* kilning
 specialty malt
    about, 192–93
    beer styles and, 29
    home-smoked, 197–98
    light crystal, 193–95
    malt-to-hop balance, 325
    organic, 311, **311–13**
    toasted, 195–96
specific gravity
    bottling beer and, 78
    higher-gravity beers, 326
    hydrometer and, 11
    low-gravity beers, 325–26
    yeast starter and, 54
spent grain. *See also* cooking with spent grain
    as animal feed, 127
    composting, 164–65
    mushroom substrate and, 165–66, 168–69, *169*
    nutritional content of, 126
    Spent Grain Dog Biscuits, 128
    Spent Grain Poultry Feed Mixture, 128
    storage of, 127
    uses for, 125

OTHER STOREY TITLES

The Backyard Homestead
EDITED BY CARLEEN MADIGAN
A complete guide to growing and raising the most local food
available anywhere — from one's own backyard.
368 pages. Paper. ISBN 978-1-60342-138-6.

Brew Ware: How to Find, Adapt & Build Homebrewing Equipment
BY KARL F. LUTZEN & MARK STEVENS
Step-by-step instructions to build tools to make brewing safer and easier.
272 pages. Paper. ISBN 978-0-88266-926-7.

The Gardener's A–Z Guide to Growing Organic Food
BY TANYA L. K. DENCKLA
An invaluable resource for growing, harvesting, and storing 765 varieties
of vegetables, fruits, herbs, and nuts.
496 pages. Paper. ISBN 978-1-58017-370-4.

The Homebrewer's Garden
BY JOE FISHER & DENNIS FISHER
Easy instructions for setting up your first trellis; growing your own hops,
malt grains, and brewing herbs; and brewing with recipes created specifically for
homegrown ingredients.
192 pages. Paper. ISBN 978-1-58017-010-9.

The Organic Farming Manual
BY ANN LARKIN HANSEN
A comprehensive guide to starting and running, or transitioning to,
a certified organic farm.
448 pages. Paper. ISBN 978-1-60342-479-0.

Tasting Beer
BY RANDY MOSHER
The first comprehensive guide to tasting, appreciating, and understanding
the world's best drink — craft beers.
256 pages. Paper. ISBN 978-1-60342-089-1.

These and other books from Storey Publishing are available
wherever quality books are sold or by calling 1-800-441-5700.
Visit us at *www.storey.com* or sign up for our newsletter
at *www.storey.com/signup*.